FRENCH, ITALIAN & GERMAN

PHRASE BOOK

CONTENTS

FRENCH

TABLE OF CONTENTS

ITALIAN

TABLE OF CONTENTS

GERMAN

Hi, I'm Rick Steves.

I'm the only monolingual speaker I know who's had the nerve to design a series of European phrase books. But that's one of the things that makes them better.

You see, after more than 30 years of travel through Europe, I've learned firsthand: (1) what's essential for communication in Europe; and (2) what's not. I've assembled the most important words and phrases in a logical, no-frills format, and I've worked with native Europeans and seasoned travelers to give you the simplest, clearest translation possible.

This three-in-one edition is a lean version of my individual French, Italian, and German phrase books. If you're lingering in a country, my individual phrase books are better at helping you connect with the locals, but if you're on a whirlwind trip, this handy three-in-one book gives you all the essential phrases.

To get the most out of this book, take the time to internalize and put into practice my pronunciation tips. But don't worry too much about memorizing grammatical rules, like the gender of a noun—forget about sex, and communicate!

While I've provided plenty of phrases, you'll find it just as effective to use only a word or two to convey your meaning and to rely on context, gestures, and smiles to help you out. To make harried postal clerks happy, don't say haltingly in the local language: "I would like to buy three stamps to mail these postcards to the United States." All you really need are the words for USA and please. Smile, point to the postcards, hold up three fingers...and you've got stamps.

This book also has six cheat sheets. Tear out the sheets and keep them handy, so you can easily memorize key phrases during otherwise idle moments. A good phrase book should help you enjoy your travel experience—not just survive it—so I've added a healthy dose of humor. And as you prepare for your trip, you may want to read the latest edition of my ***Rick Steves' Best of Europe*** guidebook or my individual guides for France, Italy, Germany, Switzerland, and Vienna, Salzburg & Tirol.

My goal is to help you become a more confident, extroverted traveler. If this phrase book helps make that happen, or if you have suggestions for making it better, I'd love to hear from you at rick@ricksteves.com.

Bon voyage. Buon viaggio. Gute Reise. Happy travels!

FRENCH

Challenging, romantic French is spoken throughout Europe and thought to be one of the most beautiful languages in the world. Half of Belgium speaks French, and French rivals English as the handiest second language in Spain, Portugal, and Italy. Even your US passport is translated into French. You're probably already familiar with this poetic language. Consider: ***bonjour, c'est la vie, bon appétit, merci, au revoir,*** and ***bon voyage!*** The most important phrase is ***s'il vous plaît*** (please; pronounced see voo play). Use it liberally—the French will notice and love it.

You can communicate quite a lot with only a few key French words: ***ça, ça va, je peux,*** and ***voilà.*** Here's how:

Ça (pronounced "sah") is a tourist's best friend. Meaning "that" or "this," it conveys worlds of meaning when combined with pointing. At the market, ***fromagerie,*** or ***pâtisserie,*** just point to what you want and say ***Ça, s'il vous plaît,*** with a smile.

Ça va (sah vah), meaning roughly "it goes," can fit almost any situation. As a question, ***Ça va?*** (Does it go?) can mean "Is this OK?" When combined with a gesture, you can use ***Ça va?*** to ask, "Can I sit here?" or "Can I touch this?" or "Can I take a picture?" or "Will this ticket get me into this museum?" and much more. As a statement, ***Ça va*** (which basically means "Yes, it's OK") is almost as versatile. When the waiter asks if you want anything more, say ***Ça va*** ("I'm good"). If someone's hassling you and you've had enough, you can just say ***Ça va*** ("That's enough").

Je peux? (zhuh puh; means "Can I?") can be used in many of the ***Ça va?*** situations, and more. Instead of saying "Can I please sit here?" just gesture toward the seat and say ***Je peux?*** Instead of asking "Do you accept credit cards?" show them your Visa and ask ***Je peux?***

While English speakers use ***Voilà*** (vwah-lah) only for a grand unveiling at a special occasion, the French say it many times each day. It means "Yes" or "Exactly" or "That's it" or "There you go." Unsure of how much your plums cost, you hold a euro coin out to the vendor and say ***Ça va?*** He responds with a cheery ***Voilà***...and you're on your way, plums in hand.

While a number of French people speak fine English, many don't. The language barrier can seem high in France, but locals are happy to give an extra boost to any traveler who makes an effort to communicate.

As with any language, the key to communicating is to go for it with a mixture of bravado and humility.

French pronunciation differs from English in some key ways:

Ç sounds like S in sun.
CH sounds like SH in shine.
G usually sounds like G in get.
But G followed by E or I sounds like S in treasure.
GN sounds like NI in onion.
H is always silent.
J sounds like S in treasure.
R sounds like an R being swallowed.
I sounds like EE in seed.
È and **Ê** sound like E in let.
É and **EZ** sound like AY in play.
ER, at the end of a word, sounds like AY in play.
Ô and **EAU** sounds like O in note.

In a Romance language, sex is unavoidable. A man is ***content*** (happy), a woman is ***contente.*** In this book, when you see a pair of words like ***content / contente,*** use the second word when talking about a woman.

French has four accents. The cedilla makes **Ç** sound like "s" ***(façade).*** The circumflex makes Ê sound like "eh" ***(crêpe),*** but has no effect on ***Â, Î, Ô,*** or ***Û.*** The grave accent stifles **È** into "eh" ***(crème),*** but doesn't change the stubborn ***À (à la carte).*** The acute accent opens **É** into "ay" ***(café).***

French is tricky because the spelling and pronunciation seem to have little to do with each other. ***Qu'est-ce que c'est?*** (What is that?) is pronounced: kehs kuh say.

The final letters of many French words are silent, so ***Paris*** sounds like pah-ree. The French tend to stress every syllable evenly: pah-ree. In contrast, Americans say ***Par***-is, emphasizing the first syllable.

In French, if a word that ends in a consonant is followed by a word that starts with a vowel, the consonant is frequently linked with the vowel. ***Mes amis*** (my friends) is pronounced: mayz-ah-mee. Some words are linked with an apostrophe. ***Ce est*** (It is) becomes ***C'est,*** as in

C'est la vie (That's life). ***Le*** and ***la*** (the masculine and feminine "the") are intimately connected to words starting with a vowel. ***La orange*** becomes ***l'orange.***

French has a few sounds that are unusual in English: the French ***u*** and the nasal vowels. To say the French ***u,*** round your lips to say "oh," but say "ee." Vowels combined with either ***n*** or ***m*** are often nasal vowels. As you nasalize a vowel, let the sound come through your nose as well as your mouth. The vowel is the important thing. The ***n*** or ***m,*** represented in this book by n for nasal, is not pronounced.

There are a total of four nasal sounds, all contained in the phrase ***un bon vin blanc*** (a good white wine).

Nasal vowels	Phonetics	To make the sound
un	uhn	nasalize the U in lung
bon	bohn	nasalize the O in bone
vin	van	nasalize the A in sack
blanc	blahn	nasalize the A in want

If you practice saying ***un bon vin blanc,*** you'll learn how to say the nasal vowels...and order a fine white wine.

Here's a guide to the rest of the phonetics in this book:

ah	like A in father
ay	like AY in play
eh	like E in let
ee	like EE in seed
ehr / air	sounds like "air" (in *merci* and *extraordinaire*)
ew	pucker your lips and say "ee"
g	like G in go
ī	like I in light
oh	like O in note
oo	like OO in too
s	like S in sun
uh	like U in but
ur	like UR in purr
zh	like S in treasure

FRENCH BASICS

HELLOS AND GOODBYES

Pleasantries

Hello.	Bonjour. bohn-zhoor
Do you speak English?	Parlez-vous anglais? par-lay-voo ahn-glay
Yes. / No.	Oui. / Non. wee / nohn
I don't speak French.	Je ne parle pas français. zhuh nuh parl pah frahn-say
I'm sorry.	Désolé. day-zoh-lay
Please.	S'il vous plaît. see voo play
Thank you (very much).	Merci (beaucoup). mehr-see (boh-koo)
Excuse me. (to pass)	Pardon. par-dohn
Excuse me. (to get attention)	Excusez-moi. ehk-skew-zay-mwah
OK?	Ça va? sah vah
OK. (two ways to say it)	Ça va. / D'accord. sah vah / dah-kor
Good.	Bien. bee-an
Very good.	Très bien. treh bee-an
Excellent.	Excellent. ehk-seh-lahn
You are very kind.	Vous êtes très gentil. vooz eht treh zhahn-tee
No problem.	Pas de problème. pah duh proh-blehm
It doesn't matter.	Ça m'est égal. sah meht ay-gahl

You're welcome.	De rien. duh ree-an
Goodbye.	Au revoir. oh ruh-vwahr

Pardon and ***Excusez-moi*** aren't interchangeable. Say ***Pardon*** to get past someone; use ***Excusez-moi*** to get someone's attention. Please is a magic word in any language, especially in French. If you know the word for what you want, such as the bill, simply say ***L'addition, s'il vous plaît*** (The bill, please).

Meeting and Greeting

The French begin every interaction with ***Bonjour, Monsieur*** (to a man) or ***Bonjour, Madame*** (to a woman). It's impossible to overstate the importance of this courtesy. To the French, a proper greeting respectfully acknowledges the recipient as a person first, and secondly as a professional. Taking the time to say a polite hello marks you as a conscientious visitor and guarantees a warmer welcome.

Good day.	Bonjour. bohn-zhoor
Good morning.	Bonjour. bohn-zhoor
Good evening.	Bonsoir. bohn-swahr
Good night.	Bonne soirée. buhn swah-ray
Hi / Bye. (informal)	Salut. sah-lew
Welcome!	Bienvenue! bee-an-vuh-new
Mr.	Monsieur muhs-yuh
Mrs.	Madame mah-dahm
Miss	Mademoiselle mahd-mwah-zehl
Good day, gentlemen and ladies.	Bonjour, Messieurs et Madames. bohn-zhoor mays-yuh ay mah-dahm
My name is ____.	Je m'appelle ____. zhuh mah-pehl ____
What's your name?	Quel est votre nom? kehl ay voh-truh nohn
Pleased to meet you.	Enchanté. ahn-shahn-tay
How are you?	Comment allez-vous? koh-mahnt ah-lay-voo

Very well, thank you.	Très bien, merci. treh bee-an mehr-see
Fine.	Bien. bee-an
And you?	Et vous? ay voo
Where are you from?	D'où êtes-vous? doo eht-voo
I am from ____.	Je suis de ____. zhuh swee duh ____
I am / We are...	Je suis / Nous sommes... zhuh swee / noo suhm
Are you...?	Êtes-vous...? eht-voo
...on vacation	...en vacances ahn vah-kahns
...on business	...en voyage d'affaires ahn vwah-yahzh dah-fair

The greeting ***Bonjour*** (Good day) turns to ***Bonsoir*** (Good evening) at dinnertime. If the French see someone they've just greeted recently, they may say ***Rebonjour.***

You might hear locals use the breezy ***Bonjour, Messieurs / Dames*** or even ***Bonjour, tout le monde*** (Hello, everybody) if both men and women are present. But to proper French people, this is too rushed and sloppy. Take the time to say ***Bonjour, Messieurs et Madames*** (Hello, gentlemen and ladies).

Moving On

I'm going to ____.	Je vais à ____. zhuh vay ah ____
How do I go to ____?	Comment aller à ____? koh-mahnt ah-lay ah ____
Let's go.	Allons-y. ah-lohn-zee
See you later.	À bientôt. ah bee-an-toh
See you tomorrow!	À demain! ah duh-man
So long! (informal)	Salut! sah-lew
Goodbye.	Au revoir. oh ruh-vwahr
Good luck!	Bonne chance! buhn shahns
Happy travels!	Bon voyage! bohn vwah-yahzh

STRUGGLING WITH FRENCH

Who Speaks What?

French	français frahn-say
English	anglais ahn-glay
Do you speak English?	Parlez-vous anglais? par-lay-voo ahn-glay
A teeny weeny bit?	Un tout petit peu? uhn too puh-tee puh
Please speak English.	Parlez anglais, s'il vous plaît. par-lay ahn-glay see voo play
Slowly.	Lentement. lahnt-mahn
Repeat?	Répétez? ray-pay-tay
I understand.	Je comprends. zhuh kohn-prahn
I don't understand.	Je ne comprends pas. zhuh nuh kohn-prahn pah
Do you understand?	Vous comprenez? voo kohn-pruh-nay
You speak English well.	Vous parlez bien l'anglais. voo par-lay bee-an lahn-glay
Does somebody nearby speak English?	Quelqu'un près d'ici parle anglais? kehl-kuhn preh dee-see parl ahn-glay
I don't speak French.	Je ne parle pas français. zhuh nuh parl pah frahn-say
I speak a little French.	Je parle un petit peu français. zhuh parl uhn puh-tee puh frahn-say
What does this mean?	Qu'est-ce que ça veut dire? kehs kuh sah vuh deer
How do you say this in French?	Comment dit-on en français? koh-mahn dee-tohn ahn frahn-say
Write it down?	Ecrivez? ay-kree-vay

A French person who is asked "Do you speak English?" assumes you mean "Do you speak English fluently?" and will likely answer no. But if you just keep on struggling in French, you'll bring out the English in most any French person.

Quintessentially French Expressions

Bon appétit!
bohn ah-pay-tee
Enjoy your meal!

Ça va?
sah vah
How are you? (informal)

Ça va. (response to Ça va?)
sah vah
I'm fine.

Sympa. / Pas sympa.
san-pah / pah san-pah
Nice. / Not nice.

C'est chouette. ("That's a female owl.")
say shweht
That's cool.

Ce n'est pas vrai!
suh nay pah vray
It's not true!

C'est comme ça.
say kohm sah
That's the way it is.

Comme ci, comme ça.
kohm see kohm sah
So so.

D'accord.
dah-kor
OK.

Formidable!
for-mee-dah-bluh
Great!

Mon Dieu!
mohn dee-uh
My God!

Tout de suite.
tood sweet
Right away.

Bonne journée.
bohn zhoor-nay
Have a good day.

Voilà.
vwah-lah
Here it is.

Oh la la!
oo lah lah
Wow!

REQUESTS

The Essentials

Can you help me?	Vous pouvez m'aider? voo poo-vay meh-day
Do you have ____?	Avez-vous ____? ah-vay-voo ____
I'd like...	Je voudrais... zhuh voo-dray
We'd like...	Nous voudrions... noo voo-dree-ohn
...this / that.	...ceci / cela. suh-see / suh-lah
How much does it cost, please?	Combien, s'il vous plaît? kohn-bee-an see voo play
Is it free?	C'est gratuit? say grah-twee
Included?	Inclus? an-klew
Is it possible?	C'est possible? say poh-see-bluh
Yes or no?	Oui ou non? wee oo nohn
Where are the toilets?	Où sont les toilettes? oo sohn lay twah-leht
men	hommes ohm
women	dames dahm

To prompt a simple answer, ask ***Oui ou non?*** (Yes or no?). To turn a word or sentence into a question, ask it in a questioning tone. ***C'est bon*** (It's good) becomes ***C'est bon?*** (Is it good?). An easy way to say "Where is the toilet?" is to ask ***Toilette, s'il vous plaît?***

Where?

Where?	Où? oo
Where is...?	Où est...? oo ay
...the tourist information office	...l'office de tourisme loh-fees duh too-reez-muh
...a cash machine	...un distributeur uhn dee-stree-bew-tur
...the train station	...la gare lah gar

Where can I buy ____?	Où puis-je acheter ____? oo pweezh ah-shuh-tay ____
Where can I find ____?	Où puis-je trouver ____? oo pweezh troo-vay ____

French makes it easy if you're looking for a ***pharmacie, hôtel,*** or ***restaurant.***

How Much?

How much does it cost, please?	Combien, s'il vous plaît? kohn-bee-an see voo play
Write it down?	Ecrivez? ay-kree-vay
I'd like...	Je voudrais... zhuh voo-dray
...a ticket.	...un billet. uhn bee-yay
...the bill.	...l'addition. lah-dee-see-ohn
This much. (gesturing)	Comme ça. kohm sah
More. / Less.	Plus. / Moins. plew / mwan
Too much.	Beaucoup trop. boh-koo troh

When?

When?	Quand? kahn
What time is it?	Quelle heure est-il? kehl ur ay-teel
At what time?	À quelle heure? ah kehl ur
____ o'clock	____ heures ____ ur
opening times	horaires d'ouverture oh-rair doo-vehr-tewr
open / closed	ouvert / fermé oo-vehr / fehr-may
What time does this open / close?	À quelle heure c'est ouvert / fermé? ah kehl ur say oo-vehr / fehr-may
Is this open daily?	C'est ouvert tous les jours? say oo-vehr too lay zhoor

What day is this closed?	C'est fermé quel jour? say fehr-may kehl zhoor
On time?	A l'heure? ah lur
Late?	En retard? ahn ruh-tar
Just a moment.	Un moment. uhn moh-mahn
now / soon / later	maintenant / bientôt / plus tard man-tuh-nahn / bee-an-toh / plew tar
today / tomorrow	aujourd'hui / demain oh-zhoor-dwee / duh-man

For tips on telling time, see "Time and Dates" on page 22.

How Long?

How long does it take?	Ça prend combien de temps? sah prahn kohn-bee-an duh tahn
How many minutes / hours?	Combien de minutes / d'heures? kohn-bee-an duh mee-newt / dur
How far?	C'est loin? say lwan

SIMPLY IMPORTANT WORDS

For numbers, days, months, and time, see the next chapter. For guidance on how to pronounce the French alphabet, see page 550.

Big Little Words

I	je zhuh
you (for formal use or a group)	vous voo
you (informal)	tu tew
we	nous noo
he	il eel
she	elle ehl

it (m / f; varies by gender of noun)	le / la luh / lah
they (m / f)	ils / elles eel / ehl
and	et ay
at	à ah
because	parce que pars kuh
but	mais may
by (train, car, etc.)	par par
for	pour poor
from	de duh
here	ici ee-see
if	si see
in	en ahn
not	pas pah
now	maintenant man-tuh-nahn
of	de / du duh / dew
only	seulement suhl-mahn
or	ou oo
out	dehors / à l'extérieur duh-or / ah lehk-stay-ree-ur
this	ceci suh-see
that	cela suh-lah
to	à ah
too	aussi oh-see
very	très treh

Opposites

good / bad	bon / mauvais bohn / moh-vay
best / worst	le meilleur / le pire luh meh-yur / luh peer
a little / lots	un peu / beaucoup uhn puh / boh-koo
more / less	plus / moins plew / mwan

cheap / expensive	bon marché / cher	bohn mar-shay / shehr
big / small	grand / petit	grahn / puh-tee
hot / cold	chaud / froid	shoh / frwah
warm / cool	tiède / frais	tee-ehd / fray
cool (nice) / not cool	sympa / pas sympa	san-pah / pah san-pah
open / closed	ouvert / fermé	oo-vehr / fehr-may
entrance / exit	entrée / sortie	ahn-tray / sor-tee
push / pull	pousser / tirer	poo-say / tee-ray
arrive / depart	arriver / partir	ah-ree-vay / par-teer
early / late	tôt / tard	toh / tar
soon / later	bientôt / plus tard	bee-an-toh / plew tar
fast / slow	vite / lent	veet / lahn
here / there	ici / là-bas	ee-see / lah-bah
near / far	près / loin	preh / lwan
inside / outside	l'intérieur / dehors	lan-tay-ree-ur / duh-or
mine / yours	le mien / le vôtre	luh mee-an / luh voh-truh
easy / difficult	facile / difficile	fah-seel / dee-fee-seel
left / right	à gauche / à droite	ah gohsh / ah drwaht
up / down	en haut / en bas	ahn oh / ahn bah
above / below	au-dessus / en-dessous	oh-duh-sew / ahn-duh-soo
young / old	jeune / vieux	zhuhn / vee-uh
new / old	neuf / vieux	nuhf / vee-uh
heavy / light	lourd / léger	loor / lay-zhay
dark / light	sombre / clair	sohn-bruh / klair
happy / sad	content / triste	kohn-tahn / treest
beautiful / ugly	beau / laid	boh / lay

nice / mean	gentil / méchant zhahn-tee / may-shahn
intelligent / stupid	intelligent / stupide an-teh-lee-zhahn / stew-peed
vacant / occupied	libre / occupé lee-bruh / oh-kew-pay
with / without	avec / sans ah-vehk / sahn

NUMBERS, MONEY & TIME

NUMBERS

0	zéro zay-roh
1	un uhn
2	deux duh
3	trois trwah
4	quatre kah-truh
5	cinq sank
6	six sees
7	sept seht
8	huit weet
9	neuf nuhf
10	dix dees
11	onze ohnz
12	douze dooz
13	treize trehz
14	quatorze kah-torz
15	quinze kanz
16	seize sehz
17	dix-sept dee-seht
18	dix-huit deez-weet
19	dix-neuf deez-nuhf
20	vingt van
21	vingt et un vant ay uhn
22	vingt-deux vant-duh
23	vingt-trois vant-trwah

30	trente trahnt
31	trente et un trahnt ay uhn
40	quarante kah-rahnt
41	quarante et un kah-rahnt ay uhn
50	cinquante san-kahnt
51	cinquante et un san-kahnt ay uhn
60	soixante swah-sahnt
61	soixante et un swah-sahnt ay uhn
70	soixante-dix swah-sahnt-dees
71	soixante et onze swah-sahnt ay ohnz
72	soixante-douze swah-sahnt-dooz
73	soixante-treize swah-sahnt-trehz
74	soixante-quatorze swah-sahnt-kah-torz
75	soixante-quinze swah-sahnt-kanz
76	soixante-seize swah-sahnt-sehz
77	soixante-dix-sept swah-sahnt-dee-seht
78	soixante-dix-huit swah-sahnt-deez-weet
79	soixante-dix-neuf swah-sahnt-deez-nuhf
80	quatre-vingts kah-truh-van
81	quatre-vingt-un kah-truh-van-uhn
82	quatre-vingt-deux kah-truh-van-duh
83	quatre-vingt-trois kah-truh-van-trwah
84	quatre-vingt-quatre kah-truh-van-kah-truh
85	quatre-vingt-cinq kah-truh-van-sank
86	quatre-vingt-six kah-truh-van-sees
87	quatre-vingt-sept kah-truh-van-seht
88	quatre-vingt-huit kah-truh-van-weet
89	quatre-vingt-neuf kah-truh-van-nuhf
90	quatre-vingt-dix kah-truh-van-dees
91	quatre-vingt-onze kah-truh-van-ohnz
92	quatre-vingt-douze kah-truh-van-dooz
93	quatre-vingt-treize kah-truh-van-trehz

94	quatre-vingt-quatorze kah-truh-van-kah-torz
95	quatre-vingt-quinze kah-truh-van-kanz
96	quatre-vingt-seize kah-truh-van-sehz
97	quatre-vingt-dix-sept kah-truh-van-dee-seht
98	quatre-vingt-dix-huit kah-truh-van-deez-weet
99	quatre-vingt-dix-neuf kah-truh-van-deez-nuhf
100	cent sahn
101	cent un sahnt uhn
102	cent deux sahn duh
200	deux cents duh sahn
300	trois cents trwah sahn
400	quatre cents kah-truh sahn
500	cinq cents sank sahn
600	six cents sees sahn
700	sept cents seht sahn
800	huit cents weet sahn
900	neuf cents nuhf sahn
1000	mille meel
2000	deux mille duh meel
2010	deux mille dix duh meel dees
2011	deux mille onze duh meel ohnz
2012	deux mille douze duh meel dooz
2013	deux mille treize duh meel trehz
2014	deux mille quatorze duh meel kah-torz
2015	deux mille quinze duh meel kanz
2016	deux mille seize duh meel sehz
2017	deux mille dix-sept duh meel dee-seht
2018	deux mille dix-huit duh meel deez-weet
2019	deux mille dix-neuf duh meel deez-nuhf
2020	deux mille vingt duh meel van
million	million meel-yohn
billion	milliard meel-yar

number one	numéro un	new-may-roh uhn
first	premier	pruhm-yay
second	deuxième	duhz-yehm
third	troisième	trwahz-yehm
once	une fois	ewn fwah
twice	deux fois	duh fwah
a quarter	un quart	uhn kar
a third	un tiers	uhn tee-ehr
half	demi	duh-mee
this much	comme ça	kohm sah
a dozen	une douzaine	ewn doo-zehn
a handful	une poignée	ewn pwahn-yay
enough	suffisament	sew-fee-zah-mahn
not enough	pas assez	pah ah-say
too much	trop	troh
more	plus	plew
less	moins	mwan
50%	cinquante pour cent	san-kahnt poor sahn
100%	cent pour cent	sahn poor sahn

French numbers are a little quirky from the seventies through the nineties. Let's pretend momentarily that the French speak English. Instead of saying 70, 71, 72, up to 79, the French say "sixty ten," "sixty eleven," "sixty twelve" up to "sixty nineteen." Instead of saying 80, the French say "four twenties." The numbers 81 and 82 are literally "four twenty one" and "four twenty two." It gets stranger. The number 90 is "four twenty ten." To say 91, 92, up to 99, the French say "four twenty eleven," "four twenty twelve" on up to "four twenty nineteen." But take heart. If little French children can learn these numbers, so can you. Besides, didn't Abe Lincoln say "Four score and seven..."?

Learning how to say your hotel room number is a good way to practice French numbers. You'll likely be asked for the number frequently (at breakfast, or to claim your key when you return to the room).

MONEY

France uses the euro currency. One ***euro*** (€, uh-roh) is divided into 100 cents (***centimes,*** sahn-teem), so "two euros and fifty cents" is ***deux euros et cinquante centimes,*** or simply ***deux-cinquante.***

Use your common cents—cents are like pennies, and the currency has coins like nickels, dimes, and half-dollars. There are also €1 and €2 coins.

Cash Machines (ATMs)

To get cash, ATMs are the way to go. At French banks, you may encounter a security door that allows one person to enter at a time. Push the ***entrez*** (enter) button, then ***attendez*** (wait), and ***voilà!*** the door opens. Every ***distributeur*** (cash machine; also called a ***point d'argent***) is multilingual, but if you'd like to learn French under pressure, look for these buttons: ***annuler*** or ***annulation*** (cancel), ***modifier*** or ***correction*** (change), ***valider*** or ***validation*** (confirm). Your PIN code is a ***code.***

Key Phrases: Money

euro(s) (€)	euro(s) uh-roh
cent(s)	centime(s) sahn-teem
cash	liquide lee-keed
Where is a...?	Oú est...? oo ay
...cash machine	...un distributeur uhn dee-stree-bew-tur
...bank	...une banque ewn bahnk
credit card	carte de crédit kart duh kray-dee
debit card	carte de débit kart duh day-bee
Do you accept credit cards?	Vous prenez les cartes de crédit? voo pruh-nay lay kart duh kray-dee

money	argent ar-zhahn
cash	liquide lee-keed
card	carte kart
PIN code	code "code"
Where is a...?	Où est...? oo ay
...cash machine	...un distributeur uhn dee-stree-bew-tur
...bank	...une banque ewn bahnk
My debit card has been...	Ma carte de débit a été... mah kart duh day-bee ah ay-tay
...demagnetized.	...démagnétisée. day-mahg-nay-tee-zay
...stolen.	...volée. voh-lay
...eaten by the machine.	...avalée par la machine. ah-vah-lay par lah mah-sheen
My card doesn't work.	Ma carte ne marche pas. mah kart nuh marsh pah

Credit and Debit Cards

Credit cards are widely accepted at larger businesses, though smaller shops, restaurants, and guest houses might prefer cash. Even if they accept credit cards, some hotels might cut you a discount for paying cash. In France, they often say ***Carte Blue***—the name of the most widely used credit card—as a generic term for any credit card. The abbreviation ***CB*** written on signs usually stands for ***carte bancaire*** (credit card).

credit card	carte de crédit / carte bancaire kart duh kray-dee / kart bahn-kair
debit card	carte de débit kart duh day-bee
receipt	reçu ruh-sew
sign	signer seen-yay

pay	payer pay-yay
cashier	caisse kehs
cash advance	crédit de caisse kray-dee duh kehs
Do you accept credit cards?	Vous prenez les cartes de crédit? voo pruh-nay lay kart duh kray-dee
Is it cheaper if I pay cash?	C'est moins cher si je paye en espèces? say mwan shehr see zhuh pay ahn ehs-pehs
I do not have a PIN.	Je n'ai pas de code PIN. zhuh nay pah duh "code" peen
Can I sign a receipt instead?	Je peux signer un reçu à la place? zhuh puh seen-yay uhn ruh-sew ah lah plahs
Print a receipt?	Imprimer un reçu? an-pree-may uhn ruh-sew
I have another card.	J'ai une autre carte. zhay ewn oh-truh kart

Much of Europe is adopting a chip-and-PIN system for credit cards, which are embedded with an electronic chip (called a ***carte à puce***). If a payment machine won't take your card, look for a cashier who can swipe it instead, or find a machine that takes cash.

TIME AND DATES

Telling Time

In France, the 24-hour clock (military time) is used for setting formal appointments (for instance, arrival times at a hotel), for the opening and closing hours of museums and shops, and for train, bus, and ferry schedules. Informally, Europeans use the 24-hour clock and our 12-hour clock interchangeably—***17:00*** is also ***5:00 de l'après-midi*** (in the afternoon).

What time is it?	Quelle heure est-il? kehl ur ay-teel
____ o'clock	____ heures ____ ur
in the morning	dans le matin dahn luh mah-tan

Key Phrases: Time and Dates

What time is it?	Quelle heure est-il? kehl ur ay-teel
____ o'clock	____ heures ____ ur
minute	minute mee-newt
hour	heure ur
It's...	Il est... eel ay
...7:00 in the morning.	...sept heures du matin. seht ur dew mah-tan
...2:00 in the afternoon.	...deux heures de l'après-midi. duhz ur duh lah-preh-mee-dee
At what time does this open / close?	À quelle heuere c'est ouvert / fermé? ah kehl ur say oo-vehr / fehr-may
day	jour zhoor
today	aujourd'hui oh-zhoor-dwee
tomorrow	demain duh-man
(this) week	(cette) semaine (seht) suh-mehn
August 21	le vingt et un août luh vant ay uhn oot

in the afternoon	dans l'après-midi dahn lah-preh-mee-dee
in the evening	dans le soir dahn luh swahr
at night	la nuit lah nwee
half	la demi lah duh-mee
quarter	le quart luh kar
minute	minute mee-newt
hour	heure ur
It's... / At...	Il est... / À... eel ay / ah
...8:00 in the morning.	...huit heures du matin. weet ur dew mah-tan
...16:00.	...seize heures. sehz ur

...4:00 in the afternoon.	...quatre heures de l'après-midi. kah-truh ur duh lah-preh-mee-dee
...10:30 in the evening.	...dix heures et demi du soir. deez ur ay duh-mee dew swahr
...a quarter past nine.	...neuf heures et quart. nuhv ur ay kar
...a quarter to eleven.	...onze heures moins le quart. ohnz ur mwan luh kar
at 6:00 sharp	à six heures précises ah sees ur pray-seez
from 8:00 to 10:00	de huit heures à dix heures duh weet ur ah dees ur
noon	midi mee-dee
midnight	minuit meen-wee
It's my bedtime.	C'est l'heure où je me couche. say lur oo zhuh muh koosh
I'll return / We'll return at 11:20.	Je reviens / Nous revenons à onze heures vingt. zhuh ruh-vee-an / noo ruh-vuh-nohn ah ohnz ur van
I'll be / We'll be there by 18:00.	Je serai / Nous serons là avant dix-huit heures. zhuh suh-ray / noo suh-rohn lah ah-vahn deez-weet ur

The word ***heures*** (roughly meaning "o'clock") is sometimes abbreviated as ***H*** in writing. So ***18 H*** means 18:00, or 6 p.m.

Timely Questions

When?	Quand? kahn
At what time?	À quelle heure? ah kehl ur
opening times	horaires d'ouverture oh-rair doo-vehr-tewr
At what time does this open / close?	À quelle heure c'est ouvert / fermé? ah kehl ur say oo-vehr / fehr-may

Is the train...?	Le train est...? luh tran ay
Is the bus...?	Le bus est...? luh bews ay
...early	...en avance ahn ah-vahns
...late	...en retard ahn ruh-tar
...on time	...à l'heure ah lur
When is checkout time?	À quelle heure on doit libérer la chambre? ah kehl ur ohn dwah lee-bay-ray lah shahn-bruh

It's About Time

now	maintenant man-tuh-nahn
soon	bientôt bee-an-toh
later	plus tard plew tar
in one hour	dans une heure dahnz ewn ur
in half an hour	dans une demi-heure dahnz ewn duh-mee-ur
in three hours	dans trois heures dahn trwahz ur
early / late	tôt / tard toh / tar
on time	à l'heure ah lur
anytime	n'importe quand nan-port kahn
immediately	immédiatement ee-may-dee-aht-mahn
every hour	toutes les heures toot layz ur
every day	tous les jours too lay zhoor
daily	quotidien koh-tee-dee-ahn
last	dernier dehrn-yay
this (m / f)	ce / cette suh / seht
next	prochain proh-shan
before	avant ah-vahn
after	après ah-preh
May 15	le quinze mai luh kanz may

The Day

day	jour zhoor
today	aujourd'hui oh-zhoor-dwee
sunrise	l'aube lohb
this morning	ce matin suh mah-tan
sunset	le coucher de soleil luh koo-shay duh soh-lay
tonight	ce soir suh swahr
yesterday	hier ee-ehr
tomorrow	demain duh-man
tomorrow morning	demain matin duh-man mah-tan
day after tomorrow	après demain ah-preh duh-man

The Week

Sunday	dimanche dee-mahnsh
Monday	lundi luhn-dee
Tuesday	mardi mar-dee
Wednesday	mercredi mehr-kruh-dee
Thursday	jeudi zhuh-dee
Friday	vendredi vahn-druh-dee
Saturday	samedi sahm-dee
week	semaine suh-mehn
last week	la semaine dernière lah suh-mehn dehrn-yehr
this week	cette semaine seht suh-mehn
next week	la semaine prochaine lah suh-mehn proh-shehn
weekend	week-end "week-end"
this weekend	ce week-end suh "week-end"

The Months

month	mois mwah
January	janvier zhahn-vee-yay
February	février fay-vree-yay
March	mars mars
April	avril ahv-reel
May	mai may
June	juin zhwan
July	juillet zhwee-yay
August	août oot
September	septembre sehp-tahn-bruh
October	octobre ohk-toh-bruh
November	novembre noh vahn-bruh
December	décembre day-sahn-bruh

For dates, say the number of the day and then the month. June 19 is ***le dix-neuf juin.***

The Year

year	année ah-nay
season	saison say-zohn
spring	printemps pran-tahn
summer	été ay-tay
fall	automne oh-tuhn
winter	hiver ee-vehr

For a list of years, see page 18.

TRANSPORTATION

GETTING AROUND

train	train tran
city bus	bus bews
shuttle bus	navette nah-veht
long-distance bus	car kar
subway	Métro may-troh
taxi	taxi tahk-see
car	voiture vwah-tewr
walk / by foot	marcher / à pied mar-shay / ah pee-ay
Where is the...?	Où est...? oo ay
...train station	...la gare lah gar
...bus station	...la gare routière lah gar root-yehr
...bus stop	...l'arrêt de bus lah-reh duh bews
...subway station	...la station de Métro lah stah-see-ohn duh may-troh
...taxi stand	...la station de taxi lah stah-see-ohn duh tahk-see
I'm going / We're going to ____.	Je vais / Nous allons à ____. zhuh vay / nooz ah-lohn ah ____
What is the cheapest / fastest / easiest way...?	Quel est le moins cher / plus rapide / plus facile...? kehl ay luh mwan shehr / plew rah-peed / plew fah-seel
...to downtown	...au centre-ville oh sahn-truh-veel
...to the train station	...à la gare ah lah gar
...to my / our hotel	...à mon / notre hôtel ah mohn / noh-truh oh-tehl
...to the airport	...à l'aéroport ah lah-ay-roh-por

Getting Tickets

When it comes to buying tickets for the bus, train, or subway, the following phrases will come in handy.

Where can I buy a ticket?	Où puis-je acheter un billet? oo pweezh ah-shuh-tay uhn bee-yay
How much (is a ticket to____)?	C'est combien (le ticket pour ____)? say kohn-bee-an (luh tee-kay poor ____)
I want to go to ____.	Je veux aller à ____. zhuh vuh ah-lay ah ____
One ticket / Two tickets (to ____).	Un billet / Deux billets (pour ____). uhn bee-yay / duh bee-yay (poor ____)
When is the next train / bus (to ____)?	A quelle heure part le prochain train / bus (pour ____)? ah kehl ur par luh proh-shan tran / bews (poor ____)
What time does it leave?	Il part à quelle heure? eel par ah kehl ur
Is it direct?	C'est direct? say dee-rehkt
Is a reservation required?	Une réservation est obligatoire? ewn ray-zehr-vah-see-ohn ay oh-blee-gah-twahr
I'd like / We'd like to reserve a seat.	Je voudrais / Nous voudrions réserver une place. zhuh voo-dray / noo voo-dree-ohn ray-zehr-vay ewn plahs
Can I buy a ticket on board?	Est-ce que je peux acheter un ticket à bord? ehs kuh zhuh puh ah-shuh-tay uhn tee-kay ah bor
Exact change only?	Montant exact seulement? mohn-tahn ehg-zahkt suhl-mahn

TRAINS

For tips and strategies about rail travel and railpasses in France, see www.ricksteves.com/rail. Note that many of the following train phrases work for bus travel as well.

Ticket Basics

At the train station, you can buy tickets at the ***espace de vente*** (sales area). Choose between the ticket office or window ***(guichet)*** and the machines (marked ***achat-retrait-échange***). On tickets, ***1ère*** means first class, and ***2ème*** means second class.

ticket	billet bee-yay
reservation	réservation ray-zehr-vah-see-ohn
ticket office	guichet gee-shay
ticket machine	guichet automatique gee-shay oh-toh-mah-teek
to validate	composter kohn-poh-stay
Where can I buy a ticket?	Où puis-je acheter un billet? oo pweezh ah-shuh-tay uhn bee-yay
Is this the line for...?	C'est la file pour...? say lah feel poor
...tickets	...les billets lay bee-yay
...reservations	...les réservations lay ray-zehr-vah-see-ohn
...information	...l'accueil lah-kuh-ee
One ticket (to ____).	Un billet (pour ____). uhn bee-yay (poor ____)
Two tickets.	Deux billets. duh bee-yay
I want to go to ____.	Je veux aller à ____. zhuh vuh ah-lay ah ____
How much (is a ticket to ____)?	C'est combien (le ticket pour ____)? say kohn-bee-an (luh tee-kay poor ____)
one-way	aller simple ah-lay san-pluh

round-trip	aller retour ah-lay ruh-toor
today / tomorrow	aujourd'hui / demain oh-zhoor-dwee / duh-man

Ticket Specifics

As trains and buses can sell out, it's smart to buy your tickets at least a day in advance even for short rides. For phrases related to discounts (e.g., children, families, or seniors), see page 34.

schedule	horaire oh-rair
When is the next train / bus (to ____)?	A quelle heure part le prochain train / bus (pour ____)? ah kehl ur par luh proh-shan tran / bews (poor ____)
What time does it leave?	Il part à quelle heure? eel par ah kehl ur
I'd like / We'd like to leave...	Je voudrais / Nous voudrions partir... zhuh voo-dray / noo voo-dree-ohn par-teer
I'd like / We'd like to arrive...	Je voudrais / Nous voudrions arriver... zhuh voo-dray / noo voo-dree-ohn ah-ree-vay
...by ____ o'clock.	...avant ____ heures. ah-vahn ____ ur
...at ____ o'clock...	...à ____ heures... ah ____ ur
...in the morning.	...le matin. luh mah-tan
...in the afternoon.	...l'après-midi. lah-preh-mee-dee
...in the evening.	...le soir. luh swahr
Is there a... train / bus?	Il y a un train / bus...? eel yah uhn tran / bews
...earlier	...plus tôt plew toh
...later	...plus tard plew tar
...overnight	...de nuit duh nwee
...cheaper	...moins cher mwahn shehr

...express	...rapide rah-peed
...direct	...direct dee-rehkt
Is it direct?	C'est direct? say dee-rehkt
Is a transfer required?	Un transfert est nécessaire? uhn trahns-fehr ay nay-suh-sair
How many transfers?	Combien de correspondances? kohn-bee-an duh koh-rehs-pohn-dahns
When? Where?	À quelle heure? Où? ah kehl ur / oo
first / second class	première / deuxième classe pruhm-yehr / duhz-yehm klahs
How long is this ticket valid?	Ce billet est bon pour combien de temps? suh bee-yay ay bohn poor kohn-bee-an duh tahn
Can you validate my railpass?	Pouvez-vous valider mon passe Eurail? poo-vay-voo vah-lee-day mohn pahs "eurail"

When buying tickets, you'll either wait in line or take a number ***(Prenez un ticket*** or ***Prenez un numéro).*** The number readout screen says ***Nous appellons le numéro...*** or simply ***Numéro*** (number currently being served) and ***Guichet*** (numbered or lettered window to report to).

Be sure you go to the correct window: ***Départ immédiat*** is for trains departing immediately, ***Autres départs*** is for other trains, ***Ventes internationales*** is international, and ***Toutes ventes*** is for any tickets.

Train Reservations

You're required to pay for a ***réservation*** for any TGV train, for selected other routes, and for couchettes (sleeping berths on night trains). On other trains, reservations aren't required, but are advisable during busy times (e.g., Friday and Sunday afternoons, Saturday mornings, weekday rush hours, and particularly holiday weekends). If you have a railpass, you're still required to reserve a seat for any TGV train (only a limited number of reservations are available for passholders, so book early) and some high-speed international trains as well—look for the Ⓡ symbol in the timetable.

Is a reservation required?	Une réservation est obligatoire? ewn ray-zehr-vah-see-ohn ay oh-blee-gah-twahr
I'd like / We'd like to reserve...	Je voudrais / Nous voudrions réserver... zhuh voo-dray / noo voo-dree-ohn ray-zehr-vay
...a seat.	...une place. ewn plahs
...an aisle seat.	...une place côté couloir. ewn plahs koh-tay kool-wahr
...a window seat.	...une place côté fenêtre. ewn plahs koh-tay fuh-neh-truh
...two seats.	...deux places. duh plahs
...a couchette (sleeping berth).	...une couchette. ewn koo-sheht
...an upper / middle / lower berth.	...une couchette en haut / milieu / en bas. ewn koo-sheht ahn oh / meel-yuh / ahn bah
...two couchettes.	...deux couchettes. duh koo-sheht
...a sleeper (with two beds).	...un compartiment privé (à deux lits). uhn kohn-par-tee-mahn pree-vay (ah duh lee)
...the entire train.	...le train entier. luh tran ahn-tee-ay

Ticket Machines

The ticket machines available at most train stations are great time-savers for short trips when ticket-window lines are long (but plan to use euros, because your American credit card probably won't work in the machines). Some have English instructions, but for those that don't, you'll see the following prompts. The default is usually what you want;

Key Phrases: Trains

train station	gare gar
train	train tran
platform	quai kay
track	voie vwah
What track does the train leave from?	Le train part de quelle voie? luh tran par duh kehl vwah
Is this the train to ____?	C'est le train pour ____? say luh tran poor ____
Which train to ____?	Quel train pour ____? kehl tran poor ____
Tell me when to get off?	Dîtes-moi quand je descends? deet-mwah kahn zhuh day-sahn
transfer (n)	correspondance koh-rehs-pohn-dahns
Change here for ____?	Transfère ici pour ____? trahns-fehr ee-see poor ____

turn the dial or touch the screen to make your choice, and press ***Validez*** to agree to each step.

Quelle est votre destination?	What's your destination?
Billet Plein Tarif	Full-fare ticket (yes for most)
1ère ou 2ème	First or second class
Aller simple ou aller retour?	One-way or round-trip?
Prix en Euro	Price in euros

Discounts

Is there a cheaper option?	Il y a un solution moins cher? eel yah uhn soh-lew-see-ohn mwan shehr
discount	réduction ray-dewk-see-ohn
reduced fare	tarif réduit tah-reef ray-dwee

refund	remboursement rahn-boor-suh-mahn
Is there a discount for...?	Il y a une réduction pour les...? eel yah ewn ray-dewk-see-ohn poor lay
...children	...enfants ahn-fahn
...youths	...jeunes zhuhn
...seniors	...personnes âgées pehr-suhn ah-zhay
...families	...familles fah-mee
...groups	...groupes groop
...advance purchase	...achat à l'avance ah-shaht ah lah-vahns
...weekends	...week-ends "week-end"
Are there any deals for this journey?	Il y a des réductions pour ce voyage? eel yah day ray-dewk-see-ohn poor suh vwah-yahzh

At the Train Station

La gare means train station. Big cities can have several. High-speed, long-distance trains use the ***gare TGV,*** which can be on the outskirts of town; ***gare ville*** or ***gare centre-ville*** is near the city center.

Where is the train station?	Où est la gare? oo ay lah gar
train information	accueil / renseignements SNCF ah-kuh-ee / rahn-sehn-yuh-mahn S N say F
customer service	conseiller clientèle kohn-say-yay klee-ahn-tehl
tickets	billets bee-yay
departures	départs day-par
arrivals	arrivées ah-ree-vay
On time?	À l'heure? ah lur
Late?	En retard? ahn ruh-tar

How late?	Combien de retard? kohn-bee-an duh ruh-tar
platform / track	quai / voie kay / vwah
What track does the train leave from?	Le train part de quelle voie? luh tran par duh kehl vwah
waiting room	salle d'attente sahl dah-tahnt
VIP lounge	salon grand voyageur sah-lohn grahn voy-ah-zhur
locker	consigne automatique kohn-seen-yuh oh-toh-mah-teek
baggage-check room	consigne de bagages / espaces bagages kohn-seen-yuh duh bah-gahzh / ehs-pahs bah-gahzh
tourist info office	office du tourisme oh-fees dew too-reez-muh
lost and found office	bureau des objets trouvés bew-roh dayz ohb-zhay troo-vay
toilets	toilettes twah-leht

In French rail stations, look for the ***Accueil*** office, where you can get information about train schedules without waiting in a long ticket line.

French trains are operated by ***SNCF*** (pronounced "S N say F"). The country is connected by an ever-growing network of high-speed trains called TGV (tay zhay vay, ***train à grande vitesse***). There are also regional and suburban lines that go by various names; for example, around Paris you'll see ***RER, Transilien, banlieue,*** and ***trains Ile-de-France.***

For security reasons, all luggage (including day packs) must carry a tag with the traveler's first and last name and current address. Free tags are available at all train stations in France.

Train and Bus Schedules

European timetables use the 24-hour clock. It's like American time until noon. After that, subtract twelve and add p.m. So 13:00 is 1 p.m., 20:00 is 8 p.m., and 24:00 is midnight.

To ask for a schedule at an information window, say ***Horaire*** (oh-rair) ***pour* ____, *s'il vous plaît*** (Schedule for ____ [city], please). French train schedules show blue (quiet), white (normal), and red (peak and holiday) times. You can save money if you get the blues (travel during off-peak hours).

à	to
à l'heure	on time
accès aux quais / trains	to the trains
arrivée	arrival
aussi	also
avant	before
de	from
départ	departure
dernier passage	last trip
desserte	initial departure time
destination (finale)	(final) destination
dimanche	Sunday
direction	goes
en retard	late
en semaine	weekdays
environ ____ minutes de retard	about ____ minutes late
et	and
heure	time / hour
heures	hours
jour férié	holiday
jours	days
jusqu'à	until
numéro / n°	train number
par	via
pas	not
pour	to
premier passage	first trip
provenance	coming from
régime	major stops en route
retard / retardé	late
samedi	Saturday
sauf	except

seulement	only
terminus	final destination
tous	every
tous les jours	daily
train direct	does not make every stop
train omnibus	makes every stop ("milk run")
voie	track number
1-5 / 6 / 7	Monday-Friday / Saturday / Sunday

All Aboard

In the station, ***accès aux quais*** or ***accès aux trains*** signs direct you to the trains. (A sign reading ***voyageurs munis de billets*** means that it's an area only for passengers with tickets in hand.) At the track, you are required to ***composter*** (validate) all train tickets and reservations. Look for the yellow, waist-high boxes marked ***compostage de billets.*** (Do not ***composte*** your railpass, but do validate it at a ticket window before the first time you use it.)

platform / track	quai / voie kay / vwah
number	numéro new-may-roh
train	train tran
train car	voiture vwah-tewr
conductor	conducteur kohn-dewk-tur
Is this the train to ____?	C'est le train pour ____? say luh tran poor ____
Which train to ____?	Quel train pour ____? kehl tran poor ____
Which train car to ____?	Quelle voiture pour ____? kehl vwah-tewr poor ____
Where is...?	Où est...? oo ay
Is this...?	C'est...? say
...my seat	...ma place mah plahs
...first / second class	...la première / deuxième classe lah pruhm-yehr / duhz-yehm klahs

...the dining car	...la voiture restaurant lah vwah-tewr rehs-toh-rahn
...the sleeper car	...la voiture-lit lah vwah-tewr-lee
...the toilet	...la toilette lah twah-leht
reserved / occupied / free	réservé / occupé / libre ray-zehr-vay / oh-kew-pay / lee-bruh
Is this (seat) free?	C'est libre? say lee-bruh
May I / May we...?	Je peux / Nous pouvon...? zhuh puh / noo poo-vohn
...sit here	...s'asseoir ici sah-swahr ee-see
...open the window	...ouvrir la fenêtre oo-vreer lah fuh-neh-truh
...eat here	...manger ici mahn-zhay ee-see
(I think) that's my seat.	(Je pense) c'est ma place. (zhuh pahns) say mah plahs
These are our seats.	Ce sont nos places. suh sohn noh plahs
Save my place?	Garder ma place? gar-day mah plahs
Save our places?	Garder nos places? gar-day noh plahs
Where are you going?	Où allez-vous? oo ah-lay-voo
I'm going / We're going to ____.	Je vais / Nous allons à ____. zhuh vay / nooz ah-lohn ah ____
Does this train stop in ____?	Ce train s'arrête à ____? suh tran sah-reht ah ____
When will it arrive in ____?	Il va arriver à ____ à quelle heure? eel vah ah-ree-vay ah ____ ah kehl ur
Where is a (handsome) conductor?	Où est un (beau) conducteur? oo ay uhn (boh) kohn-dewk-tur
Tell me when to get off?	Dîtes-moi quand je descends? deet-mwah kahn zhuh day-sahn
I'm getting off.	Je descends. zhuh day-sahn
How do I open the door?	Comment puis-je ouvrir la porte? koh-mahn pweezh oo-vreer lah port

To confirm you're boarding the right train, point to the train, and ask a conductor ***À* ____ [city]*?*** For example, ***À Chartres?*** means "To Chartres?" Some longer trains split cars en route; make sure your train car is continuing to your destination by asking ***Cette voiture va à Chartres?*** (This car goes to Chartres?).

If a non-TGV train seat is reserved, it'll usually be labeled ***réservé,*** with the cities to and from which it is reserved.

As you approach a station on the train, you will hear an announcement such as: ***Mesdames, Messieurs, dans quelques minutes, nous entrons en gare de Paris*** (In a few minutes, we will arrive in Paris).

Strikes

If a strike is pending, hoteliers or travel agencies can check for you to see when the strike goes into effect and which trains will continue to run.

strike	grève grehv
Is there a strike?	Il y a une grève? eel yah ewn grehv
Only for today?	Juste pour aujourd'hui? zhewst poor oh-zhoor-dwee
Tomorrow, too?	Demain aussi? duh-man oh-see
Are there some trains today?	Il y a quelques trains aujourd'hui? eel yah kehl-kuh tran oh-zhoor-dwee
I'm going to ____.	Je voyage à ____. zhuh voy-ahzh ah ____

CITY BUSES AND SUBWAYS

Ticket Talk

Most big cities offer deals on transportation, such as one-day tickets or cheaper fares for youths and seniors. In Paris, you'll save money by buying a ***carnet*** (kar-nay, batch of 10 tickets) at virtually any Métro station. The tickets, which are shareable, are valid on the buses, Métro, and RER (suburban railway) within the city limits.

Key Phrases: City Buses and Subways

bus	bus bews
subway	Métro may-troh
How do I get to ____?	Comment je vais à ____? koh-mahn zhuh vay ah ____
Which stop for ____?	Quel arrêt pour ____? kehl ah-reh poor ____
Tell me when to get off?	Dîtes-moi quand je descends? deet-mwah kahn zhuh day-sahn

Where can I buy a ticket?	Où puis je acheter un ticket? oo pweezh ah-shuh-tay uhn tee-kay
I want to go to ____.	Je veux aller à ____. zhuh vuh ah-lay ah ____
How much (is a ticket to ____)?	C'est combien (le ticket pour ____)? say kohn-bee-an (luh tee-kay poor ____)
single (trip)	aller simple ah-lay san-pluh
batch of 10 tickets	carnet kar nay
a day pass	un passe à la journée uhn pahs ah lah zhoor-nay
Is this ticket valid (for ____)?	Ce ticket est bon (pour ____)? suh tee-kay ay bohn (poor ____)
Can I buy a ticket on board the bus?	Est-ce que je peux acheter un ticket à bord le bus? ehs kuh zhuh puh ah-shuh-tay uhn tee-kay ah bor luh bews
Exact change only?	Montant exact seulement? mohn-tahn ehg-zahkt suhl-mahn
validate (here)	composter (ici) kohn-poh-stay (ee-see)

To enter the Paris Métro, insert your ticket in the turnstile, reclaim your ticket, pass through, and keep it until you exit the system (some stations require you to pass your ticket through a slot in the turnstile to exit). For basic ticket-buying terms, see page 29.

Transit Terms

city bus	bus bews
bus stop	arrêt de bus ah-reh duh bews
bus map	plan de bus plahn duh bews
subway	Métro may-troh
suburban train (Paris)	RER ehr-uh-ehr
subway station	station de Métro stah-see-ohn duh may-troh
subway map	plan du Métro plahn dew may-troh
subway entrance	l'entrée du Métro lahn-tray dew may-troh
subway stop	arrêt de Métro ah-reh duh may-troh
exit	sortie sor-tee
line (bus / subway)	ligne (de bus / de Métro) leen-yuh (duh bews / duh may-troh)
direction	direction dee-rehk-see-ohn
direct	direct dee-rehkt
connection	correspondance koh-rehs-pohn-dahns
public transit map	plan des lignes plahn day leen-yuh
pickpocket	pickpocket / voleur peek-poh-keht / voh-lur

Before entering the Métro system, be very clear on which line you'll be taking and what direction you're headed toward (i.e., the name of the final station on that line). At major Métro stations, several lines intersect, creating a labyrinth of underground corridors; following signs for your direction is the only way you'll find the right platform.

Once at your platform, look for the digital information board. See the first column below for examples, with the English explanation:

M-1 (or M-2, etc.)	Métro line number
La Défense (or Balard, etc.)	end station (direction)
1er train	time until arrival of the next train
2e train	time until arrival of the following train
correspondance	connections to another line, listed by direction

Riding Public Transit

How do I get to ____?	Comment je vais à ____? koh-mahn zhuh vay ah ____
How do we get to ____?	Comment nous allons à ____? koh-mahn nooz ah-lohn ah ____
Which bus to ____?	Quel bus pour ____? kehl bews poor ____
Does it stop at ____?	Il s'arrête à ____? eel sah-reht ah ____
Which bus stop for ____?	Quel arrêt pour ____? kehl ah-reh poor ____
Which subway stop for ____?	Quel arrêt de Métro pour ____? kehl ah-reh duh may-troh poor ____
Which direction for ____?	Quelle direction pour ____? kehl dee-rehk-see-ohn poor ____
Is there a transfer?	Il y a une correspondance? eel yah ewn koh-rehs-pohn-dahns
When is the...?	C'est quand le...? say kahn luh
...first / next / last...	...premier / prochain / dernier... pruhm-yay / proh-shan / dehrn-yay
...bus / subway	...bus / Métro bews / may-troh
How often does it run per hour / day?	Combien de fois par heure / jour? kohn-bee-an duh fwah par ur / zhoor

When does the next one leave?	Quand part le prochain? kahn par luh proh-shan
Where does it leave from?	D'où il part? doo eel par
Tell me when to get off?	Dîtes-moi quand je descends? deet-mwah kahn zhuh day-sahn
I'm getting off.	Je descends. zhuh day-sahn
How do I open the door?	Comment je peux ouvrir la porte? koh-mahn zhuh puh oo-vreer lah port

If you press the button to request a stop on a bus or tram, a sign lights up that says ***Arrêt demandé*** (Stop requested). Upon arrival, you may have to press a green button or pull a lever to open the door—watch locals and imitate.

Before leaving the Métro through the ***sortie*** (exit), check the helpful ***plan du quartier*** (map of the neighborhood) to get your bearings and decide which ***sortie*** you want—this can save lots of walking.

TAXIS

Taxis can take up to four people, and larger taxis take more. So you'll know what to expect, ask your hotelier about typical taxi fares. Fares go up at night and on Sundays, and drivers always charge for loading baggage in the trunk. Your fare can nearly double if you're taking a short trip with lots of bags.

If you're having a tough time hailing a taxi, ask for the nearest taxi stand ***(station de taxi)*** or seek out a big hotel where they're usually waiting for guests. The simplest way to tell a cabbie where you want to go is by stating your destination followed by "please" ***(Louvre, s'il vous plaît).*** Tipping isn't expected, but it's polite to round up. So if the fare is €19, round up to €20.

Taxi!	Taxi! tahk-see
Can you call a taxi?	Pouvez-vous appeler un taxi? poo-vay-voo ah-puh-lay uhn tahk-see

Where can I get a taxi?	Où puis-je trouver un taxi? oo pweezh troo-vay uhn tahk-see
Where is a taxi stand?	Où est une station de taxi? oo ay ewn stah-see-ohn duh tahk-see
Are you free?	Vous êtes libre? vooz eht lee-bruh
Occupied.	Occupé. oh-kew-pay
To ____, please.	À ____, s'il vous plaît. ah ____ see voo play
To this address.	À cette adresse. ah seht ah-drehs
Approximately how much does it cost to go...?	C'est environ combien pour aller...? say ahn-vee-rohn kohn-bee-an poor ah-lay
...to ____	...à ____ ah ____
...to the airport	...à l'aéroport ah lah-ay-roh-por
...to the train station	...à la gare ah lah gar
...to this address	...à cette adresse ah seht ah-drehs
Can you take ____ people?	Pouvez-vous prendre ____ passagers? poo-vay-voo prahn-druh ____ pah-sah-zhay
Any extra fee?	Il y a d'autres frais? eel yah doh-truh fray
The meter, please.	Le compteur, s'il vous plaît. luh kohn-tur see voo play
Stop here.	Arrêtez-vous ici. ah-reh-tay-voo ee-see
Here is fine.	Ici c'est bien. ee-see say bee-an
At this corner.	À ce coin. ah suh kwan
The next corner.	Au prochain coin. oh proh-shan kwan
It's too much.	C'est trop. say troh
My change, please.	La monnaie, s'il vous plaît. lah moh-nay see voo play
Keep the change.	Gardez la monnaie. gar-day lah moh-nay

FINDING YOUR WAY

Whether you're driving, walking, or biking, these phrases will help you get around.

Route-Finding Phrases

I'm going / We're going to ____.	Je vais / Nous allons à ____. zhuh vay / nooz ah-lohn ah ____
Do you have a...?	Avez-vous...? ah-vay-vooz
...city map	...un plan de la ville uhn plahn duh lah veel
...road map	...une carte routière ewn kart root-yehr
How many minutes...?	Combien de minutes...? kohn-bee-an duh mee-newt
...on foot	...à pied ah pee-yay
...by bicycle	...à bicyclette ah bee-see-kleht
...by car	...en voiture ahn vwah-tewr
How many kilometers to ____?	Combien de kilomètres à ____? kohn-bee-an duh kee-loh-meh-truh ah ____
What's the... route to Paris?	Quelle est la... route pour Paris? kehl ay lah... root poor pah-ree
...most scenic	...plus belle plew behl
...fastest	...plus directe plew dee-rehkt
...easiest	...plus facile plew fah-seel
...most interesting	...plus intéressante plewz an-tay-reh-sahnt
Point it out?	Montrez-moi? mohn-tray mwah
Where is this address?	Où se trouve cette adresse? oo suh troov seht ah-drehs

Directions

Following signs to ***centre-ville*** will land you in the heart of things.

downtown	centre-ville	sahn-truh-veel
straight ahead	tout droit	too drwah
to the left	à gauche	ah gohsh
to the right	à droite	ah drwaht
first	premier	pruhm-yay
next	prochain	proh-shan
intersection	carrefour	kar-foor
corner	au coin	oh kwan
block	paté de maisons	pah-tay duh may zohn
roundabout	rond-point	rohn-pwan
(main) square	place (principale)	plahs (pran-see-pahl)
street	rue	rew
bridge	pont	pohn
road	route	root
north / south	nord / sud	nor / sewd
east / west	est / ouest	ehst / wehst

Lost Your Way

I'm lost.	Je suis perdu.	zhuh swee pehr-dew
We're lost.	Nous sommes perdus.	noo suhm pehr-dew
Can you help me?	Vous pouvez m'aider?	voo poo-vay meh-day
Where am I?	Où suis-je?	oo sweezh
Where is ____?	Où est ____?	oo ay ____.
How do I get to ____?	Comment est-ce que j'arrive à ____?	koh-mahn ehs kuh zhah-reev ah ____
Can you show me the way?	Vous pouvez me montrer le chemin?	voo poo-vay muh mohn-tray luh shuh-man

SLEEPING

RESERVATIONS

Making a Reservation

reservation	réservation ray-zehr-vah-see-ohn
Do you have...?	Avez-vous...? ah-vay-voo
I'd like to reserve...	Je voudrais réserver... zhuh voo-dray ray-zehr-vay
...a room...	...une chambre... ewn shahn-bruh
...for one person / two people	...pour une personne / deux personnes poor ewn pehr-suhn / duh pehr-suhn
...for today / tomorrow	...pour aujourd'hui / demain poor oh-zhoor-dwee / duh-man
...for one night	...pour une nuit poor ewn nwee
two / three nights	deux / trois nuits duh / trwah nwee

Key Phrases: Sleeping

Do you have a room?	Avez-vous une chambre? ah-vay-voo ewn shahn-bruh
for one person / two people	pour une personne / deux personnes poor ewn pehr-suhn / duh pehr-suhn
today / tomorrow	aujourd'hui / demain oh-zhoor-dwee / duh-man
How much is it?	C'est combien? say kohn-bee-an
hotel	hôtel oh-tehl
inexpensive hotel	pension pahn-see-ohn
vacancy / no vacancy	chambre libre / complet shahn-bruh lee-bruh / kohn-play

June 21	le vingt et un juin luh vant ay uhn zhwan
How much is it?	C'est combien? say kohn-bee-an
Anything cheaper?	Rien de moins cher? ree-an duh mwan shehr
I'll take it.	Je la prends. zhuh lah prahn
My name is ____.	Je m'appelle ____. zhuh mah-pehl ____
Do you need a deposit?	Avez-vous besoin d'un acompte? ah-vay-voo buh-zwan duhn ah-kohnt
Do you accept credit cards?	Vous prenez les cartes de crédit? voo pruh-nay lay kart duh kray-dee
Can I reserve with a credit card and pay in cash?	Je peux faire une réservation avec une carte de crédit et payer plus tard en liquide? zhuh puh fair ewn ray-zehr-vah-see-ohn ah-vehk ewn kart duh kray-dee ay pay-ay plew tar ahn lee-keed

French hotels are rated from one to five stars (check the blue-and-white plaque by the front door). For budget travelers, one or two stars is the best value. Prices vary widely under one roof. You'll save money if you get a room with a double bed ***(grand lit)*** instead of twin beds ***(deux petits lits),*** and a bathroom with a shower ***(salle d'eau)*** instead of a bathroom with a bathtub ***(salle de bains).*** You'll pay less for a room with just a toilet and sink (***cabinet de toilette,*** or ***C. de T.***) and even less for a room with only a sink ***(lavabo seulement).***

Many people stay at a ***hôtel,*** but you have other choices:

Hôtel-château (oh-tehl-shah-toh): Castle hotel
Auberge (oh-behrzh): Small hotel with restaurant
Pension (pahn-see-ohn): Small hotel
Chambre d'hôte (shahn-bruh doht): B&B or room in a private home; a *table d'hôte* is a *chambre d'hôte* that offers an optional, reasonably priced home-cooked dinner
Gîte (zheet): Country home rental
Auberge de jeunesse (oh-behrzh duh zhuh-nehs): Hostel

Getting Specific

I'd like a...	Je voudrais une... zhuh voo-dray ewn
...single room.	...chambre single. shahn-bruh san-guhl
...double room.	...chambre double. shahn-bruh doo-bluh
...triple room.	...chambre triple. shahn-bruh tree-pluh
...room for ____ people.	...chambre pour ____ personnes. shahn-bruh poor ____ pehr-suhn
with / without / and	avec / sans / et ah-vehk / sahn / ay
king-size bed	king size keeng "size"
queen-size bed	lit de cent-soixante lee duh sahn-swah-sahnt
double bed	grand lit grahn lee
twin beds...	deux petits lits / deux lits jumeaux... duh puh-tee lee / duh lee zhew-moh
...together / separate	....ensemble / séparés ahn-sahn-bluh / say-pah-ray
single bed	petit lit / lit jumeau puh-tee lee / lee zhew-moh
without footboard	sans pied de lit sahn pee-ay duh lee
private bathroom	salle de bain privée sahl duh ban pree-vay
toilet	WC vay say
shower	douche doosh
bathtub	baignoire behn-wahr
with only a sink	avec lavabo seulement ah-vehk lah-vah-boh suhl-mahn
shower outside the room	une douche sur le palier ewn doosh sewr luh pahl-yay
balcony	balcon bahl-kohn
view	vue vew

cheap	pas cher / bon marché pah shehr / boh<u>n</u> mar-shay
quiet	tranquille trah<u>n</u>-keel
romantic	romantique roh-mah<u>n</u>-teek
on the ground floor	au rez-de-chaussée oh ray-duh-shoh-say
Do you have...?	Avez-vous...? ah-vay-voo
...an elevator	...un ascenseur uh<u>n</u> ah-sah<u>n</u>-sur
...air-conditioning	...climatisation klee-mah-tee-zah-see-oh<u>n</u>
...Internet access	...accès à l'Internet ahk-seh ah la<u>n</u>-tehr-neht
...Wi-Fi (in the room)	...Wi-Fi (dans la chambre) wee-fee (dah<u>n</u> lah shah<u>n</u>-bruh)
...parking	...un parking uh<u>n</u> par-keeng
...a garage	...un parking couvert uh<u>n</u> par-keeng koo-vehr
What is your...?	Quel est votre...? kehl ay voh-truh
...email address	...adresse email ah-drehs "email"
...cancellation policy	...conditions d'annulation koh<u>n</u>-dees-yoh<u>n</u> dah-new-lah-see-oh<u>n</u>

In France, a room with one double bed is generally smaller than a room with two twin beds ***(deux petits lits).*** An American-size double bed (55 inches wide) is called ***un grand lit.*** A queen-size bed is ***un lit de cent-soixante***—literally a 160-centimeter bed (63 inches wide). And ***le king size*** is usually two twin beds pushed together and sheeted as one big bed. You may find any of these in a French "double room." If you'll take either twins or a double, ask generically for ***une chambre pour deux*** (a room for two) to avoid being needlessly turned away. Taller guests may want to request a bed ***sans pied de lit*** (without footboard).

Nailing Down the Price

price	prix / tarif pree / tah-reef
Can I see the price list?	Je peux voir les tarifs? zhuh puh vwahr lay tah-reef
How much is...?	Combien...? kohn-bee-an
...a room for ____ people	...une chambre pour ____ personnes ewn shahn-bruh poor ____ pehr-suhn
...your cheapest room	...la chambre la moins chère lah shahn-bruh lah mwan shehr
Is breakfast included?	Le petit déjeuner est compris? luh puh-tee day-zhuh-nay ay kohn-pree
Complete price?	Tout compris? too kohn-pree
Is it cheaper if...?	C'est moins cher si je...? say mwan shehr see zhuh
...I stay three nights	...vais rester trois nuits vay rehs-tay trwah nwee
...I pay in cash	...paie en liquide pay ahn lee-keed

Arrival and Departure

arrival	arrivée ah-ree-vay
arrival date	la date d'arrivée lah daht dah-ree-vay
departure date	la date de départ lah daht duh day-par
I'll arrive / We'll arrive...	J'arrive / Nous arrivons... zhah-reev / nooz ah-ree-vohn
I'll depart / We'll depart...	Je pars / Nous partons... zhuh par / noo par-tohn
...June 16.	...le 16 (seize) juin. luh sehz zhwan
...in the morning / afternoon / evening.	...dans la matinée / l'après-midi / la soirée. dahn lah mah-tee-nay / lah-preh-mee-dee / lah swah-ray

...Friday before 6 p.m.	...vendredi avant six heures du soir. vahn-druh-dee ah-vahn seez ur dew swahr
I'll stay...	Je reste... zhuh rehst
We'll stay...	Nous restons... noo rehs-tohn
...two nights.	...deux nuits. duh nwee
We arrive Monday, depart Wednesday.	Nous arrivons lundi, et partons mercredi. nooz ah-ree-vohn luhn-dee ay par-tohn mehr-kruh-dee

For help with saying dates in French, see "Time and Dates," starting on page 22. For a sample of a reservation request email, see page 551.

Confirm, Change, or Cancel

It's smart to call a day or two in advance to confirm your reservation.

I have a reservation.	J'ai une réservation. zhay ewn ray-zehr-vah-see-ohn
My name is ____.	Je m'appelle ____. zhuh mah-pehl ____
I'd like to... my reservation.	Je voudrais... ma réservation. zhuh voo-dray... mah ray-zehr-vah-see-ohn
...confirm	...confirmer kohn-feer-may
...change	...modifier moh-dee-fee-ay
...cancel	...annuler ah-new-lay
The reservation is for...	La réservation est pour... lah ray-zehr-vah-see-ohn ay poor
...today / tomorrow.	...aujourd'hui / demain. oh-zhoor-dwee / duh-man
...August 13.	...le treize août. luh trehz oot
Did you find the reservation?	Avez-vous trouvé la réservation? ah-vay-voo troo-vay lah ray-zehr-vah-see-ohn
Is everything OK?	Ça va marcher? sah vah mar-shay

See you then.	À bientôt. ah bee-an-toh
I'm sorry, but I need to cancel.	Je suis désolé, mais j'ai besoin d'annuler. zhuh swee day-zoh-lay may zhay buh-zwan dah-new-lay
Are there cancellation fees?	Il y a des frais d'annulation? eel yah day fray dah-new-lah-see-ohn

Depending on how far ahead you cancel a reservation—and on the hotel's cancellation policy—you might pay a penalty. Most likely your credit card will be billed for one night.

AT THE HOTEL

Checking In

My name is ____.	Je m'appelle ____. zhuh mah-pehl
I have a reservation.	J'ai une réservation. zhay ewn ray-zehr-vah-see-ohn
one night	une nuit ewn nwee
two / three nights	deux / trois nuits duh / trwah nwee
Where is...?	Où est....? oo ay
...my room	...ma chambre mah shahn-bruh
...the elevator	...l'ascenseur lah-sahn-sur
...the breakfast room	...la salle du petit déjeuner lah sahl dew puh-tee day-zhuh-nay
Is breakfast included?	Le petit déjeuner est compris? luh puh-tee day-zhuh-nay ay kohn-pree
When does breakfast start and end?	Le petit déjeuner commence et termine à quelle heure? luh puh-tee day-zhuh-nay koh-mahns ay tehr-meen ah kehl ur
key	clé klay
Two keys, please.	Deux clés, s'il vous plaît. duh klay see voo play

Choosing a Room

Can I see...?	Je peux voir...? zhuh puh vwahr
...a room	...une chambre ewn shahn-bruh
...a different room	...une chambre différente ewn shahn-bruh dee-fay-rahnt
Do you have something...?	Avez-vous quelque chose de...? ah-vay-voo kehl-kuh shohz duh
...larger / smaller	...plus grand / moins grand plew grahn / mwan grahn
...better / cheaper	...meilleur / moins cher meh-yur / mwan shehr
...brighter	...plus clair plew klair
...quieter	...plus tranquille plew trahn-keel
...in the back	...derrière dehr-yehr
...with a view	...avec vue ah-vehk vew
...on a lower floor / higher floor	...sur un étage plus bas / plus haut sewr uhn ay-tahzh plew bah / plew oh
No, thank you.	Non, merci. nohn mehr-see
What a charming room!	Quelle chambre charmante! kehl shahn-bruh shar-mahnt
I'll take it.	Je la prends. zhuh lah prahn

Be aware that a room ***avec vue*** (with a view) can also come with more noise. If a ***tranquille*** room is important to you, say so.

In Your Room

air-conditioner	climatisation klee-mah-tee-zah-see-ohn
alarm clock	réveil ray-vay
balcony	balcon bahl-kohn
bathroom	salle de bains sahl duh ban
bathtub	baignoire behn-wahr
bed	lit lee
bedspread	couvre-lit koo-vruh-lee

blanket	couverture koo-vehr-tewr
chair	chaise shehz
closet	placard plah-kar
crib	berceau behr-soh
door	porte port
electrical adapter	adaptateur électrique ah-dahp-tah-tur ay-lehk-treek
electrical outlet	prise preez
faucet	robinet roh-bee-nay
hair dryer	sèche-cheveux sehsh-shuh-vuh
hanger	porte-manteau port-mahn-toh
lamp	lampe lahmp
lightbulb	ampoule ahn-pool
lock	serrure suh-rewr
pillow	oreiller oh-ray-yay
radio	radio rah-dee-oh
remote control...	télécommande... tay-lay-koh-mahnd
...for TV	...pour la télé poor lah tay-lay
...for air-conditioner	...pour la climatisation poor lah klee-mah-tee-zah-see-ohn
safe	coffre-fort koh-fruh-for
shampoo	shampooing shahn-pwan
sheets	draps drah
shower	douche doosh
sink	lavabo lah-vah-boh
sink stopper	bouchon pour le lavabo boo-shohn poor luh lah-vah-boh
soap	savon sah-vohn
telephone	téléphone tay-lay-fohn
television	télévision tay-lay-vee-zee-ohn
toilet	toilette twah-leht
toilet paper	papier toilette pahp-yay twah-leht

towel (hand)	petite serviette puh-teet sehrv-yeht
towel (bath)	serviette de bain sehrv-yeht duh ba<u>n</u>
wake-up call	réveil téléphoné ray-vay tay-lay-foh-nay
washcloth	gant de toilette gah<u>n</u> duh twah-leht
water (hot / cold)	eau (chaude / froide) oh (shohd / frwahd)
window	fenêtre fuh-neh-truh

If you don't see remote controls in the room (for the TV or air-conditioner), ask for them at the front desk. A comfortable setting for the air-conditioner is about 20 degrees Celsius. On French faucets, a **C** stands for ***chaud*** (hot)—the opposite of cold.

If you'd rather not struggle all night with a log-style French pillow, check in the closet to see if there's a fluffier American-style pillow, or ask for a ***coussin*** (koo-sa<u>n</u>).

Hotel Hassles

Combine these phrases with the words in the previous table to make simple and clear statements such as: ***La toilette ne marche pas.*** (The toilet doesn't work.)

I have a problem in the room.	J'ai un problème dans la chambre. zhay uh<u>n</u> proh-blehm dah<u>n</u> lah shah<u>n</u>-bruh
Come with me.	Venez avec moi. vuh-nay ah-vehk mwah
The room is...	La chambre est... lah shah<u>n</u>-bruh ay
It's...	C'est... say
...dirty.	...sale. sahl
...moldy.	...moisie. mwah zee
...smoky.	...enfumée. ah<u>n</u>-few-may
...stinky.	...puante. pew-ah<u>nt</u>
It's noisy.	C'est bruyante. say brew-yah<u>nt</u>
The room is too hot / too cold.	La chambre est trop chaude / trop froide. lah shah<u>n</u>-bruh ay troh shohd / troh frwahd

How can I make the room cooler / warmer?	Comment je peux rendre la chambre plus fraîche / chaude? koh-mahn zhuh puh rahn-druh lah shahn-bruh plew frehsh / shohd
There's no (hot) water.	Il n'y a pas d'eau (chaude). eel nee ah pah doh (shohd)
I can't open / shut / lock...	Je ne peux pas ouvrir / fermer / fermer à clé... zhuh nuh puh pah oo-vreer / fehr-may / fehr-may ah klay
...the door / the window.	...la porte / la fenêtre. lah port / lah fuh-neh-truh
How does this work?	Comment ça marche? koh-mahn sah marsh
This doesn't work.	Ça ne marche pas. sah nuh marsh pah
When will it be fixed?	Quand est-ce qu'il sera réparé? kahn ehs keel suh-rah ray-pah-ray
bedbugs	punaises pew-nehz
mosquitoes	moustiques moos-teek
I'm covered with bug bites.	Je suis couvert de piqures d'insectes. zhuh swee koo-vehr duh pee-kewr dan-sehkt
My... was stolen.	On m'a volé... ohn mah voh-lay
...money	...l'argent. lar-zhahn
...computer	...l'ordinateur. lor-dee-nah-tur
...camera	...l'appareil-photo. lah-pah-ray-foh-toh
I need to speak to the manager.	J'ai besoin de parler au gérant / directeur. zhay buh-zwan duh par-lay oh zhay-rahn / dee-rehk-tur
I want to make a complaint.	Je veux faire une réclamation. zhuh vuh fair ewn ray-klah-mah-see-ohn
The visitors' book, please.	Le livre d'or, s'il vous plaît. luh lee-vruh dor see voo play

Keep your valuables with you, out of sight in your room, or in a room safe (if available). For help on dealing with theft or loss, including a list of items, see page 156.

Most reputable hotels have a visitors' book in which guests can write their comments, good or bad, about their stay and the service. Asking to see the ***livre d'or*** (literally "golden book") can inspire the hotelier to find a solution for your problem.

Hotel Help

Use the "In Your Room" words (on page 55) to fill in the blanks.

I'd like...	Je voudrais... zhuh voo-dray
Do you have...?	Avez-vous...? ah-vay-voo
a / another	un / un autre uhn / uhn oh-truh
extra	supplémentaire sew-play-mahn-tair
different	différent dee-fay-rahn
Please change...	Changez, s'il vous plaît... shahn-zhay see voo play
Please don't change...	Ne changez pas, s'il vous plaît... nuh shahn-zhay pah see voo play
...the towels / the sheets.	...les serviettes / les draps. lay sehrv-yeht / lay drah
What is the charge to...?	Ça coûte combien pour...? sah koot kohn-bee-an poor
...use the telephone	...utiliser le téléphone ew-tee-lee-zay luh tay-lay-fohn
...use the Internet	...utiliser l'Internet ew-tee-lee-zay lan-tehr-neht
Do you have Wi-Fi...?	Avez-vous le Wi-Fi...? ah-vay-voo luh wee-fee
...in the room / in the lobby	...dans les chambres / à la réception dahn lay shahn-bruh / ah lah ray-sehp-see-ohn

What is the network name / the password?	Quel est le nom du réseau / le mot de passe? kehl ay luh nohn dew ray-zoh / luh moh duh pahs
Where is a nearby...?	Où se trouve le... le plus proche? oo suh troov luh... luh plew prohsh
...full-service laundry	...blanchisserie service complet blahn-shee-suh-ree sehr-vees kohn-play
...self-service laundry	...laverie automatique lah-vuh-ree oh-toh-mah-teek
...pharmacy	...pharmacie far-mah-see
...Internet café	...café Internet kah-fay an-tehr-neht
...grocery store	...supermarché / épicerie sew-pehr-mar-shay / ay-pee-suh-ree
...restaurant	...restaurant rehs-toh-rahn
Where do you go for lunch / dinner / coffee?	Vous allez où pour déjeuner / dîner / un café? vooz ah-lay oo poor day-zhuh-nay / dee-nay / uhn kah-fay
Will you call a taxi for me?	Pourriez-vous appeler un taxi pour moi? poor-yay-voo ah-puh-lay uhn tahk-see poor mwah
Where can I park?	Je peux me garer où? zhuh puh muh gah-ray oo
What time do you lock up?	Vous fermez à quelle heure? voo fehr-may ah kehl ur
Please wake me at 7:00.	Réveillez-moi à sept heures, s'il vous plaît. ray-vay-ay-mwah ah seht ur see voo play
I'd like to stay another night.	Je voudrais rester encore une nuit. zhuh voo-dray rehs-tay ahn-kor ewn nwee
Will you call my next hotel...?	Pourriez-vous appeler mon prochain hotel...? poor-yay-voo ah-puh-lay mohn proh-shan oh-tehl

...for tonight	...pour ce soir poor suh swahr
...to make / to confirm a reservation	...pour faire / confirmer une réservation poor fair / koh<u>n</u>-feer-may ewn ray-zehr-vah-see-oh<u>n</u>
Will you call another hotel for me? (if hotel is booked)	Vous pourriez contacter un autre hôtel pour moi? voo poor-yay koh<u>n</u>-tahk-tay uh<u>n</u> oh-truh oh-tehl poor mwah
I will pay for the call.	Je paierai l'appel. zhuh pay-uh-ray lah-pehl

Checking Out

When is check-out time?	A quelle heure on doit libérer la chambre? ah kehl ur oh<u>n</u> dwah lee-bay-ray lah shah<u>n</u>-bruh
Can I check out later?	Je peux libérer la chambre plus tard? zhuh puh lee-bay-ray lah shah<u>n</u>-bruh plew tar
I'll leave...	Je pars... zhuh par
We'll leave...	Nous partons... noo par-toh<u>n</u>
...today / tomorrow.	...aujourd'hui / demain. oh-zhoor-dwee / duh-ma<u>n</u>
...very early.	...très tôt. treh toh
Can I pay now?	Je peux régler la note maintenant? zhuh puh ray-glay lah noht ma<u>n</u>-tuh-nah<u>n</u>
The bill, please.	La note, s'il vous plaît. lah noht see voo play
I think this is too high.	Je pense que c'est trop. zhuh pah<u>ns</u> kuh say troh
Can you explain / itemize the bill?	Vous pouvez expliquer / détailler cette note? voo poo-vay ehk-splee-kay / day-teh-yay seht noht

Do you accept credit cards?	Vous prenez les cartes de crédit? voo pruh-nay lay kart duh kray-dee
Is it cheaper if I pay in cash?	C'est moins cher si je paie en liquide? say mwan shehr see zhuh pay ahn lee-keed
Everything was great.	C'était super. say-tay sew-pehr
Can I / Can we...?	Je peux / Nous pouvons...? zhuh puh / noo poo-vohn
...leave baggage here until ____ o'clock	...laisser les baggages ici jusqu'à ____ heure leh-say lay bah-gahzh ee-see zhews-kah ____ ur

Your bill will include a small ***taxe du séjour,*** the daily hotel tax.

FAMILIES

Do you have...?	Vous avez...? vooz ah-vay
...a family room	...une grande chambre / une suite ewn grahnd shahn-bruh / ewn sweet
...a family rate	...un tarif famille uhn tah-reef fah-mee
...a discount for children	...un tarif réduit pour enfants uhn tah-reef ray-dwee poor ahn-fahn
I have / We have...	J'ai / Nous avons... zhay / nooz ah-vohn
...one child.	...un enfant. uhn ahn-fahn
...two children.	...deux enfants. duhz ahn-fahn
____ months old	de ____ mois duh ____ mwah
____ years old	de ____ ans duh ____ ahn
Do you accept children?	Vous recevez des enfants? voo ruh-suh-vay dayz ahn-fahn
age limit	limite d'âge lee-meet dahzh
I'd like / We'd like...	Je voudrais / Nous voudrions... zhuh voo-dray / noo voo-dree-ohn
...a crib.	...un berceau. uhn behr-soh

...an extra bed.	...un lit supplémentaire. uhn lee sew-play-mahn-tair

AT THE HOSTEL

Europe's cheapest beds are in hostels, open to travelers of any age. Official hostels (affiliated with Hostelling International) are usually big and institutional. Independent hostels are more casual, with fewer rules.

hostel	auberge de jeunesse oh-behrzh duh zhuh-nehs
dorm bed	lit dortoir lee dor-twahr
How many beds per room?	Il y a combien de lits par chambre? eel yah kohn-bee-an duh lee par shahn-bruh
dorm for women only	dortoir uniquement pour les femmes dor-twahr ew-neek-mahn poor lay fahm
co-ed dorm	dortoir mixte dor-twahr meekst
double room	chambre double shahn-bruh doo-bluh
family room	salle de séjour sahl duh say-zhoor
Is breakfast included?	Le petit déjeuner est compris? luh puh-tee day-zhuh-nay ay kohn-pree
curfew	couvre-feu koov-ruh-fuh
lockout	portes fermées port fehr-may
membership card	carte de membre kart duh mahn-bruh

EATING

RESTAURANTS

French restaurants normally serve from noon to 2 p.m., and from 7 p.m. until about 10 p.m. Brasseries and some cafés serve throughout the day.

Finding a Restaurant

Where's a good... restaurant nearby?	Où se trouve un bon restaurant... près d'ici? oo suh troov uhn bohn rehs-toh-rahn... preh dee-see
...cheap	...bon marché bohn mar-shay
...local-style	...cuisine régionale kwee-zeen ray-zhee-oh-nahl
...untouristy	...pas touristique pah too-ree-steek
...romantic	...romantique roh-mahn-teek
...vegetarian	...végétarien vay-zhay-tah-ree-an
...fast	...fast-food fahst food
...self-service buffet	...buffet de libre service bew-fay duh lee-bruh sehr-vees
...Asian	...asiatique ah-zee-ah-teek
popular with locals	fréquenté par les gens du coin fray-kahn-tay par lay zhahn dew kwan
moderate price	prix modéré pree moh-day-ray
splurge	faire une folie fair ewn foh-lee
Is it better than McDonald's?	C'est mieux que Mac Do? say mee-uh kuh mahk doh

This is the sequence of a typical restaurant experience: To get the waiter's attention, simply ask ***S'il vous plaît?*** The waiter will give you a menu ***(carte)*** and then ask what you'd like to drink ***(Vous voulez quelques choses à boire?)***, if you're ready to order ***(Vous êtes prêts à com-***

Key Phrases: Restaurants

Where's a good restaurant nearby?	Où se trouve un bon restaurant près d'ici? oo suh troov uh<u>n</u> boh<u>n</u> rehs-toh-rah<u>n</u> preh dee-see
I'd like...	Je voudrais... zhuh voo-dray
We'd like...	Nous voudrions... noo voo-dree-oh<u>n</u>
...a table for one / two.	...une table pour un / deux. ewn tah-bluh poor uh<u>n</u> / duh
Is this table free?	Cette table est libre? seht tah-bluh ay lee-bruh
How long is the wait?	Combien de temps faut-il attendre? koh<u>n</u>-bee-a<u>n</u> duh tah<u>n</u> foh-teel ah-tah<u>n</u>-druh
The menu (in English), please.	La carte (en anglais), s'il vous plaît. lah kart (ah<u>n</u> ah<u>n</u>-glay) see voo play
The bill, please.	L'addition, s'il vous plaît. lah-dee-see-oh<u>n</u> see voo play
Credit card OK?	Carte de crédit OK? kart duh kray-dee "OK"

mander?), or what you'd like to eat ***(Qu'est-ce que je vous sers?).*** Later the server will ask if everything is OK ***(Tout va bien?),*** if you'd like dessert ***(Vous voulez un dessert?),*** and if you're finished ***(Vous avez terminé?).*** When you're ready, ask for the bill ***(L'addition, s'il vous plaît).***

Getting a Table

I'd like...	Je voudrais... zhuh voo-dray
We'd like...	Nous voudrions... noo voo-dree-oh<u>n</u>
...a table...	...une table... ewn tah-bluh
...for one / two.	...pour un / deux. poor uh<u>n</u> / duh

...inside / outside.	...à l'intérieur / dehors. ah la<u>n</u>-tay-ree-ur / duh-or
...by the window.	...à côté de la fenêtre. ah koh-tay duh lah fuh-neh-truh
...with a view.	...avec une vue. ah-vehk ewn vew
quiet	tranquille trah<u>n</u>-keel
Is this table free?	Cette table est libre? seht tah-bluh ay lee-bruh
Can I sit here?	Je peux m'asseoir ici? zhuh puh mah-swahr ee-see
Can we sit here?	Nous pouvons nous asseoir ici? noo poo-voh<u>n</u> nooz ah-swahr ee-see
How long is the wait?	Combien de temps faut-il attendre? koh<u>n</u>-bee-a<u>n</u> duh tah<u>n</u> foh-teel ah-tah<u>n</u>-druh
How many minutes?	Combien de minutes? koh<u>n</u>-bee-a<u>n</u> duh mee-newt
Where are the toilets?	Où sont les toilettes? oo soh<u>n</u> lay twah-leht

At a ***café*** or a ***brasserie,*** if the table is not set, it's fine to seat yourself and just have a drink. However, if it's set with a placemat and cutlery, you should wait to be seated and plan to order a meal. If you're unsure, ask the server ***Je peux m'asseoir ici?*** (Can I sit here?) before taking a seat.

Reservations

reservation	réservation ray-zehr-vah-see-oh<u>n</u>
Are reservations recommended?	Les réservations sont conseillées? lay ray-zehr-vah-see-oh<u>n</u> soh<u>n</u> koh<u>n</u>-seh-yay
I'd like to make a reservation...	Je voudrais faire une réservation... zhuh voo-dray fair ewn ray-zehr-vah-see-oh<u>n</u>
...for one person / myself.	...pour moi-même. poor mwah-mehm

...for two people.	...pour deux personnes. poor duh pehr-suhn
...for today / tomorrow.	...pour aujourd'hui / demain. poor oh-zhoor-dwee / duh-man
...for lunch / dinner.	...pour le déjeuner / le dîner. poor luh day-zhuh-nay / luh dee-nay
...at ____ o'clock.	...à ____ heures. ah ____ uhr
My name is ____.	Je m'appelle ____. zhuh mah-pehl ____
I have a reservation for ____ people.	J'ai une réservation pour ____ personnes. zhay ewn ray-zehr-vah-see-ohn poor ____ pehr-suhn

The Menu

Here are a few food categories and other restaurant lingo you may see on the menu.

menu	carte kart
The menu (in English), please.	La carte (en anglais), s'il vous plaît. lah kart (ahn ahn-glay) see voo play
fixed-price meal	menu / prix fixe muh-new / pree feeks
special of the day	plat du jour plah dew zhoor
specialty of the house	spécialité de la maison spay-see-ah-lee-tay duh lah may-zohn
fast service special	formule rapide for-mewl rah-peed
tourist menu (fixed-price meal)	menu touristique muh-new too-ree-steek
children's plate	assiette d'enfant ahs-yeht dahn-fahn
seniors' menu	une carte de seniors ewn kart duh seen-yor
breakfast	petit déjeuner puh-tee day-zhuh-nay
lunch	déjeuner day-zhuh-nay
dinner	dîner dee-nay

dishes (prepared dishes)	des plats day plah
warm / cold plates	plats chauds / froids plah shoh / frwah
appetizers	hors d'oeuvres or duh-vruh
sandwiches	sandwichs sahnd-weech
bread	pain pan
cheese	fromage froh-mahzh
soup	soupe soop
salad	salade sah-lahd
first course	entrée ahn-tray
main course	plat principal plah pran-see-pahl
fish	poisson pwah-sohn
poultry	volaille voh-lī
meat	viande vee-ahnd
seafood	fruits de mer frwee duh mehr
egg dishes	plats d'oeufs plah duhf
side dishes	plats d'accompagnement plah dah-kohn-pahn-yuh-mahn
vegetables	légumes lay-gewm
fruit	fruit frwee
dessert	dessert day-sehr
drink menu	carte des consommations kart day kohn-soh-mah-see-ohn
beverages	boissons bwah-sohn
beer	bière bee-ehr
wine	vin van
service included	service compris sehr-vees kohn-pree
service not included	service non compris sehr-vees nohn kohn-pree
hot / cold	chaud / froid shoh / frwah
comes with	servi avec sehr-vee ah-vehk
choice of	le choix de luh shwah duh

In French restaurants, you can order off the menu, which is called a ***carte,*** or you can order a multi-course, fixed-price meal, which, confusingly, is called a ***menu*** (so if you ask for a ***menu*** instead of the ***carte,*** you'll get a fixed-price meal). Most restaurants also have a few special dishes of the day, called ***plat du jour,*** or simply ***plat.***

Menus, which usually include three courses, are generally a good value and will help you pace your meal like the locals: You'll get your choice of soup, appetizer, or salad; your choice of three or four main courses with vegetables; plus a cheese course and/or a choice of desserts. Wine and other drinks are generally extra. Certain premium items add a few euros to the price, clearly noted on the menu (***supplément*** or ***sup.***). Many restaurants offer less expensive, abbreviated versions of their ***menu*** at lunchtime, allowing you to select two courses rather than three or four. These pared-down ***menus*** are sometimes called ***formules*** and feature an ***entrée et plat*** (first course and main dish) or ***plat et dessert*** (main dish and dessert).

If you order ***à la carte*** (from what we would call the "menu"), you'll have a wider selection of food. It's traditional to order an ***entrée*** (which—again, confusingly—is a starter rather than a main dish) and a ***plat principal*** (main course). The ***plats*** are generally more meat-based, while the ***entrées*** are where you can get your veggies. Elaborate meals may also have ***entremets***—tiny dishes served between courses.

Service compris (s.c.) means that the tip is included.

Ordering

waiter	Monsieur muhs-yuh
waitress	Mademoiselle / Madame mahd-mwah-zehl / mah-dahm
I'm / We're ready to order.	Je suis / Nous sommes prêt à commander. zhuh swee / noo suhm preh ah koh-mahn-day
I need / We need more time.	J'ai besoin de / Nous avons besoin de plus de temps. zhay buh-zwan duh / nooz ah-vohn buh-zwan duh plew duh tahn

I'd like / We'd like...	Je voudrais / Nous voudrions... zhuh voo-dray / noo voo-dree-ohn
...just a drink.	...une consommation seulement. ewn kohn-soh-mah-see-ohn suhl-mahn
...to see the menu.	...voir la carte. vwahr lah kart
Do you have...?	Avez-vous...? ah-vay-voo
...an English menu	...une carte en anglais ewn kart ahn ahn-glay
...a lunch special	...un plat du jour uhn plah dew zhoor
...half-portions	...des demi-portions day duh-mee-por-see-ohn
What do you recommend?	Qu'est-ce que vous recommandez? kehs kuh voo ruh-koh-mahn-day
What's your favorite dish?	Quel est votre plat favori? kehl eh voh-truh plah fah-voh-ree
What is better? (point to menu items)	Qu'est-ce qui vaut mieux? kehs kee voh mee-uh
What is...?	Qu'est-ce qui est...? kehs kee ay
Is it...?	C'est...? say
...good	...bon bohn
...affordable	...abordable ah-bor-dah-bluh
...expensive	...cher shehr
...local	...de la région / du pays duh lah ray-zhee-ohn / dew pay-ee
...fresh	...frais fray
...fast (already prepared)	...déjà préparé day-zhah pray-pah-ray
...spicy (hot)	...piquant pee-kahn
Is it filling?	C'est copieux? say koh-pee-uh
Make me happy.	Rendez-moi content. rahn-day-mwah kohn-tahn
Around ____ euros.	Environ ____ euros. ahn-vee-rohn ____ uh-roh

What is that? (pointing)	C'est quoi ça? say kwah sah
How much is it?	C'est combien? say kohn-bee-an
Nothing with eyeballs.	Rien avec des yeux. ree-an ah-vehk dayz yuh
Can I substitute (something) for ____?	Je peux substituer (quelque chose) pour ____? zhuh puh sewb-stee-tew-ay (kehl-kuh shohz) poor ____
Can I / Can we get it "to go"?	Je peux / Nous pouvons prendre ça "à emporter"? zhuh puh / noo poo-vohn prahn-druh sah ah ahn-por-tay

Once you're seated, the table is yours for the entire lunch or dinner period. The waiter or waitress is there to serve you, but only when you're ready. When going to a good restaurant with an approachable staff, I like to say, "Make me happy" ***(Rendez-moi content)*** and set a price limit.

Some eateries will let you split a dish; others won't. If you are splitting a main dish, it's polite to get one or two ***entrées*** (starters) as well. In most cases, it's fine for a person to get only a ***plat*** (main dish). You can never split a multi-course ***menu.***

If you want just a simple meal—like soup, a salad, a sandwich, or an omelet—go to a ***café*** or ***brasserie*** instead of a ***restaurant.***

There's always one more question at the end of any sales encounter (whether finishing a meal or buying cheese at a ***fromagerie***): Will there be anything else? The French have a staggering number of ways to say this, including: ***Ça sera tout?*** (Will that be all?), ***Et avec ça?*** (And with this?), ***Vous-avez terminé?*** (Have you finished?), ***Désirez-vous autre chose?*** (Would you like anything else?), ***Ça vous a plû?*** (Have you enjoyed it?), and so on. Your response can be a simple ***Ça va, merci.*** (Everything is fine, thanks.)

Tableware and Condiments

I need / We need a...	J'ai besoin / Nous avons besoin... zhay buh-zwan / nooz ah-vohn buh-zwan
...napkin.	...d'une serviette. dewn sehrv-yeht
...knife.	...d'un couteau. duhn koo-toh
...fork.	...d'une fourchette. dewn foor-sheht
...spoon.	...d'une cuillère. dewn kwee-yehr
...cup.	...d'une tasse. dewn tahs
...glass.	...d'un verre. duhn vehr
...carafe.	...d'une carafe. dewn kah-rahf
Please...	S'il vous plaît... see voo play
...another table setting.	...d'un autre couvert. duhn oh-truh koo-vehr
...another plate.	...d'une autre assiette. dewn oh-truh ahs-yeht
silverware	des couverts day koo-vehr
water	d'eau doh
bread	de pain duh pan
butter	de beurre duh bur
margarine	de margarine duh mar-gah-reen
salt / pepper	de sel / de poivre duh sehl / duh pwah-vruh
sugar	de sucre duh sew-kruh
artificial sweetener	de faux-sucre duh foh-sew-kruh
honey	de miel duh mee-ehl
mustard	de moutarde duh moo-tard
ketchup	de ketchup duh "ketchup"
mayonnaise	de mayonnaise duh mah-yoh-nehz
toothpick	d'un cure-dents duhn kewr-dahn

The Food Arrives

Your meal may begin with an ***amuse-bouche***—literally, "palate amusement" (included with your meal). After bringing your food, your server might wish you a cheery ***"Bon appétit!"***

Looks delicious!	Ça a l'air délicieux! sah ah lair day-lee-see-uh
Is it included with the meal?	C'est inclus avec le repas? say an-klew ah-vehk luh ruh-pah
I did not order this.	Je n'ai pas commandé ça. zhuh nay pah koh-mahn-day sah
We did not order this.	Nous n'avons pas commandé ça. noo nah-vohn pah koh-mahn-day sah
This is...	C'est... say
...dirty.	...sale. sahl
...greasy.	...graisseux. gray-suh
...salty.	...salé. sah-lay
...undercooked.	...pas assez cuit. pah ah-say kwee
...overcooked.	...trop cuit. troh kwee
...cold.	...froid. frwah
Can you heat this up?	Vous pouvez réchauffer ça? voo poo-vay ray-shoh-fay sah
A little.	Un peu. uhn puh
More. / Another.	Plus. / Un autre. plew / uhn oh-truh
One more, please.	Encore un, s'il vous plaît. ahn-kor uhn see voo play
The same.	La même chose. lah mehm shohz
Enough.	Assez. ah-say
Yummy!	Miam-miam! myahm-myahm
Magnificent!	Magnifique! mahn-yee-feek
My compliments to the chef!	Félicitations au chef! fay-lee-see-tah-see-ohn oh shehf

Finished.	Terminé. tehr-mee-nay
Thank you.	Merci. mehr-see

Paying

bill	addition ah-dee-see-ohn
The bill, please.	L'addition, s'il vous plaît. lah-dee-see-ohn see voo play
Together.	Ensemble. ahn-sahn-bluh
Separate checks.	Notes séparées. noht say-pah-ray
Credit card OK?	Carte de crédit OK? kart duh kray-dee "OK"
This is not correct.	Ce n'est pas exact. suh nay pah ehg-zahkt
Can you explain this?	Vous pouvez expliquez ça? voo poo-vay ehk-splee-kay sah
Can you itemize the bill?	Vous pouvez détailler cette note? voo poo-vay day-tay-yay seht noht
What if I wash the dishes?	Et si je lave la vaisselle? ay see zhuh lahv lah vay-sehl
May I have a receipt, please?	Je peux avoir une facture, s'il vous plaît? zhuh puh ah-vwahr ewn fahk-tewr see voo play
Thank you very much.	Merci beaucoup. mehr-see boh-koo

In France, slow service is good service (fast service would rush the diners). Out of courtesy, your waiter will not bring your bill until you ask for it.

Tipping

Because a service charge is already included in the bill, an additional tip is not required, but appreciated. My French friends, who understand that it bothers Americans to "undertip," suggest this: Imagine that the bill already includes a 15 percent tip, then add whatever you feel is appropriate—maybe 5 percent for good service, or up to 10 percent for exceptional service. It's often most convenient to simply round up the bill (for example, for an €18.80 check, round up to €20)—hand your payment to the waiter and say ***C'est bon*** (say bohn), meaning "It's good—keep the change." If you order your food at a counter, don't tip.

tip	pourboire poor-bwahr
service included	service compris sehr-vees kohn-pree
service not included	service non compris sehr-vees nohn kohn-pree
Is tipping expected?	Je dois laisser un pourboire? zhuh dwah lay-say uhn poor-bwahr
What percent?	Quel pourcentage? kehl poor-sahn-tahzh
Keep the change.	Gardez la monnaie. gar-day lah moh-nay
Change, please.	La monnaie, s'il vous plaît. lah moh-nay see voo play
This is for you.	C'est pour vous. say poor voo

SPECIAL CONCERNS

In a Hurry

Europeans take their time at meals, so don't expect speedy service. However, if you're in a rush, be proactive and let your server know in advance, or seek out a ***brasserie*** or restaurant that offers ***service rapide*** (fast food).

I'm / We're in a hurry.	Je suis / Nous sommes pressé. zhuh swee / noo suhm preh-say
I'm sorry.	Désolé. day-zoh-lay
I need / We need...	J'ai besoin / Nous avons besoin... zhay buh-zwan / nooz ah-vohn buh-zwan
...to be served quickly.	...d'être servi vite. deh-truh sehr-vee veet

I must / We must...	Je dois / Nous devons... zhuh dwah / noo duh-vohn
...leave in 30 minutes / one hour.	...partir dans trente minutes / une heure. par-teer dahn trahnt mee-newt / ewn ur
Will the food be ready soon?	Ce sera prêt bientôt? suh suh-rah preh bee-an-toh
The bill, please.	L'addition, s'il vous plaît. lah-dee-see-ohn see voo play

Allergies and Other Dietary Restrictions

I'm allergic to...	Je suis allergique à... zhuh sweez ah-lehr-zheek ah
I cannot eat...	Je ne peux pas manger de... zhuh nuh puh pah mahn-zhay duh
He / She cannot eat...	Il / Elle ne peut pas manger de... eel / ehl nuh puh pah mahn-zhay duh
He / She has a life-threatening allergy to...	Il / Elle a une allergie très grave à... eel / ehl ah ewn ah-lehr-zhee treh grahv ah
No...	Non... nohn
...dairy products.	...aux produits laitiers. oh proh-dwee layt-yay
...any kind of nut.	...aux toutes sortes de noix. oh toot sort duh nwah
...peanuts.	...aux cacahuètes. oh kah-kah-weht
...walnuts.	...aux noix. oh nwah
...wheat / gluten.	...au blé / au gluten. oh blay / oh glew-tehn
...shellfish.	...crustacés. krew-stah-say
...salt / sugar.	...sel / sucre. sehl / sew-kruh
I'm a diabetic.	Je suis diabétique. zhuh swee dee-ah-bay-teek

He / She is lactose intolerant.	Il / Elle est intolérant au lactose. eel / ehl ay an-toh-lay-rahnt oh lahk-tohz
No caffeine.	Décaféiné. day-kah-fay-nay
No alcohol.	Sans alcool. sahnz ahl-kohl
Organic.	Biologique. bee-oh-loh-zheek

Vegetarian Phrases

Many French people think "vegetarian" means "no red meat" or "not much meat." If you're a strict vegetarian, be very specific: Tell your server what you don't eat—and it can be helpful to clarify what you do eat. Write it out on a card and keep it handy.

I'm a...	Je suis... zhuh swee
...vegetarian. (male)	...végétarien. vay-zhay-tah-ree-an
...vegetarian. (female)	...végétarienne. vay-zhay-tah-ree-ehn
...strict vegetarian.	...strict végétarien. streekt vay-zhay-tah-ree-an
...vegan. (m / f)	...végétalien / végétalienne. vay-zhay-tah-lee-an / vay-zhay-tah-lee-ehn
Is any animal product used in this?	Il y a des produits d'origine animale dedans? eel yah day proh-dwee doh-ree-zheen ah-nee-mahl duh-dahn
What is vegetarian? (pointing to menu)	Qu'est-ce qu'il y a de végétarien? kehs keel yah duh vay-zhay-tah-ree-an
I don't eat...	Je ne mange pas... zhuh nuh mahnzh pah
I'd like this without...	Je voudrais cela sans... zhuh voo-dray suh-lah sahn
...meat.	...viande. vee-ahnd
...eggs.	...oeufs. uhf
...animal products.	...produits d'origine animale. proh-dwee doh-ree-zheen ah-nee-mahl

I eat...	Je mange... zhuh mahnzh
Do you have...?	Avez-vous...? ah-vay-voo
...anything with tofu	...quelque chose avec du tofu kehl-kuh shohz ah-vehk dew toh-few
...a veggie burger	...un hamburger végétarien uhn ahn-bur-gehr vay-zhay-tah-ree-an

Children

Do you have a...?	Vous avez...? vooz ah-vay
...children's menu	...une carte d'enfants ewn kart dahn-fahn
...children's portion	...une assiette enfant ewn ahs-yeht ahn-fahn
...half-portion	...une demi-portion ewn duh-mee-por-see-ohn
...high chair	...une chaise haute ewn shehz oht
...booster seat	...un réhausseur uhn ray-oh-sur
noodles / rice	pâtes / riz paht / ree
with butter	avec beurre ah-vehk bur
without sauce	pas de sauce pah duh sohs
sauce or dressing on the side	sauce à part sohs ah par
pizza	pizza "pizza"
...cheese only	...juste fromage zhewst froh-mahzh
...pepperoni	...chorizo shoh-ree-zoh
grilled ham and cheese sandwich	croque monsieur krohk muhs-yuh
hot dog and fries	saucisse-frites soh-sees-freet
hamburger	hamburger ahn-bur-gehr
cheeseburger	cheeseburger sheez-bur-gehr
French fries	frites freet

ketchup	ketchup "ketchup"
milk	lait lay
straw	paille pī-yuh
More napkins, please.	Des serviettes, s'il vous plaît. day sehrv-yeht see voo play

WHAT'S COOKING?

Breakfast

French hotel breakfasts are small, expensive, and often optional. The basic continental breakfast has three parts: 1) ***boisson chaude***—a hot drink, such as ***café au lait*** (coffee with milk), ***thé*** (tea), or ***chocolat chaud*** (hot chocolate); 2) ***viennoiserie***—your choice of sweet rolls, including ***croissants;*** and 3) ***une tartine***—a fancy word for a ***baguette*** with ***beurre*** (butter) and ***confiture*** (jam). You may also get some ***jus de fruit*** (fruit juice, usually orange), but it likely costs extra. Many hotels provide breakfast buffets with fruit, cereal, yogurt, and cheese (usually for a few extra euros and well worth it).

You can save money by breakfasting at a ***bar*** or ***café,*** where it's usually acceptable to bring in a ***croissant*** from the neighboring ***boulangerie*** (bakery). Or just order ***une tartine*** with your ***café au lait.*** French people almost never eat eggs for breakfast, but if you're desperate, you can get an ***omelette*** almost any time of day at a café.

I'd like / We'd like...	Je voudrais / Nous voudrions... zhuh voo-dray / noo voo-dree-ohn
breakfast	petit déjeuner puh-tee day-zhuh-nay
bread	pain pan
roll	petit pain puh-tee pan
little loaf of bread	baguette bah-geht
toast	toast "toast"
butter	beurre bur
jam	confiture kohn-fee-tewr

Key Phrases: What's Cooking?

food	nourriture noo-ree-tewr
breakfast	petit déjeuner puh-tee day-zhuh-nay
lunch	déjeuner day-zhuh-nay
dinner	dîner dee-nay
bread	pain pan
cheese	fromage froh-mahzh
soup	soupe soop
salad	salade sah-lahd
fish	poisson pwah-sohn
chicken	poulet poo-lay
meat	viande vee-ahnd
vegetables	légumes lay-gewm
fruit	fruit frwee
dessert	dessert day-sehr

honey	miel mee-ehl
fruit cup	salade de fruits sah-lahd duh frwee
pastry	pâtisserie pah-tee-suh-ree
croissant	croissant krwah-sahn
cheese	fromage froh-mahzh
yogurt	yaourt yah-oort
cereal	céréale say-ray-ahl
milk	lait lay
coffee / tea	café / thé kah-fay / tay
fruit juice	jus de fruit zhew duh frwee
orange juice (fresh)	jus d'orange (pressé) zhew doh-rahnzh (preh-say)
hot chocolate	chocolat chaud shoh-koh-lah shoh

What's Probably Not for Breakfast

You likely won't see any of these items at a traditional French breakfast table, but you may see them at international hotels or cafés catering to foreigners.

omelet	omelette oh-muh-leht
eggs	des oeufs dayz uhf
fried eggs	oeufs au plat uhf oh plah
scrambled eggs	oeufs brouillés uhf broo-yay
boiled egg...	oeuf à la coque... uhf ah lah kohk
...soft / hard	...mollet / dur moh-lay / dewr
poached egg	oeuf poché uhf poh-shay
ham	jambon zhahn-bohn

Crêpes and Quick Lunches

crêpe...	crêpe... krehp
buckwheat crêpe...	galette... gah-leht
omelet...	omelette... oh-muh-leht
quiche...	quiche... keesh
...with cheese	...au fromage oh froh-mahzh
...with ham	...au jambon oh zhahn-bohn
...with onions	...aux oignons ohz ohn-yohn
...with leeks	...aux poirreaux oh pwah-roh
...with mushrooms	...aux champignons oh shahn-peen-yohn
...with bacon, cheese, and onions	...lorraine lor-rehn
...with tuna	...au thon oh tohn
...with salmon	...au saumon oh soh-mohn
paté	pâté pah-tay
onion tart	tarte à l'oignon tart ah lohn-yohn
cheese tart	tarte au fromage tart oh froh-mahzh

Light meals are quick and easy at ***cafés, brasseries,*** and ***bars*** throughout France. (These are about the same, except that ***brasseries*** serve food all day, whereas many ***cafés*** close their kitchens between lunch and dinner—around 4 p.m. to 6 p.m.) These places generally have more limited menus than restaurants, but they offer more budget options.

A ***salade, crêpe, quiche,*** or ***omelette*** is a fairly cheap way to fill up, even in Paris. Each can be made with various extras like ham, cheese, mushrooms, and so on.

Sandwiches

I'd like a sandwich.	Je voudrais un sandwich. zhuh voo-dray uhn sahnd-weech
bread	pain pan
toasted	grillé gree-yay
cheese	fromage froh-mahzh
tuna	thon tohn
fish	poisson pwah-sohn
chicken	poulet poo-lay
turkey	dinde dand
ham	jambon zhahn-bohn
salami	salami sah-lah-mee
boiled egg	oeuf dur uhf dewr
garnished with veggies	crudités krew-dee-tay
lettuce	salade sah-lahd
tomato	tomate toh-maht
onions	oignons ohn-yohn
mustard	moutarde moo-tard
mayonnaise	mayonnaise mah-yoh-nehz
without mayonnaise	sans mayonnaise sahn mah-yoh-nehz
peanut butter	beurre de cacahuètes bur duh kah-kah-weht
jam / jelly	confiture kohn-fee-tewr

pork sandwich	sandwich au porc sahnd-weech oh por
grilled / heated	grillé / réchauffé gree-yay / ray-shoh-fay
Does this come cold or warm?	C'est servi froid ou chaud? say sehr-vee frwah oo shoh

Crunchy, grilled ***croque*** sandwiches (literally "crunch")—such as the ***croque monsieur*** (ham and cheese) or the ***croque madame*** (same as the ***monsieur*** but with a fried egg, too)—are a French café staple. Cold sandwiches, as well as small quiches, often come ready-made at ***boulangeries*** (bakeries). When buying a sandwich, you might see signs for ***emporté*** (to go) or ***sur place*** (to eat here).

Say Cheese

cheese	fromage froh-mahzh
goat	chèvre sheh-vruh
cow	vache vahsh
sheep / ewe	brebis bruh-bee
blue	bleu bluh
cheese shop	fromagerie / crémerie froh-mah-zhuh-ree / kray-muh-ree
cheese platter	plâteau de fromages plah-toh duh froh-mahzh
I like cheese that is...	J'aime le fromage qui est... zhehm luh froh-mahzh kee ay
...young. (smooth)	...ferme. fehrm
...aged. (mature, stronger flavor)	...bien fait. bee-an fay
...mild.	...doux. doo
...sharp.	...fort. for
...hard / soft / semi-soft.	...dur / mou / plutôt mou. dewr / moo / plew-toh moo

Choose for me, please.	Choisissez pour moi, s'il vous plaît. shwah-zee-say poor mwah see voo play
I would like three types of cheese for a picnic.	Je voudrais trois sortes de fromage pour une pique-nique. zhuh voo-dray trwah sort duh froh-mahzh poor ewn peek-neek
What type?	Quel sorte? kehl sort
Like this. (showing size)	Comme ça. kohm sah

When cutting you a ***tranche*** (trahnsh; slice), the ***fromagerie*** or ***crémerie*** clerk will want to know how much you want: ***Comme ça?*** (Like this?) ***Plus?*** (More?) ***Moins?*** (Less?).

Soups and Stews

soup (of the day)	soupe (du jour) soop (dew zhoor)
broth...	bouillon... boo-yohn
...chicken	...de poulet duh poo-lay
...beef	...de boeuf duh buhf
...with noodles	...aux nouilles oh noo-ee
...with rice	...au riz oh ree
thick vegetable soup	potage de légumes poh-tahzh duh lay-gewm
Provençal vegetable soup	soupe au pistou soop oh pee-stoo
onion soup	soupe à l'oignon soop ah lohn-yohn
cream of asparagus soup	crème d'asperges krehm dah-spehrzh
potato and leek soup	vichyssoise vee-shee-swahz
garlic soup	soupe à l'ail / tourin soop ah lī / too-ran
shellfish chowder	bisque beesk
seafood stew	bouillabaisse boo-yah-behs

meat and vegetable stew	pot au feu poht oh fuh
meat stew	ragoût rah-goo

Salads

Salads are usually served with a vinaigrette dressing and often eaten after the main course (to aid digestion).

salad...	salade... sah-lahd
...green / mixed	...verte / mixte vehrt / meekst
...with goat cheese	...au chèvre chaud oh sheh-vruh shoh
...chef's	...composée kohn-poh-zay
...seafood	...océane oh-say-ahn
...tuna	...de thon duh tohn
...veggie	...crudités krew-dee-tay
...with ham / cheese / egg	...avec jambon / fromage / oeuf ah-vehk zhahn-bohn / froh-mahzh / uhf
lettuce	laitue / salade lay-tew / sah-lahd
tomatoes	tomates toh-maht
onions	oignons ohn-yohn
cucumber	concombre kohn-kohn-bruh
oil / vinegar	huile / vinaigre weel / vee-nay-gruh
dressing on the side	sauce à part sohs ah par
What is in this salad?	Qu'est-ce qu'il ya dans cette salade? kehs keel yah dahn seht sah-lahd

Seafood

seafood	fruits de mer frwee duh mehr
assorted seafood	assiette de fruits de mer ahs-yeht duh frwee duh mehr

fish	poisson pwah-sohn
shellfish	crustacés / coquillages krew-stah-say / koh-kee-ahzh
anchovies	anchois ahn-shwah
clams	palourdes pah-loord
cod	cabillaud kah-bee-yoh
crab	crabe krahb
halibut	flétan flay-tahn
herring	hareng ah-rahn
lobster	homard oh-mar
mussels	moules mool
oysters	huîtres wee-truh
prawns	scampi skahn-pee
salmon	saumon soh-mohn
salty cod	morue moh-rew
sardines	sardines sar-deen
scallops	coquilles Saint-Jacques koh-keel san-zhahk
shrimp	crevettes kruh-veht
squid	calamar kah-lah-mar
trout	truite trweet
tuna	thon tohn
How much for a portion?	C'est combien la portion? say kohn-bee-an lah por-see-ohn
What's fresh today?	Qu'est-ce que c'est frais aujourd'hui? kehs kuh say fray oh-joord-wee
How do you eat this?	Comment est-ce que ça se mange? koh-mahn ehs kuh sah suh mahnzh
Do you eat this part?	Ça se mange? sah suh mahnzh
Just the head, please.	Seulement la tête, s'il vous plaît. suhl-mahn lah teht see voo play

Poultry

poultry	volaille voh-lī
chicken	poulet poo-lay
duck	canard kah-nar
goose	oie wah
turkey	dinde dand
breast	le blanc / le filet luh blahn / luh fee-lay
thigh	la cuisse lah kwees
drumstick	le pilon luh pee-lohn
white meat	viande blanche vee-ahnd blahnsh
eggs	des oeufs dayz uhf
free-range	élevé en liberté / élevé en plein air ay-luh-vay ahn lee-behr-tay / ay luh vay ahn plehn air
How long has this been dead?	Il est mort depuis longtemps? eel ay mor duh-pwee lohn-tahn

Meat

meat	viande vee-ahnd
meat cured with salt / smoked meat	viandes salées / viandes fumées vee-ahnd sah-lay / vee-ahnd few-may
beef	boeuf buhf
boar	sanglier sahn-glee-ay
cold cuts	assiette de charcuterie ahs-yeht duh shar-kew-tuh-ree
cutlet	côtelette koh-tuh-leht
frog legs	cuisses de grenouilles kwees duh greh-noo-ee
ham	jambon zhahn-bohn
lamb	agneau ahn-yoh
mixed grill	grillades gree-yahd

Avoiding Mis-Steaks

By American standards, the French undercook meats. If you're particular about the way your meat is cooked, order it more well-done than you ordinarily would.

raw	cru krew
very rare	bleu bluh
rare	saignant sehn-yahn
medium	à point ah pwan
well-done	bien cuit bee-an kwee
very well-done	très bien cuit treh bee-an kwee

mutton	mouton moo-tohn
organs	organes or-gahn
oxtail	queue de boeuf kuh duh buhf
pork	porc por
rabbit	lapin lah-pan
roast beef	rosbif rohs-beef
sausage	saucisse soh-sees
blood sausage	boudin noir boo-dan nwahr
snails	escargots ehs-kar-goh
steak	bifteck beef-tehk
thick hunk of prime steak	pavé pah-vay
flank steak	bavette bah-veht
hanger steak	onglet ohn-glay
sirloin	faux-filet foh-fee-lay
rib-eye steak	entrecôte ahn-truh-koht
tenderloin	médaillon may-dī-yohn
T-bone	côte de boeuf koht duh buhf

fillet	filet fee-lay
tenderloin of T-bone	tournedos toor-nuh-doh
veal	veau voh
venison	viande de chevreuil vee-ahnd duh shuh-vruh-ee
Is this cooked?	C'est cuit? say kwee

Veggies and Sides

vegetables	légumes lay-gewm
mixed vegetables	légumes variés lay-gewm vah-ree-ay
with vegetables	garni gar-nee
artichoke	artichaut ar-tee-shoh
arugula (rocket)	roquette roh-keht
asparagus	asperges ah-spehrzh
avocado	avocat ah-voh-kah
beans	haricots ah-ree-koh
beets	betterave beh-tuh-rahv
broccoli	brocoli broh-koh-lee
cabbage	chou shoo
carrots	carottes kah-roht
cauliflower	chou-fleur shoo-flur
corn	maïs mah-ees
cucumber	concombre kohn-kohn-bruh
eggplant	aubergine oh-behr-zheen
endive	endive ahn-deev
fennel	fenouil fuh-noo-ee
garlic	ail ī
green beans	haricots verts ah-ree-koh vehr
leeks	poireaux pwah-roh
lentils	lentilles lahn-teel
mushrooms	champignons shahn-peen-yohn

olives	olives oh-leev
onions	oignons ohn-yohn
peas	petits pois puh-tee pwah
pepper...	poivron... pwah-vrohn
...green / red / yellow	...vert / rouge / jaune vehr / roozh / zhohn
pickles	cornichons kor-nee-shohn
potato	pomme de terre pohm duh tehr
radish	radis rah-dee
rice	riz ree
spaghetti	spaghetti "spaghetti"
spinach	épinards ay-pee-nar
tomatoes	tomates toh-maht
truffles	truffes trewf
turnip	navet nah-vay
zucchini	courgette koor-zheht

Fruits

fruit	fruit frwee
fruit cup	salade de fruits sah-lahd duh frwee
fruit smoothie	smoothie aux fruits smoo-zee oh frwee
apple	pomme pohm
apricot	abricot ah-bree-koh
banana	banane bah-nahn
berries	fruits rouges frwee roozh
blueberry	myrtille meer-tee
cantaloupe	melon muh-lohn
cherry	cerise suh-reez
cranberry	canneberge kah-nuh-behrzh
date	datte daht
fig	figue feeg

grapefruit	pamplemousse pahn-pluh-moos
grapes	raisins ray-zan
lemon	citron see-trohn
melon	melon muh-lohn
orange	orange oh-rahnzh
peach	pêche pehsh
pear	poire pwahr
pineapple	ananas ah-nah-nahs
plum	prune prewn
pomegranate	grenade gruh-nahd
prune	pruneau prew-noh
raisin	raisin sec ray-zan sehk
raspberry	framboise frahn-bwahz
strawberry	fraise frehz
tangerine	mandarine mahn-dah-reen
watermelon	pastèque pah-stehk

Just Desserts

I'd like...	Je voudrais... zhuh voo-dray
We'd like...	Nous voudrions... noo voo-dree-ohn
dessert	dessert day-sehr
cookies	biscuits / petits gâteaux bees-kwee / puh-tee gah-toh
cake	gâteau gah-toh
ice cream...	glace... glahs
...scoop	...boule bool
...cone	...cornet kor-nay
...cup	...bol bohl
...vanilla	...vanille vah-nee
...chocolate	...chocolat shoh-koh-lah
...strawberry	...fraise frehz

sorbet	sorbet sor-bay
fruit cup	salade de fruits sah-lahd duh frwee
tart	tartelette tar-tuh-leht
pie	tarte tart
whipped cream	crème chantilly krehm shahn-tee-yee
pastry	pâtisserie pah-tee-suh-ree
crêpes	crêpes krehp
sweet crêpes	crêpes sucrées krehp sew-kray
candy	bonbon bohn-bohn
chocolates	chocolats shoh-koh-lah
low calorie	bas en calories bah ahn kah-loh-ree
homemade	fait maison fay may-zohn
We'll split one.	Nous le partageons. noo luh par-tah-zhohn
Two forks / spoons, please.	Deux fourchettes / cuillères, s'il vous plaît. duh foor-sheht / kwee-yehr see voo play
I shouldn't, but...	Je ne devrais pas, mais... zhuh nuh duh-vray pah may
Magnificent!	Magnifique! mahn-yee-feek
It's heavenly!	C'est divin! say dee-van

DRINKING

Every ***café*** or ***bar*** has a price list posted (and refills aren't free). In bigger cities, prices go up when you sit down. It's cheapest to stand at the ***comptoir*** (counter); drinks cost a bit more ***en salle*** (at a table indoors) or on the ***terasse*** (at a table outside). Outdoor seating is worth the extra cost in pleasant weather, with tidy sidewalk tables all set up facing the street, as if ready to watch a show.

Water

mineral water... eau minérale... oh mee-nay-rahl

...carbonated ...gazeuse gah-zuhz

...not carbonated ...non gazeuse nohn gah-zuhz

tap water (in a restaurant) une carafe d'eau ewn kah-rahf doh

(not) drinkable (non) potable (nohn) poh-tah-bluh

Is the water safe to drink? L'eau est potable? loh ay poh-tah-bluh

The French typically order ***eau minérale*** (and wine) with their meals. But if you want free tap water, ask for ***une carafe d'eau, s'il vous plaît.*** (The technical term for tap water, ***l'eau du robinet,*** sounds crass to waiters.)

Milk

whole milk lait entier lay ahnt-yay

skim milk lait écrémé lay ay-kray-may

fresh milk lait frais lay fray

cold / warm froid / chaud frwah / shoh

straw paille pī-yuh

Juice and Other Drinks

fruit juice jus de fruit zhew duh frwee

100% juice cent pour cent jus sahn poor sahn zhew

orange juice jus d'orange zhew doh-rahnzh

freshly squeezed pressé preh-say

apple juice jus de pomme zhew duh pohm

cranberry juice jus de canneberge zhew duh kah-nuh-behrzh

grape juice jus de raisin zhew duh ray-zan

Key Phrases: Drinking

drink	verre vehr
(mineral) water	eau (minérale) oh (mee-nay-rahl)
tap water (in a restaurant)	une carafe d'eau ewn kah-rahf doh
milk	lait lay
juice	jus zhew
coffee	café kah-fay
tea	thé tay
wine	vin van
beer	bière bee-ehr
Cheers!	Santé! sahn-tay

grapefruit juice	jus de pamplemousse zhew duh pahn-pluh-moos
pineapple juice	jus d'ananas zhew dah-nah-nahs
fruit smoothie	smoothie aux fruits smoo-zee oh frwee
lemonade	citron pressé see-trohn preh-say
iced tea	thé glacé tay glah-say
(diet) soda	soda ("light") soh-dah ("light")
energy drink	boisson énergétique bwah-sohn ay-nehr-zhay-teek
with / without...	avec / sans... ah-vehk / sahn
...sugar	...sucre sew-kruh
...ice	...glaçons glah-sohn
25... (small)	Vingt-cinque... vant-sank
33... (medium)	Trente-trois... trahnt-trwah
50... (large)	Cinquante... san-kahnt
...centiliters.	...centilitres. sahn-tee-lee-truh

When you order a drink, state the size in centiliters (don't say "small," "medium," or "large," because the waiter might bring a bigger drink than you want). For something small, ask for 25 ***centilitres*** (about 8 ounces); for a medium drink, order 33 ***centilitres*** (about 12 ounces—a normal can of soda); a large is 50 ***centilitres*** (about 16 ounces); and a super-size is one ***litre*** (lee-truh; about a quart—which is more than I would ever order in France).

Coffee Talk

The French define various types of espresso drinks by how much milk is added. Here are the most common coffee drinks:

coffee (espresso)	café kah-fay
a shot of espresso without milk	un café / un express uhn kah-fay / uhn ehk-sprehs
espresso shot with a "hazelnut"-size dollop of milk	une noisette ewn nwah-zeht
coffee with milk (similar to American latte)	un café crème uhn kah-fay krehm
coffee with lots of milk (in bowl-like cup)	un café au lait uhn kah-fay oh lay
coffee with whipped cream	un café avec chantilly uhn kah-fay ah-vehk shahn-tee-yee
a double espresso with milk	un grand crème uhn grahn krehm
espresso with a touch of apple brandy (calvados)	café-calva kah-fay-kahl-vah
espresso with water (like an Americano)	un café allongé / café longue uhn kah-fay ah-lohn-zhay / kah-fay lohng
instant coffee	Nescafé "Nescafé"
decaffeinated / decaf	décaféiné / déca day-kah-fay-nay / day-kah
sugar	sucre sew-kruh

Other Hot Drinks

hot water	l'eau chaude	loh shohd
hot chocolate	chocolat chaud	shoh-koh-lah shoh
tea	thé	tay
lemon	citron	see-trohn
tea bag	sachet de thé	sah-shay duh tay
plain tea	thé nature	tay nah-tewr
herbal tea	tisane	tee-zahn
lemon tea	thé au citron	tay oh see-trohn
orange tea	thé à l'orange	tay ah loh-rahnzh
peppermint tea	thé à la menthe	tay ah lah mahnt
fruit tea	thé de fruit	tay duh frwee
green tea	thé vert	tay vehr
chai tea	thé chai	tay "chai"

Wine Lingo

wine	vin	van
house wine	vin de la maison	van duh lah may-zohn
cheapest wine	vin ordinaire	van or-dee-nair
local	du pays	dew pay-ee
of the region	de la région	duh lah ray-zhee-ohn
red	rouge	roozh
white	blanc	blahn
rosé	rosé	roh-zay
sparkling	pétillant / mousseux / bouché (for cider)	pay-tee-yahn / moo-suh / boo-shay
I'd like / We'd like a wine that is ____ and ____.	Je voudrais / Nous voudrions un vin ____ et ____.	zhuh voo-dray / noo voo-dree-ohn uhn van ____ ay ____

light	léger lay-zhay
full-bodied (heavy)	robuste / costaud roh-bewst / koh-stoh
sweet	doux doo
semi-dry	demi sec duh-mee-sehk
dry	sec sehk
very dry	brut brewt
tannic	tannique tah-neek
oaky	goût du fût de chêne goo duh foo duh shehn
fruity (jammy)	confituré kohn-fee-tew-ray
fine	fin / avec finesse fan / ah-vehk fee-nehs
ready to drink (mature)	prêt à boire preh ah bwahr
not ready to drink	fermé fehr-may
from old vines	de vieille vignes duh vee-yay-ee veen-yuh
chilled	bien frais / rafraîchi bee-an fray / rah-fray-shee
at room temperature	chambré shahn-bray
cork	bouchon boo-shohn
corkscrew	tire-bouchon teer-boo-shohn
corked (spoiled from a bad cork)	bouchonné boo-shoh-nay
vineyard	vignoble veen-yoh-bluh
harvest	vendange vahn-dahnzh

The French believe that the specific qualities of wine are a unique product of its place of origin (microclimate, soil, geology, culture, and so on). This uniquely French concept is known as ***terroir*** (tehr-wahr, literally "soil") and also applies to cheese and other foods.

Ordering Wine

I would like...	Je voudrais...	zhuh voo-dray
We would like...	Nous voudrions...	noo voo-dree-ohn
...the wine list.	...la carte des vins.	lah kart day van
...a glass...	...un verre...	uhn vehr
...a small pitcher...	...un pichet...	uhn pee-shay
...a carafe...	...une carafe...	ewn kah-rahf
...a half bottle...	...une demi-bouteille...	ewn duh-mee-boo-tay
...a bottle...	...une bouteille...	ewn boo-tay
...a barrel...	...un tonneau...	uhn toh-noh
...of red wine.	...de vin rouge.	duh van roozh
...of white wine.	...de vin blanc.	duh van blahn
of the region	de la région	duh lah ray-zhee-ohn
house wine	vin de la maison	van duh lah may-zohn
What is a good vintage?	Quelles est un bon millésime?	kehl ay uhn bohn mee-lay-zeem
What do you recommend?	Qu'est-ce que vous recommandez?	kehs kuh voo ruh-koh-mahn-day
Choose for me, please.	Choisissez pour moi, s'il vous plaît.	shwah-zee-say poor mwah see voo play
Around ____ euros.	Au tour de ____ euro.	oh toor duh ____ uh-roh
Another, please.	Un autre, s'il vous plaît.	uhn oh-truh see voo play

If all you want is a basic table wine, you can order ***vin de la maison*** (house wine). It may not be available by the glass, but a ***pichet*** (small pitcher) of a quarter-liter isn't much bigger than a generously poured glass. If you don't want a whole bottle of wine for the table, look on the menu for a section of ***vins au verre*** (wines sold by the glass).

Beer

I'd like / We'd like...	Je voudrais / Nous voudrions... zhuh voo-dray / noo voo-dree-ohn
a beer	une bière ewn bee-ehr
from the tap	pression preh-see-ohn
bottle	bouteille boo-tay
light / dark	blonde / brune blohnd / brewn
local / imported	régionale / importée ray-zhee-oh-nahl / an-por-tay
a small beer	un demi uhn duh-mee
a large beer	une chope ewn shohp
lager	blonde blohnd
pilsner	pils / pilsner peel / peels-nehr
ale	bière anglaise légère / ale bee-ehr ahn-glehz lay-zhehr / ehl
wheat	bière blanche bee-ehr blahnsh
porter	bière brune bee-ehr brewn
stout	bière de malte forte bee-ehr duh mahlt fort
microbrew	bière artisanale bee-ehr ar tee-zah-nahl
low-calorie ("lite")	biere "light" bee-ehr "light"
shandy	panaché pah-nah-shay
a non-alcoholic beer	une bière non-alcoolisée ewn bee-ehr nohn-ahl-koh-lee-zay
hard apple cider	cidre see-druh

Bar Talk

Would you like to go out for a drink?	Voulez-vous prendre un verre? voo-lay-voo prahn-druh uhn vehr
I'll buy you a drink.	Je vous offre un verre. zhuh vooz oh-fruh uhn vehr

It's on me.	C'est moi qui paie. say mwah kee pay
The next one's on me.	Le suivant est sur moi. luh swee-vahnt ay sewr mwah
What would you like?	Qu'est-ce que vous prenez? kehs kuh voo pruh-nay
I'll have a ____.	Je prends un ____. zhuh prahn uhn ____
I don't drink alcohol.	Je ne bois pas d'alcool. zhuh nuh bwah pah dahl-kohl
What is the local specialty?	Quelle est la spécialité régionale? kehl ay lah spay-see-ah-lee-tay ray-zhee-oh-nahl
Straight.	Sec. sehk
With / Without...	Avec / Sans... ah-vehk / sahn
...ice.	...glaçons. glah-sohn
One more.	Encore une. ahn-kor ewn
Cheers!	Santé! sahn-tay

PICNICKING

Gather supplies early for a picnic lunch; small shops close at noon for their lunch break. For convenience, you can assemble your picnic ***(pique-nique)*** at a ***supermarché*** or ***hypermarché*** (supermarket)—but shops or a ***marché*** (open-air market) are more fun and offer the best selection. Look for a ***boulangerie*** (bakery), a ***crémerie*** or ***fromagerie*** (cheeses), a ***charcuterie*** or ***traiteur*** (deli items, salads, meats, and pâtés), an ***épicerie*** or ***magasin d'alimentation*** (grocery with fruit, veggies, and so on), and a ***pâtisserie*** (pastries). Late-night grocery stores are called ***dépanneurs*** (day-pah-nur).

Is it self-service?	C'est libre service? say lee-bruh sehr-vees
Fifty grams.	Cinquante grammes. san-kahnt grahm
One hundred grams.	Cent grammes. sahn grahm
More. / Less.	Plus. / Moins. plew / mwan
A piece.	Un morceau. uhn mor-soh

A slice.	Une tranche. ewn trahnsh
Four slices.	Quatre tranches. kah-truh trahnsh
Sliced.	Tranché. trahn-shay
Half.	La moitié. lah mwaht-yay
A handful.	Une poignée. ewn pwahn-yay
A bag.	Un sachet. uhn sah-shay
Ripe for today?	Pour manger aujourd'hui? poor mahn-zhay oh-joord-wee
Can I taste it?	Je peux goûter? zhuh puh goo-tay
Ready to eat?	Prêt à manger? preh ah mahn-zhay
Does it need to be cooked?	Il faut le faire cuire? eel foh luh fair kweer
container	barquette bar-keht
spoon / fork...	cuillère / fourchette... kwee-yehr / foor-sheht
...made of plastic	...en plastique ahn plah-steek
cup / plate...	gobelet / assiette... goh-blay / ahs-yeht
...made of paper	...en papier ahn pahp-yay
Do you have a...?	Vous avez...? vooz ah-vay
Where can I buy / find a...?	Où puis-je acheter / trouver un...? oo pwee-zhuh ah-shuh-tay / troo-vay uhn
...corkscrew	...tire-bouchon teer-boo-shohn
...can opener	...ouvre boîte oo-vruh bwaht
...bottle opener	...décapsuleur day-kahp-sew-lur

Meat and cheese are sold by the gram. One hundred grams is about a quarter pound, enough for two sandwiches. To weigh and price your produce at more modern stores, put it on the scale, push the photo or number (keyed to the bin it came from), and then stick your sticker on the food. When buying produce in a market or from a produce stand, resist the temptation to touch, and wait your turn to be served.

MENU DECODER

This handy French-English decoder won't list every word on the menu, but it'll help you get ***riz et veau*** (rice and veal) instead of ***ris de veau*** (calf pancreas).

Note that decoding a menu can be particularly challenging in France, where ingredients are lovingly described in painstaking detail. For simplicity, I've listed the most prevalent terms and commonly seen variations, but this decoder is far from exhaustive when it comes to listing every melon or mushroom under the French sun.

Menu Categories

When you pick up a menu, you'll likely see these categories of offerings.

Petit déjeuner	Breakfast
Déjeuner	Lunch
Dîner	Dinner
Entrées	First course; appetizers
Chaud	Hot
Froid	Cold
Sandwichs	Sandwiches
Salades	Salads
Potages / Soupes	Soups
Menu	Fixed-price meal(s)
Spécialités	Specialties
Plats	Dishes
Plats principals	Main dishes
Viande	Meat
Porc	Pork
Volaille	Poultry
Poisson	Fish
Fruits de mer	Seafood
Garnitures	Side dishes
Légumes	Vegetables

Carte des consommations	Drink menu
Carte des vins	Wine list
Fromages	Cheeses
Desserts	Desserts
Enfants	Children
Suggestion du jour / Plat du jour	Daily special

And for the fine print:

Couvert	Cover charge
Service (non) compris	Service (not) included
Prix net	Tax included

Small Words

à la; à l'	in the style of
au / aux / avec	with
de / d' / des / du	of
et	and
ou	or
sans	without
sur	over

If you see ***à la*** or ***à l'*** on a menu, the next word may not appear in this decoder. That's because these phrases mean "in the style of," and often are followed by flowery, artsy, obscure descriptions. Even if you knew the exact meaning, it might not make things much clearer.

FRENCH / ENGLISH

abricot apricot
accompagné de accompanied by
acide sour; acidic
affiné aged
agneau lamb
agneau de pré salé lamb raised on salt-marsh lands
agrume citrus
ail / aillet garlic; garlic shoot
aile wing (poultry or fowl)
aïoli garlic mayonnaise
airelle wild cranberry
Aisy cendré soft cow cheese coated in ash
alcool alcohol
aligot mashed potatoes with cheese
aloyau sirloin
amande almond
amer bitter
amuse-bouche appetizer
ananas pineapple
anchoïade garlic and anchovy paste
anchois anchovies
(à l') ancienne in the old style
andouille pungent tripe sausage
anémone de mer anemone
aneth dill
anglaise "English" apple pastry
(à l') anglaise boiled
anis anise
AOC certified origin, designation for top-quality wine as well as cheese and butter
apéritif before-dinner drink
appellation area in which a wine's grapes are grown
araignée de mer spider crab
armagnac brandy produced in southwest France
artichaut artichoke
artichaut à la barigoule artichoke stuffed with garlic, ham, and herbs
artisanal from a small producer
asperge asparagus
assiette plate
assiette de charcuterie cold cuts
assiette d'enfant children's plate
au gratin topped with cheese and browned
au jus meat served in its natural juices
au vinaigre pickled
aubergine eggplant
Auvergne cow cheese sold in big wheels
avocat avocado
baba au rhum rum-soaked brioche
Baeckeoffe meat-and-potato stew
bagna cauda anchovy and butter sauce
baguette long loaf of bread
bain-marie water bath
ballon roll

banane banana
Banon soft goat cheese, wrapped in chestnut leaves
bar sea bass
barbarine watermelon used in pies and preserves
(à la) barigoule brown sauce with artichokes and mushrooms
barquette basket
basilic basil
basquaise Basque-style: cooked with tomato, eggplant, red pepper, and garlic
bâtard half-length baguette
baudroie monkfish
bavarois rich "Bavarian cream" custard
bavette flank steak; skirt steak
Béarnaise sauce of egg and wine
Beaufort hard, sharp, aged cow cheese
béchamel creamy, milk-based sauce
beignet deep-fried doughnut
Bénédictine herb-based liqueur
betterave beet
beurre (doux / demi-sel / salé) butter (unsalted / salted / very salted)
beurre blanc sauce of butter, white wine, and shallots
beurre de cacahuètes peanut butter
beurre manié butter-and-flour thickening agent
beurre noisette browned butter
biche deer
bien cuit well-done (meat)
bien fait aged, mature (cheese)
bière beer
bière brune dark beer
bifteck steak (can be tough)
biologique organic
bis, pain / bisse, pain dark-grain bread
biscuit cookie
biscuit de Savoie sponge cake
bisque shellfish chowder
blanc white
blanc (de volaille) breast (chicken)
blanc d'oeuf egg white
blanquette slow-cooked stew with rich white sauce
blette chard
bleu blue (cheese); very rare (meat)
bleu d'Auvergne pungent blue cow cheese from Auvergne
boeuf beef
(de) bois "of the woods" (wild)
boisson beverage
bonbon candy
bonite bonito (skipjack tuna)
bouché sparkling (cider)
bouchée bite-size ("mouthful"), usually describes a small puff pastry
bouchée à la reine pastry shell with creamed sweetbreads and mushroom
boudin blanc bratwurst-like sausage
boudin noir blood sausage

bouillabaisse seafood stew
bouilli boiled
bouillon broth
boulangerie / boulanger bakery
boule scoop (ice cream)
boulette de viande meatball
bouquet garni "bouquet" of herbs used to flavor soups, then removed
bourguignon cooked in red wine
bourride creamy fish soup
Boursin soft, creamy, herbed cow cheese
bouteille bottle
braisé braised
brandade de morue salted cod in garlic cream
brebis, fromage de sheep-milk cheese
brick fritter
Brie (de Meaux) mild, soft (almost runny) cow cheese
brié, pain dense, crusty bread
Brillat-Savarin buttery, slightly sour variant of Brie cheese
brioche buttery roll made with eggs
Brocciu sweet, fresh goat or ewe cheese
brochet pike
brochette skewer
brocoli broccoli
brouillé scrambled
Brousse du Rove fresh, creamy goat cheese
brune dark (beer)
brunoise finely chopped vegetables
brut very dry (wine or cider)
Cabécou pungent, nutty goat cheese
cabillaud cod
cacahuète peanut
café coffee
café allongé / café longue "long" coffee (espresso with water, like an Americano)
café au lait coffee with lots of milk
café avec chantilly coffee with whipped cream
café calva espresso with a touch of brandy
café crème coffee with milk
café décaféiné / café déca decaffeinated; decaf coffee
café gourmand coffee served with 2 or 3 small pastries
café noisette coffee with a dollop of milk
caille quail
caladon honey and almond cookie
calamar squid
calisson (d'Aix) marzipan cookie
calvados apple brandy
camarguaise, salade salad with rice and veggies
Camembert pungent, semi-creamy cow cheese
(de) campagne; campagnarde country-style; rustic
canapé appetizer; finger food

canard duck
cannelé "fluted" custard and caramel pastry
cannelle cinnamon
Cantal aged, semi-hard cow cheese
câpre caper
cardamome cardamom
cargolade snail, lamb, and sausage stew
carotte carrot
carpaccio thinly sliced raw meat or fish
carré (d'agneau / de porc) loin (lamb / pork)
carrelet plaice (flatfish)
carte menu
(à la) carte individual items on the menu
cassis black currant
cassonade brown sugar
cassoulet bean and meat stew
cavaillon, melon de small cantaloupe
cave wine cellar
céleri rave celery root
cendré with ashes
Cendré de Champagne Brie-like cheese covered in ash
(aux) cendres rolled in cinders (cheese)
cépage grape variety (wine)
cèpe boletus mushroom (similar to porcini)
cerf deer
cerise cherry
cervelas garlic pork sausage
cervelle brains
Chambord raspberry liqueur
chambré room temperature
champignon mushroom
chantilly / crème chantilly whipped cream
chapelure browned breadcrumbs
charbon de bois charcoal
charcuterie prepared meats such as sausages and pâtés
charentais, melon de yellow cantaloupe
Charolais high-quality beef; also a goat cheese from the Charolais region
Chartreuse herb-based liqueur
châtaigne chestnut
château wine bottled where it was made
chaud hot
chaud-froid cooked but served cold
chausson fruit-filled pastry
chausson aux pommes apple turnover
chêne, goût du fût de oaky (wine)
cheval horse
chèvre goat
chèvre chaud, salade au salad with warm goat cheese on toasted croutons
chevreuil, viande de venison
chiffonnade sliced into thin strips
chinois Chinese
chocolat chocolate

C

(le) choix de choice of
chope large beer
chorizo spicy sausage
chou cabbage
chou frisé kale
choucroute sauerkraut
choucroute garnie sauerkraut and sausage
chou-fleur cauliflower
chouquette eggy little baked doughnut
ciboulette chives
cidre hard apple cider
citre watermelon used in pies and preserves
citron lemon
clafoutis fruit tart made with egg batter
clou de girofle clove
cochon pig
cocotte casserole
cognac wine-distilled brandy
coing quince
Cointreau orange liqueur
colin hake (fish)
complet whole (whole grain); full
composée, salade "composed" salad with various ingredients
compote stewed fruit
compote de pommes applesauce
compris included
comptoir counter
Comté "Swiss cheese" from cow's milk
concassé coarsely chopped
concombre cucumber
confit a preserve, often fowl or pork cooked in its own fat
confiture preserves; jam
confituré jammy (wine)
consommé clear broth
copieux filling
coq rooster
coq au vin chicken braised in red wine
coque cockle
coquelet cockerel (young rooster)
coquille Saint-Jacques scallop
corbeille basket
coriandre cilantro; coriander
cornichon pickle
costaud full-bodied (wine)
côte rib or chop (meat)
côte de boeuf T-bone steak
côtelette cutlet
côtes chops (for meat); hillsides (for wine)
cou neck
coulis thick sauce, usually a purée of a single ingredient
Coulommiers soft, rich, creamy, Brie-like cow cheese
courge summer squash
courgette zucchini
couronne "crown," ring-shaped baguette
court-bouillon herbed liquid used to cook fish
couteau knife
couvert cover charge
crabe crab

cramique brioche bread with raisins
crème cream; custard
crème à l'anglaise custard sauce
crème bavaroise Bavarian cream pudding
crème brûlée caramelized custard
crème caramel custard with caramel sauce
crème chantilly whipped cream
crème de cassis black currant liqueur
crème de menthe mint liqueur
crème fraîche heavy, slightly soured cream
crème (velouté) d'asperges cream of asparagus soup
créole (ice cream) rum and tropical fruit (like rum raisin)
crêpe crêpe (thin pancake)
crêpe de froment sweet crêpe (made of wheat batter)
crêpe sucrées sweet crêpe
crêpe suzette crêpe flambéed with orange brandy sauce
cresson watercress
crevette shrimp
croissant classic French crescent roll
croque madame grilled ham, cheese, and egg sandwich
croque monsieur grilled ham and cheese sandwich
croquette deep-fried ball of potato and other ingredients
Crottin de Chavignol goat cheese from the Loire Valley
croustade pastry-wrapped dish (e.g., fruit filled)
croustillant crispy
croûte crust (bread); rind (cheese)
croûte au fromage cheese pastry
croziflette buckwheat pasta with melted cheese
cru raw; superior growth (wine)
crudité raw vegetable
cuillère spoon
cuisse thigh
cuisse de grenouille frog leg
cuit cooked
cuit au four baked
culotte rump (steak)
dariole small cylindrical mold
datte date
daube stew, usually meat
dauphine, pommes (de terre) fried puffs of mashed potatoes
décortiqué peeled; shelled
déglacé deglazed
dégustation tasting; sampling
déjeuner lunch
demi half; small beer
demi-bouteille half bottle
demi-glace brown sauce
demi-sec medium-dry (wine)
désossé boned; boneless
diabolo grenadine lemon-lime soda with cherry syrup
diabolo menthe lemon-lime soda with mint syrup

D

digestif after-dinner drink
dinde turkey
dîner dinner
domaine wine estate
doré browned
doux mild, sweet (wine); mild, soft (cheese)
douze / douzaine dozen
droit de bouchon corkage fee
duchesse, pommes (de terre) baked puffs of mashed potatoes
duxelles chopped mushrooms, shallots, and cream
eau water
eau de vie fruit brandy ("water of life")
échalote shallot
Echourgnac cow cheese with brown rind
éclair oblong, iced custard-filled roll
écrivisse crayfish
édulcorant artificial sweetener
élevé en liberté / en plein air free-range
émincé chopped
Emmentaler "Swiss cheese"
(à) emporter to go
endive endive
entier whole
entrecôte rib-eye steak
entrée first course; appetizers
entremet small dish served between courses (sometimes dessert)
épaule shoulder (of beef, pork, lamb)
éperlan smelt
épice spice
épicée spicy (flavorful, well-seasoned)
épice, pain d' gingerbread
épinard spinach
Époisses (de Bourgogne) gooey, pungent, rich cow cheese
érable maple
escalope thin slice of meat
escalope normande turkey or veal in cream sauce
escargot snail
escargot raisins "snail"-shaped raisin pastry
espagnole flavorful veal-based sauce
estragon tarragon
étiquette label (wine)
express espresso
façon in the style or fashion of
fait, bien aged, mature (cheese)
fait maison homemade
(de) fantaisie fancy (can mean bread sold by the piece)
far breton baked flan, often with prunes
farce stuffing
farci stuffed
faux-filet sirloin
faux-sucre artificial sweetener
fenouil fennel
ferme farm; firm, young (cheese)
fermé not ready to drink (wine)
fermier / fermière farm-raised
feuille de vigne grape leaf
feuilleté flaky or puff pastry

fève fava bean
ficelle "string," super-thin baguette
figue fig
filet fillet
fin fine (wine)
fines herbes chopped fresh green herbs (chives, parsley, tarragon, etc.)
flambée flaming
flétan halibut
fleur de courgette stuffed and batter-fried zucchini flower
fleurie, croûte "bloomy" (soft, edible) rind (cheese)
flûte "flute," a slim baguette
foie liver
foie gras d'oie (de canard) liver from a fattened goose (duck)
fondant au chocolat molten chocolate cake
fondue small pieces of food dipped in hot liquid for cooking
fondue bourguignonne beef fondue (cooked in oil)
fondue savoyarde cheese fondue
forestière with mushrooms
fort sharp, strong (cheese)
fougasse bread with tasty tidbits baked in, often herbs
fougasse monégasque almond and anise pastry
four, cuit au baked
Fourme d'Ambert pungent cow's-milk blue cheese
frais fresh
fraise / fraise des bois strawberry / wild strawberry
framboise raspberry
friand (au fromage) cheese puff
fricadelle meatball
fricassée fricassee
frit fried; deep-fried
froid cold
fromage cheese
fromage à la crème cream cheese
fromage aux herbes cheese with herbs
fromage blanc fresh white cheese
fromage bleu blue cheese
fromage de la région cheese of the region
froment wheat
froment, pain au wheat bread
fruit fruit
fruit de la passion passion fruit
fruité fruity (wine)
fruits de mer seafood
fruits rouges berries
fumé smoked
fût wine barrel
galette a round pastry, pancake, or cake; also a buckwheat crêpe
galette de pommes de terre hash browns
gambas big prawn
Gana brand name of baguette
gariguette small strawberry
garni garnished; with vegetables
garniture side dish
gâteau cake

G

gâteau basque cherry and almond cake
gaufre waffle
gazeuse carbonated
gelée jelly; aspic
gésier gizzard
gibier game
gibier à plume game bird
gigérine watermelon used in pies and preserves
gigot (d'agneau) leg (of lamb)
gingembre ginger
girolle chanterelle mushroom
glace ice cream
glacé frozen; very cold (iced tea); glazed
glaçon ice cube
gougère savory cream puff with cheese
gourmandise sweet treat
goût du fût de chêne oaky (wine)
goûté snack
grain seed
grand large
Grand Marnier orange liqueur
gras fat
gratinée topped with cheese and browned
grenade pomegranate
grenouille frog
grillade grilled meat; mixed grill
grillé grilled
grillé pommes apple-filled pastry with "grill" pattern
griotte sour cherry (morello)
gros pain "large" baguette
groseille red currant
Gruyère "Swiss cheese"
haché minced
hachis hash
hachis Parmentier shepherd's pie
hareng herring
haricot (vert) bean (green)
herbes herbs
Hollandaise sauce of egg and butter
homard lobster
hors d'oeuvre appetizer
huile oil
huître oyster
île flottante meringue floating in cream sauce
importée imported
(à la) italienne Italian-style; grilled panini (for sandwiches)
izarra herbal brandy (Basque)
jambon de Bayonne dry-cured ham
jambon de Reims ham cooked in Champagne and wrapped in a pastry shell
jambon-mornay savory puff pastry with ham and cheese
jambon persillé ham and parsley preserved in gelatin
jardinière with vegetables
jarret shank; hock; knuckle
jaune (d'oeuf) egg yolk
jésuite triangular pastry filled with almond crème
joue cheek

julienne in matchstick-sized slices
jus juice (fruit juice, but also meat juices)
jus lié gravy
juteux juicy
kaki persimmon
kasher kosher
ker-y-pom shortbread and apple biscuit
kir white wine with black currant liqueur
kir royal champagne with black currant liqueur
kouign amann buttery, caramelized cake
Kuglehopf glacé raisin-and-almond cake with cherry liqueur
lait milk
lait demi-écrémé low-fat milk
lait écrémé nonfat milk
lait entier whole milk
lait ribot fermented milk drink; buttermilk
laitue lettuce
langoustine small, lobster-like shellfish
Langres soft cow cheese
langue tongue
lapin rabbit
lard / lardon bacon / slab bacon
laurier bay leaf
lavée, croûte washed rind (cheese)
léger light (not heavy)
légume vegetable
lentille lentil
levain, pain au sourdough ("yeast") bread
levure yeast
liaison thickening agent
light light (low-calorie)
limande dab (flatfish)
lit (sur un lit de) bed (on a bed of)
Livarot pungent, creamy cow cheese
lotte monkfish
loup sea bass
(à la) lyonnaise with onions
lyonnaise, salade salad with croutons, fried ham, and poached egg
macaron delicate sandwich cookie
macédoine mix of diced vegetables or fruit
mâche lamb's lettuce
madeleine buttery sponge cake
magret (de canard) breast (of duck)
maïs corn
maison house (specialty)
manchon wing (duck, chicken)
mandarine tangerine
mangue mango
mara des bois strawberry variety
marc regional brandy
(du) marché of the market (of the day)
mariné marinated
marinière white-wine and shallot sauce

marjolaine marjoram
marmitako Basque tuna stew
marmite stew pot
marron chestnut
médaillon tenderloin
mélangé mixed
melon cantaloupe
melon charentais yellow cantaloupe
(de) ménage homemade
mendiant chocolate with nuts and dried fruit ("beggar")
menthe mint
menu fixed-price meal
menu de dégustation tasting menu
menu du jour menu of the day
méréville watermelon used in pies and preserves
merlan whiting (cod-like fish)
mesclun mixed greens
meunière fried in butter
meurette red wine sauce
miche large round loaf of bread
mie, pain de sandwich bread
miel honey
mignardise miniature petit four
mille-feuille puff pastry with many layers; Napoleon
millésime vintage (wine)
mirepoix diced mix of celery, onions, and carrots
mixte mixed
moelleux moist, creamy, sometimes not fully cooked; sweet (wine)
moelleux au chocolat molten chocolate cake
moisi / moisi noble mold / "noble mold" that makes cheese and wine delicious
molle, à pâte gooey cheese with edible rind
Montrachet soft, tangy goat cheese, often covered in ash
Morbier semi-soft cow cheese with a charcoal streak
morceau piece
morille morel mushroom
mornay white sauce with Gruyère cheese
Morteau smoked pork sausage
morue salty cod
moule mussel
mousse mousse
mousseron meadow mushroom
mousseux sparkling
moutarde mustard
mouton mutton
multicéréales multigrain
Munster stinky, soft, aged cow cheese
mûre blackberry
muscade nutmeg
museau snout
myrtille blueberry
naturelle, croûte hard rind (cheese)
navarin lamb stew
navet turnip
Nescafé instant coffee

niçoise, salade salad with tomatoes, green beans, anchovies, olives, hard-boiled egg, and tuna
noir black
noisette hazelnut; espresso with a dollop of milk
noix walnut; nuts
noix de beurre a pat of butter
noix de coco coconut
noix de Saint-Jacques scallop
Normande cream sauce
nougat de Montélimar honey and nut nougat
nouille noodle
nouvelle new
oeuf egg
oeuf à la coque (mollet / dur) boiled egg (soft / hard)
oeuf au plat fried egg
oeuf brouillé scrambled egg
oeuf mayonnaise hard-boiled egg topped with mayo
oeufs de poisson fish roe
oie goose
oignon onion
olive olive
omelette montoise puffy omelet (Mont Saint-Michel)
onglet hanger steak
oranais apricot danish
Orangina carbonated orange juice with pulp
ordinaire ordinary
origan oregano
os à moelle marrowbone
oseille sorrel
Ossau-Iraty smooth, firm, buttery ewe's cheese
pain bread
pain au chocolat flaky pastry filled with chocolate
pain au froment wheat bread
pain au lait "milk bread"; smaller, less sweet brioche
pain au levain sourdough bread
pain aux raisins spiral, glazed raisin pastry
pain bis / pain bisse dark-grain bread
pain brié dense, crusty bread
pain complet whole-wheat bread
pain de campagne rustic country loaf
pain de mie sandwich bread
pain de seigle rye bread
pain d'épices gingerbread ("spice bread")
pain doré French toast
pain pavé "cobblestone"-shaped rye bread
pain perdu French toast
pain salé bacon, olive, and cheese roll
pain viennois soft, shiny, slightly sweeter baguette
paleron chuck (beef)
palmier "palm"-shaped buttery pastry
palourde clam
pamplemousse grapefruit
pan bagnat tuna salad sandwich (Riviera)

panaché half beer, half lemon-lime soda
pané breaded
panier basket
papaye papaya
(en) papillote cooked in parchment
paprika paprika
paquets, pieds et sheep's feet and tripe
parfumé flavored
pastèque watermelon
pastis sweet anise (licorice) drink, cut with water
pâte pastry; dough
pâté seasoned ground meat shaped into a loaf, can also be made of fish
pâte à choux eggy butter-and-flour pastry
pâte à tartiner spread (like Nutella or peanut butter)
pâte molle gooey cheese with edible rind
pâtes pasta
paupiette meat beaten thin, then rolled
pavé thick hunk of meat
Pavé d'Auge spicy, tangy, square-shaped cow cheese
pavé, pain "cobblestone"-shaped rye bread
paysanne country style
paysanne, salade salad with potatoes, walnuts, tomatoes, ham, and egg
PDT (pomme de terre) potato
pêche peach
Pélardon nutty goat cheese
pépin seed
perdrix partridge
périgourdine, salade mixed green salad with foie gras and gizzards
persil parsley
pétillant sparkling (wine, water)
petit small
petit déjeuner breakfast
petit four miniature cake
petit gâteau cookie
petit pain bread roll
petit pois pea
petit salé salt pork
pichet pitcher
picholine green, buttery olive
Picodon spicy goat cheese
pied (de cheval / de mouton) foot (horse / sheep)
pieds et paquets sheep's feet and tripe
piémontaise, salade potato salad with tomato and egg
pigeon squab (pigeon)
pignon pine nut
piment d'Espelette spicy red pepper
pineau cognac and grape juice
pintade guinea hen
piperade omelet with tomatoes and peppers
piquant spicy (hot)
pissaladière onion, olive, and anchovy bread
pissenlit dandelion leaf

pistache pistachio
pithivier spiral-shaped puff pastry pie
planche wooden board for cutting or serving
plat dish
plat du jour special of the day
plat principal main course
plateau platter
plateau de charcuterie platter of cured meats
plateau de fromages cheese platter
plateau mixte platter of both cheese and cured meats
pleurote oyster mushroom
poché poached
poêlée pan-fried
Poilâne big, round loaf of rustic bread
(à) point medium (meat)
poire pear
poire au vin rouge pear poached in red wine and spices
poireau leek
pois, petit pea
poisson fish
poitrine de boeuf brisket (beef)
poitrine de porc pork belly
poivre / au poivre pepper / pepper sauce
poivre de Cayenne cayenne pepper
poivron bell pepper
pomme apple
pomme de terre potato
pommes (de terre) dauphine fried puffs of mashed potatoes
pommes (de terre) duchesse baked puffs of mashed potatoes
pommes (de terre) sarladaise potatoes fried in duck fat
pommes frites French fries
Pont l'Evêque flavorful, smooth, earthy cow cheese
porc pork
Port Salut soft, sweet cow cheese
porto fortified wine
potage soup, usually thick
potage de légumes thick vegetable soup
potée prepared in earthenware pot
potée champenoise meat, potato, and vegetable stew
potiron winter squash
poulet chicken
poulet rôti roast chicken
poulpe octopus
pour emporter to go
poussin young chicken
pré salé raised on salt-marsh lands
pression draft (beer)
prêt à boire ready to drink; mature (wine)
prix fixe fixed price
profiterole cream puff (sometimes with ice cream)
provençale with garlic and tomatoes
prune plum

P

MENU DECODER

French / English

pruneau prune
pur pure
purée mashed
purée de pomme de terre mashed potatoes
quatre-quarts pound cake
quenelle meat or fish dumpling
quenelle de brochet fish dumpling in a creamy sauce
queue de boeuf oxtail
quiche quiche
quiche lorraine quiche with bacon, cheese, and onions
quotidien everyday
racine root
raclette melted cheese over potatoes and meats
radis radish
ragoût stew
raie sting ray
raifort horseradish
raisin grape
raisin sec raisin
râpée grated
ratatouille tomato stew with vegetables (often eggplant, zucchini, etc.)
ravioli de Royans ravioli with goat cheese filling
Reblochon soft, gooey, mild, creamy, Brie-like cow cheese
réchauffée reheated
régionale local
réglisse licorice
religieuse round éclair (shaped like a nun)
rémoulade mayonnaise sauce (often mustard-flavored)
rillette cold, shredded pork
rillon belly (pork)
ris (d'agneau / de veau) sweetbreads (lamb / veal)
riz rice
riz au lait rice pudding
riz basmati basmati rice
riz complet brown rice
riz de Camargue nutty, chewy rice
riz jasmin jasmine rice
robuste full-bodied (wine)
rognon kidney
rognon blanc testicle
romarin rosemary
Roquefort powerful, blue-veined, tangy sheep cheese
roquette arugula (rocket)
rosbif roast beef
rosé rosé (wine)
rösti hash browns
rôti roasted
rouge red
rouget red mullet
rouille mayo with garlic and spicy peppers
roulade "rolled" around a filling
roulé aux noix sweet walnut roll with nutty filling
roux butter and flour thickening agent
sablé shortcrust pastry
safran saffron
saignant rare (meat)

Saint-Jacques, coquille / noix de scallop
Saint-Marcellin soft cow cheese
Saint-Nectaire semi-soft, nutty cow cheese
Saint-Pierre John Dory (fish)
Sainte-Maure soft, creamy goat cheese
saison, de seasonal
salade salad
salade au chèvre chaud salad with warm goat cheese on toasted croutons
salade camarguaise rice and veggie salad
salade composée "composed" salad with various ingredients
salade de pissenlit warm dandelion greens with bacon
salade lyonnaise salad with croutons, fried ham, and poached egg
salade niçoise salad with tuna, green beans, tomatoes, anchovies, olives, and hard-boiled egg
salade paysanne potato, walnut, tomato, ham, and egg salad
salade périgourdine salad with foie gras and gizzards
salade piémontaise potato, tomato, and ham salad
salé savory, salty
salé cake savory loaf, often with ham and cheese or olives
sandre freshwater fish, like pike or perch
sanglier wild boar
sapeur, tablier de tripe dish
sarladaise, pommes (de terre) potatoes fried in duck fat
sauce verte tarragon-flavored mayo (sometimes with parsley)
saucisse sausage
saucisse-frites hot dog and fries
saucisson dried sausage; salami
sauge sage
saumon salmon
sauté sautéed
sauvage wild
savoyarde with melted cheese and/or potatoes
scampi prawns
scarole escarole
sec dry
seigle, pain de rye bread
sel salt
Selles-sur-Cher mild goat cheese
selon arrivage market price
semoule semolina (grain)
service compris service included
service non compris service not included
sole sole (fish)
sorbet sorbet
soubise onion-cream sauce
soufflé soufflé
soufflé au chocolat chocolate soufflé
soupe soup
soupe à l'oignon onion soup

soupe à l'ognion gratinée French onion soup
soupe au pistou Provençal vegetable soup with pesto
sous-vide vacuum-sealed and very slow-cooked in heated water (therefore very tender)
Spätzle soft egg noodles
spécialité specialty
spéculoos molasses cookie
steak haché gourmet hamburger patty
steak tartare raw minced beef
sucre sugar
tablier de sapeur tripe dish
taboulé couscous salad
tanche plump black olive
tannique tannic (wine)
tapenade olive spread
tarte pie; tart
tarte à l'oignon onion tart
tarte alsacienne fruit tart from Alsace
tarte au fromage cheese tart
tarte flambée thin-crust pizza with onion and bacon
tarte salée savory tart; quiche
tarte tatin upside-down apple pie
tartelette small tart
tartiflette scalloped potatoes with melted cheese
tartine baguette (sometimes toasted) with sweet or savory toppings
tasse cup
taureau bull meat
terrine pressed, chilled loaf of chopped meat or vegetables
tête head
thé tea
thon tuna
thym thyme
tian gratin-like vegetable dish
tiède lukewarm
tilapia tilapia
tire-bouchon corkscrew
tisane herbal tea
tomate tomato
Tomme (de Savoie) mild, semi-soft cow cheese
tonneau wine barrel
torchon cheese cloth
tourin garlic soup
tournedos steak tenderloin
tournée cut into a football shape, often potatoes or carrots
tournesol sunflower
tourte de blettes sweet and savory Swiss chard pie
tourteau crab (similar to Dungeness crab)
tourteau fromager sweet goat-cheese cake
tranche / tranché slice / sliced
tresse "braid"-shaped brioche
trévise radicchio
tripes tripe
trou Normand apple sorbet in apple brandy
truffe truffle
truite trout
ttoro Basque seafood stew
turbot turbot (flatfish)

unilatéral, (grillé) à l' (grilled) on one side
vache cow
Valençay firm, nutty, goat cheese
vanille vanilla
(à la) vapeur steamed
varié assorted
VDQS quality standards for regional wines
veau veal
végétarien vegetarian
velouté smooth sauce or soup
venalson venison
vendange harvest (wine)
verre glass
verrine small glass serving dish
vert green
viande meat
viande de chevreuil venison
viandes fumées smoked meats
viandes salées salt-cured meats
vichyssoise potato and leek soup
(de) vieille vignes from old vines (wine)
viennoise coated with egg and breadcrumbs
(de) vigne from the vine
vignoble vineyard
vin wine
vin de la maison house wine
vin du pays wine from a given area
vin ordinaire house wine
vlnaigre vinegar
vinaigrette vinaigrette
volaille poultry
vol-au-vent cylindrical, filled pastry
yaourt yogurt

SIGHTSEEING

WHERE?

Where is / are the...?	Où est / sont...? oo ay / sohn
tourist information office	l'office de tourisme loh-fees duh too-reez-muh
toilets	les toilettes lay twah-leht
main square	la place principale lah plahs pran-see-pahl
old town center	la vieille ville lah vee-yay veel
entrance	l'entrée lahn-tray
exit	la sortie lah sor-tee
museum	le musée luh mew-zay
cathedral	la cathédrale lah kah-tay-drahl
church	l'église lay-gleez
castle	le château luh shah-toh

Key Phrases: Sightseeing

ticket	billet bee-yay
How much is it?	C'est combien? say kohn-bee-an
price	prix pree
Is there a guided tour (in English)?	Il y a une visite guidée (en anglais)? eel yah ewn vee-zeet gee-day (ahn ahn-glay)
When?	Quand? kahn
What time does this open / close?	À quelle heuere c'est ouvert / fermé? ah kehl ur say oo-vehr / fehr-may

palace	le palais luh pah-lay
best view	la meilleure vue lah meh-yur vew
viewpoint	le point de vue luh pwan duh vew

AT SIGHTS

Tickets and Discounts

ticket office	guichet / billetterie gee-shay / bee-yeh-teh-ree
ticket	billet bee-yay
combo-ticket	billet combiné bee-yay kohn-bee-nay
price	prix pree
discount	réduction ray-dewk-see-ohn
Is there a discount for...?	Il y a une réduction pour...? eel yah ewn ray-dewk-see-ohn poor
...children	...les enfants layz ahn-fahn
...youths	...les jeunes lay juhn
...students	...les étudiants layz ay-tew-dee-ahn
...families	...les familles lay fah-mee
...seniors	...les gens âgés lay zhahn ah-zhay
...groups	...les groupes lay groop
I am...	J'ai... zhay
He / She is...	Il / Elle a... eel / ehl ah
... ____ years old.	... ____ ans. ____ ahn
I am extremely old.	Je suis très âgé. zhuh swee trehz ah-zhay
Is the ticket good all day?	Le billet est valable toute la journée? luh bee-yay ay vah-lah-bluh toot lah zhoor-nay
Can I get back in?	Je peux rentrer? zhuh puh rahn-tray

Information and Tours

information	les renseignements lay rahn-sehn-yuh-mahn
tour	une visite ewn vee-zeet
in English	en anglais ahn ahn-glay
Is there a...?	Il y a...? eel yah
...city walking tour	...une promenade guidée de la ville ewn proh-muh-nahd gee-day duh lah veel
...guided tour	....une visite guidée ewn vee-zeet gee-day
...audioguide	...un audioguide uhn oh-dee-oh-geed
...local guide (who is available)	...un guide local (qui est disponible) uhn geed loh-kahl (kee ay dee-spoh-nee-bluh)
...city guidebook (for Paris)	...un guide touristique (de Paris) uhn geed too-rees-teek (duh pah-ree)
...museum guidebook	...un guide de musée uhn geed duh mew-zay
Is it free?	C'est gratuit? say grah-twee
How much is it?	C'est combien? say kohn-bee-an
How long does it last?	Ça dure combien de temps? sah dewr kohn-bee-an duh tahn
When is the next tour in English?	La prochaine visite en anglais est à quelle heure? lah proh-shehn vee-zeet ahn ahn-glay ay ah kehl ur

Some sights are tourable only by groups with a guide ***(un guide).*** Individuals usually end up with the next French tour. To get an English tour, call in advance to see if one's scheduled; individuals can often tag along with a large tour group.

Visiting Sights

opening times	horaires d'ouverture oh-rair doo-vehr-tewr
last entry	la dernière entrée lah dehrn-yehr ahn-tray
At what time does this open / close?	À quelle heuere c'est ouvert / fermé? ah kehl ur say oo-vehr / fehr-may
What time is the last entry?	La dernière entrée est à quelle heure? lah dehrn-yehr ahn-tray ay ah kehl ur
Do I have to check this bag?	Est-ce que je dois déposer ce sac à la consigne? ehs kuh zhuh dwah day-poh-zay suh sahk ah lah kohn-seen-yuh
bag check	consigne kohn-seen-yuh
floor plan	plan plahn
floor	étage ay-tahzh
collection	collection koh-lehk-see-ohn
exhibition...	exposition... ehks-poh-zee-see-ohn
...temporary / special	...temporaire / spéciale tahn-poh-rair / spay-see-ahl
...permanent	...permamente pehr-mah-nahnt
café	café kah-fay
elevator	ascenseur ah-sahn-sur
toilet	toilette twah-leht
Where is ___?	Où est ___? oo ay ___
I'd like to see ___.	Je voudrais voir ___. zhuh voo-dray vwahr ___
Photo / Video OK?	Photo / Vidéo OK? foh-toh / vee-day-oh "OK"
(No) flash.	(Pas de) flash. (pah duh) flahsh
(No) tripod.	(Pas de) trépied. (pah duh) tray-pee-yay

Will you take my / our photo?	Vous pouvez prendre ma / notre photo? voo poo-vay prahn-druh mah / noh-truh foh-toh
Please let me in. (if room or sight is closing)	S'il vous plaît, laissez-moi entrer. see voo play leh-say-mwah ahn-tray
I promise I'll be fast.	Je promets d'aller vite. zhuh proh-may dah-lay veet
It was my mother's dying wish that I see this.	C'était le dernier souhait de ma mère que je voies ça. say-tay luh dehrn-yay soo-way duh mah mehr kuh zhuh vwah sah

Once at the sight, get your bearings by viewing ***le plan*** (floor plan). ***Vous êtes ici*** means "You are here." Many museums have an official, one-way route that all visitors take—just follow signs for ***Sens de la visite.***

RECREATION AND ENTERTAINMENT

RECREATION

Outdoor Fun

Where is the best place for...?	Où est le meilleur endroit pour...? oo ay luh meh-yur ahn-drwah poor
...biking	...faire du vélo fair dew vay-loh
...walking	...marcher mar-shay
...hiking	...faire de la randonnée fair duh lah rahn-doh-nay
...running	...courrir / faire du jogging koo-reer / fair dew zhoh-geeng
...picnicking	...pique-niquer peek-nee-kay
...sunbathing	...se bronzer suh brohn-zay
Where is a...?	Où est...? oo ay
...park	...un parc uhn park
...playground	...une aire de jeux ewn air duh juh
...snack shop	...un snack uhn "snack"
...toilet	...une toilette ewn twah-leht
Where can I rent...?	Où puis-je louer...? oo pweezh loo-ay
...a bike	...un vélo uhn vay-loh
...that	...ça sah
What's fun to do...?	Qu'est-ce qu'il y a d'amusant à faire...? kehs keel yah dah-mew-zahnt ah fair
...for a boy / a girl...	...pour un garçon / une fille... poor uhn gar-sohn / ewn fee
... ____ years old	...de ____ ans duh ____ ahn

Renting

Whether you're renting a bike or a boat, here's what to ask.

Where can I rent a...?	Où puis-je louer...? oo pweezh loo-ay
Can I rent a...?	Je peux louer...? zhuh puh loo-ay
...bike	...un vélo uhn vay-loh
...boat	...un bâteau uhn bah-toh
How much per...?	C'est combien par...? say kohn-bee-an par
...hour	...heure ur
...half-day	...demie-journée duh-mee-zhoor-nay
...day	...jour zhoor
Is a deposit required?	Une caution est obligatoire? ewn koh-see-ohn ay oh-blee-gah-twahr

At most parks, people (usually men) play ***boules*** (pronounced "bool," also called ***pétanque***). Each player takes turns tossing an iron ball, with the goal of getting it as close as possible to the small, wooden target ball ***(cochonnet).***

At bigger parks, you can sometimes rent toy sailboats ***(voiliers de bassin)*** or see puppet shows ***(guignols)***—fun to watch in any language.

Swimming

swimming	natation nah-tah-see-ohn
to swim	nager nah-zhay
Where's a...?	Où est...? oo ay
...swimming pool	...une piscine ewn pee-seen
...water park	...un parc aquatique uhn park ah-kwah-teek
...(good) beach	...une (belle) plage ewn (behl) plahzh
...nude beach	...une plage naturiste ewn plahzh nah-tewr-eest

Is it safe for swimming?	On peut nager en sécurité? ohn puh nah-zhay ahn say-kew-ree-tay

Bicycling

bicycle / bike	bicyclette / vélo bee-see-kleht / vay-loh
mountain bike	VTT (vélo tout-terrain) vay tay tay (vay-loh too-tuh-ran)
I'd like to rent a bike.	Je voudrais louer un vélo. zhuh voo-dray loo-ay uhn vay-loh
two bikes	deux vélos duh vay-loh
kid's bike	vélo d'enfant vay-loh dahn-fahn
helmet	casque kahsk
map	carte kart
lock	antivol ahn-tee-vohl
chain	chaîne shehn
pedal	pédale pay-dahl
wheel	roue roo
tire	pneu pnuh
air / no air	air / pas d'air air / pah dair
pump	pompe pohmp
brakes	les freins lay fran
How does this work?	Ça marche comment? sah marsh koh-mahn
How many gears?	Combien de vitesses? kohn-bee-an duh vee-tehs
Is there a bike path?	Il y a une piste cyclable? eel yah ewn peest see-klah-bluh
I don't like hills or traffic.	Je n'aime pas les côtes ni la circulation. zhuh nehm pah lay koht nee lah seer-kew-lah-see-ohn
I brake for bakeries.	Je m'arrête à chaque boulangerie. zhuh mah-reht ah shahk boo-lahn-zhuh-ree

RECREATION

Way to Go!

Whether you're biking or hiking, you'll want to know the best way to go.

Can you recommend a route / a hike that is...?	Pouvez-vous recommander un itinéraire / une randonnée qui est...? poo-vay-voo ruh-koh-mahn-day uhn ee-tee-nay-rair / ewn rahn-doh-nay kee ay
...easy	...facile fah-seel
...moderate	...modéré moh-day-ray
...strenuous	...difficile dee-fee-seel
...safe	...sans danger sahn dahn-zhay
...scenic	...panoramique / beau pah-noh-rah-meek / boh
...about ____ kilometers	...environ ____ kilomètres ahn-vee-rohn ____ kee-loh-meh-truh
How many hours / minutes?	Combien d'heures / de minutes? kohn-bee-an dur / duh mee-newt
uphill / level / downhill	montée / niveau / descente mohn-tay / nee-voh / day-sahnt

Hiking

go hiking	faire de la randonnée fair duh lah rahn-doh-nay
a hike	une randonnée ewn rahn-doh-nay
a trail	un sentier uhn sahn-tee-ay
Where can I buy a...?	Où puis-je acheter...? oo pweezh ah-shuh-tay
...hiking map	...une carte de randonnée / carte IGN ewn kart duh rahn-doh-nay / kart ee zhay ehn
...compass	...une boussole ewn boo-sohl

Where's the trailhead?	Où commence le sentier? oo koh-mahns luh sahn-tee-ay
How do I get there?	Comment est-ce que j'y arrive? koh-mahn ehs kuh zhee ah-reev

Most hiking trails are well-marked with signs listing the destination and the duration in hours ***(parcours de ____ heures)*** and minutes ***(parcours de ____ minutes)***.

ENTERTAINMENT

event guide	guide des événements geed dayz ay-vay-nuh-mahn
What's happening tonight?	Qu'est-ce qui ce passe ce soir? kehs kee suh pahs suh swahr
What do you recommend?	Qu'est-ce que vous recommandez? kehs kuh voo ruh-koh-mahn-day
Where is it?	C'est où? say oo
How do I get there?	Comment est-ce que j'y arrive? koh-mahn ehs kuh zhee ah-reev
How do we get there?	Comment est-ce que nous y arrivons? koh-mahn ehs kuh nooz ee ah-ree-vohn
Is it free?	C'est gratuit? say grah-twee
Are there seats available?	Il y a des places disponibles? eel yah day plahs dee-spoh-nee-bluh
Where can I buy a ticket?	Où puis-je acheter un billet? oo pweezh ah-shuh-tay uhn bee-yay
Do you have tickets for today / tonight?	Avez-vous des billets pour aujourd'hui / ce soir? ah-vay-voo day bee-yay poor oh-zhoor-dwee / suh swahr
best seats	les meilleures places lay may-yur plahs
cheap seats	les places bon marché lay plahs bohn mar-shay
sold out	complet kohn-play

When does it start?	Ça commence à quelle heure? sah koh-mahns ah kehl ur
When does it end?	Ça se termine à quelle heure? sah suh tehr-meen ah kehl ur
Where do people stroll?	Les gens se balladent où? lay zhahn suh bah-lahd oo
Where's a good place for...?	Où se trouve un bon endroit pour...? oo suh troov uhn bohn ahn-drwah poor
...dancing	...danser dahn-say
...(live) music	...musique (en directe) mew-zeek (ahn dee-rehkt)
bar with a live band	bar avec un groupe musical bar ah-vehk uhn groop mew-zee-kahl
nightclub	boîte bwaht
cabaret	caberet kah-buh-ray
(no) cover charge	(pas de) admission (pah duh) ahd-mee-see-ohn
concert	concert kohn-sehr
opera	d'opéra doh-pay-rah
symphony	symphonique san-foh-neek
show	spectacle spehk-tah-kluh
performance	séance say-ahns
theater	théâtre tay-ah-truh

SHOPPING

SHOP TILL YOU DROP

Shop Talk

opening hours	les heures d'ouverture layz ur doo-vehr-tewr
sale	solde sohld
discounted	prix réduit pree ray-dwee
big discounts	prix choc pree shohk
cheap	bon marché bohn mar-shay
affordable	abordable ah-bor-dah-bluh
(too) expensive	(trop) cher (troh) shehr
good value	bon rapport qualité prix bohn rah-por kah-lee-tay pree
window shopping	lèche-vitrines lehsh-vee-treen
Pardon me (for bothering you).	Excusez-moi (de vous déranger). ehk-skew-zay-mwah (duh voo day-rahn-zhay)
Where can I buy ____?	Où puis-je acheter ____? oo pweezh ah-shuh-tay ____
How much is it?	C'est combien? say kohn-bee-an
I'm just browsing.	Je regarde. zhuh ruh-gard
We're just browsing.	Nous regardons. noo ruh-gar-dohn
I'd like ____.	Je voudrais ____. zhuh voo-dray ____
Do you have...?	Vous avez...? vooz ah-vay
...more	...plus plew
...something cheaper	...quelque chose de moins cher kehl-kuh shohz duh mwan shehr
...something nicer	...quelque chose plus agréable kehl-kuh shohz plew ah-gray-ah-bluh

Key Phrases: Shopping

How much is it?	C'est combien? say kohn-bee-an
I'm just browsing.	Je regarde. zhuh ruh-gard
Can I see more?	Je peux en voir d'autres? zhuh puh ahn vwahr doh-truh
I'll think about it.	Je vais réfléchir. zhuh vay ray-flay-sheer
I'll take it.	Je le prends. zhuh luh prahn
Do you accept credit cards?	Vous prenez les cartes? voo pruh-nay lay kart
Can I try it on?	Je peux l'essayer? zhuh puh lay-say-yay
It's too expensive / big / small.	C'est trop cher / grand / petit. say troh shehr / grahn / puh-tee

Can I see more?	Je peux en voir d'autres? zhuh puh ahn vwahr doh-truh
May I see this more closely?	Pourrais-je voir de plus près? poo-rayzh vwahr duh plew preh
This one.	Celui ci. suhl-wee see
I'll think about it.	Je vais réfléchir. zhuh vay ray-flay-sheer
I'll take it.	Je le prends. zhuh luh prahn
What time do you close?	Vous fermez à quelle heure? voo fehr-may ah kehl ur
What time do you open tomorrow?	Vous allez ouvrir à quelle heure demain? vooz ah-lay oo-vreer ah kehl ur duh-man

Bargain hunters keep an eye out for ***soldes*** (sale), ***liquidation de stock*** (liquidation sale), ***tout doit disparaître*** (everything must go), ***prix choc*** (a shockingly good price), or ***réductions*** (reduced). When the French go window-shopping, they call it ***lèche-vitrines*** (window-licking).

Except in department stores, ask first before you pick up an item: ***Pourrais-je voir de plus près?*** (May I see this more closely?).

Pay Up

Where do I pay?	Où se trouve la caisse? oo suh troov lah kehs
cashier	caisse kehs
Do you accept credit cards?	Vous prenez les cartes? voo pruh-nay lay kart
VAT (Value-Added Tax)	TVA (Taxe sur la Valeur Ajoutée) tay vay ah (tahks sewr lah vah-lur ah-zhoo-tay)
Can I get...?	Je peux avoir...? zhuh puh ah-vwahr
I need the paperwork for...	J'ai besoin de remplir un formulaire pour... zhay buh-zwan duh rahn-pleer uhn for-mew-lair poor
...a VAT refund	...la détaxe lah day-tahks
Can you ship this?	Vous pouvez l'envoyer? voo poo-vay lahn-voy-ay

When you're ready to pay, look for a ***caisse*** (cashier). The cashier may ask you something like ***Auriez-vous quinze centimes?*** (Do you have 15 cents?), or ***Voulez-vous un sac?*** (Do you want a bag?).

If you make a major purchase from a single store, you may be eligible for a VAT refund; for details, see www.ricksteves.com/vat.

WHERE TO SHOP

Types of Shops

Where is a...?	Où est...? oo ay
barber shop	un salon de coiffeur pour hommes uhn sah-lohn duh kwah-fur poor ohm
beauty salon	un salon de coiffeur pour dames uhn sah-lohn duh kwah-fur poor dahm

bookstore...	une librairie... ewn lee-bray-ree
used bookstore...	une boutique de livres d'occasion... ewn boo-teek duh lee-vruh doh-kah-zee-ohn
...with books in English	...avec des livres en anglais ah-vehk day lee-vruh ahn ahn-glay
camera shop	un magasin de photo uhn mah-gah-zan duh foh-toh
clothing boutique	une boutique de vêtements ewn boo-teek duh veht-mahn
coffee shop	un café uhn kah-fay
department store	un grand magasin uhn grahn mah-gah-zan
electronics store	un magasin d'équipements électroniques uhn mah-gah-zan day-keep-mahn ay-lehk-troh-neek
flea market	un marché aux puces uhn mar-shay oh pews
jewelry shop (fine)	une boutique de joaillerie ewn boo-teek duh zhoh-ī-ree
jewelry shop (cheap)	une bijouterie bon marché ewn bee-zhoo-tuh-ree bohn mar-shay
launderette (self-service)	une laverie automatique ewn lah-vuh-ree oh-toh-mah-teek
laundry (full-service)	une blanchisserie ewn blahn-shee-suh-ree
mobile phone shop	un magasin de portables uhn mah-gah-zan duh por-tah-bluh
newsstand	une maison de la presse ewn may-zohn duh lah prehs
open-air market	un marché en plein air uhn mar-shay ahn plan air
pharmacy	une pharmacie ewn far-mah-see

shoe store	un magasin de chaussures uhn mah-gah-zan duh shoh-sewr
shopping mall	un centre commercial uhn sahn-truh koh-mehr-see-ahl
souvenir shop	une boutique de souvenirs ewn boo-teek duh soo-vuh-neer
toy store	un magasin de jouets uhn mah-gah-zan duh zhoo-ay
travel agency	une agence de voyages ewn ah-zhahns duh voy-yahzh
wine store	une caviste ewn kah-veest

In France, most small shops close for a long lunch (noon until about 2 p.m.), and all day on Sundays and Mondays. For tips and phrases on shopping for a picnic—at grocery stores or open-air markets—see page 100.

Street Markets

There are two types of street markets. The more common and colorful ***les marchés*** feature products from local farmers and artisans. ***Les marchés brocantes*** specialize in quasi-antiques and flea-market bric-a-brac.

Did you make this?	C'est vous qui l'avez fait? say voo kee lah-vay fay
Is this made in France?	C'est fabriqué en France? say fah-bree-kay ahn frahns
How much is it?	C'est combien? say kohn-bee-an
Cheaper?	Moins cher? mwan shehr
Will you take ____? (name price)	Est-ce que vous prendriez ____? ehs kuh voo prahn-dree-ay ____
Is it cheaper if I buy several?	C'est moins cher si j'en achète plusieurs? say mwan shehr see zhahn ah-sheht plewz-yur

It's a good price.	C'est un bon prix. say uhn bohn pree
My last offer.	Ma dernière offre. mah dehrn-yehr oh-fruh
I'll take it.	Je le prends. zhuh luh prahn
We'll take it.	Nous le prenons. noo luh pruh-nohn
I'm nearly broke.	Je suis presque fauché. zhuh swee prehsk foh-shay

It's OK to bargain at street markets, though not every vendor will drop prices. Expect to pay cash and be wary of pickpockets. For help with numbers and prices, see page 16.

WHAT TO BUY

Clothing

clothing	vêtement veht-mahn
This one.	Celui-ci. suhl-wee-see
Can I try it on?	Je peux l'essayer? zhuh puh lay-say-yay
Do you have a...?	Vous avez...? vooz ah-vay
...mirror	...un miroir uhn meer-wahr
...fitting room	...une salle d'essayage ewn sahl day-say-ahzh
It's too...	C'est trop... say troh
...expensive.	...cher. shehr
...big / small.	...grand / petit. grahn / puh-tee
...short / long.	...court / long. koor / lohn
...tight / loose.	...serré / grand. suh-ray / grahn
...dark / light.	...foncé / clair. fohn-say / klair
Do you have a different color / a different pattern?	Avez-vous une couleur différente / un motif différent? ah-vay-voo ewn koo-lur dee-fay-rahnt / uhn moh-teef dee-fay-rahn
What's this made of?	C'est en quoi ça? say ahn kwah sah

Is it machine washable?	C'est lavable en machine? say lah-vah-bluh ahn mah-sheen
Will it shrink?	Ça va rétrécir? sah vah ray-tray-seer
Will it fade in the wash?	Ça va déteindre au lavage? sah vah day-tan-druh oh lah-vahzh
Dry clean only?	Nettoyage à sec seulement? neh-twah-yahzh ah sehk suhl-mahn

For a list of colors, see page 141.

Types of Clothes and Accessories

For a...	Pour... poor
...man.	...un homme. uhn ohm
...woman.	...une femme. ewn fahm
...teenager. (m / f)	...un adolescent / une adolescente. uhn ah-doh-luh-sahn / ewn ah-doh-luh-sahnt
...child. (m / f)	...un petit garçon / une petite fille. uhn puh-tee gar-sohn / ewn puh-teet fee
...baby boy / girl.	...un bébé garçon / fille. uhn bay-bay gar-sohn / fee
I'm looking for a...	Je cherche... zhuh shehrsh
I want to buy a...	Je veux acheter... zhuh vuh ah-shuh-tay
belt	une ceinture ewn san-tewr
bra	un soutien-gorge uhn soo-tee-an-gorzh
dress	une robe ewn rohb
earrings	boucles d'oreille boo-kluh doh-ray
gloves	des gants day gahn
handbag	un sac à main uhn sahk ah man
hat	un chapeau uhn shah-poh
jacket	une veste ewn vehst
jeans	un jean uhn "jean"

jewelry	bijoux bee-zhoo
necklace	collier kohl-yay
nylons	des bas nylon day bah nee-lohn
pajamas	un pyjama uhn pee-zhah-mah
pants	un pantalon uhn pahn-tah-lohn
raincoat	un imperméable uhn an-pehr-may-ah-bluh
ring	bague bahg
scarf	un foulard uhn foo-lar
shirt	une chemise ewn shuh-meez
shoelaces	des lacets day lah-say
shoes	des chaussures day shoh-sewr
shorts	un short uhn short
skirt	une jupe ewn zhewp
socks	des chaussettes day shoh-seht
sweater	un pull uhn pewl
swimsuit	un maillot de bain uhn mī-yoh duh ban
tie	une cravate ewn krah-vaht
tights	un collant uhn koh-lahn
T-shirt	un T-shirt uhn "T-shirt"
underwear	des sous vêtements day soo veht-mahn
wallet	un portefeuille uhn por-tuh-fuh-ee
watch	montre mohn-truh

Clothing Sizes

extra-small	extra-small "extra-small"
small	small "small"
medium	medium "medium"
large	large "large"
extra-large	extra-large "extra-large"

I need a bigger / smaller size.	J'ai besoin d'une plus grande / plus petite taille. zhay buh-zwan dewn plew grahnd / plew puh-teet tī
What's my size?	Quelle est ma taille? kehl ay mah tī

For help converting US sizes to European, see page 552.

Colors

black	noir nwahr
blue	bleu bluh
brown	marron mah-rohn
gray	gris gree
green	vert vehr
orange	orange oh-rahnzh
pink	rose rohz
purple	violet vee-oh-lay
red	rouge roozh
white	blanc blahn
yellow	jaune zhohn
dark(er)	(plus) foncé (plew) fohn-say
light(er)	(plus) clair (plew) klair
bright(er)	(plus) coloré (plew) koh-loh-ray

SHIPPING AND MAIL

If you need to ship packages home, head for ***la Poste*** (post office), which is often marked ***PTT*** (for its old name, *Postes, Télégraphes et Téléphones*). Otherwise, you can often get stamps at a ***tabac*** (tobacco shop).

post office	la Poste / PTT lah pohst / pay tay tay
Where is the post office?	Où est la Poste? oo ay lah pohst

stamps	timbres tan-bruh
postcard	carte postale kart poh-stahl
letter	lettre leht-ruh
package	colis koh-lee
window / line	guichet / file gee-shay / feel
Which window for ____?	Quel guichet pour ____? kehl gee-shay poor ____
Is this the line for ____?	C'est la file pour ____? say lah feel poor ____
I need...	J'ai besoin... zhay buh-zwan
...to buy stamps.	...d'acheter des timbres. dah-shuh-tay day tan-bruh
...to mail a package.	...d'envoyer un colis. dahn-vwah-yay uhn koh-lee
to the United States	pour les Etats-Unis poor layz ay-tah-zew-nee
Pretty stamps, please.	De jolis timbres, s'il vous plaît. duh zhoh-lee tan-bruh see voo play
Can I buy a box?	Puis-je acheter une boîte? pweezh ah-shuh-tay ewn bwaht
This big.	De cette taille. duh seht tī
Do you have tape?	Avez-vous du scotch? ah-vay-voo dew skohtch

TECHNOLOGY

TECH TERMS

Portable Devices and Accessories

I need a...	J'ai besoin de...	zhay buh-zwan duh
Do you have a...?	Avez-vous...?	ah-vay-voo
Where can I buy a...?	Où puis-je acheter...?	oo pweezh ah-shuh-tay
battery (for my ____)	une pile (pour mon ____)	ewn peel (poor mohn ____)
battery charger	un chargeur de piles	uhn shar-zhur duh peel
charger	un chargeur	uhn shar-zhur
computer	un ordinateur	uhn or-dee-nah-tur
convertor	un convertisseur	uhn kohn-vehr-tee-sur
CD / DVD	un CD / DVD	uhn say day / day vay day
ebook reader	un ereader	uhn ee-ree-dehr
electrical adapter	un adaptateur électrique	uhn ah-dahp-tah-tur ay-lehk-treek
flash drive	une carte mémoire flash	ewn kart may-mwahr flahsh
headphones / earbuds	un casque / les écouteurs	uhn kahsk / layz ay-koo-tur
iPod / MP3 player	iPod / un balladeur MP3	"iPod" / uhn bah-lah-dur ehm pay trwah
laptop	un ordinateur portable / laptop	uhn or-dee-nah-tur por-tah-bluh / "laptop"
memory card	une carte mémoire	ewn kart may-mwahr

mobile phone	un portable uhn por-tah-bluh
SIM card	une carte SIM ewn kart seem
speakers (for my ____)	des haut-parleurs (pour mon ____) dayz oh-par-lur (poor mohn ____)
tablet	une tablette ewn tah-bleht
(mini) USB cable	un (petit) câble USB uhn (puh-tee) kah-bluh ew ehs bay
USB key	clé USB klay ew ehs bay
video game	un jeu vidéo uhn zhuh vee-day-oh
Wi-Fi	Wi-Fi wee-fee

Familiar brands (like iPad, Facebook, YouTube, Instagram, or whatever the latest craze is) are just as popular in Europe as they are back home. Invariably, these go by their English names (sometimes with a French accent).

Cameras

camera	un appareil-photo uhn ah-pah-ray-foh-toh
digital camera	un appareil-photo numérique uhn ah-pah-ray-foh-toh new-may-reek
video camera	une caméra vidéo ewn kah-may-rah vee-day-oh
lens cap	un bouchon d'objectif uhn boo-shohn dohb-zhehk-teef
film (for cameras)	la pellicule lah peh-lee-kewl
Can I / Can you download my photos onto a CD?	Puis-je / Pouvez-vous graver mes photos sur un CD? pweezh / poo-vay-voo grah-vay may foh-tohs sewr uhn say day
Will you take my / our photo?	Vous pouvez prendre ma / notre photo? voo poo-vay prahn-druh mah / noh-truh foh-toh

Can I take a photo of you?	Je peux prendre votre photo? zhuh puh prahn-druh voh-truh foh-toh
Smile!	Souriez! soo-ree-ay

You'll find words for batteries, chargers, and more in the previous list.

TELEPHONES

Telephone Terms

telephone	téléphone tay-lay-fohn
phone call...	appel téléphonique... ah-pehl tay-lay-foh-neek
...local	...local loh-kahl
...domestic	...national nah-see-oh-nahl
...international	...international an-tehr-nah-see-oh-nahl
...toll-free	...gratuit grah-twee
...with a credit card	...avec une carte de crédit ah-vehk ewn kart duh kray-dee
...collect	...en PCV ahn pay say vay
mobile phone	un portable uhn por-tah-bluh
mobile number	numéro de portable new-may-roh duh por-tah-bluh
landline	numéro fixe new-may-roh feeks
fax	fax fahks

Travelers have several phoning options. A mobile phone provides the best combination of practicality and flexibility. Public pay phones are available, but increasingly rare (and often require buying an insertable phone card called a ***télékarte***—tay-lay-kart). You can also make calls online (using Skype or a similar program) and from your hotel room (using an international phone card called a ***carte á code***—kart ah kohd). As this is a fast-changing scene, check my latest tips at www.ricksteves.com/phoning.

France has a direct-dial 10-digit phone system (no area codes). For phone tips—including a calling chart for dialing European numbers—see page 548.

Making Calls

Where is the nearest phone?	Où est le téléphone le plus proche? oo ay luh tay-lay-fohn luh plew prohsh
May I use your phone?	Je peux téléphoner? zhuh puh tay-lay-foh-nay
Can you talk for me?	Vous pouvez parler pour moi? voo poo-vay par-lay poor mwah
It's busy.	C'est occupé. say oh-kew-pay
This doesn't work.	Ça ne marche pas. sah nuh marsh pah
out of service	hors service or sehr-vees
Try again?	Essayez de nouveau? ay-say-yay duh noo-voh

If the number you're calling is out of service, you'll likely hear this recording: ***Le numéro que vous demandez n'est pas attribué.***

On the Phone

Hello, this is ____.	Âllo, c'est ____. ah-loh say ____
My name is ____.	Je m'appelle ____. zhuh mah-pehl ____
Do you speak English?	Parlez-vous anglais? par-lay-voo ahn-glay
Sorry, I speak only a little French.	Désolé, je parle seulement un petit peu de français. day-zoh-lay zhuh parl suhl-mahn uhn puh-tee puh duh frahn-say
Speak slowly, please.	Parlez lentement, s'il vous plaît. par-lay lahnt-mahn see voo play
Wait a moment.	Un moment. uhn moh-mahn

The French answer a call by saying ***Allô*** (Hello).

Key Phrases: Telephones

telephone	téléphone tay-lay-fohn
phone call	appel téléphonique ah-pehl tay-lay-foh-neek
mobile phone	un portable uhn por-tah-bluh
Where is the nearest phone?	Où est le téléphone le plus proche? oo ay luh tay-lay-fohn luh plew prohsh
May I use your phone?	Je peux téléphoner? zhuh puh tay-lay-foh-nay
Where is a mobile phone shop?	Où est un magasin de portables? oo ay uhn mah-gah-zan duh por-tah-bluh

You'll find the phrases you need to reserve a hotel room on page 48, or a table at a restaurant on page 66. To spell your name over the phone, refer to the code alphabet on page 550.

Mobile Phones

Your US mobile phone should work in Europe if it's GSM-enabled, tri-band or quad-band, and on a calling plan that includes international service. Alternatively, you can buy a phone in Europe. If your phone is unlocked ***(debloqué),*** you can save money by buying a cheap European SIM card (which usually comes with some calling credit) at a mobile-phone shop or a newsstand. After inserting a SIM card in your phone, you'll have a European number and pay lower European rates.

mobile phone	un portable uhn por-tah-bluh
smartphone	un smartphone uhn "smartphone"
roaming	itinérance / roaming ee-tee-nay-rahns / "roaming"
text message	SMS / texto "SMS" / tehk-stoh

Where is a mobile phone shop?	Où est un magasin de portables? oo ay uhn mah-gah-zan duh por-tah-bluh
I'd like to buy...	Je voudrais acheter... zhuh voo-dray ah-shuh-tay
...a (cheap) mobile phone.	...un portable (pas cher). uhn por-tah-bluh (pah shehr)
...a SIM card.	...une carte SIM. ewn kart seem
prepaid credit	unités prépayées ew-nee-tay pray-pay-ay
calling time	temps d'appel tahn dah-pehl
contract	abonnement ah-buhn-mahn
locked	bloqué bloh-kay
unlocked	debloqué day-bloh-kay
Is this phone unlocked?	Est-ce que ce téléphone est débloqué? ehs kuh suh tay-lay-fohn ay day-bloh-kay
Can you unlock this phone?	Pouvez-vous débloquer ce téléphone? poo-vay-voo day-bloh-kay suh tay-lay-fohn
How do I...?	Comment puis-je...? koh-mahn pweezh
...make calls	...appeler ah-puh-lay
...receive calls	...recevoir les appels ruh-suh-vwahr layz ah-pehl
...send a text message	...envoyer un SMS / texto ahn-vwoh-yay uhn "SMS" / tehk-stoh
...check my voicemail	...vérifier ma boîte vocale vehr-ee-fee-ay mah bwaht voh-kahl
...set the language to English	...paramétrer la langue en anglais pah-rah-may-tray lah lahng ahn ahn-glay
...mute the ringer	...appuyer sur la touche sourdine ah-pwee-yay sewr lah toosh soor-deen
...change the ringer	...changer la sonnerie shahn-zhay lah suhn-ree
...turn it on	...allumer ah-lew-may
...turn it off	...éteindre ay-tan-druh

GETTING ONLINE

Internet Terms

Internet access	accès à l'Internet ahk-seh ah lan-tehr-neht
Wi-Fi	Wi-Fi wee-fee
email	email ee-mehl
computer	ordinateur or-dee-nah-tur
Internet café	café Internet kah-fay an-tehr-neht
surf the Web	surfer le web sewr-fay luh wehb
username	nom d'utilisateur nohn dew-tee-lee-zah-tur
password	mot de passe moh duh pahs
network key	mot de passe pour le réseau moh duh pahs poor luh ray-zoh
secure network	un réseau sûr / un réseau en sécurité uhn ray-zoh sewr / uhn ray-zoh ahn say-kew-ree-tay
website	site web seet wehb
homepage	page d'accueil pahzh dah-kuh-ee
download	télécharger tay-lay-shar-zhay

Key Phrases: Getting Online

Where is a Wi-Fi hotspot?	Où se trouve un point Wi-Fi? oo suh troov uhn pwan wee-fee
Where can I get online?	Où puis-je me connecter? oo pweezh muh koh-nehk-tay
Where is an Internet café?	Où se trouve un café Internet? oo suh troov uhn kah-fay an-tehr-neht
Can I check my email?	Je peux regarder mon email ? zhuh puh ruh-gar-day mohn ee-mehl

print	imprimer an-pree-may
My email address is ____.	Mon adresse email est ____. mohn ah-drehs ee-mehl ay ____
What's your email address?	Quelle est votre adresse email? kehl ay voh-truh ah-drehs ee-mehl

Note that a few terms look the same as in English, but are pronounced differently: ***www*** (doo-bluh-vay, doo-bluh-vay, doo-bluh-vay); ***Wi-Fi*** (wee-fee); ***CD*** (say day); ***DVD*** (day vay day); ***MP3*** (ehm pay trwah); and ***USB*** (ew ehs bay).

Tech Support

Help me, please.	Aidez-moi, s'il vous plaît. eh-day-mwah see voo play
How do I...?	Comment je...? koh-mahn zhuh
...start this	...démarre ça day-mar sah
...get online	...me connecte muh koh-nehkt
...get this to work	...fais marcher ça fay mar-shay sah
...stop this	....arrête ça ah-reht sah
...send this	...envoie ça ahn-vwah sah
...print this	...imprime ça an-preem sah
...make this symbol	...fais ce symbole fay suh san-bohl
...copy and paste	...fais un copier-coller fay uhn kohp-yay-koh-lay
...type @	...tape arobase tahp ah-roh-bahz
This doesn't work.	Ça ne marche pas. sah nuh marsh pah

For do-it-yourself tips, see "French Keyboards" on page 153.

Using Your Own Portable Device

If you have a smartphone, tablet computer, laptop, or other wireless device, you can get online at many hotels, cafés, and public hotspots.

Most Internet access is Wi-Fi (wee-fee), but occasionally you'll connect by plugging an Ethernet cable directly into your laptop. While Internet access is often free, sometimes you'll have to pay.

laptop	ordinateur portable / laptop or-dee-nah-tur por-tah-bluh / "laptop"
tablet	tablette tah-bleht
smartphone	smartphone "smartphone"
Where is a Wi-Fi hotspot?	Où se trouve un point Wi-Fi? oo suh troov uhn pwan wee-fee
Do you have Wi-Fi?	Avez-vous le Wi-Fi? ah-vay-voo luh wee-fee
What is the...?	C'est quoi le...? say kwah luh
...network name	...nom du réseau nohn dew ray-zoh
...username	...nom d'utilisateur nohn dew-tee-lee-zah-tur
...password	...mot de passe moh duh pahs
Do I need a cable?	J'ai besoin d'un câble? zhay buh-zwan duhn kah-bluh
Do you have a...?	Vous avez un...? vooz ah-vay uhn
Can I borrow a...?	Je peux emprunter un...? zhuh puh ahn-pruhn-tay uhn
...charging cable	...câble pour charger kah-bluh poor shar-zhay
...Ethernet cable	...câble ethernet kah-bluh "ethernet"
...USB cable	...câble USB kah-bluh ew ehs bay
Free?	Gratuit? grah-twee
How much?	Combien? kohn-bee-an
Do I have to buy something to use the Internet?	J'ai besoin d'acheter quelque chose pour utiliser l'Internet? zhay buh-zwan dah-shuh-tay kehl-kuh shohz poor ew-tee-lee-zay lan-tehr-neht

Using a Public Internet Terminal

Many hotels have terminals in the lobby for guests to get online; otherwise, an Internet café is usually nearby.

Where can I get online?	Où puis-je me connecter? oo pweezh muh koh-nehk-tay
Where is an Internet café?	Où se trouve un café Internet? oo suh troov uhn kah-fay an-tehr-neht
Can I use this computer to...?	Je peux utiliser cet ordinateur pour...? zhuh puh ew-tee-lee-zay seht or-dee-nah-tur poor
...get online	...me connecter muh koh-nehk-tay
...check my email	...regarder mon email ruh-gar-day mohn ee-mehl
...download photos	...télécharger des photos tay-lay-shar-zhay day foh-toh
...print (something)	...imprimer (quelque chose) an-pree-may (kehl-kuh shohz)
boarding passes	cartes d'embarquement kart dahn-bar-kuh-mahn
tickets	billets bee-yay
reservation confirmation	confirmer une réservation kohn-feer-may ewn ray-zehr-vah-see-ohn
Free?	Gratuit? grah-twee
How much (for... minutes)?	C'est combien (pour... minutes)? say kohn-bee-an (poor... mee-newt)
...10	...dix dees
...15	...quinze kanz
...30	...trente trahnt
...60	...soixante swah-sahnt
Can you switch the keyboard to American?	Vous-pourriez changer le clavier au format américain? voo-poo-ree-ay shahn-zhay luh klah-vee-ay oh for-maht ah-may-ree-kan

If you're using a public Internet terminal, the keyboard, menus, and on-screen commands will likely be designed for French speakers. Some computers allow you to make the French keyboard work as if it were an American one (ask the clerk if it's possible).

French Keyboards

On French keyboards, most command keys differ, and some keys are in a different location. For example, the **M** key is where the semicolon is on American keyboards. The **A** and **Q** keys and the **Z** and **W** keys are reversed from American keyboards. Here's a rundown of how major commands are labeled on a French keyboard:

YOU'LL SEE...	IT MEANS...	YOU'LL SEE...	IT MEANS...
Entrée	Enter	←	Backspace
Maj	Shift	Inser	Insert
Verr Maj	Shift Lock	↖	Home
Verr Num	Num Lock	Fin	End
Echap	Esc	Page Haut	Page Up
Suppr	Delete	Page Bas	Page Down

The **Alt** key to the right of the space bar is actually a different key, called **Alt Gr** (for Alternate Graphics). Press this key to insert the extra symbol that appears on some keys (such as the **€** in the corner of the **E** key).

A few often-used keys look the same, but have different names in French:

@ sign	signe arobase	seen-yuh ah-roh-bahz
dot	point	pwan
hyphen (-)	tiret	tee-ray
underscore (_)	souligne	soo-leen-yuh
slash (/)	barre oblique / "slash"	bar oh-bleek / "slahsh"

French speakers have several names for the @ sign, but the most common is ***arobase.*** When saying an email address, you say ***arobase*** in the middle.

To type @, press **Alt Gr** and the **à/0** key. Belgian keyboards may require pressing **Alt Gr** and the **é/2** key. If that doesn't work, try copying-and-pasting the @ sign from elsewhere on the page.

HELP!

EMERGENCIES

France's medical emergency phone number is **15;** for police, dial **17.** ***SOS médecins*** are doctors who make emergency house calls. If you need help, someone will call an ***SOS médecin*** (SOS mayd-san) for you. If you're lost, see the phrases on page 46.

Medical Help

Help!	Au secours! oh suh-koor
Help me, please.	Aidez-moi, s'il vous plaît eh-day-mwah see voo play
emergency	urgence ewr-zhahns
accident	accident ahk-see-dahn
medical clinic / hospital	clinique médicale / hôpital klee-neek may-dee-kahl / oh-pee-tahl
Call...	Appelez... ah-puh-lay
...a doctor.	...un docteur. uhn dohk tur
...the police.	...la police. lah poh-lees
...an ambulance.	...le SAMU. luh sah-moo
I need / We need...	J'ai besoin / Nous avons besoin... zhay buh-zwan / nooz ah-vohn buh-zwan
...a doctor.	...un docteur. uhn dohk-tur
...to go to the hospital.	...d'aller à l'hôpital. dah-lay ah loh-pee-tahl
It's urgent.	C'est urgent. say ewr-zhahn
injured	blessé bleh-say
bleeding	saigne sehn-yuh
choking	étouffe ay-toof
unconscious	inconscient an-kohn-see-ahn
not breathing	ne respire pas nuh rehs-peer pah

Thank you for your help.	Merci pour votre aide. mehr-see poor voh-truh ehd
You are very kind.	Vous êtes très gentil. vooz eht treh zhahn-tee

If you need someone to come and get you because you're having a heart attack, you need the ***SAMU,*** which stands for ***Service d'Aide Médicale Urgente. Ambulance*** is also a word in French, but not for emergencies. ***Les ambulances*** are for transporting people without cars to doctor's visits. For other health-related words, see the Personal Care and Health chapter.

Theft and Loss

thief	voleur voh-lur
pickpocket	pickpocket peek-poh-keht
police	police poh-lees
embassy	ambassade ahn-bah-sahd
Stop, thief!	Arrêtez, au voleur! ah-reh-tay oh voh-lur
Call the police!	Appelez la police! ah-puh-lay lah poh-lees
I've been robbed.	On m'a volé. ohn mah voh-lay
We've been robbed.	Nous avons été volé. nooz ah-vohn ay-tay voh-lay
A thief took...	Un voleur à pris... uhn voh-lur ah pree
Thieves took...	Des voleurs ont pris... day voh-lur ohn pree
I've lost my...	J'ai perdu mon... zhay pehr-dew mohn
We've lost our...	Nous avons perdu nos... nooz ah-vohn pehr-dew noh
money	argent ar-zhahn
credit card	carte de crédit kart duh kray-dee
passport	passeport pahs-por

Key Phrases: Help!

Help!	Au secours! oh suh-koor
emergency	urgence ewr-zhahns
clinic / hospital	clinique médicale / hôpital klee-neek may-dee-kahl / oh-pee-tahl
Call a doctor.	Appelez un docteur. ah-puh-lay uhn dohk-tur
ambulance	SAMU sah-moo
police	police poh-lees
thief	voleur voh-lur
Stop, thief!	Arrêtez, au voleur! ah-reh-tay oh voh-lur

ticket	billet bee-yay
railpass	passe Eurail pahs "Eurail"
baggage	bagages bah-gahzh
purse	sac sahk
wallet	portefeuille por-tuh-fuh-ee
watch	montre mohn-truh
jewelry	bijoux bee-zhoo
camera	appareil-photo ah-pah-ray-foh-toh
mobile phone	téléphone portable tay-lay-fohn por-tah-bluh
iPod / iPad	iPod / iPad "iPod" / "iPad"
tablet	tablette tah-bleht
computer	ordinateur or-dee-nah-tur
laptop	ordinateur portable / laptop or-dee-nah-tur por-tah-bluh / "laptop"
faith in humankind	foi en l'humanité fwah ahn lew-mah-nee-tay

I want to contact my embassy.	Je veux contacter mon ambassade. zhuh vuh kohn-tahk-tay mohn ahn-bah-sahd
I need to file a police report (for my insurance).	Je veux porter plainte à la police (pour mon assurance). zhuh vuh por-tay plahnt ah lah poh-lees (poor mohn ah-sewr-rahns)
Where is the police station?	Où se trouve la gendarmerie? oo suh troov lah zhahn-dar-muh-ree

To replace a passport, you'll need to go in person to your embassy. Cancel and replace your credit and debit cards by calling your credit-card company (as of this printing, these are the 24-hour US numbers that you can call collect: Visa—tel. 303/967-1096, MasterCard—tel. 636/722-7111, American Express—tel. 336/393-1111). If you'll want to submit an insurance claim for lost or stolen gear, be sure to file a police report, either on the spot or within a day or two. For more info, see www.ricksteves.com/help. Precautionary measures can minimize the effects of loss—back up your photos and other files frequently.

Fire!

fire	feu fuh
smoke	fumée few-may
exit	sortie sor-tee
emergency exit	sortie de secours sor-tee duh suh-koor
fire extinguisher	extincteur ehks-tank-tur
Call the fire department.	Appelez les pompiers. ah-puh-lay lay pohn-pee-yay

HELP FOR WOMEN

Generally the best way to react to unwanted attention is loudly and quickly.

No!	Non! nohn
Stop it!	Arrêtez! ah-reh-tay
Enough!	Ça suffit! sah sew-fee
Don't touch me.	Ne me touchez pas. nuh muh too-shay pah
Leave me alone.	Laissez-moi tranquille. lay-say-mwah trahn-keel
Go away.	Allez-vous en. ah-lay-vooz ahn
Get lost!	Dégagez! day-gah-zhay
Drop dead!	Foutez-moi la paix! foo-tay-mwah lah pay
Police!	Police! poh-lees

Safety in Numbers

If a guy is bugging you, approach a friendly-looking couple, family, or business for a place to stay safe.

A man is bothering me.	Un homme est en train de me harceler. uhn ohm ayt ahn tran duh muh ar-suh-lay
May I...?	Est-ce que je peux...? ehs kuh zhuh puh
...join you	...vous joindre voo zhwan-druh
...sit here	...m'asseoir ici mah-swahr ee-see
...wait here until he's gone	...attendez ici jusqu'à ce qu'il parte ah-tahn-day ee-see zhew-skah skeel part

You Want to Be Alone

I want to be alone.	Je veux être seule. zhuh vuh eh-truh suhl
I'm not interested.	Ça ne m'intéresse pas. sah nuh man-tay-rehs pah
I'm married.	Je suis mariée. zhuh swee mah-ree-ay
I'm waiting for my husband.	J'attends mon mari. zhah-tahn mohn mah-ree
I'm a lesbian.	Je suis lesbienne. zhuh swee lehz-bee-ehn
I have a contagious disease.	J'ai une maladie contagieuse. zhay ewn mah-lah-dee kohn-tah-zhee-uhz

PERSONAL CARE AND HEALTH

PERSONAL CARE

aftershave lotion	lotion d'après rasage loh-see-ohn dah-preh rah-zahzh
antiperspirant	anti-transpirant ahn-tee-trahn-spee-rahn
breath freshener / mints	rafraîchisseurs d'haleine / bonbons à la menthe rah-freh-shee-sur dah-lehn / bohn-bohn ah la mahnt
cologne	cologne koh-lohn-yuh
comb	peigne pehn-yuh
conditioner for hair	après-shampoing ah-preh-shahn-pwan
dental floss	fil dentaire feel dahn-tair
deodorant	déodorant day-oh-doh-rahn
face cleanser	lait nettoyant lay neh-twah-yahn
facial tissue	kleenex "kleenex"
fluoride rinse	rince-bouche fluoré rans-boosh flew-oh-ray
hair dryer	sèche-cheveux sehsh-shuh-vuh
hairbrush	brosse à cheveux brohs ah shuh-vuh
hand lotion	crème pour les mains krehm poor lay man
hand sanitizer	désinfectant pour les mains day-zan-fehk-tahn poor lay man
lip balm	beaume pour les lèvres bohm poor lay leh-vruh
lip gloss	gloss à lèvres "gloss" ah leh-vruh

lipstick	rouge à lèvres· roozh ah leh-vruh
makeup	maquillage mah-kee-ahzh
mirror	mirroir meer-wahr
moisturizer (with sunblock)	crème hydratante (avec protection solaire) krehm ee-drah-tahnt (ah-vehk proh-tehk-see-ohn soh-lair)
nail clipper	coupe-ongles koop-ohn-gluh
nail file	lime à ongles leem ah ohn-gluh
nail polish	vernis à ongles vehr-nee ah ohn-gluh
nail polish remover	dissolvant dee-sohl-vahn
perfume	parfum par-fuhn
Q-tips (cotton swabs)	coton-tiges koh-tohn-teezh
razor	rasoir rahz-wahr
sanitary pads	serviettes hygiéniques sehrv-yeht ee-zhay-neek
scissors	ciseaux see-zoh
shampoo	shampoing shahn-pwan
shaving cream	mousse à raser moos ah rah-zay
soap	savon sah-vohn
sunscreen	crème solaire krehm soh-lair
tampons	tampons tahn-pohn
tissues	mouchoirs en papier moosh-wahr ahn pahp-yay
toilet paper	papier hygiénique pahp-yay ee-zhay-neek
toothbrush	brosse à dents brohs ah dahn
toothpaste	dentifrice dahn-tee-frees
tweezers	pince à épiler pans ah ay-pee-lay

HEALTH

Throughout Europe, people with simple ailments go first to the pharmacist, who can diagnose and prescribe remedies. Pharmacists are usually friendly and speak English. If necessary, the pharmacist will send you to a doctor or a clinic.

After 7:00 p.m., most pharmacies are closed, but you'll find the name, address, and phone number on their front door of the nearest after-hours ***pharmacie de garde.*** In an emergency, go to the police station, which will call ahead to the pharmacist. At the pharmacy, ring the doorbell and the pharmacist will open the door. ***Voilà.***

Getting Help

Where is a...?	Où est...? oo ay
...(24-hour) pharmacy	...une pharmacie (de garde) ewn far-mah-see (duh gard)
...clinic	...une clinique médicale ewn klee-neek may-dee-kal
...hospital	...l'hôpital loh-pee-tahl
I am sick.	Je suis malade. zhuh swee mah-lahd

Key Phrases: Health

I am sick.	Je suis malade. zhuh swee mah-lahd
I need a doctor (who speaks English).	J'ai besoin d'un docteur (qui parle anglais). zhay buh-zwan̲ duhn̲ dohk-tur (kee parl ahn̲-glay)
pain	douleur doo-lur
It hurts here.	J'ai mal ici. zhay mahl ee-see
medicine	médicament may-dee-kah-mahn̲
Where is a pharmacy?	Où est une pharmacie? oo ay ewn far-mah-see

He / She is sick.	Il / Elle est malade. eel / ehl ay mah-lahd
I need a doctor...	J'ai besoin d'un docteur... zhay buh-zwan duhn dohk-tur
We need a doctor...	Nous avons besoin d'un docteur... nooz ah-vohn buh-zwan duhn dohk-tur
...who speaks English.	...qui parle anglais. kee parl ahn-glay
Please call a doctor.	S'il vous plaît appelez un docteur. see voo play ah-puh-lay uhn dohk-tur
Could a doctor come here?	Un docteur pourrait venir? uhn dohk-tur poo-ray vuh-neer
It's urgent.	C'est urgent. say ewr-zhahn
ambulance	SAMU sah-moo
dentist	dentiste dahn-teest
health insurance	assurance maladie ah-sew-rahns mah-lah-dee
Receipt, please.	Une facture, s'il vous plait. ewn fahk-tewr see voo play

Ailments

I have...	J'ai... zhay
He / She has...	Il / Elle a... eel / ehl ah
I need medicine for...	J'ai besoin d'un médicament pour... zhay buh-zwan duhn may-dee-kah-mahn poor
allergy	une allergie ewn ah-lehr-zhee
bee sting	une piqûre d'abeille ewn pee-kewr dah-bay
bite(s) from...	morsure(s)... mor-sewr
...bedbugs	...des punaises de lit day pew-nehz duh lee
...dog	...de chien duh shee-an

...mosquitoes	...des moustiques day moos-teek
...spider	...d'araignée dar-ayn-yay
...tick	...de tique duh teek
blisters	des ampoules dayz ahn-pool
body odor	l'odeur corporelle loh-dur kor-por-ehl
burn	une brûlure ewn brew-lewr
chapped lips	les lèvres gerçées lay lehv ruh zhehr-say
chest pains	maux de poitrine moh duh pwah-treen
chills	des frissons day free-sohn
a cold	un rhume uhn rewm
congestion	la congestion lah kohn-zheh-stee-ohn
constipation	la constipation lah kohn-stee-pah-see-ohn
cough	la toux lah too
cramps...	des crampes... day krahnp
...muscle	...musculaires mew-skew-lair
...stomach	...d'estomac deh-stoh-mah
...menstrual	...menstruelles mahn-strew-ehl
diarrhea	la diarrhée lah dee ah-ray
dizziness	le vertige luh vehr-teezh
earache	l'otite loh-teet
eczema	l'eczéma lehk-zay-mah
fever	une fièvre ewn fee-eh-vruh
flu	la grippe lah greep
food poisoning	empoisonement alimentaire ahn-pwah-zohn-mahn ah-lee-mahn-tair
gas	le gaz luh gahz
hay fever	le rhume des foins luh rewm day fwan
headache	mal à la tête mahl ah lah teht
heartburn	le reflux gastrique luh ruh-flew gah-streek

hemorrhoids	hémorroïdes ay-mor-wahd
hot flashes	bouffées de chaleur boo-fay duh shah-lur
indigestion	une indigestion ewn an-dee-zheh-stee-ohn
infection	une infection ewn an-fehk-see-ohn
inflammation	une inflammation ewn an-flah-mah-see-ohn
insomnia	de l'insomnie duh lan-sohm-nee
lice	des poux day poo
lightheaded	tête légère teht lay-zhehr
migraine	une migraine ewn mee-grehn
motion sickness	mal des transports mahl day trahns-por
nausea	la nausée lah noh-zay
numbness	engourdissement ahn-goor-dees-mahn
pain	la douleur lah doo-lur
pimples	des boutons day boo-tohn
pneumonia	la pneumonie lah pnuh-moh-nee
pus	pus pews
rash	boutons boo-tohn
sinus problems	problèmes de sinus proh-blehm duh see-news
sneezing	l'éternuement lay-tehr-new-mahn
sore throat	mal à la gorge mahl ah lah gorzh
splinter	écharde ay-shard
stomachache	mal à l'estomac mahl ah leh-stoh-mah
(bad) sunburn	un (méchant) coup de soleil uhn (may-shahn) koo duh soh-lay
swelling	une enflure ewn ahn-flewr
tendonitis	tendinite tahn-dee-neet
toothache	mal aux dents mahl oh dahn
urinary tract infection	une infection urinaire ewn an-fehk-see-ohn ew-ree-nair

frequent urination	fréquente envie d'uriner fray-kahnt ahn-vee dew-ree-nay
painful urination	miction douloureuse meek-see-ohn doo-loor-uhz
vomiting	le vomissement luh voh-mees-mahn
wart(s)	verrue(s) veh-rew
I'm going bald.	Je deviens chauve. zhuh duh-vee-an shohv

It Hurts

pain	douleur doo-lur
painful	douloureux doo-loo-ruh
It hurts here.	J'ai mal ici. zhay mahl ee-see
My ____ hurts. (body parts listed on next page)	Mon ____ me fait mal. mohn ____ muh fay mahl
aching (soreness)	courbaturé koor-bah-tew-ray
bleeding	saignement sehn-yuh-mahn
blocked	bloqué bloh-kay
broken	cassé kah-say
bruise	contusion kohn-tew-zee-ohn
chafing	irritations ee-ree-tah-see-ohn
cracked	fêlé feh-lay
fractured	fracturé frahk-tew-ray
infected	infecté an-fehk-tay
inflamed	enflammé ahn-flah-may
punctured (a rusty nail)	entaillé (un clou rouillé) ahn-tī-yay (uhn kloo roo-yay)
scraped	éraflé ay-rah-flay
sore	irrité ee-ree-tay
sprained	foulé foo-lay

swollen gonflé gohn-flay

weak (no energy) faible feh-bluh

diagnosis diagnostic dee-ahg-noh-steek

What can I do? Que puis-je faire? kuh pweezh fair

Is it serious? C'est sérieux? say say-ree-uh

Is it contagious? C'est contagieux? say kohn-tah-zhee-uh

Body Parts

ankle cheville shuh-vee

appendix appendice ah-pahn-dees

arm bras brah

back dos doh

bladder vessie veh-see

blood sang sahn

body corps kor

bone os oh

bowel movement selle sehl

brain cerveau sehr-voh

breast seins san

chest poitrine pwah-treen

ear oreille oh-ray

elbow coude kood

eye oeil oy

face visage vee-zahzh

fingers doigts dwah

fingernail ongle de doigt ohn-gluh duh dwah

foot pied pee-ay

hand main man

head tête teht

heart coeur kur

hip	hanche ahnsh
intestines	intestins an-tehs-tan
kidney	reins ran
knee	genou zhuh-noo
leg	jambe zhahmb
lips	lèvres leh-vruh
liver	foie fwah
lung	poumon poo-mohn
mouth	bouche boosh
muscles	muscles mew-skluh
neck	cou koo
nose	nez nay
ovary	ovaire oh-vair
penis	pénis pay-nee
poop	ka-ka kah-kah
shoulder	épaule ay-pohl
skin	peau poh
stomach	estomac eh-stoh-mah
teeth	dents dahn
testicles	testicules teh-stee-kewl
throat	gorge gorzh
toes	doigts de pied dwah duh pee-ay
toenail	ongle de pied ohn-gluh duh pee-ay
tongue	langue lahng
urine	urine ew-reen
uterus	utérus ew-tay-rew
vagina	vagin vah-zhan
waist	taille tī-yuh
wrist	poignet pwahn-yay
right / left	droite / gauche drwaht / gohsh

First-Aid Kit and Medications

American name-brand medications are rare in Europe, but you'll find equally good local equivalents. Rather than looking for Sudafed, ask for Actifed (decongestant). Instead of Nyquil, request Vicks or Dolirhume (cold medicine). For prescription drugs, ask your doctor for the generic name (for example, atorvastatin instead of Lipitor), which is more likely to be understood internationally. If using a European thermometer, see page 553 for help with temperature conversions.

medicine	médicament may-dee-kah-mahn
pill	comprimé kohn-pree-may
prescription	ordonnance or-doh-nahns
to refill	remplir de nouveau rahn-pleer duh noo-voh
pharmacy	pharmacie far-mah-see
24-hour pharmacy	pharmacie de garde far-mah-see duh gard
antacid	anti-acide ahn-tee-ah-seed
anti-anxiety medicine	anxiolytique (Xanax) ahnk-see-oh-lee-teek ("Xanax")
antibiotic	antibiotique ahn-tee-bee-oh-teek
antihistamine (like Benadryl)	antihistaminique (Cetirizine) ahn-tee-ees-tah-mee-neek (suh-tee-ree-zeen)
aspirin	aspirine ah-spee-reen
non-aspirin substitute	Tylenol tee-leh-nohl
adult diapers (like Depends)	couches pour adultes koosh poor ah-dewlt
bandage	bandage bahn-dahzh
Band-Aids	pansements pahn-suh-mahn
cold medicine	remède contre le rhume ruh-mehd kohn-truh luh rewm

cough drops	pastilles pour la toux pah-stee poor lah too
decongestant (like Sudafed)	décongestant day-kohn-zhehs-tahn
diarrhea medicine	médicament pour la diarrhée may-dee-kah-mahn poor lah dee-ah-ray
disinfectant	désinfectant day-zan-fehk-tahn
first-aid cream	crème antiseptique krehm ahn-tee-sehp-teek
gauze / tape	gaze / sparadra gahz / spah-rah-drah
hemorrhoid medicine	Préparation H (no kidding) pray-pah-rah-see-ohn ahsh
hydrogen peroxide	eau oxygénée oh ohk-see-zhay-nay
ibuprofen (like Advil)	ibuprofène ee-bew-proh-fehn
inhaler	inhalateur an-ahl-ah-tur
insulin	insuline an-sew-leen
itch reliever	quelque chose pour soulager des démangeaisons kehl-kuh shohz poor soo-lah-zhay day day-mahn-zhay-zohn
laxative	laxatif lahk-sah-teef
moleskin (for blisters)	pansement ampoules pahns-mahn ahn-pool
mosquito repellant	anti-moustique ahn-tee-moos-teek
pain killer	calmant kahl-mahn
stomachache medicine	médicament pour les maux d'estomac may-dee-kah-mahn poor lay moh deh stoh mah
support bandage	pansement élastique pahns-mahn ay-lah-steek
syringe	seringue suh-rang
tetanus shot	vaccin contre le tétanos vahk-san kohn-truh luh tay-tah-nohs
thermometer	thermomètre tehr-moh-meh-truh

Vaseline	Vaseline vah-zuh-leen
vitamins	vitamines vee-tah-meen
Does it sting?	Est-ce que ça pique? ehs kuh sah peek
Take one pill every ____ hours for ____ days.	Prendre un comprimé toutes les ____ heures pendant ____ jours. prahn-druh uhn kohn-pree-may toot lay ____ ur pahn-dahn ____ zhoor

SPECIFIC NEEDS

The Eyes Have It

optician	opticien ohp-tee-see-an
eye / eyes	oeil / yeux uh-ee / yuh
eye drops (for inflammation)	gouttes pour les yeux (pour l'inflammation) goot poor layz yuh (poor lan-flah-mah-see-ohn)
artificial tears	larmes artificielles larmz ar-tee-fee-see-ehl
glasses	lunettes lew-neht
sunglasses	lunettes de soleil lew-neht duh soh-lay
reading glasses	lunettes de vue lew-neht duh vew
glasses case	étui à lunettes ay-twee ah lew-neht
(broken) lens	verre (cassé) vehr (kah-say)
to repair	réparer ray-pah-ray
replacement	remplacement rahn-plahs-mahn
prescription	ordonnance or-doh-nahns
contact lenses...	lentilles de contact... lahn-tee duh kohn-tahkt
...soft	...souples soop-luh
...hard	...dures dewr

all-purpose solution	solution pour tout soh-lew-see-ohn poor too
contact lens case	boîte à lentilles de contact bwaht ah lahn-tee duh kohn-tahkt
I don't see well.	Je ne vois pas bien. zhuh nuh vwah pah bee-an
nearsighted	myope mee-yohp
farsighted	presbyte prehs-beet
20 / 20 vision	vision vingt sur vingt veez-yohn van sewr van

On Intimate Terms

personal lubricant (like KY Jelly)	lubrifiant personnel / sexuel lew-bree-fee-ahn pehr-soh-nehl / sehk-sew-ehl
contraceptives	contraceptifs kohn-trah-sehp-teef
condoms	préservatifs / capotes pray-zehr-vah-teef / kah-poht
birth-control pills	les pilules lay pee-lewl
prescription refill	renouvellement d'ordonnance ruh-noo-vehl-mahn dor-doh-nahns
morning-after pill	pilule du lendemain pee-lewl dew lahn-duh-man
herpes (inactive)	herpès (inactif) ehr-pehs (an-ahk-teef)
HIV / AIDS	VIH / SIDA vay ee ahsh / see-dah
STD (sexually transmitted disease)	MST (maladie sexuellement transmissible) ehm ehs tay (mah-lah-dee sehk-sew-ehl-mahn trahns-mee-see-bluh)

For Women

menstruation	menstruation mahn-strew-ah-see-ohn
period	les règles lay reh-gluh
tampons	tampons tahn-pohn
sanitary pads	serviettes hygiéniques sehrv-yeht ee-zhay-neek
I need medicine for...	J'ai besoin d'un médicament pour... zhay buh-zwan duhn may-dee-kah-mahn poor
...menstrual cramps.	...des crampes menstruelles. day krahnp mahn-strew-ehl
...a yeast infection.	...une candidose. ewn kahn-dee-dohz
...a urinary tract infection.	...une infection urinaire. ewn an-fehk-see-ohn ew-ree-nair
cranberry juice	jus d'airelles zhew dair-ehl
I'd like to see a female...	Je voudrais voir une femme... zhuh voo-dray vwahr ewn fahm
...doctor.	...docteur. dohk-tur
...gynecologist.	...gynécologue. zhee-nay-koh-lohg
I've missed a period.	J'ai du retard dans mes règles. zhay dew ruh-tar dahn may reh-gluh
pregnancy test	test de grossesse tehst duh groh-sehs
ultrasound	écographie ay-koh-grah-fee
I am / She is... pregnant.	Je suis / Elle est... enceinte. zhuh swee / ehl ay... ahn-sant
... ____ weeks / months	...de ____ semaines / mois duh ____ suh-mehn / mwah
miscarriage	fausse couche fohs koosh
abortion	avortement ah-vor-tuh-mahn
menopause	ménopause may-noh-pohz

ITALIAN

User-friendly Italian is easy to get the hang of. Some Italian words are so familiar, you'd think they were English. If you can say ***pizza, lasagna,*** and ***spaghetti,*** you can speak Italian.

Italian pronunciation differs from English in some key ways:

C usually sounds like C in cat.
But C followed by E or I sounds like CH in chance.
CH sounds like C in cat.
G usually sounds like G in get.
But G followed by E or I sounds like G in gentle.
GH sounds like G in spaghetti.
GLI sounds like LI (pronounced lee) in million. The G is silent.
GN sounds like GN in lasagna.
H is never pronounced.
I sounds like EE in seed.
R is rolled as in brrravo!
SC usually sounds like SK in skip.
But SC followed by E or I sounds like SH in shape.
Z usually sounds like TS in hits, and sometimes like the sound of DZ in kids.

You can communicate a lot with only a few key Italian words: ***prego, va bene, così, questo/quello,*** and ***vorrei.***

Prego (**preh**-goh) is the all-purpose polite word. It can mean "May I help you?" or "Here you go" or "You're welcome" or "After you" (when someone's holding the door for you).

Va bene (vah **beh**-nay), meaning "It's good," is used constantly. It's the all-purpose "OK" that you'll hear a hundred times a day.

Così (koh-**zee**) basically means "like this." It can be handy, for instance, when ordering food (to show them how much of the eggplant you want on your ***antipasti*** plate).

Questo (**kweh**-stoh, this) and ***quello*** (**kweh**-loh, that) combine conveniently with gestures. Just point to what you want and say ***quello.***

Vorrei (voh-**reh**-ee) is an easy way to say "I would like." It's the standard and polite way to make a request in Italian. ***Vorrei un caffè, per favore*** (I would like a coffee, please).

A few language tips will help you learn some Italian and get the most out of this book. For instance, have you ever noticed that most Italian words end in a vowel? It's ***o*** if the word is masculine and ***a*** if it's feminine. So, a baby boy is a ***bambino*** and a baby girl is a ***bambina.*** A man is ***generoso*** (generous), a woman is ***generosa.*** In this book, we show some gender-bender words like this: ***generoso[a].***

Adjective endings agree with the noun. It's ***cara amica*** (a dear female friend) and ***caro amico*** (a dear male friend). Sometimes the adjective comes after the noun, as in ***vino rosso*** (red wine). Adjectives and nouns ending in ***e*** don't change with the gender, such as ***gentile*** (kind) or ***cantante*** (singer)—the same word applies to either sex.

Plurals are formed by changing the final letter of the noun: ***a*** becomes ***e,*** and ***o*** becomes ***i.*** So it's one ***pizza*** and two ***pizze,*** and one ***cappuccino*** and two ***cappuccini.*** If you're describing any group of people that includes at least one male, the adjective should end with ***i.*** But if the group is female, the adjective ends with ***e.*** A handsome man is ***bello*** and an attractive group of men (or men and women) is ***belli.*** A beautiful woman is ***bella*** and a bevy of beauties is ***belle.***

The key to Italian inflection is to remember this simple rule: Most Italian words have their accent on the second-to-last syllable. To override this rule, Italians sometimes insert an accent: ***città*** (city) is pronounced chee-**tah.**

Italians are animated and even dramatic. You may think two Italians are arguing when in reality they're agreeing enthusiastically. Be confident and have fun communicating. The Italians really do want to understand you, and are forgiving of a Yankee-fied version of their language.

Here's a quick guide to the phonetics used in this book:

ah	like A in father
ay	like AY in play
eh	like E in let
ee	like EE in seed
ehr	sounds like "air"
ew	like EW in few
g	like G in go
ī	like I in light

oh	like O in note
oo	like OO in too
or	like OR in core
ow	like OW in now
s	like S in sun
ts	like TS in hits

ITALIAN BASICS

HELLOS AND GOODBYES

Pleasantries

Hello.	Buon giorno. bwohn **jor**-noh
Do you speak English?	Parla inglese? **par**-lah een-**gleh**-zay
Yes. / No.	Si. / No. see / noh
I don't speak Italian.	Non parlo l'italiano. nohn **par**-loh lee-tah-lee-**ah**-noh
I'm sorry.	Mi dispiace. mee dee-spee-**ah**-chay
Please.	Per favore. pehr fah-**voh**-ray
Thank you (very much).	Grazie (mille). **graht**-see-ay (**mee**-lay)
Excuse me. (to pass)	Permesso. pehr-**meh**-soh
Excuse me. (to get attention)	Mi scusi. mee **skoo**-zee
OK?	Va bene? vah **beh**-nay
OK. (Things are going well.)	Va bene. vah **beh**-nay
Good.	Bene. **beh**-nay
Great.	Benissimo. beh-**nee**-see-moh
Excellent.	Perfetto. pehr-**feh**-toh
You are very kind.	Lei è molto gentile. **leh**-ee eh **mohl**-toh jehn-**tee**-lay
It's (not) a problem.	(Non) c'è problema. (nohn) cheh proh-**bleh**-mah
It doesn't matter.	Non importa. nohn eem-**por**-tah

You're welcome.	Prego. **preh**-goh
Goodbye!	Arrivederci! ah-ree-veh-**dehr**-chee

Please is a magic word in any language. If you know the word for what you want, such as the bill, simply say ***Il conto, per favore*** (The bill, please). ***Per favore*** is the basic "please." You might hear locals say ***per piacere*** (for my pleasure), which is used to sweetly ask for a favor. ***Per favore*** often comes at the beginning of a request, while ***per piacere*** (pehr pee-ah-cheh-ree) normally goes at the end.

Grazie, an important word that means "thank you," often sounds like **graht**-see; Italians barely pronounce the final syllable: **graht**-see(ay).

Meeting and Greeting

Good morning. / Good day.	Buon giorno. bwohn **jor**-noh
Good afternoon.	Buon pomeriggio. bwohn poh-meh-**ree**-joh
Good evening.	Buona sera. **bwoh**-nah **seh**-rah
Good night.	Buona notte. **bwoh**-nah **noh**-tay
Hi. / Bye. (informal)	Ciao. chow
Hello. (informal)	Salve. **sahl**-vay
Welcome.	Benvenuto. behn-veh-**noo**-toh
Mr.	Signore seen-**yoh**-ray
Mrs.	Signora seen-**yoh**-rah
Miss	Signorina seen-yoh-**ree**-nah
My name is ____.	Mi chiamo ____. mee kee-**ah**-moh ____
What's your name?	Come si chiama? **koh**-may see kee-**ah**-mah
Pleased to meet you.	Piacere. pee-ah-**cheh**-ray
How are you?	Come sta? **koh**-may stah
Very well, thank you.	Molto bene, grazie. **mohl**-toh **beh**-nay **graht**-see-ay

Fine, thanks.	Bene, grazie. **beh**-nay **graht**-see-ay
And you?	E Lei? ay **leh**-ee
Where are you from?	Di dove È? dee **doh**-vay eh
I am from ____.	Vengo da ____. **vehn**-goh dah ____
I am / We are...	Sono / Siamo... **soh**-noh / see-**ah**-moh
Are you...?	Lei È...? **leh**-ee eh
...on vacation	...in vacanza een vah-**kahnt**-sah
...on business	...qui per lavoro kwee pehr lah-**voh**-roh

People use the greeting ***buon giorno*** (good morning / good day) before noon. After lunch, some people shift to ***buon pomeriggio*** (good afternoon), but many stick with ***buon giorno*** until mid afternoon, when they switch to ***buona sera*** (good afternoon / evening). Some shorten it to a very casual ***sera.*** At bedtime, say ***buona notte*** (good night). Informal greetings (***ciao*** and ***salve***) are the same all day long.

In Italy, saying hello is important. When entering a shop, always offer a ***buon giorno*** or ***buona sera*** before getting down to business.

Moving On

I'm going to ____.	Vado a ____. **vah**-doh ah ____
How do I go to ____?	Come arrivo a ____? **koh**-may ah-**ree**-voh ah ____
Let's go.	Andiamo. ahn-dee-**ah**-moh
See you later.	A più tardi. ah pew **tar**-dee
See you tomorrow!	A domani! ah doh-**mah**-nee
So long! (informal)	Ci vediamo! chee veh-dee-**ah**-moh
Goodbye.	Arrivederci. ah-ree-veh-**dehr**-chee
Good luck!	Buona fortuna! **bwoh**-nah for-**too**-nah
Happy travels!	Buon viaggio! bwohn vee-**ah**-joh

STRUGGLING WITH ITALIAN

Who Speaks What?

Italian	l'italiano lee-tah-lee-**ah**-noh
English	inglese een-**gleh**-zay
Do you speak English?	Parla inglese? **par**-lah een-**gleh**-zay
A teeny weeny bit?	Nemmeno un pochino? neh-**meh**-noh oon poh-**kee**-noh
Please speak English.	Parli inglese, per favore. **par**-lee een-**gleh**-zay pehr fah-**voh**-ray
Speak slowly, please.	Parli lentamente, per favore. **par**-lee lehn-tah-**mehn**-tay pehr fah-**voh**-ray
Repeat?	Ripeta? ree-**peh**-tah
I understand.	Capisco. kah-**pees**-koh
I don't understand.	Non capisco. nohn kah-**pees**-koh
Do you understand?	Capisce? kah-**pee**-shay
You speak English well.	Lei parla bene l'inglese. **leh**-ee **par**-lah **beh**-nay leen-**gleh**-zay
Does somebody here speak English?	C'è qualcuno qui che parla inglese? cheh kwal-**koo**-noh kwee kay **par**-lah een-**gleh**-zay
I don't speak Italian.	Non parlo l'italiano. nohn **par**-loh lee-tah-lee-**ah**-noh
I speak a little Italian.	Parlo un po' d'italiano. **par**-loh oon poh dee-tah-lee-**ah**-noh
What does this mean?	Cosa significa? **koh**-zah seen-**yee**-fee-kah
How do you say this in Italian?	Come si dice in italiano? **koh**-may see **dee**-chay een ee-tah-lee-**ah**-noh
Write it for me?	Me lo scrive? may loh **skree**-vay

Very Italian Expressions

Prego. **preh**-goh	You're welcome. / Please. / After you. / All right. / Can I help you?
Pronto. **prohn**-toh	Hello. (answering phone) / Ready. (other situations)
Ecco. **eh**-koh	Here it is.
Certo. **chehr**-toh	Sure.
Dica. **dee**-kah	Tell me.
Allora... ah-**loh**-rah	Well... (like our "uh" before a sentence)
Senta. **sehn**-tah	Listen.
Va bene. vah **beh**-nay	OK.
Va tutto bene. vah **too**-toh **beh**-nay	Everything's fine.
Basta. **bah**-stah	That's enough.
È tutto. eh **too**-toh	That's all.
Altro? **ahl**-troh	Do you need anything else?
la dolce vita lah **dohl**-chay **vee**-tah	the sweet life
il dolce far niente eel **dohl**-chay far nee-**ehn**-tay	the sweetness of doing nothing

Italians sometimes illustrate their expressions with gestures. If frustrated, they might say ***Mi sono cadute le braccia!*** (I throw my arms down!)—thrusting their arms toward the floor in an "I give up" gesture.

Italians use the suffix ***issimo*** to intensify their description. If something is good, it's ***bravo,*** but if it's very good, it's ***bravissimo.***

REQUESTS

The Essentials

Can you help me?	Può aiutarmi? pwoh ah-yoo-**tar**-mee
Do you have ____?	Avete ____? ah-**veh**-tay ____
I'd like / We'd like...	Vorrei / Vorremmo... voh-**reh**-ee / voh-**reh**-moh
...this / that.	...questo / quello. **kweh**-stoh / **kweh**-loh
How much does it cost?	Quanto costa? **kwahn**-toh **koh**-stah
Is it free?	È gratis? eh **grah**-tees
Is it included?	È incluso? eh een-**kloo**-zoh
Is it possible?	È possibile? eh poh-**see**-bee-lay
Yes or no?	Si o no? see oh noh
Where is the toilet?	Dov'è la toilette? doh-**veh** lah twah-**leh**-tay
men	uomini / signori **woh**-mee-nee / seen-**yoh**-ree
women	donne / signore **doh**-nay / seen-**yoh**-ray

To prompt a simple answer, ask ***Si o no?*** (Yes or no?). To turn a word or sentence into a question, ask it in a questioning tone. An easy way to ask "Where is the toilet?" is to say ***Toilette?***

A versatile word is ***Posso?*** (Can I?), combined with a gesture. Say it to someone when you point to a table (to mean "Can I sit here?"), or to your camera ("Can I take a picture?"), or to your combo-ticket ("Is this sight covered by this ticket?"). When ordering a menu item, you can say ***Posso avere*** ____? (Can I have ____?). At a café, you'd say ***Posso avere un caffè?*** (Can I have a coffee?)

Where?

Where?	Dove? **doh**-vay
Where is...?	Dov'è...? doh-**veh**

...the tourist information office	...l'ufficio informazioni loo-**fee**-choh een-for-maht-see-**oh**-nee
...the train station	...la stazione lah staht-see-**oh**-nay
...a cash machine	...un bancomat oon **bahn**-koh-maht
Where can I buy ____?	Dove posso comprare ____? **doh**-vay **poh**-soh kohm-**prah**-ray ____
Where can I find ____?	Dove posso trovare ____? **doh**-vay **poh**-soh troh-**vah**-ray ____

Italian makes it easy if you're looking for a ***farmacia, hotel, ristorante,*** or ***supermercato.***

How Much?

How much (does it cost)?	Quanto (costa)? **kwahn**-toh (**koh**-stah)
Write it for me?	Me lo scrive? may loh **skree**-vay
I'd like...	Vorrei... voh-**reh**-ee
...a ticket.	...un biglietto. oon beel-**yeh**-toh
...the bill.	...il conto. eel **kohn**-toh
This much. (gesturing)	Così. koh-**zee**
More. / Less.	Di più. / Di meno. dee pew / dee **meh**-noh
Too much.	Troppo. **troh**-poh

When?

When?	Quando? **kwahn**-doh
What time is it?	Che ora sono? kay **oh**-rah **soh**-noh
At what time?	A che ora? ah kay **oh**-rah
open / closed	aperto / chiuso ah-**pehr**-toh / kee-**oo**-zoh
What time does this open / close?	A che ora apre / chiude? ah kay **oh**-rah **ah**-pray / kee-**oo**-day

Is this open daily?	È aperto tutti i giorni? eh ah-**pehr**-toh **too**-tee ee **jor**-nee
What day is this closed?	Che giorno chiudete? kay **jor**-noh kee-oo-**deh**-tay
On time?	In orario? een oh-**rah**-ree-oh
Late?	In ritardo? een ree-**tar**-doh
Just a moment.	Un momento. oon moh-**mehn**-toh
now / soon / later	adesso / presto / più tardi ah-**deh**-soh / **preh**-stoh / pew **tar**-dee
today / tomorrow	oggi / domani **oh**-jee / doh-**mah**-nee

For tips on telling time, see "Time and Dates" on page 195.

How Long?

How long does it take?	Quanto ci vuole? **kwahn**-toh chee **vwoh**-lay
How many minutes?	Quanti minuti? **kwahn**-tee mee-**noo**-tee
How many hours?	Quante ore? **kwahn**-tay **oh**-ray
How far?	Quanto dista? **kwahn**-toh **dee**-stah

SIMPLY IMPORTANT WORDS

For numbers, days, months, and time, see the next chapter. For guidance on how to pronounce the Italian alphabet, see page 550.

Big Little Words

I	io **ee**-oh
you (formal)	Lei **leh**-ee
you (informal)	tu too
we	noi **noh**-ee
he	lui **loo**-ee
she	lei **leh**-ee

it	esso / essa **eh**-soh / **eh**-sah
they	loro **loh**-roh
and	e ay
at	a ah
because	perchè pehr-**keh**
but	ma mah
by (train, car, etc.)	in een
for	per pehr
from	da dah
here	qui kwee
if	se say
in	in een
not	non nohn
now	adesso ah-**deh**-soh
of	di dee
only	solo **soh**-loh
or	o oh
out	fuori foo-**oh**-ree
this	questo **kweh**-stoh
that	quello **kweh**-loh
there	lì lee
to	a ah
too	anche **ahn**-kay
very	molto **mohl**-toh

Opposites

good / bad	buono / cattivo **bwoh**-noh / kah-**tee**-voh
best / worst	il migliore / il peggiore eel meel-**yoh**-ray / eel peh-**joh**-ray
a little / a lot	poco / tanto **poh**-koh / **tahn**-toh
more / less	più / meno pew / **meh**-noh

cheap / expensive	economico / caro eh-koh-**noh**-mee-koh / **kah**-roh
big / small	grande / piccolo **grahn**-day / **pee**-koh-loh
hot / cold	caldo / freddo **kahl**-doh / **freh**-doh
warm / cool	caldo / fresco **kahl**-doh / **freh**-skoh
open / closed	aperto / chiuso ah-**pehr**-toh / kee-**oo**-zoh
entrance / exit	entrata / uscita ehn-**trah**-tah / oo-**shee**-tah
push / pull	spingere / tirare **speen**-jeh-ray / tee-**rah**-ray
arrive / depart	arrivare / partire ah-ree-**vah**-ray / par-**tee**-ray
early / late	presto / tardi **preh**-stoh / **tar**-dee
soon / later	presto / più tardi **preh**-stoh / pew **tar**-dee
fast / slow	veloce / lento veh-**loh**-chay / **lehn**-toh
here / there	qui / lì kwee / lee
near / far	vicino / lontano vee-**chee**-noh / lohn-**tah**-noh
inside / outside	dentro / fuori **dehn**-troh / foo-**oh**-ree
mine / yours	mio / suo **mee**-oh / **soo**-oh
this / that	questo / quello **kweh**-stoh / **kweh**-loh
easy / difficult	facile / difficile **fah**-chee-lay / dee-**fee**-chee-lay
left / right	sinistra / destra see-**nee**-strah / **deh**-strah
up / down	su / giù soo / joo
above / below	sopra / sotto **soh**-prah / **soh**-toh
young / old	giovane / anziano **joh**-vah-nay / ahnt-see-**ah**-noh
new / old	nuovo / vecchio **nwoh**-voh / **veh**-kee-oh
heavy / light	pesante / leggero peh-**zahn**-tay / leh-**jeh**-roh

dark / light	scuro / chiaro **skoo**-roh / kee-**ah**-roh
happy / sad	felice / triste fee-**lee**-chay / **tree**-stay
beautiful / ugly	bello(a) / brutto(a) **beh**-loh / **broo**-toh
nice / mean	carino(a) / cattivo(a) kah-**ree**-noh / kah-**tee**-voh
smart / stupid	intelligente / stupido(a) een-tehl-ee-**jehn**-tay / **stoo**-pee-doh
vacant / occupied	libero / occupato **lee**-beh-roh / oh-koo-**pah**-toh
with / without	con / senza kohn / **sehnt**-sah

NUMBERS, MONEY & TIME

NUMBERS

0	zero **zeh**-roh
1	uno **oo**-noh
2	due **doo**-ay
3	tre tray
4	quattro **kwah**-troh
5	cinque **cheen**-kway
6	sei **seh**-ee
7	sette **seh**-tay
8	otto **oh**-toh
9	nove **noh**-vay
10	dieci dee-**eh**-chee
11	undici **oon**-dee-chee
12	dodici **doh**-dee-chee
13	tredici **treh**-dee-chee
14	quattordici kwah-**tor**-dee-chee
15	quindici **kween**-dee-chee
16	sedici **seh**-dee-chee
17	diciassette dee-chah-**seh**-tay
18	diciotto dee-**choh**-toh
19	diciannove dee-chah-**noh**-vay
20	venti **vehn**-tee
21	ventuno vehn-**too**-noh
22	ventidue vehn-tee-**doo**-ay
23	ventitre vehn-tee-**tray**

30	trenta **trehn**-tah
31	trentuno trehn-**too**-noh
40	quaranta kwah-**rahn**-tah
41	quarantuno kwah-rahn-**too**-noh
50	cinquanta cheen-**kwahn**-tah
60	sessanta seh-**sahn**-tah
70	settanta seh-**tahn**-tah
80	ottanta oh-**tahn**-tah
90	novanta noh-**vahn**-tah
100	cento **chehn**-toh
101	centouno chehn-toh-**oo**-noh
102	centodue chehn-toh-**doo**-ay
200	duecento doo-eh-**chehn**-toh
300	trecento treh-**chehn**-toh
400	quattrocento kwah-troh-**chehn**-toh
500	cinquecento cheen-kweh-**chehn**-toh
600	seicento seh-ee-**chehn**-toh
700	settecento seh-teh-**chehn**-toh
800	ottocento oh-toh-**chehn**-toh
900	novecento noh-veh-**chehn**-toh
1000	mille **mee**-lay
2000	duemila doo-eh-**mee**-lah
2010	duemiladieci doo-eh-mee-lah-dee-**eh**-chee
2011	duemilaundici doo-eh-mee-lah-**oon**-dee-chee
2012	duemiladodici doo-eh-mee-lah-**doh**-dee-chee
2013	duemilatredici doo-eh-mee-lah-**treh**-dee-chee
2014	duemilaquattordici doo-eh-mee-lah-kwah-**tor**-dee-chee
2015	duemilaquindici doo-eh-mee-lah-**kween**-dee-chee
2016	duemilasedici doo-eh-mee-lah-**seh**-dee-chee

2017	duemiladiciassette doo-eh-mee-lah-dee-chah-**seh**-tay
2018	duemiladiciotto doo-eh-mee-lah-dee-**choh**-toh
2019	duemiladiciannove doo-eh-mee-lah-dee-chah-**noh**-vay
2020	duemilaventi doo-eh-mee-lah-**vehn**-tee
million	milione mee-lee-**oh**-nay
billion	miliardo mee-lee-**ar**-doh
number one	numero uno **noo**-meh-roh **oo**-noh
first	primo **pree**-moh
second	secondo seh-**kohn**-doh
third	terzo **tehrt**-soh
once	una volta **oo**-nah **vohl**-tah
twice	due volte **doo**-ay **vohl**-tay
a quarter	un quarto oon **kwar**-toh
a third	un terzo oon **tehrt**-soh
half	mezzo **mehd**-zoh
this much	tanto così **tahn**-toh koh-**zee**
a dozen	una dozzina **oo**-nah dohd-**zee**-nah
a handful	una manciata **oo**-nah mahn-**chah**-tah
enough	basta **bah**-stah
not enough	non basta nohn **bah**-stah
too much	troppo **troh**-poh
more	di più dee pew
less	di meno dee **meh**-noh
50%	cinquanta per cento cheen-**kwahn**-tah pehr **chehn**-toh
100%	cento per cento **chehn**-toh pehr **chehn**-toh

Learning how to say your hotel-room number is a good way to practice Italian numbers. You'll likely be asked for the number frequently (at breakfast, or to claim your key when you return to your room).

MONEY

Italy uses the euro currency (€). One ***euro*** is divided into 100 cents ***(centesimi).*** Italians keep the term ***euro*** as singular, while ***centesimi*** is always plural. To say €2.50, it's ***due euro e cinquanta centesimi*** or, for short, ***due euro e cinquanta.***

Use your common cents—***centesimi*** are like pennies, and other coins are like nickels, dimes, and half-dollars. There are also €1 and €2 coins.

Cash Machines (ATMs)

To get cash, ATMs are the way to go. All cash machines (called ***banco-mats***) have multilingual instructions. However, the keys may be marked in Italian: ***esatto*** (correct), ***conferma*** (confirm), ***esegui*** (continue), and ***annullare*** (cancel).

money	soldi / denaro **sohl**-dee / deh-**nah**-roh
cash	contante kohn-**tahn**-tay
card	carta **kar**-tah
PIN code	codice segreto / codice PIN koh-**dee**-chay seh-**greh**-toh / koh-**dee**-chay peen
Where is...?	Dov'è...? doh-**veh**
...a cash machine	...un bancomat oon **bahn**-koh-maht
...a bank	...una banca **oo**-nah **bahn**-kah
My debit card has been...	La mia carta di debito è stata... lah **mee**-ah **kar**-tah dee **deh**-bee-toh eh **stah**-tah
...demagnetized.	...smagnetizzata. zmahn-yeht-eed-**zah**-tah
...stolen.	...rubata. roo-**bah**-tah
...eaten by the machine.	...trattenuta dal bancomat. trah-teh-**noo**-tah dahl **bahn**-koh-maht
My card doesn't work.	La mia carta non funziona. lah **mee**-ah **kar**-tah nohn foont-see-**oh**-nah

Credit and Debit Cards

Credit cards are widely accepted at larger businesses, though many smaller shops, restaurants, and hotels prefer cash.

credit card	carta di credito **kar**-tah dee **kreh**-dee-toh
debit card	carta di debito **kar**-tah dee **deh**-bee-toh
receipt	ricevuta ree-cheh-**voo**-tah
sign	firmare feer-**mah**-ray
pay	pagare / saldare pah-**gah**-ray / sahl-**dah**-ray
cashier	cassiere kah-see-**eh**-ray
cash advance	prelievo preh-lee-**eh**-voh
Do you accept credit cards?	Accettate carte di credito? ah-cheh-**tah**-tay **kar**-tay dee **kreh**-dee-toh

Key Phrases: Money

euro (€)	euro eh-**oo**-roh
cents	centesimi chehn-**teh**-zee-mee
cash	contante kohn-**tahn**-tay
Where is...?	Dov'è...? doh-**veh**
...a cash machine	...un bancomat oon **bahn**-koh-maht
...a bank	...una banca **oo**-nah **bahn**-kah
credit card	carta di credito **kar**-tah dee **kreh**-dee-toh
debit card	carta di debito **kar**-tah dee **deh**-bee-toh
Do you accept credit cards?	Accettate carte di credito? ah-cheh-**tah**-tay **kar**-tay dee **kreh**-dee-toh

Cheaper if I pay cash?	C'è uno sconto se pago in contanti? cheh **oo**-noh **skohn**-toh say **pah**-goh een kohn-**tahn**-tee
I do not have a PIN.	Non ho un codice segreto. nohn oh oon koh-**dee**-chay seh-**greh**-toh
Can I sign a receipt instead?	Posso firmare una ricevuta invece? **poh**-soh feer-**mah**-ray **oo**-nah ree-cheh-**voo**-tah een-**veh**-chay
Print a receipt?	Stampare una ricevuta? stahm-**pah**-ray **oo**-nah ree-cheh-**voo**-tah
I have another card.	Ho un'altra carta. oh oon-**ahl**-trah **kar**-tah

Much of Europe is adopting "chip-and-PIN" credit cards, which are embedded with an electronic security chip. If an automated payment machine won't take your magnetic-stripe card, look for a cashier who can swipe it instead, or find a machine that takes cash.

TIME AND DATES

Telling Time

In Italy, the 24-hour clock (military time) is used for setting formal appointments (for instance, arrival times at a hotel), for the opening and closing hours of museums and shops, and for train, bus, and ferry schedules. Informally, Italians use the same 12-hour clock we do, but they don't say "o'clock"—they instead say ***mattina*** (morning), ***pomeriggio*** (afternoon), and so on. So they might meet a friend at ***tre di pomeriggio*** (three in the afternoon) to catch a train that leaves at ***le sedici*** (16:00).

What time is it?	Che ore sono? kay **oh**-ray **soh**-noh
(in the) morning	(di) mattina (dee) mah-**tee**-nah
(in the) afternoon	(di) pomeriggio (dee) poh-meh-**ree**-joh
(in the) evening	(di) sera (dee) **seh**-rah
(at) night	(di) notte (dee) **noh**-tay
half	mezza **mehd**-zah

Key Phrases: Time and Dates

What time is it?	Che ore sono? kay **oh**-ray **soh**-noh
minute	minuto mee-**noo**-toh
hour	ora **oh**-rah
It's 1:00	È l'una. eh **loo**-nah
It's...	Sono... **soh**-noh
...7:00 in the morning.	...le sette di mattina. lay **seh**-tay dee mah-**tee**-nah
...2:00 in the afternoon.	...le due di pomeriggio. lay **doo**-ay dee poh-meh-**ree**-joh
When does this open / close?	A che ora apre / chiude? ah kay **oh**-rah **ah**-pray / kee-**oo**-day
day	giorno **jor**-noh
today	oggi **oh**-jee
tomorrow	domani doh-**mah**-nee
(this) week	(questa) settimana (**kweh**-stah) seh-tee-**mah**-nah
August 21	il ventuno agosto eel vehn-**too**-noh ah-**goh**-stoh

quarter	un quarto oon **kwar**-toh
minute	minuto mee-**noo**-toh
hour	ora **oh**-rah
It's / At...	Sono / Alle... **soh**-noh / **ah**-lay
...8:00 in the morning.	...le otto di mattina. lay **oh**-toh dee mah-**tee**-nah
...16:00.	...le sedici. lay **seh**-dee-chee
...4:00 in the afternoon.	...le quattro di pomeriggio. lay **kwah**-troh dee poh-meh-**ree**-joh

...10:30 in the evening.	...le dieci e mezza di sera. lay dee-**eh**-chee ay **mehd**-zah dee **seh**-rah
...a quarter past nine.	...le nove e un quarto. lay **noh**-vay ay oon **kwar**-toh
...a quarter to eleven.	...le undici meno un quarto. lay **oon**-dee-chee **meh**-noh oon **kwar**-toh
at 6:00 sharp	alle sei in punto **ah**-lay **seh**-ee een **poon**-toh
from 8:00 to 10:00	dalle otto alle dieci **dah**-lay **oh**-toh **ah**-lay dee-**eh**-chee
noon	mezzogiorno mehd-zoh-**jor**-noh
midnight	mezzanotte mehd-zah-**noh**-tay
It's my bedtime.	Per me è ora di andare a dormire. pehr may eh **oh**-rah dee ahn-**dah**-ray ah dor-**mee**-ray
I will be / We will be...	Sarò / Saremo... sah-**roh** / sah-**reh**-moh
...back at 11:20.	...di ritorno alle undici e venti. dee ree-**tor**-noh **ah**-lay **oon**-dee-chee ay **vehn**-tee
...there by 18:00.	...lì per le diciotto. lee pehr lay dee-**choh**-toh

In Italy, the ***pomeriggio*** (afternoon) turns to ***sera*** (evening) generally about 4:00 or 5:00 p.m. (5:30 p.m. is ***cinque e mezza di sera***).

Timely Questions

When?	Quando? **kwahn**-doh
When is...?	Quand'è...? kwahn-**deh**
At what time?	A che ora? ah kay **oh**-rah
opening time	ora di apertura **oh**-rah dee ah-pehr-**too**-rah

When does this open / close?	Quando apre / chiude? **kwahn**-doh **ah**-pray / kee-**oo**-day
Is the train...?	È... il treno? eh... eel **treh**-noh
Is the bus...?	È... l'autobus? eh... **low**-toh-boos
...early	...in anticipo een ahn-**tee**-chee-poh
...late	...in ritardo een ree-**tar**-doh
...on time	...in orario een oh-**rah**-ree-oh
When is checkout time?	A che ora bisogna liberare la camera? ah kay **oh**-rah bee-**zohn**-yah lee-beh-**rah**-ray lah **kah**-meh-rah

It's About Time

now	adesso ah-**deh**-soh
soon	presto / tra poco **preh**-stoh / trah **poh**-koh
later	più tardi pew **tar**-dee
in one hour	tra un'ora trah oon-**oh**-rah
in half an hour	tra mezz'ora trah mehd-**zoh**-rah
in three hours	tra tre ore trah tray **oh**-ray
early	presto **preh**-stoh
late	tardi **tar**-dee
on time	puntuale poon-too-**ah**-lay
anytime	a qualsiasi ora ah kwahl-**see**-ah-zee **oh**-rah
immediately	immediatamente **ee**-meh-dee-ah-tah-**mehn**-tay
every hour	ogni ora **ohn**-yee **oh**-rah
every day	ogni giorno **ohn**-yee **jor**-noh
daily	giornaliero jor-nahl-ee-**ehr**-oh
last	scorso **skor**-soh
this	questo **kweh**-stoh

next	prossimo **proh**-see-moh
before	prima **pree**-mah
after	dopo **doh**-poh
May 15	il quindici maggio eel **kween**-dee-chee **mah**-joh

The Day

day	giorno **jor**-noh
today	oggi **oh**-jee
sunrise	alba **ahl**-bah
this morning	stamattina stah-mah-**tee**-nah
sunset	tramonto trah-**mohn**-toh
tonight	stasera stah-**seh**-rah
last night	stanotte stah-**noh**-tay
yesterday	ieri ee-**eh**-ree
tomorrow	domani doh-**mah**-nee
tomorrow morning	domani mattina doh-**mah**-nee mah-**tee**-nah
day after tomorrow	dopodomani doh-poh-doh-**mah**-nee

The Week

Sunday	domenica doh-**meh**-nee-kah
Monday	lunedì loo-neh-**dee**
Tuesday	martedì mar-teh-**dee**
Wednesday	mercoledì mehr-koh-leh-**dee**
Thursday	giovedì joh-veh-**dee**
Friday	venerdì veh-nehr-**dee**
Saturday	sabato **sah**-bah-toh
week	settimana seh-tee-**mah**-nah

last week	la settimana scorsa lah seh-tee-**mah**-nah **skor**-sah
this week	questa settimana **kweh**-stah seh-tee-**mah**-nah
next week	la settimana prossima lah seh-tee-**mah**-nah **proh**-see-mah
weekend	weekend "weekend"
this weekend	questo weekend **kweh**-stoh "weekend"

Weekdays plus Saturday are called ***feriali*** (literally "working days"); Sundays and holidays are ***festivi.***

The Months

month	mese **meh**-zay
January	gennaio jeh-**nah**-yoh
February	febbraio feh-**brah**-yoh
March	marzo **mart**-soh
April	aprile ah-**pree**-lay
May	maggio **mah**-joh
June	giugno **joon**-yoh
July	luglio **lool**-yoh
August	agosto ah-**goh**-stoh
September	settembre seh-**tehm**-bray
October	ottobre oh-**toh**-bray
November	novembre noh-**vehm**-bray
December	dicembre dee-**chehm**-bray

For dates, say ***il*** followed by the number and month; for example, July 4 is ***il quattro luglio.***

The Year

year	anno **ahn**-noh
season	stagione stah-jee-**oh**-nee
spring	primavera pree-mah-**veh**-rah
summer	estate eh-**stah**-tay
fall	autunno ow-**too**-noh
winter	inverno een-**vehr**-noh

For a list of years, see the “Numbers” section on pages 191-192.

TRANSPORTATION

GETTING AROUND

train	treno **treh**-noh
city bus	autobus **ow**-toh-boos
long-distance bus	pullman / autobus **pool**-mahn / **ow**-toh-boos
subway	Metropolitana / Metro meh-troh-poh-lee-**tah**-nah / **meh**-troh
taxi	taxi **tahk**-see
car	macchina **mah**-kee-nah
boat	barca **bar**-kah
ferry	traghetto trah-**geh**-toh
car ferry	autotraghetto ow-toh-trah-**geh**-toh
hydrofoil	aliscafo ah-lee-**skah**-foh
walk / by foot	camminare / a piedi kah-mee-**nah**-ray / ah pee-**eh**-dee
Where is the...?	Dov'è il / la...? doh-**veh** eel / lah
...train station	...stazione staht-see-**oh**-nay
...bus station	...stazione degli autobus staht-see-**oh**-nay **dehl**-yee **ow**-toh-boos
...bus stop	...fermata fehr-**mah**-tah
...subway station	...stazione della Metro staht-see-**oh**-nay **deh**-lah **meh**-troh
...taxi stand	...fermata dei taxi fehr-**mah**-tah **deh**-ee **tahk**-see
I'm going / We're going to ____.	Vado / Andiamo a ____. **vah**-doh / ahn-dee-**ah**-moh ah ____

Getting Tickets

When you're buying tickets for the bus, train, or subway, the following phrases will come in handy.

Where can I buy a ticket?	Dove posso comprare un biglietto? **doh**-vay **poh**-soh kohm-**prah**-ray oon beel-**yeh**-toh
How much (is a ticket to ____)?	Quant'è (il biglietto per ____)? kwahn-**teh** (eel beel-**yeh**-toh pehr ____)
I want to go to ____.	Voglio andare a ____. **vohl**-yoh ahn-**dah**-ray ah ____
One ticket / Two tickets (to ____).	Un biglietto / Due biglietti (per ____). oon beel-**yeh**-toh / **doo**-ay beel-**yeh** tee (pehr ____)
When is the next train / bus (to ____)?	Quando è il prossimo treno / autobus (per ____)? **kwahn**-doh eh eel **proh**-see-moh **treh**-noh / **ow**-toh-boos (pehr ____)
What time does it leave?	A che ora parte? ah kay **oh**-rah **par**-tay
Is it direct?	È diretto? eh dee-**reh**-toh
Is a reservation required?	Ci vuole la prenotazione? chee **vwoh**-lay lah preh-noh-taht-see-**oh**-nay
I'd like / We'd like to reserve a seat.	Vorrei / Vorremmo prenotare un posto. voh-**reh**-ee / voh-**reh**-moh preh-noh-**tah**-ray oon **poh**-stoh
Can I buy a ticket on board?	Posso comprare un biglietto a bordo? **poh**-soh kohm-**prah**-ray oon beel-**yeh**-toh ah **bor**-doh
Exact change only?	Solo importo esatto? **soh**-loh eem-**por**-toh eh-**zah**-toh

What is the cheapest / fastest / easiest way...?	Qual'è il modo più economico / più veloce / più facile...? kwah-**leh** eel **moh**-doh pew eh-koh-**noh**-mee-koh / pew veh-**loh**-chay / pew **fah**-chee-lay
...to downtown	...al centro ahl **chehn**-troh
...to the train station	...alla stazione **ah**-lah staht-see-**oh**-nay
...to my / to our hotel	...al mio / al nostro hotel ahl **mee**-oh / ahl **noh**-stroh **oh**-tehl
...to the airport	...all'aeroporto ahl-ay-roh-**por**-toh

TRAINS

For tips and strategies about rail travel and railpasses in Italy, see www.ricksteves.com/rail. Note that many of the following train phrases work for long-distance bus travel as well.

Ticket Basics

ticket	biglietto beel-**yeh**-toh
reservation	prenotazione preh-noh-taht-see-**oh**-nay
ticket office	biglietteria beel-yeh-teh-**ree**-yah
ticket machine	biglietteria automatica beel-yeh-teh-**ree**-yah ow-toh-**mah**-tee-kah
to validate	timbrare / convalidare teem-**brah**-ray / kohn-vah-lee-**dah**-ray
Where can I buy a ticket?	Dove posso comprare un biglietto? **doh**-vay **poh**-soh kohm-**prah**-ray oon beel-**yeh**-toh
Is this the line for...?	È questa la fila per...? eh **kweh**-stah lah **fee**-lah pehr
...tickets	...biglietti beel-**yeh**-tee
...reservations	...prenotazioni preh-noh-taht-see-**oh**-nee

Key Phrases: Trains

train station	stazione staht-see-**oh**-nay
train	treno **treh**-noh
platform / track	binario bee-**nah**-ree-oh
What track does it leave from?	Da che binario parte? dah kay bee-**nah**-ree-oh **par**-tay
Is this the train to ____?	Questo è il treno per ____? **kweh**-stoh eh eel **treh**-noh pehr ____
Which train to ____?	Quale treno per ____? **kwah**-lay **treh**-noh pehr ____
Tell me when to get off?	Mi dice quando devo scendere? mee **dee**-chay **kwahn**-doh **deh**-voh **shehn**-deh-ray
transfer (n)	scalo **skah**-loh
Change here for ____?	Cambio qui per ____? **kahm**-bee-oh kwee pehr ____

...information	...informazioni een-for-maht-see-**oh**-nee
One ticket (to ____).	Un biglietto (per ____). oon beel-**yeh**-toh (pehr ____)
Two tickets.	Due biglietti. **doo**-ay beel-**yeh**-tee
I want to go to ____.	Voglio andare a ____. **vohl**-yoh ahn-**dah**-ray ah ____
How much (is a ticket to ____)?	Quant'è (il biglietto per ____)? kwahn-**teh** (eel beel-**yeh**-toh pehr ____)
one-way	andata ahn-**dah**-tah
round-trip	andata e ritorno ahn-**dah**-tah ay ree-**tor**-noh
today / tomorrow	oggi / domani **oh**-jee / doh-**mah**-nee

Ticket Specifics

As trains and buses can sell out, it's smart to buy your tickets a day in advance even for short rides. For phrases related to discounts (such as for children, families, or seniors), see page 209.

schedule	orario oh-**rah**-ree-oh
When is the next train / bus (to ____)?	Quando è il prossimo treno / autobus (per ____)? **kwahn**-doh eh eel **proh**-see-moh **treh**-noh / **ow**-toh-boos (pehr ____)
What time does it leave?	A che ora parte? ah kay **oh**-rah **par**-tay
I'd like / We'd like to leave...	Vorrei / Vorremmo partire... voh-**reh**-ee / voh-**reh**-moh par-**tee**-ray
I'd like / We'd like to arrive...	Vorrei / Vorremmo arrivare... voh-**reh**-ee / voh-**reh**-moh ah-ree-**vah**-ray
...by ____... (name time)	...per le ____... pehr lay ____
...at ____... (name time)	...alle ____... **ah**-lay ____
...in the morning / afternoon / evening.	...di mattina / pomeriggio / sera. dee mah-**tee**-nah / poh-meh-**ree**-joh / **seh**-rah
Is there a... train / bus?	C'è un treno / autobus...? cheh oon **treh**-noh / **ow**-toh-boos
...earlier	...prima **pree**-mah
...later	...più tardi pew **tar**-dee
...overnight	...notturno noh-**toor**-noh
...cheaper	...più economico pew eh-koh-**noh**-mee-koh
...express	...espresso eh-**spreh**-soh
...direct	...diretto dee-**reh**-toh
Is it direct?	È diretto? eh dee-**reh**-toh

Is a transfer required?	Devo cambiare? **deh**-voh kahm-bee-**ah**-ray
How many transfers?	Quante volte devo cambiare treno? **kwahn**-tay **vohl**-tay **deh**-voh kahm-bee-**ah**-ray **treh**-noh
When? / Where?	Quando? / Dove? **kwahn**-doh / **doh**-vay
first / second class	prima / seconda classe **pree**-mah / seh-**kohn**-dah **klah**-say
How long is this ticket valid?	Per quanto tempo è valido questo biglietto? pehr **kwahn**-toh **tehm**-poh eh **vah**-lee-doh **kweh**-stoh beel-**yeh**-toh
Can you validate my railpass?	Può convalidare la mia tessera ferroviaria? pwoh kohn-vah-lee-**dah**-ray lah **mee**-ah **teh**-seh-rah feh-roh-vee-**ah**-ree-ah

At the train station, you can buy tickets at the windows in the ***atrio biglietteria*** or ***salone biglietti*** (ticketing hall) or at machines ***(biglietterie automatiche).*** At large stations, be sure you go to the correct window: ***biglietti*** are tickets, ***prenotazioni*** is for reservations, ***nazionali*** is for domestic trips, and ***internazionali*** is international. On tickets, ***1a*** (or ***prima classe***) means first class, and ***2a*** (or ***seconda classe***) means second class.

Rather than wait in line, you may find it faster to use machines to buy tickets, railpass reservations, and more. Look for the big "self service" signs, or the even faster ***biglietto veloce*** kiosks. Some machines take credit cards, others take cash, and some take both—before using a machine, be sure it accepts your method of payment. (When the machine prompts you—"Fidelity Card?"—choose no.) For nearby destinations only, use the machines marked ***Rete regionale*** (cash only, push button for English).

For a small fee, it's also possible to book rail tickets through a travel agency ***(agenzia di viaggi).***

Train Reservations

Some fast trains require a ***prenotazione*** (reservation)—often noted by an Ⓡ in the schedule. Even if a reservation isn't required, it can be a good idea to reserve a seat on busy routes at popular times. (If you're using a railpass, you must pay an extra ***supplemento*** to reserve.)

Is a reservation required?	Ci vuole la prenotazione? chee **vwoh**-lay lah preh-noh-taht-see-**oh**-nay
I'd like / We'd like to reserve...	Vorrei / Vorremmo prenotare... voh-**reh**-ee / voh-**reh**-moh preh-noh-**tah**-ray
...a seat.	...un posto. oon **poh**-stoh
...an aisle seat.	...un posto corridoio. oon **poh**-stoh koh-ree-**doh**-yoh
...a window seat.	...un posto finestrino. oon **poh**-stoh fee-neh-**stree**-noh
...two seats.	...due posti. **doo**-ay **poh**-stee
...a couchette. (sleeping berth)	...una cuccetta. **oo**-nah koo-**cheh**-tah
...an upper / middle / lower berth.	...una cuccetta di sopra / in mezzo / di sotto. **oo**-nah koo-**cheh**-tah dee **soh**-prah / een **mehd**-zoh / dee **soh**-toh
...two couchettes.	...due cuccette. **doo**-ay koo-**cheh**-tay
...a sleeper compartment. (private)	...un compartimento in vagone letto. oon kohm-par-tee-**mehn**-toh een vah-**goh**-nay **leh**-toh
...a sleeper compartment (with two beds).	...un compartimento in vagone letto (con due cuccette). oon kohm-par-tee-**mehn**-toh een vah-**goh**-nay **leh**-toh (kohn **doo**-ay koo-**cheh**-tay)
...the entire train.	...tutto il treno. **too**-toh eel **treh**-noh

Discounts

Is there a cheaper ticket?	C'è un biglietto più economico? cheh oon beel-**yeh**-toh pew eh-koh-**noh**-mee-koh
discount	sconto **skohn**-toh
reduced fare	tariffa ridotta tah-**ree**-fah ree-**doh**-tah
refund	rimborso reem-**bor**-soh
Is there a discount for...?	Fate sconti per...? **fah**-tay **skohn**-tee pehr
...children	...bambini bahm-**bee**-nee
...minors	...minorenni mee-noh-**reh**-nee
...seniors	...anziani ahnt-see-**ah**-nee
...families	...famiglie fah-**meel**-yay
...groups	...gruppi **groo**-pee
...advance purchase	...acquisto anticipato ah-**kwee**-stoh ahn-tee-chee-**pah**-toh
...weekends	...fine settimana **fee**-nay seh-tee-**mah**-nah
Are there any deals for this journey?	Ci sono delle offerte per questo viaggio? chee **soh**-noh **deh** lay oh-**fehr**-tay pehr **kweh**-stoh vee-**ah**-joh

At the Train Station

Where is the train station?	Dov'è la stazione? doh-**veh** lah staht-see-**oh**-nay
train information	informazioni treni / informazioni e servizi een-for-maht-see-**oh**-nee **treh**-nee / een-for-maht-see-**oh**-nee ay sehr-**veet**-see
customer assistance	assistenza clienti ah-sees-**tehnt**-sah klee-**ehn**-tee
tickets	biglietti beel-**yeh**-tee

ticket hall	atrio biglietteria / salone biglietti **ah**-tree-oh beel-yeh-teh-**ree**-yah / sah-**loh**-nay beel-**yeh**-tee
ticket sales	biglietteria beel-yeh-teh-**ree**-yah
(time of) departure / arrival	(orario di) partenza / arrivo (oh-**rah**-ree-oh dee) par-**tehnt**-sah / ah-**ree**-voh
On time?	È in orario? eh een oh-**rah**-ree-oh
Late?	In ritardo? een ree-**tar**-doh
How late?	Quanto ritardo? **kwahn**-toh ree-**tar**-doh
platform / track	binario bee-**nah**-ree-oh
What track does it leave from?	Da che binario parte? dah kay bee-**nah**-ree-oh **par**-tay
waiting room	sala di attesa / sala d'aspetto **sah**-lah dee ah-**teh**-zah / **sah**-lah dah-**speh**-toh
lockers	armadietti ar-mah-dee-**eh**-tee
baggage check	deposito bagagli / consegna deh-**poh**-zee-toh bah-**gahl**-yee / kohn-**sehn**-yah
tourist information	informazioni per turisti een-for-maht-see-**oh**-nee pehr too-**ree**-stee
lost and found office	ufficio oggetti smarriti oo-**fee**-choh oh-**jeh**-tee smah-**ree**-tee
toilet	toilette twah-**leh**-tay

The general term for "railroad" in Italian is ***ferrovia.*** Most trains in Italy are operated by the national rail company, ***Ferrovie dello Stato Italiane***—abbreviated ***FS*** or ***FSI*** and usually just called ***Trenitalia*** (trehn-ee-**tahl**-yah).

Types of Trains

Trains are classified according to how fast and how far they travel; here are the abbreviations you may see, roughly in order from slowest to fastest.

R / REG	regionali (pokey milk-run trains)
RV	regionale veloce (medium-speed)
IR	InterRegio (medium-speed)
D	diretto (medium-speed)
E / EXP	espresso (medium-speed)
IC	InterCity (fast)
EC	EuroCity (fast)
ES	Eurostar Italia (super-fast)
ES / AV / EAV	Eurostar Italia Alta Velocità (super-fast)

The speedy **ES** and **EAV** routes use three types of trains: the fast ***Frecciabianca*** (White Arrow), faster ***Frecciargento*** (Silver Arrow), and fastest ***Frecciarossa*** (Red Arrow).

Train and Bus Schedules

European timetables use the 24-hour clock. It's like American time until noon. After that, subtract 12 and add "p.m." For example, 13:00 is 1 p.m., and 19:00 is 7 p.m.

You can check train schedules throughout Italy at the handy ticket machines. Newsstands sell up-to-date regional and all-Italy timetables ***(orario ferroviaro).***

At the station, look for the big yellow posters labeled ***Partenze*** (departures; ignore the white posters, which show arrivals). Organized in this order, each schedule has these columns:

Ora	Time of departure
Treno	Type and number of train
Classi Servizi	Services available (for example, dining car, *cuccetta* sleeping berths, etc.); if you see an R here, the train requires a reservation

Principali Fermate Destinazioni	Major stops and final destination
Servizi Diretti e Annotazioni	Additional notes (see bottom of poster)
Binario / Bin	Track number

On any timetable—posted or printed—you might also see some of these terms:

a	to; can mean "arrival"
anche	also
annulata	cancelled
arrive / arrivi	arrival(s)
avvisi al pubblico / al viaggiatori	advisory to the public / to travelers
circa ____ minuti di ritardo	about ____ minutes late
(non) circola nei giorni festivi	does (not) run on holidays
coincidenze	connections
corsia	bus stall or platform
corse rapide	fast route (bus)
da	from
destinazione	destination
direzione e / o stazione d'arrivo	direction and / or final destination
eccetto / escluso	except
feriali	weekdays including Saturday
ferma	stops
ferma anche a ____	also stops in ____
ferma in tutte le stazioni	stops at all the stations
festivi	Sundays and holidays
fino	until
G	runs even in case of strike
giornaliero	daily
giorni	days
in ritardo	late
minuti	minutes
NB	note
non ferma a ____	doesn't stop in ____

ogni	every
ordinaria	makes every stop (bus)
ore	hours
partenza / p	departure
per	for
più tardi (dell'orario stabilito)	later (than scheduled)
provenienza	originating from
rapida	fast route (bus)
riduzioni (delle corse)	reduced service
ritardo / rit	delay
servizio automobilistico	bus service
servizio periodico	periodic service
si effettua anche ___	also runs on ___
solo	only
tempo	time
transita da ___	stops at ___
transiti	stops
treni in arrivo	arriving trains
treni in partenza	departing trains
tutti i giorni	daily
va	goes
via	by way of
1-5 / 6 / 7	Monday-Friday / Saturday / Sunday

Avvisi (advisory) means something is not running normally. When perusing train schedules, it helps to know the Italian names of cities, such as ***Firenze*** (Florence), ***Venezia*** (Venice), ***Napoli*** (Naples), ***Monaco di Baviera*** (Munich), and ***Parigi*** (Paris).

All Aboard

To find the platforms, look for the signs ***ai treni*** (to the trains) or ***ai binari*** (to the platforms).

You'll need to validate ***(timbrare)*** most types of unreserved tickets on the platform in the machines marked ***convalida biglietti.*** If you're on the train and you forget to validate your ticket, go right away to the train conductor—before he comes to you—or you'll pay a fine.

The ***composizione principali treni*** (train-car configuration) diagram can show you where to wait for your car along the platform, though they're not always accurate.

platform / track	binario bee-**nah**-ree-oh
number	numero **noo**-meh-roh
train car	vagone vah-**goh**-nay
conductor	capotreno kah-poh-**treh**-noh
Is this the train to ____?	Questo è il treno per ____? **kweh**-stoh eh eel **treh**-noh pehr ____
Which train to ____?	Quale treno per ____? **kwah**-lay **treh**-noh pehr ____
Which train car to ____?	Quale vagone per ____? **kwah**-lay vah-**goh**-nay pehr ____
Where can I validate my ticket?	Dove posso timbrare il biglietto? **doh**-vay **poh**-soh teem-**brah**-ray eel beel-**yeh**-toh
Where is...?	Dov'è...? doh-**veh**
Is this...?	È questo...? eh **kweh**-stoh
...my seat	...il mio posto eel **mee**-oh **pohs**-toh
...first / second class	...la prima / seconda classe lah **pree**-mah / seh-**kohn**-dah **klah**-say
...the dining car	...il vagone ristorante eel vah-**goh**-nay ree-stoh-**rahn**-tay
...the sleeper car	...il vagone letto eel vah-**goh**-nay **leh**-toh
...the toilet	...la toilette lah twah-**leh**-tay
reserved / occupied / free	prenotato / occupato / libero preh-noh-**tah**-toh / oh-koo-**pah**-toh / **lee**-beh-roh
Is this (seat) free?	È libero? eh **lee**-beh-roh
May I / May we...?	Posso / Possiamo...? **poh**-soh / poh-see-**ah**-moh

...sit here	...sedermi / sederci qui seh-**dehr**-mee / seh-**dehr**-chee kwee
...open the window	...aprire il finestrino ah-**pree**-ray eel fee-neh-**stree**-noh
...eat here	...mangiare qui mahn-**jah**-ray kwee
(I think) this is my seat.	(Penso che) questo è il mio posto. (**pehn**-soh kay) **kweh**-stoh eh eel **mee**-oh **poh**-stoh
These are our seats.	Sono i nostri posti. **soh**-noh ee **noh**-stree **poh**-stee
Save my place?	Mi tiene il posto? mee tee-**eh**-nay eel **poh**-stoh
Save our places?	Ci tiene i posti? chee tee-**eh**-nay ee **poh**-stee
Where are you going?	Dove va? **doh**-vay vah
I'm going / We're going to ____.	Vado / Andiamo a ____. **vah**-doh / ahn-dee-**ah**-moh ah ____
When will it arrive (in ____)?	Quando arriva (a ____)? **kwahn**-doh ah-**ree**-vah (ah ____)
Where is a (handsome) conductor?	Dov'è un (bel) capotreno? doh-**veh** oon (behl) kah-poh-**treh**-noh
Tell me when to get off?	Mi dice quando devo scendere? mee **dee**-chay **kwahn**-doh **deh**-voh **shehn**-deh-ray
I'm getting off.	Devo scendere. **deh**-voh **shehn**-deh-ray
How do I open the door?	Come si apre la porta? **koh**-may see **ah**-pray lah **por**-tah

As you approach a station on the train, you will hear an announcement such as ***Stiamo per arrivare alla Stazione di Milano Centrale*** (We are about to arrive at Milan Central Station).

Strikes

Strikes *(scioperi)* are common, and generally last a day. Train employees will simply shrug and say ***Sciopero.*** But a few sporadic trains often do lumber down the tracks during most strikes. Hoteliers and travel agencies can tell you when a strike will go into effect and which trains will continue to run (they're also marked "G" in train schedules).

strike	sciopero **shoh**-peh-roh
Is there a strike?	C'è lo sciopero? cheh loh **shoh**-peh-roh
Only for today?	È solo per oggi? eh **soh**-loh pehr **oh**-jee
Tomorrow, too?	Anche domani? **ahn**-kay doh-**mah**-nee
Are there some trains today?	C'è qualche treno oggi? cheh **kwahl**-kay **treh**-noh **oh**-jee
I'm going to ___.	Vado a ___. **vah**-doh ah ___

Strikes often come with demonstrations ***(manifestazioni)***, which can close down streets and impede your progress.

LONG-DISTANCE BUSES

In Italy, buses can connect many smaller towns more efficiently and affordably than trains. In many hill towns, trains leave you at a station in the valley far below, while buses bring you right into the thick of things. If you're not sure where to buy tickets, ask ***Chi vende i biglietti dell'autobus per ___?*** (Who sells bus tickets to ___?). Some piazzas have more than one bus stop; confirm the departure point ***(Dov'è la fermata?)***.

Remember that many phrases that apply to train travel can be used for bus travel as well. For ticket-buying help, see page 203.

long-distance bus	pullman / autobus **pool**-mahn / **ow**-toh-boos
bus station	stazione degli autobus staht-see-**oh**-nay **dehl**-yee **ow**-toh-boos
stall	corsia / stallo kor-**see**-ah / **stah**-loh
stop	fermata fehr-**mah**-tah

Who sells bus tickets to ____?	Chi vende i biglietti dell'autobus per ____? kee **vehn**-day ee beel-**yeh**-tee dehl-ow-toh-boos pehr ____
How many minutes will we be here?	Quanti minuti ci fermiamo qui? **kwahn**-tee mee-**noo**-tee chee fehr-mee-**ah**-moh kwee
Where is the bus stop?	Dov'è la fermata? doh-**veh** lah fehr-**mah**-tah
Where does the connection leave from?	Da dove parte la coincidenza? dah **doh**-vay **par**-tay lah koh-een-chee-**dehnt**-sah

Buses marked ***via autostrada*** or ***via superstrada*** on schedules take speedy expressways—they'll get you there faster than ***ordinaria*** buses, which take back roads and make every stop. On schedules, ***transiti*** are the major stops en route. (For more tips on interpreting schedules, see page 211.) Sundays and holidays are problematic; schedules are sparse, buses are jam-packed, and ticket offices are often closed. Plan ahead and buy your ticket in advance.

CITY BUSES AND SUBWAYS

Ticket Talk

Most big cities offer deals on transportation, such as one-day tickets ***(biglietto giornaliero),*** cheaper fares for youths and seniors, or a discount for buying a batch of tickets (called a ***carnet,*** which you can share with friends). You can buy tickets and passes at some newsstands, tobacco shops (***tabacchi,*** marked by a black-and-white ***T*** sign), and major Metro stations and bus stops.

Where can I buy a ticket?	Dove posso comprare un biglietto? **doh**-vay **poh**-soh kohm-**prah**-ray oon beel-**yeh**-toh
I want to go to ____.	Voglio andare a ____. **vohl**-yoh ahn-**dah**-ray ah ____

Key Phrases: City Buses and Subways

bus	autobus **ow**-toh-boos
subway	Metropolitana / Metro meh-troh-poh-lee-**tah**-nah / **meh**-troh
How do I get to ____?	Come si va a ____? **koh**-may see vah ah ____
Which stop for ____?	Qual'è la fermata per ____? kwah-**leh** lah fehr-**mah**-tah pehr ____
Tell me when to get off?	Mi dice quando devo scendere? mee **dee**-chay **kwahn**-doh **deh**-voh **shehn**-deh-ray

How much (is a ticket to ____)?	Quant'è (il biglietto per ____)? kwahn-**teh** (eel beel-**yeh**-toh pehr ____)
single trip	biglietto singolo beel-**yeh**-toh **seen**-goh-loh
short-ride ticket	biglietto per tragitto breve beel-**yeh**-toh pehr trah-**jee**-toh **breh**-vay
day ticket	biglietto giornaliero beel-**yeh**-toh jor-nahl-**yeh**-roh
Is there a...?	C'è un...? cheh oon
...day ticket	...biglietto giornaliero beel-**yeh**-toh jor-nahl-**yeh**-roh
...discount if I buy more tickets	...sconto se compro più biglietti **skohn**-toh say **kohm**-proh pew beel-**yeh**-tee
Can I buy a ticket on board (the bus)?	Posso comprare un biglietto a bordo (dell'autobus)? **poh**-soh kohm-**prah**-ray oon beel-**yeh**-toh ah **bor**-doh (dehl-**ow**-toh-boos)

Exact change only?	Solo importo esatto? **soh**-loh eem-**por**-toh eh-**zah**-toh
validate (here)	timbrare (qui) teem-**brah**-ray (kwee)

In many cities, you are required to ***timbrare*** (validate) your ticket by sticking it into a validation machine as you enter the subway station, bus, or tram. If you have an all-day or multi-day ticket, validate it only the first time you use it. For basic ticket-buying terms, see page 203.

Transit Terms

Most big cities have the usual public-transit systems, such as the ***Metropolitana*** (subway) and ***autobus*** (city bus). Some cities have unique types of transit, like the ***elettrico*** minibuses in Rome that connect tight old neighborhoods. Venice has boats instead of buses—you'll zip around on ***vaporetti*** (motorized ferries) and ***traghetti*** (gondola ferries).

city bus	autobus **ow**-toh-boos
electric minibus	elettrico eh-**leh**-tree-koh
bus stop	fermata fehr-**mah**-tah
subway	Metropolitana / Metro meh-troh-poh-lee-**tah**-nah / **meh**-troh
subway station	stazione della Metro staht-see-**oh**-nay **deh**-lah **meh**-troh
public-transit map	mappa dei trasporti **mah**-pah **deh**-ee trah-**spor**-tee
entrance	entrata ehn-**trah**-tah
stop	fermata fehr-**mah**-tah
exit	uscita oo-**shee**-tah
line (subway)	linea **lee**-neh-ah
number (bus)	numero **noo**-meh-roh
direction	direzione dee-reht-see-**oh**-nay
direct	diretto dee-**reh**-toh

connection	coincidenza koh-een-chee-**dehnt**-sah
pickpocket	borseggiatore bor-seh-jah-**toh**-ray

The ***mappa dei trasporti*** is a map of the city's public transit, often accompanied by the ***orario*** (timetable) and ***tariffe*** (fares). At night, most transit stops running, except for a few ***linee notturne*** (night lines).

Public Transit

How do I get to ____?	Come si va a ____? **koh**-may see vah ah ____
How do we get to ____?	Come andiamo a ____? **koh**-may ahn-dee-**ah**-moh ah ____
Which bus to ____?	Quale autobus per ____? **kwah**-lay **ow**-toh-boos pehr ____
Does it stop at ____?	Si ferma a ____? see **fehr**-mah ah ____
Which stop for ____?	Qual'è la fermata per ____? kwah-**leh** lah fehr-**mah**-tah pehr ____
Which direction for ____?	Da che parte è ____? dah kay **par**-tay eh ____
Is a transfer required?	Devo cambiare? **deh**-voh kahm-bee-**ah**-ray
When is...?	Quando parte...? **kwahn**-doh **par**-tay
...the first / next / last...	...il primo / il prossimo / l'ultimo... eel **pree**-moh / eel **proh**-see-moh / **lool**-tee-moh
...bus / subway	...autobus / Metro **ow**-toh-boos / **meh**-troh
How often does it run (per hour / per day)?	Ogni quanto passa (all'ora / al giorno)? **ohn**-yee **kwahn**-toh **pah**-sah (ah-**loh**-rah / ahl **jor**-noh)
When does the next one leave?	Quando parte il prossimo? **kwahn**-doh **par**-tay eel **proh**-see-moh
Where does it leave from?	Da dove parte? dah **doh**-vay **par**-tay

Tell me when to get off?	Mi dice quando devo scendere? mee **dee**-chay **kwahn**-doh **deh**-voh **shehn**-deh-ray
I'm getting off.	Devo scendere. **deh**-voh **shehn**-deh-ray
How do I open the door?	Come si apre la porta? **koh**-may see **ah**-pray lah **por**-tah

If you press the button to request a stop on a bus, a sign lights up that says *fermata richiesta* (stop requested). Upon arrival, you may have to press a button or pull a lever to open the door—watch locals and imitate.

TAXIS

Taxis usually take up to four people, and larger taxis take more. So you'll know what to expect, ask your hotelier about typical taxi fares.

If you have trouble flagging down a taxi, ask for directions to a *fermata dei taxi* (taxi stand) or seek out a big hotel where taxis wait for guests. The simplest way to tell a cabbie where you want to go is to state your destination followed by "please" *(Uffizi, per favore).* Tipping isn't expected, but it's polite to round up—if the fare is €19, give €20.

Taxi!	Taxi! **tahk**-see
Can you call a taxi?	Può chiamare un taxi? pwoh kee-ah-**mah**-ray oon **tahk**-see
Where can I get a taxi?	Dove posso prendere un taxi? **doh**-vay **poh**-soh **prehn**-deh-ray oon **tahk**-see
Where is a taxi stand?	Dov'è una fermata dei taxi? doh-**veh** **oo**-nah fehr-**mah**-tah **deh**-ee **tahk**-see
Are you free?	È libero? eh **lee**-beh-roh
Occupied.	Occupato. oh-koo-**pah**-toh
To ____, please.	A ____, per favore. ah ____ pehr fah-**voh**-ray

To this address.	A questo indirizzo. ah **kweh**-stoh een-dee-**reed**-zoh
I know there's a meter, but about how much is it to go...?	So che c'è il tassametro, ma più o meno quanto costa andare...? soh kay cheh eel tah-sah-**meh**-troh mah pew oh **meh**-noh **kwahn**-toh **koh**-stah ahn-**dah**-ray
...to ____	...a ____ ah ____
...to the airport	...all'aeroporto ahl-ay-roh-**por**-toh
...to the train station	...alla stazione ferroviaria **ah**-lah staht-see-**oh**-nay feh-roh-vee-**ah**-ree-ah
...to this address	...a questo indirizzo ah **kweh**-stoh een-dee-**reed**-zoh
Can you take ____ people?	Può portare ____ persone? pwoh por-**tah**-ray ____ pehr-**soh**-nay
Any extra fee?	C'è un sovrapprezzo? cheh oon soh-vrah-**prehd**-zoh
The meter, please.	Il tassametro, per favore. eel tah-sah-**meh**-troh pehr fah-**voh**-ray
Stop here.	Si fermi qui. see **fehr**-mee kwee
Here is fine.	Va bene qui. vah **beh**-nay kwee
At this corner.	A questo angolo. ah **kweh**-stoh **ahn**-goh-loh
The next corner.	Al prossimo angolo. ahl **proh**-see-moh **ahn**-goh-loh
Too much.	Troppo. **troh**-poh
My change, please.	Il resto, per favore. eel **reh**-stoh pehr fah-**voh**-ray
Keep the change.	Tenga il resto. **tehn**-gah eel **reh**-stoh

FINDING YOUR WAY

Whether you're driving, walking, or biking, these phrases will help you get around.

Route-Finding Phrases

I'm going / We're going to ____.	Vado / Andiamo a ____. **vah**-doh / ahn-dee-**ah**-moh ah ____
Do you have a...?	Avete una...? ah-**veh**-tay **oo**-nah
...city map	...cartina della città kar-**tee**-nah **deh**-lah chee-**tah**
...road map	...cartina stradale kar-**tee**-nah strah-**dah**-lay
How many minutes...?	Quanti minuti...? **kwahn**-tee mee-**noo**-tee
How many hours...?	Quante ore...? **kwahn**-tay **oh**-ray
...on foot	...a piedi ah pee-**eh**-dee
...by bicycle	...in bicicletta een bee-chee-**kleh**-tah
...by car	...in macchina een **mah**-kee-nah
How many kilometers to ____?	Quanti chilometri per ____? **kwahn**-tee kee-**loh**-meh-tree pehr ____
What is the... route to Rome?	Qual'è la strada... per andare a Roma? kwah-**leh** lah **strah**-dah... pehr ahn-**dah**-ray ah **roh**-mah
...most scenic	...più panoramica pew pah-noh-**rah**-mee-kah
...fastest	...più veloce pew veh-**loh**-chay
...easiest	...più facile pew **fah**-chee-lay
...most interesting	...più interessante pew een-teh-reh-**sahn**-tay
Point it out?	Me lo mostra? may loh **moh**-strah
Where is this address?	Dov'è questo indirizzo? doh-**veh** **kweh**-stoh een-dee-**reed**-zoh

You can summit some hill towns by using a ***scala mobile*** (long escalator), ***ascensore*** (elevator), or ***funicolare*** (funicular).

Directions

Following signs to ***centro*** will land you in the heart of things. On a map, ***(voi) siete qui*** means "you are here."

downtown	centro **chehn**-troh
straight ahead	sempre dritto **sehm**-pray **dree**-toh
(to the) left / right	(a) sinistra / destra (ah) see-**nee**-strah / **deh**-strah
first	prima **pree**-mah
next	prossima **proh**-see-mah
intersection	incrocio een-**kroh**-choh
corner	angolo **ahn**-goh-loh
block	isolato ee-zoh-**lah**-toh
roundabout	rotonda roh-**tohn**-dah
(main) square	piazza (principale) pee-**aht**-sah (preen-chee-**pah**-lay)
street	strada / via **strah**-dah / **vee**-ah
bridge	ponte **pohn**-tay
road	strada **strah**-dah
highway	autostrada ow-toh-**strah**-dah
north	nord nord
south	sud sood
east	est ehst
west	ovest **oh**-vehst

Lost Your Way

I'm lost.	Mi sono perso(a). mee **soh**-noh **pehr**-soh
We're lost.	Ci siamo persi. chee see-**ah**-moh **pehr**-see
Excuse me, can you help me?	Scusi, mi può aiutare? **skoo**-zee mee pwoh ah-yoo-**tah**-ray
Where am I?	Dove sono? **doh**-vay **soh**-noh
Where is ____?	Dov'è ____? doh **veh** ____
How do I get to ____?	Come si va a ____? **koh**-may see vah ah ____
Can you show me the way?	Mi può indicare la strada? mee pwoh een-dee-**kah**-ray lah **strah**-dah

SLEEPING

RESERVATIONS

Making a Reservation

reservation	prenotazione preh-noh-taht-see-**oh**-nay
Do you have...?	Avete...? ah-**veh**-tay
I'd like to reserve...	Vorrei prenotare... voh-**reh**-ee preh-noh-**tah**-ray
...a room for...	...una camera per... **oo**-nah **kah**-meh-rah pehr
...one person / two people	...una persona / due persone **oo**-nah pehr-**soh**-nah / **doo**-ay pehr-**soh**-nay
...today / tomorrow	...oggi / domani **oh**-jee / doh-**mah**-nee
...one night	...una notte **oo**-nah **noh**-tay
two / three nights	due / tre notti **doo**-ay / tray **noh**-tee
June 21	il ventuno giugno eel vehn-**too**-noh **joon**-yoh
How much is it?	Quanto costa? **kwahn**-toh **koh**-stah
Anything cheaper?	Niente di più economico? nee-**ehn**-tay dee pew eh-koh-**noh**-mee-koh
I'll take it.	La prendo. lah **prehn**-doh
My name is ____.	Mi chiamo ____. mee kee-**ah**-moh ____
Do you need a deposit?	Bisogna lasciare un acconto? bee-**zohn**-yah lah-**shah**-ray oon ah-**kohn**-toh
Do you accept credit cards?	Accettate carte di credito? ah-cheh-**tah**-tay **kar**-tay dee **kreh**-dee-toh

Key Phrases: Sleeping

Do you have a room?	Avete una camera? ah-**veh**-tay **oo**-nah **kah**-meh-rah
for one person / two people	per una persona / due persone pehr **oo**-nah pehr-**soh**-nah / **doo**-ay pehr-**soh**-nay
today / tomorrow	oggi / domani **oh**-jee / doh-**mah**-nee
one night / two nights	una notte / due notti **oo**-nah **noh**-tay / **doo**-ay **noh**-tee
How much is it?	Quanto costa? **kwahn**-toh **koh**-stah
hotel	hotel / albergo oh-**tehl** / ahl-**behr**-goh
small hotel	pensione / locanda pehn-see-**oh**-nay / loh-**kahn**-dah
vacancy / no vacancy	camere disponibili / completo **kah**-meh-ray dee-spoh-**nee**-bee-lee / kohm-**pleh**-toh

Can I reserve with a credit card and pay in cash?	Posso prenotare con la carta di credito e pagare in contanti? **poh**-soh preh-noh-**tah**-ray kohn lah **kar**-tah dee **kreh**-dee-toh ay pah-**gah**-ray een kohn-**tahn**-tee

Many people stay at a ***hotel*** (also called ***albergo***), but you have other choices as well. These include a small hotel (***pensione*** or ***locanda***), a country inn ***(locanda di campagna),*** or a working farm with accommodations ***(agriturismo).*** Staying at a family-run place offers double the cultural experience for half the price of a hotel. Rooms rented in a home may be called ***camere*** (rooms), ***soggiorno*** (stay), or simply ***B&B.*** Other options include a hostel ***(ostello),*** a vacation apartment ***(casa vacanze),*** or accommodations in a convent (often called ***instituto***).

Getting Specific

I'd like a...	Vorrei una... voh-**reh**-ee **oo**-nah
...single room.	...camera singola. **kah**-meh-rah **seen**-goh-lah
...double room.	...camera doppia. **kah**-meh-rah **doh**-pee-ah
...triple room.	...camera tripla. **kah**-meh-rah **treep**-lah
...room for ____ people.	...camera per ____ persone. **kah**-meh-rah pehr ____ pehr-**soh**-nay
with / without / and	con / senza / e kohn / **sehnt**-sah / ay
double bed	letto matrimoniale **leh**-toh mah-tree-moh-nee-**ah**-lay
twin beds	letti singoli **leh**-tee **seen**-goh-lee
...together / separate	...uniti / separati oon-**ee**-tee / seh-pah-**rah**-tee
single bed	letto singolo **leh**-toh **seen**-goh-loh
bed without a footboard	letto senza piedi **leh**-toh **sehnt**-sah pee-**ay**-dee
private bathroom	bagno in camera **bahn**-yoh een **kah**-meh-rah
toilet	toilette / gabinetto twah-**leh**-tay / gah-bee-**neh**-toh
shower	doccia **doh**-chah
bathtub	vasca da bagno **vah**-skah dah **bahn**-yoh
with only a sink	con solo un lavandino kohn **soh**-loh oon lah-vahn-**dee**-noh
shower outside the room	doccia comune **doh**-chah koh-**moo**-nay
balcony	balcone bahl-**koh**-nay
view	vista **vee**-stah
cheap	economica eh-koh-**noh**-mee-kah
quiet	tranquilla trahn-**kwee**-lah
romantic	romantica roh-**mahn**-tee-kah

on the ground floor	al piano terra ahl pee-**ah**-noh **teh**-rah
Do you have...?	Avete...? ah-**veh**-tay
...an elevator	...l'ascensore lah-shehn-**soh**-ray
...air-conditioning	...l'aria condizionata **lah**-ree-ah kohn-deet-see-oh-**nah**-tah
...Internet access	...l'accesso al Internet lah-**cheh**-soh ahl **een**-tehr-neht
...Wi-Fi (in the room)	...il Wi-Fi (in camera) eel **wee**-fee (een **kah**-meh-rah)
...parking	...un parcheggio oon par-**keh**-joh
...a garage	...un garage oon gah-**rahj**
What's your email address?	Qual'è il suo indirizzo email? kwah-**leh** eel **soo**-oh een-dee-**reed**-zoh "email"
What is your cancellation policy?	Quali sono i termini per la cancellazione della prenotazione? **kwah**-lee **soh**-noh ee **tehr**-mee-nee pehr lah kahn-cheh-laht-see-**oh**-nay **deh**-lah preh-noh-taht-see-**oh**-nay

In Italy, a true double or queen-size bed is relatively rare. Sometimes, a "double bed" is two twin beds in separate frames, pushed together.

Taller guests may want to request a ***letto senza piedi*** (bed without a footboard).

Nailing Down the Price

price	prezzo **prehd**-zoh
Can I see the price list?	Posso vedere le tariffe? **poh**-soh veh-**deh**-ray lay tah-**ree**-fay
How much is...?	Quanto costa...? **kwahn**-toh **koh**-stah
...a room for ____ people	...una camera per ____ persone **oo**-nah **kah**-meh-rah pehr ____ pehr-**soh**-nay

...your cheapest room	...la camera più economica lah **kah**-meh-rah pew eh-koh-**noh**-mee-kah
Is breakfast included?	La colazione è inclusa? lah koh-laht-see-**oh**-nay eh een-**kloo**-zah
Complete price?	Prezzo completo? **prehd**-zoh kohm-**pleh**-toh
Is it cheaper if...?	È più economico se...? eh pew eh-koh-**noh**-mee-koh say
...I stay three nights	...mi fermo tre notti mee **fehr**-moh tray **noh**-tee
...I pay cash	...pago in contanti **pah**-goh een kohn-**tahn**-tee

Arrival and Departure

(date of) arrival	(data di) arrivo (**dah**-tah dee) ah-**ree**-voh
(date of) departure	(data di) partenza (**dah**-tah dee) par-**tent**-sah
I'll arrive / We'll arrive...	Arrivo / Arriviamo... ah-**ree**-voh / ah-ree-vee-**ah**-moh
I'll depart / We'll depart...	Parto / Partiamo... **par**-toh / par-tee-**ah**-moh
...June 16.	...il sedici giugno. eel **seh**-dee-chee **joon**-yoh
...in the morning / afternoon / evening.	...la mattina / il pomeriggio / la sera. lah mah-**tee**-nah / eel poh-meh-**ree**-joh / lah **seh**-rah
...Friday before 6 p.m.	...venerdì entro le sei di sera. veh-nehr-**dee ehn**-troh lay **seh**-ee dee **seh**-rah
I'll stay / We'll stay two nights.	Starò / Staremo due notti. stah-**roh** / stah-**reh**-moh **doo**-ay **noh**-tee

We arrive Monday, depart Wednesday.	Arriviamo lunedì, partiamo mercoledì. ah-ree-vee-**ah**-moh loo-neh-**dee** par-tee-**ah**-moh mehr-koh-leh-**dee**

For help with saying dates in Italian, see the "Time and Dates" section starting on page 195. For a sample of a reservation request email, see page 551.

Confirm, Change, or Cancel

It's smart to call a day or two in advance to confirm your reservation.

I have a reservation.	Ho una prenotazione. oh **oo**-nah preh-noh-taht-see-**oh**-nay
My name is ____.	Mi chiamo ____. mee kee-**ah**-moh ____
I'd like to... my reservation.	Vorrei... una prenotazione. voh-**reh**-ee... **oo**-nah preh-noh-taht-see-**oh**-nay
...confirm	...confermare kohn-fehr-**mah**-ray
...change	...cambiare kahm-bee-**ah**-ray
...cancel	...annullare ah-noo-**lah**-ray
The reservation is for...	La prenotazione è per... lah preh-noh-taht-see-**oh**-nay eh pehr
...today / tomorrow.	...oggi / domani. **oh**-jee / doh-**mah**-nee
...August 13.	...il tredici agosto. eel **treh**-dee-chee ah-**goh**-stoh
Did you find the reservation?	Avete trovato la prenotazione? ah-**veh**-tay troh-**vah**-toh lah preh-noh-taht-see-**oh**-nay
Is everything OK?	Va bene? vah **beh**-nay
See you then.	Ci vediamo allora. chee veh-dee-**ah**-moh ah-**loh**-rah

I'm sorry that I need to cancel.	Mi dispiace ma devo cancellare la mia prenotazione. mee dee-spee-**ah**-chay mah **deh**-voh kahn-cheh-**lah**-ray lah **mee**-ah preh-noh-taht-see-**oh**-nay
Is there a penalty (for canceling the reservation)?	C'è una penalità da pagare (in caso di cancellazione)? cheh **oo**-nah peh-nah-lee-**tah** dah pah-**gah**-ray (een **kah**-zoh dee kahn-cheh-laht-see-**oh**-nay)

Depending on how far ahead you cancel a reservation—and on the hotel's cancellation policy—you might pay a penalty.

AT THE HOTEL

Checking In

My name is ____.	Mi chiamo ____. mee kee-**ah**-moh ____
I have a reservation.	Ho una prenotazione. oh **oo**-nah preh-noh-taht-see-**oh**-nay
one night	una notte **oo**-nah **noh**-tay
two / three nights	due / tre notti **doo**-ay / tray **noh**-tee
When will the room be ready?	Quando sarà pronta la camera? **kwahn**-doh sah-**rah** **prohn**-tah lah **kah**-meh-rah
Where is...?	Dov'è...? doh-**veh**
...my room	...la mia camera lah **mee**-ah **kah**-meh-rah
...the elevator	...l'ascensore lah-shehn-**soh**-ray
...the breakfast room	...la sala colazione lah **sah**-lah koh-laht-see-**oh**-nay
Is breakfast included?	La colazione è inclusa? lah koh-laht-see-**oh**-nay eh een-**kloo**-zah

When does breakfast start and end?	Quando comincia e finisce la colazione? **kwahn**-doh koh-**meen**-chah ay fee-**nee**-shay lah koh-laht-see-**oh**-nay
key	chiave kee-**ah**-vay
Two keys, please.	Due chiavi, per favore. **doo**-ay kee-**ah**-vee pehr fah-**voh**-ray

Choosing a Room

Can I see...?	Posso vedere...? **poh**-soh veh-**deh**-ray
...a room	...una camera **oo**-nah **kah**-meh-rah
...a different room	...un'altra camera oon-**ahl**-trah **kah** meh-rah
Do you have something...?	Avete qualcosa...? ah-**veh**-tay kwahl-**koh**-zah
...larger / smaller	...di più grande / di più piccolo dee pew **grahn**-day / dee pew **pee**-koh-loh
...better / cheaper	...di più bello / di più economico dee pew **beh** loh / dee pew eh-koh-**noh**-mee-koh
...brighter	...di più luminoso dee pew loo-mee-**noh**-zoh
...quieter	...di più tranquillo dee pew trahn-**kwee**-loh
...in the back	...sul retro sool **reh**-troh
...with a view (of the sea)	...con vista (sul mare) kohn **vee**-stah (sool **mah**-ray)
...on a lower / higher floor	...ad un piano più basso / più alto ahd oon pee-**ah**-noh pew **bah**-soh / pew **ahl**-toh
No, thank you.	No, grazie. noh **graht**-see-ay

What a charming room!	Che bella camera! kay **beh**-lah **kah**-meh-rah
I'll take it.	La prendo. lah **prehn**-doh

When selecting a room, be aware that ***con vista*** (with a view) can also come with more noise. If a ***tranquilla*** room is important to you, say so.

In Your Room

air-conditioner	condizionatore kohn-deet-see-oh-nah-**toh**-ray
alarm clock	sveglia **svehl**-yah
balcony	balcone bahl-**koh**-nay
bathroom	bagno **bahn**-yoh
bathtub	vasca da bagno **vah**-skah dah **bahn**-yoh
bed	letto **leh**-toh
bedspread	copriletto koh-pree-**leh**-toh
blanket	coperta koh-**pehr**-tah
chair	sedia **seh**-dee-ah
closet	armadio ar-**mah**-dee-oh
crib	culla **koo**-lah
door	porta **por**-tah
electrical adapter	adattatore elettrico ah-dah-tah-**toh**-ray eh-**leh**-tree-koh
electrical outlet	presa **preh**-zah
faucet	rubinetto roo-bee-**neh**-toh
hair dryer	phon fohn
hanger	stampella stahm-**peh**-lah
lamp	lampada **lahm**-pah-dah
lightbulb	lampadina lahm-pah-**dee**-nah
lock	serratura seh-rah-**too**-rah
pillow	cuscino koo-**shee**-noh
radio	radio **rah**-dee-oh

remote control...	telecomando... teh-leh-koh-**mahn**-doh
...for the TV	...per la televisione pehr lah teh-leh-vee-zee-**oh**-nay
...for the air-conditioning	...per l'aria condizionata pehr **lah**-ree-ah kohn-deet-see-oh-**nah**-tah
safe	cassaforte kah-sah-**for**-tay
shampoo	shampo **shahm**-poh
sheets	lenzuola lehnt-**swoh**-lah
shower	doccia **doh**-chah
sink	lavabo **lah**-vah-boh
sink stopper	tappo **tah**-poh
soap	sapone sah-**poh**-nay
sponge (for the shower)	spugna (per la doccia) **spoon**-yah (pehr lah **doh**-chah)
telephone	telefono teh-**leh**-foh-noh
television	televisione teh-leh-vee-zee-**oh**-nay
toilet	gabinetto gah-bee-**neh**-toh
toilet paper	carta igienica **kar**-tah ee-**jeh**-nee-kah
towel (hand)	asciugamano per il viso ah-shoo-gah-**mah**-noh pehr eel **vee**-zoh
towel (bath)	telo bagno **teh**-loh **bahn**-yoh
wake-up call	sveglia telefonica **svehl**-yah teh-leh-**foh**-nee-kah
water (hot / cold)	acqua (calda / fredda) **ahk**-wah (**kahl**-dah / **freh**-dah)
window	finestra fee-**neh**-strah

If you don't see remote controls (for the TV or air-conditioner) in the room, ask for them at the front desk. A comfortable setting for the air-conditioner is about 20 degrees Celsius. On Italian faucets, a **C** stands for ***caldo*** (hot)—the opposite of "cold."

Hotel Hassles

Combine these phrases with the words in the previous table to make simple and clear statements such as: ***Gabinetto non funziona*** (Toilet doesn't work).

There is a problem in my room.	C'è un problema nella mia camera. cheh oon proh-**bleh**-mah **neh**-lah **mee**-ah **kah**-meh-rah
Come with me.	Venga con me. **vehn**-gah kohn may
The room is...	La camera è... lah **kah**-meh-rah eh
...dirty.	...sporca. **spor**-kah
...noisy.	...rumorosa. roo-moh-**roh**-zah
...stinky.	...maleodorante. mah-leh-oh-doh-**rahn**-tay
...too hot / too cold.	...troppo calda / troppo fredda. **troh**-poh **kahl**-dah / **troh**-poh **freh**-dah
How can I make the room cooler / warmer?	Come devo fare per avere la camera più fresca / più calda? **koh**-may **deh**-voh **fah**-ray pehr ah-**veh**-ray lah **kah**-meh-rah pew **frehs**-kah / pew **kahl**-dah
The room is moldy / musty.	Nella camera c'è la muffa / odore di chiuso. **neh**-lah **kah**-meh-rah cheh lah **moo**-fah / oh-**doh**-ray dee kee-**oo**-zoh
It's smoky.	C'è l'odore di fumo. cheh loh-**doh**-ray dee **foo**-moh
There's no (hot) water.	Non c'è acqua (calda). nohn cheh **ahk**-wah (**kahl**-dah)
I can't open / shut / lock...	Non riesco ad aprire / a chiudere / a chiudere a chiave... nohn ree-**eh**-skoh ahd ah-**pree**-ray / ah kee-oo-**deh**-ray / ah kee-oo-**deh**-ray ah kee-**ah**-vay
...the door / the window.	...la porta / la finestra. lah **por**-tah / lah fee-**neh**-strah

How does this work?	Come funziona? **koh**-may foont-see-**oh**-nah
This doesn't work.	Non funziona. nohn foont-see-**oh**-nah
When will it be fixed?	Quando verrà riparato? **kwahn**-doh veh-**rah** ree-pah-**rah**-toh
bedbugs	cimici **chee** mee-chee
mosquitoes	zanzare zahnt-**sah**-ray
I'm covered with bug bites.	Sono pieno[a] di punture di insetti. **soh**-noh pee-**eh**-noh dee poon-**too**-ray dee een-**seh**-tee
My... was stolen.	Mi hanno rubato... mee **ahn**-noh roo-**bah**-toh
...money	...i soldi. ee **sohl**-dee
...computer	...il computer. eel kohm-**poo**-tehr
...camera	...la macchina fotografica. lah **mah**-kee-nah foh-toh-**grah**-fee-kah
I need to speak to the manager.	Devo parlare con il direttore. **deh**-voh par-**lah** ray kohn eel dee-reh-**toh**-ray
I want to make a complaint.	Vorrei fare un reclamo. voh-**reh**-ee **fah**-ray oon reh-**klah**-moh

Keep your valuables with you or out of sight in your room, or in a room safe (if available). For help on dealing with theft or loss, including a list of items, see page 347.

Hotel Help

Use the "In Your Room" words (on page 234) to fill in the blanks.

I'd like...	Vorrei... voh-**reh**-ee
Do you have...?	Avete...? ah-**veh**-tay
a / another	un / un altro oon / oon **ahl**-troh
extra	extra **ehk**-strah

different	altra **ahl**-trah
Please change...	Per favore può cambiare... pehr fah-**voh**-ray pwoh kahm-bee-**ah**-ray
Please don't change...	Per favore può non cambiare... pehr fah-**voh**-ray pwoh nohn kahm-bee-**ah**-ray
...the towels / sheets.	...gli asciugamani / le lenzuola. lee ah-shoo-gah-**mah**-nee / lay lent-soo-**oh**-lah
What is the charge to...?	Quanto costa...? **kwahn**-toh **koh**-stah
...use the telephone	...usare il telefono oo-**zah**-ray eel teh-**leh**-foh-noh
...use the Internet	...usare Internet oo-**zah**-ray **een**-tehr-neht
Do you have Wi-Fi...?	Avete il Wi-Fi...? ah-**veh**-tay eel **wee**-fee
...in the room / lobby	...in camera / nella reception een **kah**-meh-rah / **neh**-lah reh-sehp-see-**ohn**
What is the network name / password?	Qual'è il network name / la password? kwah-**leh** eel "network" **nah**-may / lah "password"
Is a... nearby?	C'è un / una... qui vicino? cheh oon / **oo**-nah... kwee vee-**chee**-noh
...full-service laundry	...lavanderia lah-vahn-deh-**ree**-ah
...self-service laundry	...lavanderia self-service lah-vahn-deh-**ree**-ah sehlf-**sehr**-vees
...pharmacy	...farmacia far-mah-**chee**-ah
...Internet café	...Internet café **een**-tehr-neht kah-**fay**
...grocery store	...alimentari / supermercato ah-lee-mehn-**tah**-ree / soo-pehr-mehr-**kah**-toh
...restaurant	...ristorante ree-stoh-**rahn**-tay

Where do you go for lunch / dinner / coffee?	Dove si va per il pranzo / la cena / il caffè? **doh**-vay see vah pehr eel **prahnt**-soh / lah **cheh**-nah / eel kah-**feh**
Will you call a taxi for me?	Mi può chiamare un taxi? mee pwoh kee-ah-**mah**-ray oon **tahk**-see
Where can I park?	Dove posso parcheggiare? **doh**-vay **poh**-soh par-keh-**jah**-ray
What time do you lock up?	A che ora chiude? ah kay **oh**-rah kee-**oo**-day
Please wake me at 7:00.	Mi svegli alle sette, per favore. mee **svehl**-yee **ah**-lay **seh**-tay pehr fah-**voh**-ray
I'd like to stay another night.	Vorremmo fermarci un'altra notte. voh-**reh**-moh fehr-**mar**-chee oon-**ahl**-trah **noh**-tay
Will you call my next hotel...?	Può chiamare il mio prossimo hotel...? pwoh kee-ah-**mah**-ray eel **mee**-oh **proh**-see-moh oh-**tehl**
...for tonight	...per stasera pehr stah-**seh**-rah
...to make / to confirm a reservation	...per fare / confermare una prenotazione pehr **fah**-ray / kohn-fehr-**mah**-ray **oo**-nah preh-noh-taht-see-**oh**-nay
Will you please call another hotel for me? (if hotel is booked)	Chiamerebbe un altro albergo per me per favore? kee-ah-meh-**reh**-bay oon **ahl**-troh ahl-**behr**-goh pehr may pehr fah-**voh**-ray
I will pay for the call.	Pago la chiamata. **pah**-goh lah kee-ah-**mah**-tah

Checking Out

When is check-out time?	A che ora devo lasciare la camera? ah kay **oh**-rah **deh**-voh lah-**shah**-ray lah **kah**-meh-rah
Can I check out later?	Posso lasciare la camera più tardi? **poh**-soh lah-**shah**-ray lah **kah**-meh-rah pew **tar**-dee
I'll leave / We'll leave...	Parto / Partiamo... **par**-toh / par-tee-**ah**-moh
...today / tomorrow.	...oggi / domani. **oh**-jee / doh-**mah**-nee
...very early.	...molto presto. **mohl**-toh **preh**-stoh
Can I pay now?	Posso pagare subito? **poh**-soh pah-**gah**-ray **soo**-bee-toh
The bill, please.	Il conto, per favore. eel **kohn**-toh pehr fah-**voh**-ray
I think this is too high.	Credo che il conto sia troppo alto. **kreh**-doh kay eel **kohn**-toh **see**-ah **troh**-poh **ahl**-toh
Can you explain the bill?	Può spiegare il conto? pwoh spee-eh-**gah**-ray eel **kohn**-toh
Can you itemize the bill?	Posso avere il conto in dettaglio? **poh**-soh ah-**veh**-ray eel **kohn**-toh een deh-**tahl**-yoh
Do you accept credit cards?	Accettate carte di credito? ah-cheh-**tah**-tay **kar**-tay dee **kreh**-dee-toh
Is it cheaper if I pay cash?	È più economico se pago in contanti? eh pew eh-koh-**noh**-mee-koh say **pah**-goh een kohn-**tahn**-tee
Everything was great.	Tutto magnifico. **too**-toh mahn-**yee**-fee-koh

Can I / can we...?	Posso / Possiamo...? **poh**-soh / poh-see-**ah**-moh
...leave baggage here until ____ o'clock	...lasciare il bagaglio qui fino a ____ lah-**shah**-ray eel bah-**gahl**-yoh kwee **fee**-noh ah ____

FAMILIES

Do you have...?	Avete...? ah-**veh**-tay
...a family room	...una camera per una famiglia **oo**-nah **kah**-meh-rah pehr **oo**-nah fah-**meel**-yah
...a family discount	...uno sconto per famiglie **oo**-noh **skohn**-toh pehr fah-**meel**-yay
...a discount for children	...uno sconto per bambini **oo**-noh **skohn**-toh pehr bahm-**bee**-nee
I have / We have...	Ho / Abbiamo... oh / ah-bee-**ah**-moh
...one child.	...un bambino. oon bahm-**bee**-noh
...two children.	...due bambini. **doo**-ay bahm-**bee**-nee
____ months old	di ____ mesi dee ____ **meh**-zee
____ years old	di ____ anni dee ____ **ahn**-nee
Do you accept children?	I bambini sono ammessi? ee bahm-**bee**-nee **soh**-noh ah-**meh**-see
Is there an age limit?	C'è un limite d'età? cheh oon **lee**-mee-tay deh-**tah**
I'd like / We'd like...	Vorrei / Vorremmo... voh-**reh**-ee / voh-**reh**-moh
...a crib.	...una culla. **oo**-nah **koo**-lah
...an extra bed.	...un letto in più. oon **leh**-toh een pew

AT THE HOSTEL

Europe's cheapest beds are in hostels, open to travelers of any age. Official hostels (affiliated with Hostelling International) are usually big and institutional. Independent hostels are more casual, with fewer rules.

hostel	ostello oh-**steh**-loh
dorm bed	letto in un dormitorio **leh**-toh een oon dor-mee-**toh**-ree-oh
How many beds per room?	Quanti letti per camera? **kwahn**-tee **leh**-tee pehr **kah**-meh-rah
dorm for women only	dormitorio per sole donne dor-mee-**toh**-ree-oh pehr **soh**-lay **doh**-nay
co-ed dorm	dormitorio misto dor-mee-**toh**-ree-oh **mee**-stoh
double room	camera doppia **kah**-meh-rah **doh**-pee-ah
family room	camera per una famiglia **kah**-meh-rah pehr **oo**-nah fah-**meel**-yah
Is breakfast included?	La colazione è inclusa? lah koh-laht-see-**oh**-nay eh een-**kloo**-zah
curfew	coprifuoco koh-pree-**fwoh**-koh
lockout	chiusura notturna kee-oo-**zoo**-rah noh-**toor**-nah
membership card	tessera **teh**-seh-rah

EATING

RESTAURANTS

In general, Italians eat meals a bit later than we do. At 7:00 or 8:00 in the morning, they have a light breakfast (a roll and coffee), often while standing at a café or bar. Lunch, which is usually the main meal of the day, begins around 13:00 and can last for a couple of hours. Then they eat a late, light dinner (around 20:00-21:30, sometimes earlier in winter). To bridge the gap, people drop into a bar in the late afternoon for a ***spuntino*** (snack) and aperitif.

Most restaurant kitchens are closed between lunch and dinner. Good restaurants don't reopen for dinner before 19:00.

Finding a Restaurant

Where's a good... restaurant nearby?	Dov'è un buon ristorante... qui vicino? doh-**veh** oon bwohn ree-stoh-**rahn**-tay... kwee vee-**chee**-noh
...cheap	...economico eh-koh-**noh**-mee koh
...local-style	...con cucina casereccia kohn koo-**chee**-nah kah-zeh-**reh**-chah
...untouristy	...non per turisti nohn pehr too-**ree**-stee
...romantic	...romantico roh-**mahn**-tee-koh
...vegetarian	...vegetariano veh-jeh-tah-ree-**ah**-noh
...fast	...veloce veh-**loh**-chay
...fast-food (Italian-style)	...tavola calda **tah**-voh-lah **kahl**-dah
...self-service buffet	...self-service sehlf-**sehr**-vees
...Asian	...asiatica ah-zee-**ah**-tee-kah
with terrace	con terrazza kohn teh-**rahd**-zah

with a salad bar	con un banco delle insalate kohn oon **bahn**-koh **deh**-lay een-sah-**lah**-tay
candlelit	a lume di candela ah **loo**-may dee kahn-**deh**-lah
popular with locals	che piace alla gente del posto kay pee-**ah**-chay **ah**-lah **jehn**-tay dehl **poh**-stoh
moderate price	a buon mercato ah bwohn mer-**kah**-toh
a splurge	caro **kah**-roh
Is it better than McDonald's?	È meglio di McDonald's? eh **mehl**-yoh dee "McDonald's"

Getting a Table

I'd like / We'd like...	Vorrei / Vorremmo... voh-**reh**-ee / voh-**reh**-moh
...a table...	...un tavolo... oon **tah**-voh-loh
...for one / two.	...per uno / due. pehr **oo**-noh / **doo**-ay
...inside / outside.	...dentro / fuori. **dehn**-troh / **fwoh**-ree
...by the window.	...vicino alla finestra. vee-**chee**-noh **ah**-lah fee-**neh**-strah
...with a view.	...con la vista. kohn lah **vee**-stah
quiet	tranquillo trahn-**kee**-loh
Is this table free?	È libero questo tavolo? eh **lee**-beh-roh **kweh**-stoh **tah**-voh-loh
Can I sit here?	Posso sedermi qui? **poh**-soh seh-**dehr**-mee kwee
Can we sit here?	Possiamo sederci qui? poh-see-**ah**-moh seh-**dehr**-chee kwee
How long is the wait?	Quanto c'è da aspettare? **kwahn**-toh cheh dah ah-speh-**tah**-ray
How many minutes?	Quanti minuti? **kwahn**-tee mee-**noo**-tee

Key Phrases: Restaurants

Where's a good restaurant nearby?	Dov'è un buon ristorante qui vicino? doh-**veh** oon bwohn ree-stoh-**rahn**-tay kwee vee-**chee**-noh
I'd like...	Vorrei... voh-**reh**-ee
We'd like...	Vorremmo... voh-**reh**-moh
...a table for one / two.	...un tavolo per uno / due. oon **tah**-voh-loh pehr **oo**-noh / **doo**-ay
Is this table free?	È libero questo tavolo? eh **lee**-beh-roh **kweh**-stoh **tah**-voh-loh
How long is the wait?	Quanto c'è da aspettare? **kwahn**-toh cheh dah ah-speh-**tah**-ray
The menu (in English), please.	Il menù (in inglese), per favore. eel meh-**noo** (een een-**gleh**-zay), pehr fah-**voh**-ray
The bill, please.	Il conto, per favore. eel **kohn**-toh pehr fah-**voh**-ray
Do you accept credit cards?	Accettate carte di credito? ah-cheh-**tah**-tay **kar**-tay dee **kreh**-dee-toh

Where is the toilet?	Dov'è la toilette? doh-**veh** lah twah-**leh**-tay

Reservations

reservation	prenotazione preh-noh-taht-see-**oh**-nay
Are reservations recommended?	È meglio prenotare? eh **mehl**-yoh preh-noh-**tah**-ray

I'd like to make a reservation...	Vorrei prenotare... voh-**reh**-ee preh-noh-**tah**-ray
...for myself.	...per me. pehr may
...for two people.	...per due persone. pehr **doo**-ay pehr-**soh**-nay
...for today / tomorrow.	...per oggi / domani. pehr **oh**-jee / doh-**mah**-nee
...for lunch / dinner.	...per pranzo / cena. pehr **prahnt**-soh / **cheh**-nah
...at ____. (specific time)	...alle ____. **ah**-lay ____
My name is ____.	Mi chiamo ____. mee kee-**ah**-moh ____
I have a reservation for ____ people.	Ho una prenotazione per ____ persone. oh **oo**-nah preh-noh-taht-see-**oh**-nay pehr ____ pehr-**soh**-nay

The Menu

A full Italian meal—and menu—is divided into three courses:

Antipasti: Appetizers such as *bruschetta*, grilled veggies, deep-fried tasties, or a plate of olives, cold cuts, and cheeses

Primo piatto: A "first dish," generally consisting of pasta, rice (especially *risotto*), or soup

Secondo piatto: A "second dish," equivalent to our main course, of meat and fish / seafood dishes

A side dish ***(contorno)*** may come with the ***secondo*** or cost extra. After all that food, ***dolci*** (desserts) seem gluttonous—but still very tempting.

menu	menù meh-**noo**
The menu (in English), please.	Il menù (in inglese), per favore. eel meh-**noo** (een een-**gleh**-zay) pehr fah-**voh**-ray
appetizers	antipasti ahn-tee-**pah**-stee

first course	primo piatto **pree**-moh pee-**ah**-toh
main course	secondo piatto seh-**kohn**-doh pee-**ah**-toh
side dishes	contorni kohn-**tor**-nee
specialty (of the house)	specialità (della casa) speh-chah-lee-**tah** (**deh**-lah **kah**-zah)
daily specials	piatti del giorno pee-**ah**-tee dehl **jor**-noh
menu of the day	menù del giorno meh-**noo** dehl **jor**-noh
tourist menu / fixed-price menu	menù turistico / menù fisso meh-**noo** too-**ree**-stee-koh / meh-**noo** **fee**-soh
breakfast	colazione koh-laht-see-**oh**-nay
lunch	pranzo **prahnt**-soh
dinner	cena **cheh**-nah
dishes	piatti pee-**ah**-tee
hot / cold dishes	piatti caldi / freddi pee-**ah**-tee **kahl**-dee / **freh**-dee
sandwiches	panini pah-**nee**-nee
bread	pane **pah**-nay
salad	insalata een-sah-**lah**-tah
soup	zuppa **tsoo**-pah
meat	carni **kar**-nee
poultry	pollame poh-**lah**-may
fish	pesce **peh**-shay
seafood	frutti di mare **froo**-tee dee **mah**-ray
vegetables	verdure vehr-**doo**-ray
cheese	formaggio for-**mah**-joh
dessert	dolce **dohl**-chay
bar snacks	stuzzichini stood-zee-**kee**-nee
drink menu	lista delle bevande **lee**-stah **deh**-lay beh-**vahn**-day
beverages	bevande / bibite beh-**vahn**-day / **bee**-bee-tay

beer	birra **bee**-rah
wine	vino **vee**-noh
cover charge	coperto koh-**pehr**-toh
service (not) included	servizio (non) incluso sehr-**veet**-see-oh (nohn) een-**kloo**-zoh
comes with	servito con sehr-**vee**-toh kohn
choice of	a scelta ah **shehl**-tah

For most travelers, a three-course meal is simply too much food. To avoid overeating (and to stretch your budget), share dishes. A good rule of thumb is for each person to order any two courses. For example, a couple can order and share one ***antipasto,*** one ***primo,*** one ***secondo,*** and one dessert or two ***antipasti*** and two ***primi.***

A ***menù del giorno*** (menu of the day) offers you a choice of appetizer, entrée, and dessert at a fixed price and is usually a good deal. A tourist-oriented ***menù turistico*** works the same way, but often includes less interesting or adventurous options.

Ordering

waiter	cameriere kah-meh-ree-**eh**-ray
waitress	cameriera kah-meh-ree-**eh**-rah
I'm ready / We're ready to order.	Sono pronto / Siamo pronti per ordinare. **soh**-noh **prohn**-toh / see-**ah**-moh **prohn**-tee pehr or-dee-**nah**-ray
I / We need a little more time.	Mi / Ci serve un altro minuto. mee / chee **sehr**-vay oon **ahl**-troh mee-**noo**-toh
I'd like / We'd like...	Vorrei / Vorremmo... voh-**reh**-ee / voh-**reh**-moh
...just a drink.	...soltanto qualcosa da bere. sohl-**tahn**-toh kwahl-**koh**-zah dah **beh**-ray
...to see the menu.	...vedere il menù. veh-**deh**-ray eel meh-**noo**
...to eat.	...mangiare. mahn-**jah**-ray

...only a first course.	...solo un primo piatto. **soh**-loh oon **pree**-moh pee-**ah**-toh
Do you have...?	Avete...? ah-**veh**-tay
...an English menu	...un menù in inglese oon meh-**noo** een een-**gleh**-zay
...a menu of the day	...un menù del giorno oon meh-**noo** dehl **jor**-noh
...half portions	...mezze porzioni **mehd**-zay port-see-**oh**-nee
What do you recommend?	Che cosa raccomanda? kay **koh**-zah rah-koh-**mahn**-dah
What's your favorite dish?	Qual'è il suo piatto preferito? kwah-**leh** eel **soo**-oh pee-**ah**-toh preh-feh-**ree**-toh
What is better? (point to items on menu)	Qual'è meglio? kwah-**leh mehl**-yoh
What is...?	Che cosa c'è di...? kay **koh**-zah cheh dee
Is it...?	È...? eh
...good	...buono **bwoh**-noh
...affordable	...poco caro **poh**-koh **kah**-roh
...expensive	...caro **kah**-roh
...local	...di locale dee loh-**kah**-lay
...fresh	...di fresco dee **freh**-skoh
...fast	...di veloce dee veh-**loh**-chay
...spicy (hot)	...piccante pee-**kahn**-tay
Is it filling?	Riempie molto? ree-**ehm**-pee-ay **mohl**-toh
Make me happy.	Mi faccia felice. mee **fah**-chah feh-**lee**-chay
Around ____ euros.	Intorno ai ____ euro. een-**tor**-noh ī ____ eh-**oo**-roh
What is that? (pointing)	Che cos'è quello? kay koh-**zeh kweh**-loh
How much is it?	Quanto costa? **kwahn**-toh **koh**-stah

Nothing with eyeballs.	Niente con gli occhi. nee-**ehn**-tay kohn lee **oh**-kee
Can I substitute (something) for the ____?	Posso sostituire (qualcosa d'altro) per il ____? **poh**-soh soh-stee-**twee**-ray (kwahl-**koh**-zah **dahl**-troh) pehr eel ____
Can I / Can we get it to go?	Posso / Possiamo averlo da portar via? **poh**-soh / poh-see-**ah**-moh ah-**vehr**-loh dah por-**tar** **vee**-ah

When going to a good restaurant with an approachable staff, I like to say ***Mi faccia felice*** (Make me happy), and set a price limit.

Here are a few things you may hear from your server during the meal: First, he'll ask what you'd like to drink ***(Da bere?)***. When ready to take your order, he'll ask ***Prego?*** He'll prompt you with ***E dopo?*** (And then?) to see what else you might want; just reply ***È tutto*** (That's all). When you're finished eating, place your utensils on your plate with the handles pointing to your right as the Italians do. This tells the waiter you're done. He'll confirm by asking ***Finito?*** He'll usually ask if you'd like dessert ***(Qualcosa di dolce?)*** and coffee ***(Un caffè?)***, and if you want anything else ***(Altro?)***.

Tableware and Condiments

I'd like a...	Vorrei un / una... voh-**reh**-ee oon / **oo**-nah
We'd like a...	Vorremmo un / una... voh-**reh**-moh oon / **oo**-nah
...napkin.	...tovagliolo. toh-vahl-**yoh**-loh
...knife.	...coltello. kohl-**teh**-loh
...fork.	...forchetta. for-**keh**-tah
...spoon.	...cucchiaio. koo-kee-**ah**-yoh
...cup.	...tazza. **tahd**-zah
...glass.	...bicchiere. bee-kee-**eh**-ray
Please...	Per favore... pehr fah-**voh**-ray

...another table setting.	...un altro coperto. oon **ahl**-troh koh-**pehr**-toh
...another plate.	...un altro piatto. oon **ahl**-trah pee-**ah**-toh
silverware	posate poh-**zah**-tay
carafe	caraffa kah-**rah**-fah
water	acqua **ah**-kwah
bread	pane **pah**-nay
breadsticks	grissini gree-**see**-nee
butter	burro **boo**-roh
margarine	margarina mar-gah-**ree**-nah
salt / pepper	sale / pepe **sah**-lay / **peh**-pay
sugar	zucchero **tsoo**-keh-roh
artificial sweetener	dolcificante dohl-chee-fee-**kahn**-tay
honey	miele mee-**eh**-lay
mustard	senape **seh**-nah-pay
mayonnaise	maionese mah-yoh-**neh**-zay
toothpick	stuzzicadente stood-zee-kah-**dehn**-tay

The Food Arrives

Looks delicious!	Ha un ottimo aspetto! ah oon **oh**-tee-moh ah-**speh**-toh
Is this included with the meal?	È incluso nel pasto questo? eh een-**kloo**-zoh nehl **pah**-stoh **kweh**-stoh
I did not order this.	Io questo non l'ho ordinato. **ee**-oh **kweh**-stoh nohn loh or dee-**nah**-toh
This is...	Questo è... **kweh**-stoh eh
...dirty.	...sporco. **spor**-koh
...greasy.	...grasso. **grah**-soh
...salty.	...salato. sah-**lah**-toh
...undercooked.	...troppo crudo. **troh**-poh **kroo**-doh

...overcooked.	...troppo cotto. **troh**-poh **koh**-toh
...cold.	...freddo. **freh**-doh
Can you heat it up?	Lo può scaldare? loh pwoh skahl-**dah**-ray
A little.	Un po'. oon poh
More. / Another.	Di più. / Un altro. dee pew / oon **ahl**-troh
One more, please.	Ancora un altro, per favore. ahn-**koh**-rah oon **ahl**-troh pehr fah-**voh**-ray
The same.	Lo stesso. loh **steh**-soh
Enough.	Basta. **bah**-stah
Yummy!	Buono! **bwoh**-noh
Very good!	Molto buono! **mohl**-toh **bwoh**-noh
Delicious!	Delizioso! deh-leet-see-**oh**-zoh
My compliments to the chef!	Complimenti al cuoco! kohm-plee-**mehn**-tee ahl **kwoh**-koh
A great memory!	Grande ricordo! **grahn**-day ree-**kor**-doh
Finished.	Finito. fee-**nee**-toh
I'm full.	Sono sazio. **soh**-noh **saht**-see-oh
I'm stuffed! ("I'm as full as an egg!")	Sono pieno(a) come un uovo! **soh**-noh pee-**eh**-noh **koh**-may oon **woh**-voh
Thank you.	Grazie. **graht**-see-ay

Paying

bill	conto **kohn**-toh
The bill, please.	Il conto, per favore. eel **kohn**-toh pehr fah-**voh**-ray
Together.	Conto unico. **kohn**-toh **oo**-nee-koh
Separate checks.	Conto separato. **kohn**-toh seh-pah-**rah**-toh
Do you accept credit cards?	Accettate carte di credito? ah-cheh-**tah**-tay **kar**-tay dee **kreh**-dee-toh

This is not correct.	Questo non è giusto. **kweh**-stoh nohn eh **joo**-stoh
Can you explain this?	Lo può spiegare? loh pwoh spee-eh-**gah**-ray
Can you itemize the bill?	Può spiegare il conto in dettaglio? pwoh spee-eh-**gah**-ray eel **kohn**-toh een deh-**tahl**-yoh
What if I wash the dishes?	E se lavassi i piatti? ay say lah-**vah**-see ee pee-**ah**-tee
Could I have a receipt, please?	Posso avere una ricevuta, per favore? **poh**-soh ah-**veh**-ray **oo**-nah ree-cheh-**voo**-tah pehr fah-**voh**-ray

Tipping

Two extra charges are commonly found at Italian restaurants: the ***coperto*** and the ***servizio.*** Both should be clearly noted on the menu and/or your check.

The ***coperto*** (cover charge), sometimes called ***pane e coperto*** (bread and cover), offsets overhead expenses. Most restaurants add it as a flat fee (usually €1-3 per person).

The ***servizio*** (service charge) of about 10 percent is for the waitstaff. The words ***servizio incluso*** on the menu and/or the receipt indicate that the listed prices include the fee. You can add a tip, if you choose, by adding a euro or two for each person in your party. While Italians don't think about tips in terms of percentages—and many don't tip at all—this extra tip is usually around 5 percent.

If you see the words ***servizio non incluso*** on the menu or bill, you're expected to tip about 10 percent. And in Italian bars and any eatery where you don't sit at a table, there's no need to tip.

tip	mancia **mahn**-chah
service (not) included	servizio (non) incluso sehr-**veet**-see-oh (nohn) een-**kloo**-zoh

Is tipping expected?	Bisogna lasciare una mancia? bee-**zohn**-yah lah-**shah**-ray **oo**-nah **mahn**-chah
What percent?	Che percentuale? kay pehr-chehn-too-**ah**-lay
Keep the change.	Tenga il resto. **tehn**-gah eel **reh**-stoh
Change, please.	Il resto, per favore. eel **reh**-stoh pehr fah-**voh**-ray
This is for you.	Questo è per lei. **kweh**-stoh eh pehr **leh**-ee

SPECIAL CONCERNS

In a Hurry

Europeans take their time at meals, so don't expect speedy service. If you're in a rush, let your server know. To hurry things up, ask for your bill when the waiter brings your food.

I'm / We're in a hurry.	Sono / Siamo di fretta. **soh**-noh / see-**ah**-moh dee **freh**-tah
I'm sorry.	Mi dispiace. mee dee-spee-**ah**-chay
I need to be served quickly.	Ho bisogno di essere servito(a) rapidamente. oh bee-**zohn**-yoh dee **eh**-seh-ray sehr-**vee**-toh rah-pee-dah-**mehn**-tay
We need to be served quickly.	Avremmo bisogno di essere serviti rapidamente. ah-**vreh**-moh bee-**zohn**-yoh dee **eh**-seh-ray sehr-**vee**-tee rah-pee-dah-**mehn**-tay
I must / We must...	Devo / Dobbiamo... **deh**-voh / doh-bee-**ah**-moh
...leave in 30 minutes / one hour.	...andarcene tra trenta minuti / un'ora. ahn-dar-**cheh**-nay trah **trehn**-tah mee-**noo**-tee / oo-**noh**-rah

When will the food be ready?	Tra quanto è pronto il cibo? trah **kwahn**-toh eh **prohn**-toh eel **chee**-boh
The bill, please.	Il conto, per favore. eel **kohn**-toh pehr fah-**voh**-ray

Allergies and Other Dietary Restrictions

I'm allergic to...	Sono allergico(a) a... **soh**-noh ah-**lehr**-jee-koh ah
I cannot eat...	Non posso mangiare... nohn **poh**-soh mahn-**jah**-ray
He cannot / She cannot eat...	Lui / Lei non può mangiare... **loo**-ee / **leh**-ee nohn pwoh mahn-**jah**-ray
He / She has a severe allergy to...	Ha un'allergia molto seria a... ah oon-ah-**lehr**-jee-ah **mohl**-toh **seh**-ree-ah ah
No...	Niente... nee-**ehn**-tay
...dairy products.	...latticini. lah-tee-**chee**-nee
...nuts.	...noci e altra frutta secca. **noh**-chee ay **ahl**-trah **froo**-tah **seh**-kah
...peanuts.	...arachidi. ah-**rah**-kee-dee
...walnuts.	...noci. **noh**-chee
...wheat / gluten.	...frumento / glutine. froo-**mehn**-toh / gloo-**tee**-nay
...seafood.	...frutti di mare. **froo**-tee dee **mah**-ray
...shellfish.	...molluschi e crostacei. moh-**loo**-skee ay kroh-**stah**-cheh-ee
...salt / sugar.	...sale / zucchero. **sah**-lay / **tsoo**-keh-roh
I am diabetic.	Ho il diabete. oh eel dee-ah-**beh**-tay
He / She is lactose intolerant.	Lui / Lei ha un'intolleranza ai latticini. **loo**-ee / **leh**-ee ah oon-een-toh-leh-rahnt-sah ī lah-tee-**chee**-nee

No caffeine.	Senza caffeina. **sehnt**-sah kah-feh-**ee**-nah
No alcohol.	Niente alcool. nee-**ehn**-tay **ahl**-kohl
Organic.	Biologico. bee-oh-**loh**-jee-koh

Vegetarian Phrases

I'm a...	Sono... **soh**-noh
...vegetarian.	...vegetariano(a). veh-jeh-tah-ree-**ah**-noh
...strict vegetarian.	...strettamente vegetariano(a). streh-tah-**mehn**-tay veh-jeh-tah-ree-**ah**-noh
...vegan.	...vegano(a). veh-**gah**-noh
Is any meat or animal fat used in this?	Contiene carne o grassi animali? kohn-tee-**eh**-nay **kar**-nay oh **grah**-see ah-nee-**mah**-lee
What is vegetarian? (pointing to menu)	Quali piatti sono vegetariani? **kwah**-lee pee-**ah**-tee **soh**-noh veh-jeh-tah-ree-**ah**-nee
I don't eat...	Io non mangio... **ee**-oh nohn **mahn**-joh
I'd like this without...	Vorrei questo ma senza... voh-**reh**-ee **kweh**-stoh mah **sehnt**-sah
...meat.	...carne. **kar**-nay
...eggs.	...uova. **woh**-vah
...animal products.	...prodotti animali. proh-**doh**-tee ah-nee-**mah**-lee
I eat...	Io mangio... **ee**-oh **mahn**-joh
Do you have...?	Avete...? **ah**-veh-tay
...anything with tofu	...qualcosa con il tofu kwahl-**koh**-zah kohn eel **toh**-foo
...veggie burgers	...hamburger vegetariani ahm-**boor**-gehr veh-jeh-tah-ree-**ah**-nee

Children

Children's menus and special dishes for ***bambini*** are rare in Italy. Most Italian parents request a ***mezza porzione*** (half-portion, not always available), or simply order from the regular menu and customize it for their kids.

Do you have a children's menu?	Avete un menù per bambini? ah-**veh**-tay oon meh-**noo** pehr bahm-**bee**-nee
children's portions	delle porzioni per bambini **deh**-lay port-see-**oh**-nee pehr bahm-**bee**-nee
half-portions	mezze porzioni **mehd**-zay port-see-**oh**-nee
high chair	un seggiolone oon seh-joh-**loh**-nay
booster seat	un seggiolino oon seh-joh-**lee**-noh
noodles	pasta **pah**-stah
rice	del riso dehl **ree**-zoh
with butter	con il burro kohn eel **boo**-roh
without sauce	senza sugo **sehnt**-sah **soo**-goh
sauce / dressing on the side	il sugo / il condimento a parte eel **soo**-goh / eel kohn-dee-**mehn**-toh ah **par**-tay
pizza	pizza "pizza"
...cheese only	...Margherita mar-geh-**ree**-tah
...pepperoni	...con salame piccante kohn sah-**lah**-may pee-**kahn**-tay
cheese sandwich...	un panino... al formaggio oon pah-**nee**-noh... ahl for-**mah**-joh
...toasted	...scaldato skahl-**dah**-toh
hot dog	wurstel **voor**-stehl
hamburger	hamburger ahm-**boor**-gehr
french fries	patate fritte pah-**tah**-tay **free**-tay
ketchup	ketchup "ketchup"

small milk	un po' di latte oon poh dee **lah**-tay
straw	cannuccia kah-**noo**-chah
More napkins, please.	Degli altri tovaglioli, per favore. **dehl**-yee **ahl**-tree toh-vahl-**yoh**-lee pehr fah-**voh**-ray

WHAT'S COOKING?

Breakfast

I'd like / We'd like...	Vorrei / Vorremmo... voh-**reh**-ee / voh-**reh**-moh
breakfast	colazione koh-laht-see-**oh**-nay
bread	pane **pah**-nay
baguette	baguette bah-**geh**-tay
roll	pane / panino **pah**-nay / pah-**nee**-noh
sweet roll	brioche **bree**-ohsh
croissant	cornetto kor-**neh**-toh
toast	toast "toast"
butter	burro **boo**-roh
jam	marmellata mar-meh-**lah**-tah
honey	miele mee-**eh**-lay
fruit cup	macedonia mah-cheh-**doh**-nee-ah
milk	latte **lah**-tay
coffee / tea	caffè / tè kah-**feh** / teh
fruit juice	succo di frutta **soo**-koh dee **froo**-tah
fresh orange juice	spremuta di arancia spreh-**moo**-tah dee ah-**rahn**-chah
blood orange juice	succo di arance rosse **soo**-koh dee ah-**rahn**-chay **roh**-say
hot chocolate	cioccolata calda choh-koh-**lah**-tah **kahl**-dah

Key Phrases: What's Cooking?

food	cibo **chee**-boh
breakfast	colazione koh-laht-see-**oh**-nay
lunch	pranzo **prahnt**-soh
dinner	cena **cheh**-nah
bread	pane **pah**-nay
cheese	formaggio for-**mah**-joh
soup	minestra / zuppa mee-**neh**-strah / **tsoo**-pah
salad	insalata een-sah-**lah**-tah
fish	pesce **peh**-shay
chicken	pollo **poh**-loh
meat	carni **kar**-nee
vegetables	verdure vehr-**doo**-ray
fruit	frutta **froo**-tah
dessert	dolci **dohl**-chee

If you want to skip your hotel breakfast, do as the Italians do: Stop into a bar or café to drink a cappuccino and munch a ***cornetto*** (croissant) while standing at the bar.

What's Probably Not For Breakfast

These items are not typical on a traditional Italian breakfast table, but you may find them at international hotels or cafés catering to foreigners.

omelet	omelette / frittata oh-meh-**leh**-tay / free-**tah**-tah
eggs...	uova... **woh**-vah
...fried	...fritte **free**-tay
...scrambled	...strapazzate strah-pahd-**zah**-tay

...poached	...in camicia een kah-**mee**-chah
...hard-boiled	...sode **soh**-day
...soft-boiled	...alla coque **ah**-lah kohk
ham	prosciutto cotto proh-**shoo**-toh **koh**-toh
cheese	formaggio for-**mah**-joh
yogurt	yogurt **yoh**-goort
cereal	cereali cheh-reh-**ah**-lee

Sandwiches

The generic Italian sandwich comes on a baguette—it's called a ***panino.*** Another common sandwich—especially in central Italy—is the ***foccacia,*** made on the puffy bread of the same name.

sandwich (on a baguette)	panino pah-**nee**-noh
I'd like a sandwich.	Vorrei un panino. voh-**reh**-ee oon pah-**nee**-noh
white bread	pane bianco **pah**-nay bee-**ahn**-koh
whole-grain bread	pane integrale **pah**-nay een-teh-**grah**-lay
toasted ham and cheese	toast con prosciutto cotto e formaggio "toast" kohn proh-**shoo**-toh **koh**-toh ay for-**mah**-joh
cheese	formaggio for-**mah**-joh
tuna	tonno **toh**-noh
fish	pesce **peh**-shay
chicken	pollo **poh**-loh
turkey	tacchino tah-**kee**-noh
ham	prosciutto proh-**shoo**-toh
air-cured beef	bresaola breh-zah-**oh**-lah

salami	salame sah-**lah**-may
lettuce	lattuga lah-**too**-gah
tomato	pomodoro poh-moh-**doh**-roh
onion	cipolla chee-**poh**-lah
mustard	senape **seh**-nah-pay
mayonnaise	maionese mah-yoh-**neh**-zay
on sandwich bread / on a roll	con pane in cassetta / panino al latte kohn **pah**-nay een kah-**seh**-tah / pah-**nee**-noh ahl **lah**-tay
toasted / grilled / heated	scaldato / alla griglia / caldo skahl-**dah**-toh / **ah**-lah **greel**-yah / **kahl**-doh
Does this come cold or hot?	Si mangia freddo o caldo? see **mahn**-jah **freh**-doh oh **kahl**-doh
That. (pointing)	Quello. **kway**-loh
What is that?	Che cos'è? kay **koh**-zeh
What is good with that?	Cosa è buono con questo? **koh**-zah eh **bwoh**-noh kohn **kweh**-stoh
What do you suggest?	Cosa mi consiglia? **koh**-zah mee kohn-**seel**-yah
very filling (big sandwich)	molto pieno **mohl**-toh pee-**eh**-noh
just a taste (small sandwich)	solo un assaggino **soh**-loh oon ah-sah-**jee**-noh
well heated / cooked	molto caldo / cotto **mohl**-toh **kahl**-doh / **koh**-toh
not overcooked	non troppo caldo nohn **troh**-poh **kahl**-doh

To grab a sandwich, stop by a ***panificio*** (bakery) or a ***bar***—or, better yet, a ***paninoteca*** or ***foccaceria,*** where they can custom-make you a sandwich.

Say Cheese

cheese	formaggio for-**mah**-joh
cheese shop	formaggeria for-mah-jeh-**ree**-ah
Do you have a cheese that is...?	Avete un formaggio...? ah-**veh**-tay oon for-**mah**-joh
...mild / sharp	...dolce / saporito **dohl**-chay / sah-poh-**ree**-toh
...fresh / aged	...fresco / stagionato **freh**-skoh / stah-joh-**nah**-toh
...soft / hard	...morbido / duro **mor**-bee-doh / **doo**-roh
...from a cow / sheep / goat	...di mucca / di pecora / di capra dee **moo**-kah / dee **peh**-koh-rah / dee **kah**-prah
...sliced	...affettato ah-feh-**tah**-toh
...smoked	...affumicato ah-foo-mee-**kah**-toh
May I taste it?	Posso avere un assagio? **poh**-soh ah-**veh**-ray oon ah-**sah**-joh
What is your favorite cheese?	Qual'è il suo formaggio preferito? kwah-**leh** eel **soo**-oh for-**mah**-joh preh-feh-**ree**-toh
I would like three or four types of cheese for a picnic.	Vorrei tre o quattro tipi di formaggi per un picnic. voh-**reh**-ee tray oh **kwah**-troh **tee**-pee dee for-**mah**-jee pehr oon **peek**-neek
Choose for me, please.	Scelga lei, per favore. **shehl**-gah **leh**-ee pehr fah-**voh**-ray
This much. (showing size)	Tanto così. **tahn**-toh koh-**zee**
More. / Less.	Di più. / Di meno. dee pew / dee **meh**-noh
Can you please slice it?	Lo può affettare, per favore? loh pwoh ah-feh-**tah**-ray pehr fah-**voh**-ray

Prosciutto

Prosciutto is a popular type of ***salumi*** (literally "salted meats"), an Italian staple. Produced mainly in the north of Italy, this thinly sliced ham can be sweet or salty.

prosciutto (crudo) proh-**shoo**-toh (**kroo**-doh)
air-cured hamhock, thinly sliced

prosciutto dolce proh-**shoo**-toh **dohl**-chay
sweet prosciutto

prosciutto salato / stagionato
proh-**shoo**-toh sah-**lah**-toh / stah-joh-**nah**-toh
salty prosciutto

prosciutto di Parma proh-**shoo**-toh dee **par**-mah
premium, super-lean, sweet prosciutto

prosciutto toscano proh-**shoo**-toh toh-**skah**-noh
Tuscan prosciutto, generally dark and salty

culatello koo-lah-**teh**-loh
made with the finest pork and sometimes wine-cured

Purists claim that the best ***prosciutto*** comes from ***cinta senese*** (Sienese-branded) pigs, with black hooves.

Pizza

For a fresh, fast, and frugal meal, drop by a ***pizzeria.*** Get it to go (***da portar via***—for the road), or eat it on the spot. To get cold pizza warmed up say ***Caldo, per favore*** (Hot, please). Here are some types and toppings to look for:

bianca / ciaccina bee-**ahn**-kah / chah-**chee**-nah
"white" pizza (no tomatoes)

capricciosa kah-pree-**choh**-zah
"chef's choice"—usually ham, mushrooms, olives, and artichokes

(alla) diavola (**ah**-lah) dee-**ah**-voh-lah
spicy (usually spicy salami)

funghi **foon**-gee (hard "g")
mushrooms

margherita mar-geh-**ree**-tah
tomato sauce, mozzarella, and basil

peperoni peh-peh-**roh**-nee
green or red peppers (not spicy salami!)

quattro formaggi / stagioni **kwah**-troh for-**mah**-jee / stah-**joh**-nee
pizza divided into quarters with four different cheeses / toppings

salame piccante / salamino
sah-**lah**-may pee-**kahn**-tay / sah-lah-**mee**-noh
spicy salami (similar to American pepperoni)

salsiccia sahl-**see**-chah
sausage

vegetariana / ortolana veh-jeh-tah-ree-**ah**-nah / or-toh-**lah**-nah
veggie

For take-out ***(pizza al taglio),*** you'll most likely find ***pizza rustica:*** pizza baked in a big rectangular pan and sold by weight. Order 100 grams ***(un etto)*** for a snack-size piece; 200 grams ***(due etti)*** makes a light meal. Or show the size you want with your hands and say ***Tanto così*** (**tahn**-toh koh-**zee;** This much).

If you want a pepperoni pizza, don't order ***peperoni*** (which means peppers)—instead, go for ***diavola*** or ***salame piccante.***

Pasta

Italy is the land of ***pasta,*** with more than 600 different shapes and sizes. Here are a few:

capellini / capelli d'angelo
kah-peh-**lee**-nee / kah-**peh**-lee **dahn**-jeh-loh
extremely thin spaghetti ("little hairs" / "angel hair")

cannelloni kah-neh-**loh**-nee
wide tube similar to manicotti; often used in baked dishes

farfalle far-**fah**-lay
"butterfly" or bowtie shape

fusilli foo-**zee**-lee
spiral shapes ideal for cream or cheese sauces

manicotti mah-nee-**koh**-tee
large tubes ("sleeves"); usually stuffed (often with ricotta) and baked

mostaccioli moh-stah-**choh**-lee
"moustache"-like smooth penne

orzo **ord**-zoh
tiny "barley" shape (looks like rice)

penne **pehn**-nay; draw out **nn** sound to avoid saying *pene* (penis)
angle-cut tubes ("quills")

rigatoni ree-gah-**toh**-nee
"ridged," square-cut, hollow tubes

rotini roh-**tee**-nee
like fusilli, but shorter

tagliatelle tahl-yah-**teh**-lay
wide, flat noodles

ziti **zee**-tee
long, hollow tubes (wider than *penne*)

Italians prefer their pasta cooked ***al dente*** ("to the tooth"—still quite firm compared to American tastes).

Pasta Sauces

These popular pasta dishes appear on many menus. Note that words describing a pasta sauce or preparation are usually preceded by ***in*** or ***alla*** (in the style of).

aglio e olio **ahl**-yoh ay **oh**-lee-oh
garlic and olive oil

alfredo ahl-**freh**-doh
butter, cream, and *parmigiano*

arrabbiata ah-rah-bee-**ah**-tah
"angry," spicy tomato sauce with chili peppers

bologness boh-lohn-**yeh**-zay
meat and tomato sauce

brodo **broh**-doh
in broth

burro e salvia **boo**-roh ay **sahl**-vee-ah
butter and sage

carbonara kar-boh-**nah**-rah
bacon, egg, cheese, and pepper

dell'ortolano deh-lor-tah-**lah**-noh
"green grocer-style," with vegetables

diavola dee-**ah**-voh-lah
"devil-style," spicy hot

forno **for**-noh
oven-baked

frutti di mare **froo**-tee dee **mah**-ray
seafood sauce

(ai) funghi (ī) **foon**-gee (hard "g")
with mushrooms

genovese jeh-noh-**veh**-zay
with pesto

marinara mah-ree-**nah**-rah
usually a tomato sauce, often with garlic and onions; can also refer to a dish with seafood

panna **pah**-nah
cream

pescatore peh-skah-**toh**-ray
seafood ("fishermen's"-style)

pesto **peh**-stoh
basil ground with *parmigiano,* garlic, pine nuts, and olive oil

pomodoro poh-moh-**doh**-roh
tomato only

puttanesca poo-tah-**neh**-skah
"harlot"-style tomato sauce with anchovies, olives, and capers

quattro formaggi **kwah**-troh for-**mah**-jee
four cheeses

ragù rah-**goo**
meaty tomato sauce

scoglio **skohl**-yoh
with mussels, clams, and tomatoes

sugo **soo**-goh
sauce, usually tomato

tartufo / tartufata tar-**too**-foh / tar-too-**fah**-tah
with truffles

vongole **vohn**-goh-lay
with clams and spices

Soups

soup...	zuppa... **tsoo**-pah
...of the day	...del giorno dehl **jor**-noh
...chicken	...di pollo dee **poh**-loh
...beef	...di carne dee **kar**-nay
...fish	...di pesce dee **peh**-shay
...vegetable	...di verdure dee vehr-**doo**-ray
...with noodles	...con pastina kohn pah-**stee**-nah
...with rice	...con riso kohn **ree**-zoh
vegetable soup	minestrone mee-neh-**stroh**-nay
stew	stufato stoo-**fah**-toh
broth	brodo **broh**-doh

Salad

Insalate (salads) are usually served as a side dish with the main course (if you don't order a ***secondo,*** the waiter will ask when you'd like the salad served). Salad dressing is normally just the oil and vinegar at the table; if it's missing, ask for the ***oliera.***

salad...	insalata... een-sah-**lah**-tah
...green	...verde **vehr**-day
...mixed	...mista **mee**-stah
...niçoise	...nizzarda need-**zar**-dah
...with ham and cheese	...con prosciutto e formaggio kohn proh-**shoo**-toh ay for-**mah**-joh
...with egg	...con uova kohn **woh**-vah
lettuce	lattuga lah-**too**-gah
tomato	pomodoro poh-moh-**doh**-roh
onion	cipolla chee-**poh**-lah
cucumber	cetriolo cheh-tree-**oh**-loh
carrot	carota kah-**roh**-tah
oil / vinegar	olio / aceto **oh**-lee-oh / ah-**cheh**-toh
oil and vinegar	oliera oh-lee-**eh**-rah
dressing (on the side)	condimento (a parte) kohn-dee-**mehn**-toh (ah **par**-tay)
What is in this salad?	Che cosa c'è in questa insalata? kay **koh**-zah cheh een **kweh**-stah een-sah-**lah**-tah

Salad bars at fast-food restaurants and ***autostrada*** rest stops can be a good budget bet.

Meat

meat	carne **kar**-nay
cold cuts / cured meats	salumi / affettati sah-**loo**-mee / ah-feh-**tah**-tee
cutlet	cotoletta koh-toh-**leh**-tah
ribs	costolette koh-stoh-**leh**-tay
shoulder	spalla **spah**-lah
shank (leg meat)	stinco **steen**-koh
bacon, salt-cured	pancetta pahn-**cheh**-tah

beef	manzo **mahnt**-soh
beef steak	bistecca di manzo bee-**steh**-kah dee **mahnt**-soh
sirloin steak	entrecote ehn-treh-**koh**-tay
rib-eye steak	costata koh-**stah**-tah
tenderloin	filetto fee-**leh**-toh
T-bone	bistecca (alla fiorentina) bee-**steh**-kah (**ah**-lah fee-oh-rehn-**tee**-nah)
roast beef	roast beef "roast beef"
air-cured beef	bresaola breh-zah-**oh**-lah
boar	cinghiale cheen-gee-**ah**-lay
goat (kid)	capretto kah-**preh**-toh
ham...	prosciutto... proh-**shoo**-toh
...dried, air-cured	...crudo **kroo**-doh
...smoked	...affumicato ah-foo-mee-**kah**-toh
...cooked	...cotto **koh**-toh
...roasted	...arrosto ah-**roh**-stoh
lamb	agnello ahn-**yeh**-loh
mutton	montone mohn-**toh**-nay
oxtail	coda di bue **koh**-dah dee **boo**-ay
pork	maiale mī-**yah**-lay
suckling pig	porchetta / maialino por-**keh**-tah / mī-yah-**lee**-noh
sausage	salsiccia sahl-**see**-chah
blood sausage	sanguinaccio sahn-gwee-**nah**-choh
rabbit	coniglio koh-**neel**-yoh
veal	vitello vee-**teh**-loh
veal, thin-sliced	scaloppine skah-loh-**pee**-nay
venison	selvaggina sehl-vah-**jee**-nah
Is this cooked?	È cotto questo? eh **koh**-toh **kweh**-stoh

On a menu, the price of steak is often listed per *etto* (100 grams, about a quarter-pound); the letters ***s.q.*** (for ***secondo quantità)*** mean "according

Avoiding Mis-Steaks

alive	vivo **vee**-voh
raw	crudo **kroo**-doh
very rare	molto al sangue **mohl**-toh ahl **sahn**-gway
rare	al sangue ahl **sahn**-gway
medium	cotto **koh**-toh
well-done	ben cotto behn **koh**-toh
very well-done	completamente cotto kohm-pleh-tah-**mehn**-tay **koh**-toh

to quantity." It is most common to order four or five ***etti*** of steak to share. There's often a minimum-weight order—ask.

Poultry

poultry	pollame poh-**lah**-may
chicken	pollo **poh**-loh
duck	anatra **ah**-nah-trah
goose	oca **oh**-kah
turkey	tacchino tah-**kee**-noh
partridge	pernice pehr-**nee**-chay
breast	petto **peh**-toh
thigh	sovracoscia soh-vrah-**koh**-shah
drumstick	coscia **koh**-shah
white / dark meat	carne bianca / scura **kar**-nay bee-**ahn**-kah / **skoo**-rah
liver (pâté)	fegato (patè) **feh**-gah-toh (pah-**teh**)
eggs	uova **woh**-vah

free-range eggs	uova di galline allevate a terra **woh**-vah dee gah-**lee**-nay ah-leh-**vah**-tay ah **teh**-rah
How long has this been dead?	Da quanto tempo è morto questo? dah **kwahn**-toh **tehm**-poh eh **mor**-toh **kweh**-stoh

Fish and Seafood

seafood	frutti di mare **froo**-tee dee **mah**-ray
assorted seafood	misto di frutti di mare **mee**-stoh dee **froo**-tee dee **mah**-ray
fish	pesce **peh**-shay
shellfish	crostacei kroh-**stah**-cheh-ee
anchovies	acciughe ah-**choo**-gay
bream (fish)	orata oh-**rah**-tah
clams	vongole **vohn**-goh-lay
cod	merluzzo mehr-**lood**-zoh
crab / spider crab	granchio / granseola **grahn**-kee-oh / grahn-seh-**oh**-lah
crayfish	gambero di fiume gahm-**beh**-roh dee fee-**oo**-may
cuttlefish	seppia **sehp**-yah
dogfish	palombo pah-**lohm**-boh
eel	anguilla ahn-**gwee**-lah
hake	nasello nah-**zeh**-loh
halibut	ippoglosso / halibut ee-poh-**gloh**-soh / **ah**-lee-boot
herring	aringa ah-**reen**-gah
lobster	aragosta ah-rah-**goh**-stah
monkfish	rana pescatrice **rah**-nah peh-skah-**tree**-chay
mussels	cozze **kohd**-zay

octopus	polpo **pohl**-poh
oysters	ostriche **oh**-stree-kay
prawns	scampi / gamberi **skahm**-pee / gahm-**beh**-ree
jumbo prawns	gamberoni gahm-beh-**roh**-nee
salmon	salmone sahl-**moh**-nay
salt cod	baccalà bah-kah-**lah**
sardines	sardine sar-**dee**-nay
scad (like mackerel)	sgombro **zgohm**-broh
scallops	capesante kah-peh-**zahn**-tay
sea bass	branzino brahnt-**see**-noh
shrimp / small shrimp...	gamberi / gamberetti... gahm-**beh**-ree / gahm-beh-**reh**-tee
...in the shell	...interi een-**teh**-ree
...peeled	...sgusciati zgoo-**shah**-tee
sole	sogliola sohl-**yoh**-lah
squid	calamari kah-lah-**mah**-ree
swordfish	pesce spada **peh**-shay **spah**-dah
trout	trota **troh**-tah
tuna	tonno **toh**-noh
turbot (like flounder)	rombo **rohm**-boh
How much for a portion?	Quanto per una porzione? **kwahn**-toh pehr **oo**-nah port-see-**oh**-nay
What's fresh today?	Cosa c'è di fresco oggi? **koh**-zah cheh dee **freh**-skoh **oh**-jee
How do you eat this?	Come si mangia? **koh**-may see **mahn**-jah
Do you eat this part?	Si mangia anche questa parte? see **mahn**-jah **ahn**-kay **kweh**-stah **par**-tay
Just the head, please.	Solo la testa, per favore. **soh**-loh lah **teh**-stah pehr fah-**voh**-ray

Like steak, seafood is often served by the ***etto*** (100 grams). To find out how much a typical portion costs, ask ***Quanto per una porzione?***

Veggies and Sides

Expect main dishes to be served without vegetables or other side dishes. That's why ***contorni*** (sides) appear separately on the menu.

vegetables	verdure vehr-**doo**-ray
mixed vegetables	misto di verdure **mee**-stoh dee vehr-**doo**-ray
artichoke	carciofo kar-**choh**-foh
giant artichoke	carciofo romanesco kar-**choh**-foh roh-mah-**neh**-skoh
arugula (rocket)	rucola **roo**-koh-lah
asparagus	asparagi ah-spah-**rah**-jee
avocado	avocado ah-voh-**kah**-doh
bean	fagiolo fah-**joh**-loh
beet	barbabietola bar-bah-bee-**eh**-toh-lah
broccoli	broccoli **broh**-koh-lee
cabbage	verza **vehrt**-sah
capers	capperi **kah**-peh-ree
carrot	carota kah-**roh**-tah
cauliflower	cavolfiore kah-vohl-fee-**oh**-ray
chickpea (garbanzo)	cece **cheh**-cheh
corn	granoturco / mais grah-noh-**toor**-koh / "mice"
cucumber	cetriolo cheh-tree-**oh**-loh
eggplant	melanzana meh-lahnt-**sah**-nah
endive	indivia een-**dee**-vee-ah
fennel	finocchio fee-**noh**-kee-oh
French fries	patate fritte pah-**tah**-tay **free**-tay
garlic	aglio **ahl**-yoh

green bean	fagiolino fah-joh-**lee**-noh
lentil	lenticchia lehn-**tee**-kee-ah
mushroom	fungo **foon**-goh
olive	oliva oh-**lee**-vah
onion	cipolla chee-**poh**-lah
peas	piselli pee-**zeh**-lee
pepper (green / red)	peperone (verde / rosso) peh-peh-**roh**-nay (**vehr**-day / **roh**-soh)
pepper (hot)	peperoncino peh-peh-rohn-**chee**-noh
pickle	cetriolino cheh-tree-oh-**lee**-noh
polenta	polenta poh-**lehn**-tah
potato / roasted potatoes	patata / patate arrosto pah-**tah**-tah / pah-**tah**-tay ah-**roh**-stoh
rice	riso **ree**-zoh
spinach	spinaci spee-**nah**-chee
tomato	pomodoro poh-moh-**doh**-roh
turnip	rapa **rah**-pah
truffle	tartufo tar-**too**-foh
zucchini	zucchine tsoo-**kee**-nay

Polenta (cornmeal) is a popular side dish in the north, either served warm and soft, or cut into firm slabs and grilled.

Fruits

fruit	frutta **froo**-tah
fruit salad	macedonia mah-cheh-**doh**-nee-ah
fruit smoothie	frullato di frutta froo-**lah**-toh dee **froo**-tah
apple	mela **meh**-lah
apricot	albicocca ahl-bee-**koh**-kah
banana	banana bah-**nah**-nah

berries	frutti di bosco **froo**-tee dee **boh**-skoh
blackberry	mora **moh**-rah
blueberry	mirtillo meer-**tee**-loh
cantaloupe	melone meh-**loh**-nay
cherry	ciliegia chee-lee-**eh**-jah
...sour cherry	...amarena / visciola ah-mah-**reh**-nah / vee-**shoh**-lah
date	dattero **dah**-teh-roh
fig	fico **fee**-koh
grapefruit	pompelmo pohm-**pehl**-moh
grapes	uva **oo**-vah
honeydew melon	melone d'inverno meh-**loh**-nay deen-**vehr**-noh
lemon	limone lee-**moh**-nay
mango	mango **mahn**-goh
orange	arancia ah-**rahn**-chah
peach	pesca **peh**-skah
pear	pera **peh**-rah
persimmon	caco **kah**-koh
pineapple	ananas **ah**-nah-nahs
plum	susina soo-**zee**-nah
pomegranate	melograno meh-loh-**grah**-noh
prune	prugna **proon**-yah
raisin	uvetta oo-**veh**-tah
raspberry	lampone lahm-**poh**-nay
strawberry	fragola **frah**-goh-lah
tangerine	mandarino mahn-dah-**ree**-noh
watermelon	cocomero / anguria koh-koh-**meh**-roh / ahn-**goo**-ree-ah

Just Desserts

I'd like / We'd like...	Vorrei / Vorremmo... voh-**reh**-ee / voh-**reh**-moh
dessert	dolce **dohl**-chay
cake	torta **tor**-tah
cookies	biscotti bee-**skoh**-tee
ice cream	gelato jeh-**lah**-toh
sorbet	sorbetto sor-**beh**-toh
fruit salad	macedonia mah-cheh-**doh**-nee-ah
tart	crostata kroh-**stah**-tah
pie	torta **tor**-tah
whipped cream	panna **pah**-nah
chocolate mousse	mousse di cioccolato moos dee choh-koh-**lah**-toh
pudding	budino boo-**dee**-noh
candy	caramella kah-rah-**meh**-lah
chocolates	cioccolatini choh-koh-lah-**tee**-nee
low calorie	poche calorie **poh**-kay kah-loh-**ree**-ay
homemade	fatto in casa **fah**-toh een **kah**-zah
We'll split one.	Ne dividiamo uno. nay dee-vee-dee-**ah**-moh **oo**-noh
Two forks / spoons, please.	Due forchette / cucchiai, per favore. **doo**-ay for-**keh**-tay / koo-kee-**ī**-ee pehr fah-**voh**-ray
I shouldn't, but...	Non dovrei, ma... nohn doh-**vreh**-ee mah
Super tasty!	Super gustoso! **soo**-pehr goo-**stoh**-zoh
Exquisite!	Squisito! skwee-**zee**-toh
Sinfully good ("A sin of the throat").	Un peccato di gola. oon peh-**kah**-toh dee **goh**-lah

Gelato

cone	cono **koh**-noh
cup	coppa / copetta **koh**-pah / koh-**peh**-tah
one scoop	una pallina **oo**-nah pah-**lee**-nah
two scoops	due palline **doo**-ay pah-**lee**-nay
one flavor / two flavors	un gusto / due gusti oon **goo**-stoh / **doo**-ay **goo**-stee
chocolate	cioccolato choh-koh-**lah**-toh
coffee	caffè kah-**feh**
hazelnut	nocciola noh-**choh**-lah
mint	menta **mehn**-tah
strawberry	fragola **frah**-goh-lah
vanilla	vaniglia vah-**neel**-yah
vanilla with chocolate shreds	stracciatella strah-chah-**teh**-lah
with whipped cream	con panna kohn **pah**-nah
sorbet	sorbetto sor-**beh**-toh
slushy ice with sweet syrup	granita / grattachecca grah-**nee**-tah / grah-tah-**keh**-kah
mix of slushy ice and gelato	cremolata kreh-moh-**lah**-tah
What is that?	Che cos'è? kay koh-**zeh**
A little taste?	Un assaggio? oon ah-**sah**-joh
How many flavors can I have?	Quanti gusti posso avere? **kwahn**-tee **goo**-stee **poh**-soh ah-**veh**-ray
Which flavors go well together?	Quali gusti stanno bene insieme? **kwah**-lee **goo**-stee **stah**-noh **beh**-nay een-see-**eh**-may
a cone / a cup for ____ euros (fill in amount)	un cono / una coppa da ____ euro oon **koh**-noh / **oo**-nah **koh**-pah dah ____ eh-**oo**-roh

To avoid having your request for a cone turn into a €10 "tourist special," survey the size options and be very clear in your order: for example, ***un cono da due euro*** (a €2 cone).

DRINKING

Water

mineral water...	acqua minerale...	**ah**-kwah mee-neh-**rah**-lay
...with carbonation / sparkling	...con gas / frizzante	kohn gahs / freed-**zahn**-tay
...without carbonation / natural	...senza gas / naturale	**sehnt**-sah gahs / nah-too-**rah**-lay
lightly carbonated water	acqua leggermente effervescente	**ah**-kwah leh-jehr-**mehn**-tay eh-fehr-veh-**shehn**-tay
(half) liter	(mezzo) litro	(**mehd**-zoh) **lee**-troh
tap water	acqua del rubinetto	**ah**-kwah dehl roo-bee-**neh**-toh
(not) drinkable	(non) potabile	(nohn) poh-**tah**-bee-lay
Is this water safe to drink?	È potabile quest'acqua?	eh poh-**tah**-bee-lay kweh-**stah**-kwah

You can ask for ***acqua del rubinetto*** (tap water) in restaurants, but your server may give you a funny look. It's customary and never expensive to order a ***litro*** (liter) or ***mezzo litro*** (half liter) of bottled water with your food.

Milk

whole milk	latte intero	**lah**-tay een-**teh**-roh
skim milk	latte magro	**lah**-tay **mah**-groh
fresh milk	latte fresco	**lah**-tay **freh**-skoh
milk shake	frullato / frappè	froo-**lah**-toh / frah-**peh**

Key Phrases: Drinking

drink	bibita **bee**-bee-tah
(mineral) water	acqua (minerale) **ah**-kwah (mee-neh-**rah**-lay)
tap water	acqua del rubinetto **ah**-kwah dehl roo-bee-**neh**-toh
milk	latte **lah**-tay
juice	succo **soo**-koh
coffee	caffè kah-**feh**
tea	tè teh
wine	vino **vee**-noh
beer	birra **bee**-rah
Cheers!	Cin cin! cheen cheen

cold / hot	freddo / caldo **freh**-doh / **kahl**-doh
straw	cannuccia kah-**noo**-chah

Juice and Other Drinks

(fruit) juice	succo (di frutta) **soo**-koh (dee **froo**-tah)
freshly squeezed juice	spremuta spreh-**moo**-tah
100% juice	100% succo di frutta **chehn**-toh pehr **chehn**-toh **soo**-koh dee **froo**-tah
orange juice	succo di arancia **soo**-koh dee ah-**rahn**-chah
freshly squeezed orange juice	spremuta di arancia spreh-**moo**-tah dee ah-**rahn**-chah
apple juice	succo di mela **soo**-koh dee **meh**-lah

blood orange juice	succo di arance rosse **soo**-koh dee ah-**rahn**-chay **roh**-say
grape juice	succo d'uva **soo**-koh **doo**-vah
pineapple juice	succo d'ananas **soo**-koh **dah**-nah-nahs
fruit smoothie	frullato di frutta froo-**lah**-toh dee **froo**-tah
lemonade	limonata lee-moh-**nah**-tah
iced tea	tè freddo teh **freh**-doh
(diet) soda	bibita gassata ("light") bee-bee-tah gah-**sah**-tah ("light")
energy drink	bibita energetica **bee**-bee-tah eh-nehr-**jeh**-tee-kah
with / without...	con / senza... kohn / **sehnt**-sah
...sugar	...zucchero **tsoo**-keh-roh
...ice	...ghiaccio gee-**ah**-choh (hard "g")

Coffee

When you're ordering coffee in bars in bigger cities, you'll notice that the price board ***(lista dei prezzi)*** lists two price levels: the cheaper price for the stand-up ***bar*** and the more expensive for the ***tavolo*** (table) or ***terrazza*** (out on the terrace or sidewalk). If standing at the bar, don't order from the bartender—instead, order and pay first at the ***cassa*** (cash register), then take your receipt to the person who makes the coffee. Refills are never free (except at hotel breakfasts).

espresso...	caffè... kah-**feh**
...with milk	...latte **lah**-tay
...with foamed milk	...cappuccino kah-poo-**chee**-noh
...American-style (with hot water)	...americano ah-meh-ree-**kah**-noh
...with sugar	...con zucchero kohn **tsoo**-keh-roh
...iced and sweetened	...freddo **freh**-doh

...double shot	...doppio **dohp**-yoh
instant	solubile soh-**loo**-bee-lay
decaffeinated	decaffeinato / Hag deh-kah-feh-**nah**-toh / ahg
price list...	lista dei prezzi... **lee**-stah **deh**-ee **preht**-see
...at the bar / at a table / on the terrace	...al bar / al tavolo / in terrazza ahl bar / ahl **tah**-voh-loh / een teh-**raht**-sah
Same price if I sit or stand?	Costa uguale al tavolo o al banco? **koh**-stah oo-**gwah**-lay ahl **tah**-voh-loh oh ahl **bahn**-koh
Very hot, please.	Molto caldo, per favore. **mohl**-toh **kahl**-doh pehr fah-**voh**-ray
Hotter, please.	Più caldo, per favore. pew **kahl**-doh pehr fah-**voh**-ray

In Italian, ***caffè*** means espresso. If you ask for ***un latte,*** you'll get a glass of hot milk; instead, order ***un caffè latte.*** For the closest thing to a cup of drip coffee, request ***un caffè americano.***

Italians like their coffee only warm—to get it hot, request ***molto caldo*** (very hot) or ***più caldo, per favore*** (hotter, please).

Coffee Specialties

While coffee is popular any time of day, Italians drink the kinds with lots of milk only in the morning. But ***baristas*** are willing—perhaps with a raised eyebrow—to serve milky drinks to tourists in the afternoon.

caffè kah-**feh**
a shot of espresso in a little cup

caffè americano kah-**feh** ah-meh-ree-**kah**-noh
espresso diluted with lots of hot water, in a larger cup (similar to American-style drip coffee)

caffè corretto kah-**feh** koh-**reh**-toh
espresso "corrected" with a shot of liqueur (typically grappa, amaro, or Sambuca)

caffè freddo kah-**feh** **freh**-doh
sweet, iced espresso

caffè latte kah-**feh** **lah**-tay
espresso mixed with hot milk, no foam, in a tall glass

caffè lungo kah-**feh** **loon**-goh
espresso diluted with a little hot water, in a small cup

caffè macchiato kah-**feh** mah-kee-**ah**-toh
espresso "marked" with just a splash of milk, served in a small cup

cappuccino kah-poo-**chee**-noh
espresso with foamed milk on top

cappuccino freddo kah-poo-**chee**-noh **freh**-doh
iced cappuccino

latte macchiato **lah**-tay mah-kee-**ah**-toh
layers of hot milk and foam, "marked" by an espresso shot, in a tall glass

Other Hot Drinks

hot water	acqua calda **ah**-kwah **kahl**-dah
hot chocolate (with whipped cream)	cioccolata calda (con panna) choh-koh-**lah**-tah **kahl**-dah (kohn **pah**-nah)
tea	tè teh
lemon	limone lee-**moh**-nay
tea bag	bustina di tè boo-**stee**-nah dee teh
herbal tea	tisana tee-**zah**-nah
chamomile	camomilla kah-moh-**mee**-lah
black tea	tè nero teh **neh**-roh
green tea	tè verde teh **vehr**-day
lemon tea	tè al limone teh ahl lee-**moh**-nay
citrus tea	tè agli agrumi teh **ahl**-yee ah-**groo**-mee
fruit tea	tè alla frutta teh **ah**-lah **froo**-tah
mint tea	tè alla menta teh **ah**-lah **mehn**-tah

Wine Lingo

The ancient Greeks who colonized Italy more than 2,000 years ago called it ***Oenotria,*** land of the grape. Italian wines are named by grape, place, descriptive term, or a combination of these.

wine	vino **vee**-noh
table wine	vino da tavola **vee**-noh dah **tah**-voh-lah
house wine	vino della casa **vee**-noh **deh**-lah **kah**-zah
local	locale loh-**kah**-lay
of the region	della regione **deh**-lah reh-**joh**-nay
red	rosso **roh**-soh
white	bianco bee-**ahn**-koh
rosé	rosato roh-**zah**-toh
sparkling	frizzante / spumante freed-**zahn**-tay / spoo-**mahn**-tay
sparkling white wine	prosecco proh-**seh**-koh
I like ____. (fill in type of wine)	Mi piace il ____. mee pee-**ah**-chay eel ____
I like something that is ____ and ____.	Preferisco qualcosa di ____ e ____. preh-feh-**ree**-skoh kwahl-**koh**-zah dee ____ ay ____
sweet	dolce / abboccato / amabile **dohl**-chay / ah-boh-**kah**-toh / ah-**mah**-bee-lay
semi-dry	semi-secco seh-mee-**seh**-koh
(very) dry	(molto) secco (**mohl**-toh) **seh**-koh
light / heavy	leggero / gustoso leh-**jeh**-roh / goo-**stoh**-zoh
full-bodied	corposo / pieno kor-**poh**-zoh / pee-**eh**-noh
young	giovane **joh**-vah-nay
mature	maturo mah-**too**-roh
fruity	fruttato froo-**tah**-toh

earthy	terroso teh-**roh**-zoh
tannic	tannico **tah**-nee-koh
elegant	elegante eh-leh-**gahn**-tay
smooth	morbido **mor**-bee-doh
chilled	ghiacciato gee-ah-**chah**-toh (hard "g")
at room temperature	a temperatura ambiente ah tehm-peh-rah-**too**-rah ahm-bee-**ehn**-tay
cork	tappo **tah**-poh
corkscrew	cavatappi kah-vah-**tah**-pee
vineyard	vigneto veen-**yeh**-toh
harvest	vendemmia vehn-**deh**-mee-ah
wine-tasting	degustazione deh-goo-staht-see-**oh**-nay

Visit an ***enoteca*** (wine shop or bar) to sample regional wines.

Ordering Wine

I'd like / We'd like...	Vorrei / Vorremo... voh-**reh**-ee / voh-**reh**-moh
...the wine list.	...la lista dei vini. lah **lee**-stah **deh**-ee **vee**-nee
...a glass...	...un bicchiere... oon bee-kee-**eh**-ray
...a small glass...	...un bicchiere piccolo... oon bee-kee-**eh**-ray **pee**-koh-loh
...a quarter liter...	...un quartino... oon kwar-**tee**-noh
...a half liter...	...un mezzo... oon **mehd**-zoh
...a liter...	...un litro... oon **lee**-troh
...a carafe...	...una caraffa... **oo**-nah kah-**rah**-fah
...a bottle...	...una bottiglia... **oo**-nah boh-**teel**-yah
...of red wine.	...di rosso. dee **roh**-soh
...of white wine.	...di bianco. dee bee-**ahn**-koh

...of house wine / table wine.	...di vino della casa / vino da tavola. dee **vee**-noh **deh**-lah **kah**-zah / **vee**-noh dah **tah**-voh-lah
I'd like to sample a typical local wine.	Vorrei provare un vino locale tipico. voh-**reh**-ee proh-**vah**-ray oon **vee**-noh loh-**kah**-lay **tee**-pee-koh
What do you recommend?	Cosa raccomanda? **koh**-zah rah-koh-**mahn**-dah
Choose for me, please.	Scelga lei, per favore. **shehl**-gah **leh**-ee pehr fah-**voh**-ray
Around ____ euros.	Intorno ai ____ euro. een-**tor**-noh ī ____ eh-**oo**-roh
Another, please.	Un altro, per favore. oon **ahl**-troh pehr fah-**voh**-ray

Beer

I'd like / We'd like...	Vorrei / Vorremo... voh-**reh**-ee / voh-**reh**-moh
beer...	birra... **bee**-rah
...from the tap	...alla spina **ah**-lah **spee**-nah
bottle	bottiglia boh-**teel**-yah
can	lattina lah-**tee**-nah
light / dark	chiara / scura kee-**ah**-rah / **skoo**-rah
local / imported	locale / importata loh-**kah**-lay / eem-por-**tah**-tah
small / large	piccola / grande **pee**-koh-lah / **grahn**-day
wheat	birra di frumento **bee**-rah dee froo-**mehn**-toh
microbrew	birra artigianale **bee**-rah ar-tee-jah-**nah**-lay

glass of draft beer	birra alla spina **bee**-rah **ah**-lah **spee**-nah
small (11 oz) beer	birra piccola **bee**-rah **pee**-koh-lah
medium (1 pint) beer	birra media **bee**-rah **meh**-dee-ah
large (1 liter) beer	birra grande **bee**-rah **grahn**-day
half-liter bottle	bottiglia da mezzo litro boh-**teel**-yah dah **mehd**-zoh **lee**-troh
shandy (beer with lemon soda)	panachè pah-**nahsh**
low-calorie ("light")	leggera leh-**jeh**-rah
non-alcoholic beer	analcolica ahn-ahl-**koh**-lee-kah

Italians drink mainly lager beers. You'll find local brews (Peroni or Moretti) and imports such as Heineken.

Bar Talk

bar	bar bar
Shall we go for a drink?	Andiamo a prendere qualcosa da bere? ahn-dee-**ah**-moh ah **prehn**-deh-ray kwahl-**koh**-zah dah **beh**-ray
I'll buy you a drink.	Ti offro qualcosa da bere. tee **oh**-froh kwahl-**koh**-zah dah **beh**-ray
It's on me.	Pago io. **pah**-goh **ee**-oh
The next one's on me.	Offro io la prossima. **oh**-froh **ee**-oh lah **proh**-see-mah
What would you like?	Che cosa prendi? kay **koh**-zah **prehn**-dee
I'll have ____.	Prendo ____. **prehn**-doh ____
I don't drink.	Non bevo. nohn **beh**-voh

What is the local specialty?	Qual'è la specialità locale? **kwah**-leh lah speh-chah-lee-**tah** loh-**kah**-lay
Straight.	Liscio. **lee**-shoh
With / Without ice.	Con / Senza ghiaccio. kohn / **sehnt**-sah gee-**ah**-choh (hard "g")
One more.	Un altro. oon **ahl**-troh
Cheers!	Cin cin! cheen cheen

PICNICKING

While you can opt for a one-stop ***supermercato,*** it's more fun to assemble your ***picnic*** (pronounced **peek**-neek) and practice your Italian visiting an ***alimentari*** (small grocery), individual shops, or a ***mercato*** (open-air market).

Is it self-service?	È self-service? eh sehlf-**sehr**-vees
Fifty grams.	Cinquanta grammi. cheeng-**kwahn**-tah **grah**-mee
One hundred grams.	Un etto. oon **eh**-toh
More. / Less.	Di più. / Di meno. dee pew / dee **meh**-noh
A piece.	Un pezzo. oon **pehd**-zoh
A slice.	Una fetta. **oo**-nah **feh**-tah
Four slices.	Quattro fette. **kwah**-troh **feh**-tay
A thin slice.	Una fettina. **oo**-nah feh-**tee**-nah
Cut into slices (fine).	Affettato (sottile). ah-feh-**tah**-toh (soh-**tee**-lay)
Half.	Metà. meh-**tah**
A bunch. (a lot)	Un bel pò. oon behl poh
Enough.	Basta. **bah**-stah
A bag, please.	Un sacchetto, per favore. oon sah-**keh**-toh pehr fah-**voh**-ray
To take out.	Da portar via. dah por-**tar vee**-ah

Ripe for today?	Da mangiare oggi? dah mahn-**jah**-ray **oh**-jee
May I taste it?	Posso assaggiarlo? **poh**-soh ah-sah-**jar**-loh
Does it need to be cooked?	Bisogna cucinarlo prima di mangiarlo? bee-**zohn**-yah koo-chee-**nar**-loh **pree**-mah dee mahn-**jar**-loh
container	contenitore kohn-teh-nee-**toh**-ray
spoon / fork...	cucchiaio / forchetta... koo-kee-ī-yoh / for-**keh**-tah
...made of plastic	...di plastica dee **plah**-stee-kah
cup / plate...	bicchiere / piatto... bee-kee-**eh**-ray / pee-**ah**-toh
...made of paper	...di carta dee **kar**-tah
Do you have a...?	Avete un...? ah-**veh**-tay oon
Where can I buy / find a...?	Dove posso comprare / trovare un...? **doh**-vay **poh**-soh kohm-**prah**-ray / troh-**vah**-ray oon
...corkscrew	...cavatappi kah-vah-**tah**-pee
...can opener	...apriscatole ah-pree-skah-**toh**-lay
...bottle opener	...apribottiglie ah-pree-boh-**teel**-yay

Meat and cheese are sold by the gram. One hundred grams ***(un etto)*** is enough for two sandwiches. When buying cold cuts, you can order by the ***fettina*** (thin slice). For two people, I might get ***cinque fettine*** (five slices) of prosciutto.

At markets, it's customary to let merchants choose produce for you. Say ***per oggi*** (pehr **oh**-jee; for today), and they will grab you something ready to eat.

MENU DECODER

This handy Italian-English decoder won't list every word on the menu, but it will help you get ***trota*** (trout) instead of ***tripa*** (tripe).

Menu Categories

When you pick up a menu, you'll likely see these categories of offerings, and they'll generally appear in this order.

Colazione	Breakfast
Pranzo	Lunch
Cena	Dinner
Antipasti	Appetizers
Piatti Caldi	Hot Dishes
Piatti Freddi	Cold Dishes
Panini	Sandwiches
Insalate	Salads
Minestre / Zuppe	Soups
Menù a Prezzo Fisso	Fixed-Price Meal(s)
Specialità	Specialties
Piatti	Dishes
Primo Piatto (Primi)	First Course(s)
Secondo Piatto (Secondi)	Main Course(s)
Carne	Meat
Pollame	Poultry
Pesce	Fish
Frutti di Mare	Seafood
Contorni	Side Dishes
Riso	Rice Dishes
Verdure	Vegetables
Pane	Bread
(Lista delle) Bevande	Drinks (Menu)
(Lista dei) Vini	Wine (List)
Dolci	Dessert

La Nostra	"Our"
Selezione di...	Selection of...

And for the fine print:

cover charge	coperto
service (not) included	servizio (non) incluso
tax included	I.V.A. inclusa

Small Words

alla / alle / della / delle	in the style of
con / senza	with / without
di	of
e	and
l'etto	price per 100 grams
in	in
-ine, -ette, -elle	small
-one	big
oppure	or
s.q. (secondo quantità)	price according to quantity
su	served over

If you see a phrase that begins with ***alla*** or ***della,*** the next word may not appear in this decoder. That's because these phrases mean "in the style of," and are often flowery, artsy, or obscure descriptions. Even if you knew the exact meaning, it might not make things much clearer.

ITALIAN / ENGLISH

abbacchio alla romana grilled spring lamb chops
abboccato sweet (wine)
acciuga anchovy
acero maple
aceto vinegar
acqua water
acqua del rubinetto tap water
acqua minerale (naturale / effervescente) mineral water (still / carbonated)
affettati cold cuts; cured meats
affettato sliced
affogato poached
affogato al caffè ice cream with coffee
affumicato smoked (often refers to salty smoked fish)
aglio garlic
aglio e olio with garlic and olive oil (pasta)
aglio fresco garlic shoot
agnello lamb
agnolotti stuffed pasta shaped like a "priest's hat"
agrodolce sweet and sour
agrumi citrus
albicocca apricot
albume egg white
alcool alcohol
alfabeto letter-shaped pasta
alfredo butter, cream, and *parmigiano* sauce (pasta)
amabile sweet (wine)
amarena sour cherry
amaro bitter; also a type of digestif
amatriciana sauce of pork cheek, pecorino cheese, and tomato (pasta)
anacardo cashew
analcolica alcohol-free
ananas pineapple
anatra duck
aneto dill
anguilla eel
anguillette in umido stewed baby eels
anguria watermelon
anice anise
animelle (di vitello) sweetbreads (of veal)
annata vintage (wine)
antipasti appetizers
antipasto (frutti) di mare assortment of fish and shellfish
antipasto misto assortment of meats and veggies
arachide peanut
aragosta lobster
arancia orange
arancia rossa blood orange
aranciata orange soda
arancini deep-fried balls of rice, tomato sauce, and mozzarella
aringa / aringhe herring
arista pork loin
arrabbiata "angry," spicy pasta sauce with tomatoes and hot peppers

A

arrosto roasted
arrosto misto assortment of roasted meats
asiago hard, mild cow cheese
asiago mezzano young, firm, and creamy asiago
asiago stravecchio aged, pungent, and granular asiago
asparagi asparagus
assortiti assorted
astice lobster
babà (al rhum) mushroom-shaped, rum-soaked cake
baccalà rehydrated Atlantic salt cod
baccalà alla livornese salt cod with tomato and herbs
baccalà mantecato whipped spread of cod and mayonnaise
bacio chocolate hazelnut candy
barbabietola beet
barbina very skinny spaghetti often coiled into nest-like "beards"
basilico basil
bavette flank steak
bavette / bavettine skinnier tagliatelle
bel paese mild, white, creamy cow cheese
ben cotto / molto ben cotto well-done / very well-done (meat)
bevande beverages
bianco white
bibite beverages
bicchiere glass
bietola chard
bignè (alla crema) (cream) puff
bignole cream puff
bigoli (in salsa) thick pasta strands made of whole wheat or buckwheat (with anchovy sauce)
biologico organic
birra beer
birra alla spina beer on tap
bis split course
biscotto cookie
bistecca (di manzo) (beef) steak
bistecca alla fiorentina Florence-style, very rare T-bone steak
bistecca di fesa di manzo rump steak
bocconcini small balls of mozzarella; also refers to bite-size stew meat
bollente boiling hot
bollito boiled
bollito misto various boiled meats with sauces
bolognese meat and tomato sauce (pasta)
bombolone / bomba filled doughnut
boscaiola mushroom and sausage sauce (pasta and pizza)
(di) bosco wild ("of the forest")
bottarga cured fish roe
bottiglia bottle
(alla) brace broiled
braciola chop
branzino sea bass
brasato braised

bresaola air-cured beef, thinly sliced
brioche sweet roll
broccolo romanesco cross between broccoli and cauliflower
brodo broth
bruciatini cured pork, similar to pancetta
bruciato burned
bruschetta toast brushed with olive oil and garlic or chopped tomatoes
bucatini long, thick, hollow pasta tubes
buccellato wreath-shaped anise-and-raisin bread
budino pudding
burrata soft, creamy mozzarella
burro butter
burro d'arachidi peanut butter
burro e salvia butter and sage (pasta)
bussoli Easter cookies
bustina di tè tea bag
buzzara seafood (often shrimp) and tomato pasta sauce
cacciatora "hunter-style" chicken or rabbit, with red wine, rosemary, garlic, tomato, and often mushrooms
cacio e pepe cheese and pepper (pasta)
caciocavallo semi-hard cow cheese
caciucco Tuscan fish soup
caco persimmon
caffè espresso
caffè americano espresso diluted with hot water (closest to American-style drip coffee)
caffè con panna espresso with a dollop of whipped cream
caffè corretto espresso with a shot of liqueur
caffè corto extra-strong espresso
caffè freddo sweet, iced espresso
caffè latte espresso with hot milk
caffè lungo espresso diluted with some hot water
caffè macchiato espresso with just a splash of milk
caffè schiumato caffè macchiato with extra foam
caffè solubile instant coffee
caffeina caffeine
calamarata "squid"-shaped pasta with spicy tomato sauce and squid
calamari squid
caldo hot
calzone pizza turnover
camomilla chamomile
campanelle "bell"-shaped pasta
canederli large dumplings with ham, liver, spinach, or cheese
cannella cinnamon
cannelloni big, stuffed pasta tube

C

cannoli fried pastry tubes filled with whipped ricotta, candied fruit, and chocolate
cannoncini baked pastry tubes filled with cream
cantucci / cantuccini Tuscan almond cookies
capellini / capelli d'angelo extremely thin spaghetti
capesante scallops
capocollo peppery, air-cured pork shoulder
caponata eggplant and vegetable salad
cappelletti meat-filled dumplings
cappero caper
cappuccino espresso with foamed milk
capra goat
capretto kid (goat)
capricciosa chef's choice; combo
caprino goat cheese
capriolo roe deer
carabaccia Tuscan onion soup
caraffa carafe
caramelle candy
carbonara sauce with bacon, egg, cheese, and pepper (pasta)
carbonella charcoal
carciofi alla giudia artichokes flattened and deep-fried
carciofi alla romana artichokes stuffed with garlic, mint, and parsley
carciofo artichoke
carciofo romanesco giant artichoke
cardamomo cardamom
carne meat
carne bianca white meat
carne di cervo venison
carne equina horse meat
carne in umido meat stew
carne scura dark meat
carota carrot
carpaccio thinly sliced air-cured meat
carrè affumicato pork shank that's smoked then boiled
carrè di rack of
carrettiera spicy sauce with garlic, olive oil, and little tomatoes (pasta)
(al) cartoccio steamed in parchment
(della) casa of the house
casarecce short pasta with S-shaped cross-section
casereccio home-style
cassata ice cream, sponge cake, ricotta, fruit, and pistachios; also a gelato flavor with dried fruits (Sicily)
castagne chestnut
castellane pasta shaped like a castle tower
cavatappi corkscrew; "corkscrew"-shaped pasta
cavatelli croissant-shaped pasta
cavolfiore cauliflower
cavolini di bruxelles Brussels sprouts
cavolo cabbage
cavolo nero Tuscan kale

cavolo riccio kale
cazzotto calzone-like folded pizza
cece chickpea (garbanzo bean)
cecina savory chickpea crëpe
cedro citron (lemon-like citrus fruit)
cellentani corkscrew-shaped pasta
cena dinner
cereali cereal
cereali misti multigrain
cervella brains
cervo deer
cetriolino pickle
cetriolo cucumber
(lo) chef consiglia "the chef recommends"
chiacchiere fritters with powdered sugar
Chianina top-quality Tuscan beef
chiantigiana Chianti-style
chicche small potato dumplings; sometimes describes sweets
chiodo di garofano clove (spice)
ciabatta crusty, flat, rustic bread
ciambella filled doughnut
ciambellone pound cake
cibo food
ciccheti small appetizers (Venice)
ciccioli (frolli) compressed dried pork belly; crispy pork belly
ciliegia cherry
cinese Chinese
cinghiale boar
cioccolata chocolate
cipolla onion
cipollina chive
cippolloti mini-onions marinated in oil
ciuffi tufts
classico wine from a defined, select area
cocciole holly, "seashell"-shaped pasta
cocomero watermelon
coda alla vaccinara oxtail braised with garlic, wine, tomato, and celery
coda di bue oxtail
collo neck
(di) Colonnata best-quality lardo (seasoned lard)
(al) coltello hand-sliced to order
con panna with whipped cream
conchiglie; cocciole hollow, "seashell"-shaped pasta
condito seasoned
congelato frozen
coniglio rabbit
cono cone
conserva preserves
consigliamo "we recommend"
contadina "peasant-style"; rustic
coppa small bowl; also peppery, air-cured pork shoulder
coppa di testa headcheese (organs in aspic)
coriandolo cilantro; coriander
cornetti generic term for pastries
cornetto croissant
corposo full-bodied (wine)

C

corretto, caffè espresso with a shot of liqueur
corto, caffè extra-strong espresso
corzetti pasta that resembles stamped coins
coscia drumstick
cosciotto di agnello leg of lamb
costata rib-eye steak
costoletta rib
cotechino pork sausage
cotoletta chop or cutlet; often a breaded veal chop
cotto cooked; medium (meat)
cotto al forno oven-baked
cotto sul momento cooked on request (à la minute)
cozza mussel
cozze ripiene mussels stuffed with herbs, cheese, and bread crumbs
crauti rossi red-cabbage sauerkraut
crema custard
crème caramel custard with carmelized topping
cremolata mix of slushy ice and gelato
crescenza mild, soft cheese
crescione watercress
crespella baked crêpe, often stuffed with ricotta
croccante crisp; crispy
croccantino "crunchy" gelato flavor with toasted peanut bits
crocchetta croquette (deep-fried mashed potato ball)
crosta crust (bread); rind (cheese)
crostacei shellfish
crostata (di marmellata) tart (with jam)
crostata di ricotta cheesecake-like dessert
crostino toast with pâté
crudo raw; air-cured (prosciutto)
cucina kitchen
culatello air-cured, high-quality prosciutto
cumino cumin
cuoco cook; chef
da portar via to go
daterini sweet cherry tomatoes
dattero date
decaffeinato decaffeinated
deglassato deglazed
delicato mild (cheese)
delizia al limone cake with lemon-flavored whipped cream
dello chef chef's choice
(al) dente cooked firm, "to the tooth" (pasta)
diavola "devil-style," spicy hot; with pepperoni-like salami (pizza)
digestivo digestif (after-dinner drink)
disossato boneless
ditali / ditalini "thimble"-shaped pasta
dolce sweet; dessert
dolci sweets (often sweet rolls)
dolci dal carrello dessert cart
dolcificante artificial sweetener

dozzina dozen
dragoncello tarragon
effervescente carbonated
eliche "propeller"-shaped pasta
emmenthal Swiss cheese
entrecote sirloin steak
erba cipollina chive
erbe herbs
etto 100 grams
extravergine extra virgin (top-quality olive oil)
facile da bere drinkable (wine)
fagiano pheasant
fagioli all'uccelletto "bird-style" beans with tomato and sage
fagiolino green bean; also a green bean-shaped pasta
fagiolo bean
fagiolo lima lima bean
fagottino puff pastry turnover
faraona guinea hen
farcito stuffed
farfalle "butterfly"- or bowtie-shaped pasta
farinata savory chickpea crêpe (Liguria); also a porridge
farro spelt (nutty-tasting grain)
fatto in casa homemade
fava fava bean
fave al guanciale fava beans simmered with cured pork cheek and onion
fedelini thin, long pasta noodle
fegatelli liver meatballs
fegato (patè) liver (pâté)
fegato alla veneziana liver and onions
fettina slice
fettuccine flat egg noodles cut into "small ribbons"
fettuce wider fettucine noodle
fettucelle skinnier fettucine noodle
fico fig
filetto tenderloin; fillet
filetto di baccalà salt cod fried in batter
filone loaf of bread
finocchio fennel
finocchiona salami with fennel seeds
fiorentina "Florence-style"
fiori "flower"-shaped pasta
fiori di zucca fried squash blossoms filled with mozzarella and anchovies
foccacia rustic, flat bread (or a sandwich made with that bread)
foccacina small foccacia sandwich
foglia di vite grape leaf
foglia / verdura a foglia leaf / leafy vegetable
fontina (Val d'Aosta) semi-hard, nutty, Gruyère-style cheese
formaggi, quattro four cheeses (pizza or pasta)
formagglo cheese
formaggio di capra / formaggio di caprino goat cheese
formaggio di fossa cheese aged underground
formaggio di testa headcheese (organs in aspic)

F

formaggio fresco cream cheese
(al) forno oven-baked
fragola strawberry
frangelico hazelnut liqueur
frappè milkshake
frattaglie offal (organs)
freddo cold; iced (coffee drinks)
fresco fresh
fricassea fricassee
frittata omelet
frittata con le erbe eggs pan-cooked with fresh herbs
frittella fritter
fritti little deep-fried snacks
fritto fried
fritto misto deep-fried calamari, prawns, and assorted small fish
frittole small doughnuts eaten during Carnevale
frittura deep-fried food
frizzante sparkling
frullato di frutta fruit smoothie
frumento wheat
frutta fruit
fruttato fruity (young wine)
frutti di bosco berries
frutti di mare seafood
(ai) funghi (with) mushrooms
fungo mushroom
fungo porcino porcini mushroom
fusilli spiral-shaped pasta
fusilli bucati long, tightly coiled hollow pasta
fuso melted
galletti pasta shaped like a rooster's comb; chanterelle mushrooms
galletto cockerel (rooster)
gamberetto small shrimp
gambero shrimp
gambero di fiume crayfish
gamberone big shrimp
garganelli flat egg pasta rolled into a tube
gassata carbonated
gattafin deep-fried pastry filled with greens
gelatina jelly
gelato ice cream
gemelli pasta shaped like a double helix ("twins")
genovese with pesto sauce; with a thick crust (pizza)
ghiacciato chilled
ghiaccio ice
gigli conical "lily"-shaped pasta
(del) giorno (of the) day
giovane young (wine)
girasole sunflower; also a ravioli shape
glassato glazed
glutine gluten
gnocchi little potato dumplings
gomiti "elbow" macaroni
gorgonzola blue cheese
grana padano grainy, hard cheese, similar to *parmigiano-reggiano* but a cheaper version
granchio crab
grande large
granita flavored shaved ice
granoturco corn
grappa brandy distilled from fermented grapes

grasso cooking fat
(al) gratin topped with browned cheese
gratinate au gratin (with melted cheese)
grattachecca slushy ice with sweet syrup
grattuggiato grated
gricia with cured pork and *pecorino romano* cheese (pasta)
griglia grilled
grissini breadsticks
groviera Swiss cheese
guanciale tender, air-cured pork cheek
guarnizione garnish
guscio shell; peel; rind
gusto flavor (gelato)
gustoso flavorful; heavy (wine)
Hag decaffeinated coffee
impanato breaded
impepata (di cozze) mussel soup (with mussels in the shell)
importato imported
incluso included
indivia endive
insalata salad
insalata caprese salad of sliced tomato, mozzarella, and basil
insalata di mare seafood salad
insalata mista mixed salad
insalata russa vegetable salad with mayonnaise
insalata verde green salad
integrale whole-grain
involtini stuffed; rolls, wraps; meat or fish fillets with fillings
involtini al sugo veal cutlets rolled with prosciutto and cheese in tomato sauce
inzimino marinated in tomatoes and greens
ippoglosso halibut
kaiserschmarrn eggy crêpe with raisins, jam, and powdered sugar
kasher kosher
lampone raspberry
lampredotto cow's stomach
lardellato larded
lardo (di Colonnata) strips of seasoned lard (top-quality)
latte milk
latte fresco fresh milk
latte intero whole milk
latte macchiato hot milk and foam, layered in a tall glass, "marked" by an espresso shot
latte magro skim milk
latticini dairy products
lattuga lettuce
lattuga romana Romaine lettuce
leggermente mild; mildly
leggero light (not heavy)
legume pulses
lenticchia lentil
lepre / sugo di lepre hare / rich sauce with hare
(su) letto on a bed of
lieviti breakfast pastries
lievito yeast
limonata lemon soda
limoncello lemon liqueur
limone lemon

L

lingua tongue
linguettine skinny linguine
linguine narrow, flat spaghetti
liquirizia licorice
locale local
lombarda, zuppa Tuscan bean soup
lombatina sirloin
lombo / lombata loin
lonzino air-cured pork loin
luccio pike
lumaca snail
lungo, caffè espresso diluted with water
maccheroni tube-shaped pasta
macchiato, caffè espresso with a splash of milk
macchiato, latte hot milk and foam, layered in a tall glass, "marked" by an espresso shot
macedonia fruit salad
macinato minced
mafalde / mafaldine wide, flat, rectangular noodles ruffled on both sides
maggiorana marjoram
maiale pork
maiale sotto sale salt pork
maionese mayonnaise
mais sweet corn
malaga gelato flavor resembling rum raisin
maltagliati "roughly cut" pasta
mandarino tangerine
mandorla almond
mango mango
manicotti big, stuffed pasta tube
manzo beef
margarina margarine
margherita with tomato sauce, mozzarella, and basil (pizza)
marinara tomato sauce—on pasta, sometimes with seafood; on pizza, without cheese
marinato marinated
marmellata jam
marocchino "Moroccan" coffee with espresso, foamed milk, and cocoa powder
(al) Marsala sweet Marsala wine sauce
marziani pasta spirals resembling "Martian" antennae
mascarpone sweet, buttery dessert cheese
maturo mature (wine)
mela apple
mela cotogna quince
melanzana eggplant
melograno pomegranate
melone cantaloupe; melon
melone d'inverno honeydew melon
menta mint
menù del giorno menu of the day
menù fisso fixed-price meal
meridionale southern Italian
meringa meringue
merluzzo cod
mezzani hollow, tubular pasta
mezzano young, firm, creamy asiago cheese

mezzelune stuffed pasta shaped like "half-moons"
mezzo half
midollo marrow; marrowbone
miele honey
millefoglie layers of sweet, buttery pastry
minestra soup
minestrone classic Italian vegetable soup
mirtillo blueberry
missoltino salted, air-dried shad-like lake fish
misticanza mixed green salad of arugula, curly endive, and anchovies
misto mixed; assorted
mocaccino espresso with foamed milk and chocolate
moleche col pien fried soft-shell crabs
mollusco shellfish
montone mutton
mora blackberry
morbido soft (cheese); smooth (wine)
mortadella baloney-like pork loaf
moscardino (bianco) octopus
mostaccioli "moustache"-like penne pasta
mozzarella (di bufala) mozzarella cheese (from water buffalo milk)
napoletana / napoli with mozzarella, anchovies, and tomato sauce (pizza)
nasello hake (whitefish)
naturale still (bottled water)
'nduja spicy, spreadable salami
nero black
nero di seppia cuttlefish ink
nocciola hazelnut
nocciolina peanut
noce walnut
noce di cocco coconut
noce moscata nutmeg
nocino walnut liqueur
nodino knuckle
norma tomato, eggplant, and ricotta cheese sauce (pasta)
oca goose
oggi today
olio oil
oliva olive
olive con peperoni olives stuffed with red hot peppers
olive nero black olives
olive verde very green olives
omelette omelet
orata bream (fish)
orecchiette "ear"-shaped pasta
origano oregano
(dell') ortolano "green grocer-style," with vegetables
orzo tiny, barley-shaped pasta; barley
ossi di morto "bones of the dead" Tuscan cookies
ossobuco (alla genovese) veal shank (braised in broth with vegetables)
ostricha oyster
otto "8"-shaped pastry

paccheri short, very wide pasta tubes
pagliata / pajata calf intestines
pallina scoop (ice cream)
palombo dogfish
pan di spagna sponge cake
pancetta salt-cured pork belly meat
pancetta arrotolata pancetta rolled into a tight, sausage-like bundle and sliced
pane bread; rolls
pane alle olive olive bread
pane aromatico herb or vegetable bread
pane bianco white bread
pane casereccio home-style bread
pane di segale rye bread
pane integrale whole-grain bread
pane scuro brown bread
pane toscano rustic bread made without salt
panettone Milanese yeast cake with raisins and candied fruit (Christmas)
panforte dense fruit and nut cake
panificio bakery
panini farciti premade sandwiches
panino roll; baguette sandwich
panna cream; whipped cream
panna cotta custard-like dessert, served with berries or other toppings
pansotti ravioli with ricotta and greens
panzanella bread salad with tomatoes
panzerotto calzone-like folded pizza
papaia papaya
pappa al pomodoro soup of tomatoes, olive oil, and bread
pappardelle very wide, flat noodles
parmigiana with tomato, cheese and breadcrumbs
parmigiano-reggiano hard, sharp, aged cow cheese
passito sweet dessert wine
pasta e fagioli bean and pasta soup
pasta fresca fresh-made pasta
pasta secca dry-stored pasta
pasta sfoglia puff pastry
paste sweet rolls (Florence); plural of "pasta"
pasticcino pastry
pasticcio di carne hash
pasticciotto small custard pie
pastina small soup noodle
patata potato
patate arrosto roasted potatoes
patate fritte French fries
patate sabbiose deep-fried potato chunks
patè di fegato chicken liver paste
pecora sheep
pecorino ewe cheese

pecorino fresco fresh, soft, mild ewe cheese
pecorino romano hard, aged ewe cheese
pecorino stagionato aged, sharp ewe cheese
pellizzoni thicker spaghetti
penne angle-cut pasta tubes
pennette smaller penne
pennoni larger penne
pepato with pepper
pepe pepper (spice)
pepe di caienna cayenne pepper
peperonata peppers with tomato sauce
peperoncino hot chili pepper
peperone bell pepper
peposo highly peppered beef stew
pera pear
perciatelli hollow, tubular pasta noodles
pernice partridge
pesante heavy (rich, hard to digest)
pesca peach
pescatore seafood sauce ("fisherman-style")
pesce fish
pesce lupo catfish
pesce spada swordfish
pesce spada alla ghiotta swordfish with tomatoes, olives, and capers
pesto basil and pine nut sauce
petto (di ____) breast (of ____)
pezzo piece
piacentino di enna hard, spicy sheep cheese with saffron and pepper
(a) piacere to order (as you like)
piadina stuffed, soft, flat bread
piatto plate
piatto di formaggi misti cheese plate
piccante spicy hot
piccione / piccioncino squab (young pigeon)
piccolo small
pici hand-rolled thick pasta strands
pieno full-bodied (wine)
pignolo macaroon
pinolo pine nut
pisello pea
pistacchio pistachio
pizza al taglio pizza by the slice
pizza bianca "white" pizza (no tomato sauce)
pizza ciaccina Tuscan "white" pizza (no tomato sauce)
pizza rustica "rustic" pizza, sold by weight
pizzelle thin, delicate waffle cookie
pizzoccheri short, thick buckwheat tagliatelle
platessa plaice (whitefish)
poche calorie low calorie
polenta slow-cooked cornmeal
pollame poultry
pollastrella game hen
pollo chicken

pollo alla cacciatora "hunter-style" chicken with red wine, rosemary, garlic, tomato, and often mushrooms
polpa di riccio sea urchin
polpo octopus
pomodorino vesuvio very sweet cherry tomatoes
pomodoro tomato
pomodoro gratinato tomatoes grilled and dusted with breadcrumbs
pompelmo grapefruit
pompelmo rosa pink grapefuit
porchetta roast suckling pig
porcini porcini mushroom
porro leek
prezzemolo parsley
prezzo al peso priced by the weight
prezzo di mercato market price
profiterole cream-filled pastry with warm chocolate sauce
prosciutto cured ham
prosciutto cotto cooked ham
prosciutto crudo air-cured ham
prosciutto di Parma top-quality prosciutto
prosciutto dolce "sweet" (less salty) air-cured ham
prosciutto e melone / fichi air-cured ham wrapped around melon / fresh figs
prosciutto salato "salty" air-cured ham
prosciutto toscano dark and salty air-cured ham
provolone / provola rich, firm, aged cow cheese
prugna prune
puntarella curly endive served with anchovy dressing
purè di patate mashed potatoes
puro pure
puttanesca "harlot"-style tomato sauce with anchovies, olives, and capers (pasta)
quaglia quail
quattro formaggi four cheeses (pizza or pasta)
quattro stagioni with four separate toppings (pizza)
quinto quarto offal ("fifth quarter")
radiatore radiator-shaped pasta
radicchio bitter, deep-purple lettuce
radice root
rafano horseradish
ragù meaty tomato sauce (pasta)
ragusano semi-hard cow cheese
rana pescatrice monkfish
rapa turnip
ravanello radish
ribes nero black currant
ribes rosso red currant
ribollita "reboiled" stew of white beans, veggies, bread, and olive oil
ricciarelli white macaroon-and-almond cookie
riccio di mare sea urchin ("sea hedgehog")
ricoperto coated

ricotta white cheese resembling cottage cheese
rigatino croccante crispy bacon (Tuscany)
rigatoncini shorter rigatoni
rigatoni "ridged," square-cut pasta tubes
ripassate sautéed with garlic and olive oil (usually a green vegetable)
ripieno stuffed; filled
risi e bisi rice and peas (Venice)
riso rice
riso basmati basmati rice
riso condito seasoned rice
riso integrale brown rice
riso jasmine jasmine rice
risotto short-grain rice, simmered in broth
risotto ai porcini simmered rice with porcini mushrooms
risotto al nero di seppia rice simmered in cuttlefish ink
risotto alla milanese simmered rice with saffron
rocciata apple strudel with raisins
rognone kidney
romana "Roman style"
rombo turbot (flounder-like fish)
rosa rose
rosato rosé (wine)
rosmarino rosemary
rosolato browned
rospo frogfish (small marine fish)
rosso red
rotelli "wagon wheel"-shaped pasta
rotini short, spiral-shaped pasta
rubinetto, acqua del tap water
russa, insalata vegetable salad with mayonnaise
sagnarelli thick, flat, short noodles with wavy edges
salame cured sausage, sometimes spicy
salame di Sant'Olcese Genoa salami
salame piccante spicy salami (similar to American pepperoni)
salamino small salami
salato salty
sale salt
salmone salmon
salmone in bellavista braised salmon, usually elegantly presented
salsa bruna gravy
salsa di pomodoro tomato and garlic sauce
salsiccia link sausage
saltato sautéed ("skipped")
saltimbocca alla romana thinly sliced sautéed veal layered with prosciutto and sage
salumi cold cuts
salumi misti assortment of sliced, cured meats
salvia sage
sambuca anise liqueur
(al) sangue / molto al sangue rare / very rare (meat)
sanguinaccio blood sausage

saporito sharp (cheese)
sarda / sardina sardine
sarde in saor sardines marinated with onions
sbrisolona / sbriciolona crumbly; can refer to crumble cake and / or a less-aged, "crumbly" fennel salami
scaldato toasted
scalogno shallot
scaloppine thin-sliced veal
scamerita (di maiale) pork shoulder
scamorza mozzarella-like cow cheese, often smoked
scampi prawns
scarola escarole
schiacciata thin, "squashed" bread sprinkled with sea salt and olive oil
schiuma milky foam on espresso
sciachetrà sweet dessert wine
scialatelli like linguine, but squared instead of rounded
scoglio pasta sauce with mussels, clams, and tomatoes
scottaditto "scorch your fingers" (can't wait to eat them)
scottato blanched
scremato skimmed
secco dry (wine)
selvaggina game
selvatico wild-grown
seme seed
semifreddo frozen mousse-like dessert
semola semolina
senape mustard
senza glutine gluten-free
seppia cuttlefish, sometimes squid
seppie al nero cuttlefish served in its own ink
sfoglia puff pastry, often filled with fruit
sfogliatella crispy pastry filled with sweet ricotta
sformato / sformatino casserole
sfornato baked
sfusato juicy lemon (Amalfi Coast)
sgombro scad (like mackerel)
sgroppino after-dinner drink of vodka and lemon gelato
sgusciato peeled (shellfish)
siciliana with capers, olives, and often anchovies (pizza)
sogliola sole (fish)
soppressata in the south, a coarsely ground, spicy salami; in Tuscany *(soppressata toscana)*, headcheese
sorbetto sherbet
sorrentina "Sorrento-style," pasta sauce with tomatoes, basil, and mozzarella
sott'aceto pickled
sott'oli pickled
sovracoscia thigh (poultry)
spaghetti alla chitarra spaghetti cut with a stringed ("guitar") device
spaghettini skinny spaghetti
spaghettoni thicker spaghetti

spagnolo Spanish-style (spicy) salami
spalla shoulder (of beef, pork, lamb)
spalla di manzo beef chuck
specialità specialty
speck smoked, thinly sliced pork shoulder
sperlano smelt
spezia spice
speziato spicy (flavorful)
spezzatino stew
spiedini alla griglia grilled on a skewer
spiedino skewer
spigola bass
spigoloso sharp (wine)
(alla) spina from the tap (beer)
spinaci spinach
spirali / spiralini "spiral"-shaped tube of pasta
spremuta freshly squeezed juice
spritz white wine and liquor spritzer
spuntino snack
stagionato aged, sharp, and hard (cheese)
(di) stagione seasonal
stinco shank (leg meat)
straccetti sautéed slices of meat with arugula and tomatoes or mushrooms
stracchino spreadable, soft cow cheese
stracciatella vanilla gelato with shreds of chocolate
stracciatella alla romana egg-drop meat broth topped with *parmigiano* cheese
strangolapreti twisted pasta
strapazzate scrambled
strascicate sautéed (with meat sauce); scrambled
stravecchio well-aged (cheese)
stringozzi "shoestring"-shaped pasta noodles
stricchetti bow-tie pasta
strozzapreti pasta shaped like a priest's collar ("priest-strangler")
stufato (di agnello) (lamb) stew
stuzzicadente toothpick
su letto on a bed of
succo juice
succoso juicy
sughetto gravy; sauce
(al) sugo with sauce (usually tomato)
suppli deep-fried balls of rice, tomato sauce, and mozzarella
suprema (di pollo) (chicken) breast with cream sauce
susina plum
tacchino turkey
tagliata thin slices of grilled tenderloin, typically on bed of arugula
tagliatelle wide, flat noodles
tagliere wooden platter with meats and cheeses
taglierini thinner tagliatelle noodles
(al) taglio by the slice

taleggio rich, creamy, cow cheese
tannico tannic (wine)
tartina canapé
tartine farcite finger sandwiches
tartufata with truffles
tartufo truffle
tartufo (con panna) dark-chocolate gelato ball with a cherry inside (and whipped cream on top)
tavola calda buffet-style eatery
tazza cup
tazzina small coffee cup
tè tea
tè agli agrumi citrus tea
tè al limone lemon tea
tè alla frutta fruit tea
tè alla menta mint tea
tè freddo iced tea
tè nero black tea
tè verde green tea
tegame alla Vernazza anchovies served with potatoes, tomatoes, white wine, oil, and herbs
temperatura ambiente room temperature
terroso earthy
testa head
testa in cassetta / coppa di testa / formaggio di testa headcheese (organs in aspic)
testicolo testicle
tiepido lukewarm
timo thyme
tiramisù espresso-soaked cake with chocolate, cream, and Marsala
tisana herbal tea
tomino goat cheese
tonno tuna
torchietti "torch"-shaped pasta
torello bullock (young bull)
torrefazione roasted
torrone nougat and almond sweet
torta cake; pie
torta de ceci savory chickpea crêpe
torta della nonna custard tart with pine nuts
torta di mele apple cake
torta di ricotta ricotta cake with chocolate chips
torta salata quiche
tortelli / tordelli small, C-shaped pasta filled with meat or cheese
tortellini smaller tortelli
tortelloni larger tortelli
tortiglioni narrow rigatoni pasta
toscana "Tuscan style"; also chicken-liver paste
totani squid
tovagliolo napkin
tramezzini small, crustless sandwiches
trancia slice
trenette long, flat, thin noodle similar to linguine
triglia red mullet (fish)
tripoline long, flat, thick noodle ruffled on one side

trippa tripe
trippa alla fiorentina tripe and vegetables sautéed in a tomato sauce, sometimes baked with *parmigiano-reggiano*
trippa alla romana tripe braised with onions, carrots, and mint
tritato / trito chopped
trofie / trofiette twisted noodle
trota trout
tuorlo egg yolk
umbria pasta sauce of anchovies, garlic, tomatoes, and truffles
umbricelli thick, chewy, rolled pasta
(in) umido stewed
ungherese Hungarian-style (smoky) salami
uova di galline allevate a terra free-range eggs
uova di pesce fish roe
uova di riccio di mare sea urchin roe
uova fritte fried eggs
uova strapazzate scrambled eggs
uovo egg
uovo alla coque (molle / sodo) boiled egg (soft / hard)
uovo in camicia poached egg
uva grape
uvetta raisin
Valtellina, bresaola della best-quality air-cured beef
vaniglia vanilla
(al) vapore steamed
vegetariano vegetarian
veloce fast
vendemmia harvest (wine)
ventriglio gizzard
verace authentic; fresh
verde green
verdura vegetable
vermicelli long noodles slightly thicker than spaghetti
vermicelloni thicker vermicelli
verza cabbage
viennese with tomato, mozzarella, and German-style sausage (pizza)
vigneto vineyard
Vin Santo sweet dessert wine
vino wine
vino da tavola table wine
vino della casa house wine
vino riserva high-quality, aged wine
vino selezionato select wine (good year)
vino sfuso house wine in a jug
visciola sour cherry
vitello veal
vitello di mare porbeagle shark ("sea veal"), similar to swordfish
vitello milanese breaded and pan-fried veal cutlet
vitello tonnato thin-sliced roasted veal with tuna-caper mayonnaise
vongola clam
wurstel hot dog; German-style sausage

zabaglione custard dessert of egg yolks, sugar, and sweet wine
zafferano saffron
zampone sausage-stuffed pig's leg
zenzero ginger
zeppola deep-fried doughnut filled with oozing custard
ziti long, hollow pasta tubes
zucca summer squash
zucca gialla yellow pumpkin
zucca invernale winter squash
zucchero sugar
zucchero di canna brown sugar
zucchina zucchini
zuppa soup
zuppa alla volterrana stew of white beans, veggies, bread, and olive oil
zuppa di pesce fish soup or stew
zuppa inglese trifle (rum-soaked cake layered with whipped cream and fruit)
zuppa lombarda Tuscan bean soup

SIGHTSEEING

WHERE?

Where is the...?	Dov'è...? doh-**veh**
Where are the...?	Dove sono...? **doh**-vay **soh**-noh
tourist information office	l'ufficio informazioni loo-**fee**-choh een-for-maht-see-**oh**-nee
toilet	la toilette lah twah-**leh**-tay
main square	la piazza principale lah pee-**aht**-sah preen-chee-**pah**-lay
old town center	il centro storico eel **chehn**-troh **stoh**-ree-koh
entrance	l'entrata lehn-**trah**-tah
exit	l'uscita loo-**shee**-tah
town hall	il municipio eel moo-nee-**chee**-pee-oh
museum	il museo eel moo-**zeh**-oh
art gallery	galleria d'arte gah-leh-**ree**-ah **dar**-tay
painting gallery	pinacoteca pee-nah-koh-**teh**-kah
cathedral	il duomo / la cattedrale eel **dwoh**-moh / lah kah-teh-**drah**-lay
church	la chiesa lah kee-**eh**-zah
castle	il castello eel kah-**steh**-loh
palace	il palazzo eel pah-**lahd**-zoh
best view	la vista più bella lah **vee**-stah pew **beh**-lah
viewpoint	il punto panoramico eel **poon**-toh pah-noh-**rah**-mee-koh

A major town square can be called a ***piazza*** or ***campo,*** while a smaller square might be a ***piazzetta*** or ***campiello.***

AT SIGHTS

Tickets and Discounts

ticket office	biglietteria beel-yeh-teh-**ree**-yah
ticket	biglietto beel-**yeh**-toh
combo-ticket	biglietto cumulativo beel-**yeh**-toh koo-moo-lah-**tee**-voh
reduced ticket	biglietto ridotto beel-**yeh**-toh ree-**doh**-toh
museum pass	pass per più musei pahs pehr pew moo-**zeh**-ee
price	prezzo **prehd**-zoh
discount	sconti **skohn**-tee
Is there a discount for...?	Fate sconti per...? **fah**-tay **skohn**-tee pehr
...children	...bambini bahm-**bee**-nee
...youths	...giovani **joh**-vah-nee
...students	...studenti stoo-**dehn**-tee
...families	...famiglie fah-**meel**-yay
...seniors	...anziani ahnt-see-**ah**-nee
...groups	...comitive koh-mee-**tee**-vay
I am...	Io ho... **ee**-oh oh
He / She is...	Lui / Lei ha... **loo**-ee / **leh**-ee ah
... ____ years old.	... ____ anni. ____ **ahn**-nee
...extremely old.	...vecchissimo(a). veh-**kee**-see-moh
reservation	prenotazione preh-noh-taht-see-**oh**-nay
Is it possible to make a reservation?	Si può prenotare? see pwoh preh-noh-**tah**-ray
How do I make a reservation?	Come si prenota? **koh**-may see preh-**noh**-tah
What time?	A che ora? ah kay **oh**-rah
Where?	Dove? **doh**-vay

Key Phrases: Sightseeing

ticket	biglietto beel-**yeh**-toh
How much is it?	Quanto costa? **kwahn**-toh **koh**-stah
Is there a guided tour in English?	Avete una visita guidata in inglese? ah-**veh**-tay **oo**-nah vee-**zee**-tah gwee-**dah**-tah een een-**gleh**-zay
When?	Quando? **kwahn**-doh
What time does this open / close?	A che ora apre / chiude? ah kay **oh**-rah **ah**-pray / kee-**oo**-day

Is the ticket good all day?	È valido per tutto il giorno? eh **vah** lee doh pehr **too**-toh eel **jor**-noh
Can I get back in?	Posso rientrare? **poh**-soh ree-ehn-**trah**-ray

For some very crowded museums (such as Florence's Uffizi Gallery or Rome's Vatican Museum), it's possible to make reservations online, and sometimes by phone. Ask locals or check your guidebook for details—it could save you hours in line.

Some cities sell admission passes that let you skip ticket-buying lines at multiple museums. At some popular places (such as Rome's Colosseum or Venice's Doge's Palace), you can get in more quickly by buying your ticket or pass at a less-crowded sight.

Information and Tours

information	informazioni een-for-maht-see-**oh**-nee
tour	tour toor
tour guide	guida turistica **gwee**-dah too-**ree**-stee-kah
in English	in inglese een een-**gleh**-zay

Is there a...?	C'è una...? cheh **oo**-nah
...city walking tour	...visita guidata della città **vee**-zee-tah gwee-**dah**-tah **deh**-lah chee-**tah**
...guided tour	...visita guidata **vee**-zee-tah gwee-**dah**-tah
...audioguide	...audioguida ow-dee-oh-**gwee**-dah
...city guidebook	...guida della città **gwee**-dah **deh**-lah chee-**tah**
...museum guidebook	...guida del museo **gwee**-dah dehl moo-**zeh**-oh
Is it free?	È gratis? eh **grah**-tees
How much is it?	Quanto costa? **kwahn**-toh **koh**-stah
How long does it last?	Quanto dura? **kwahn**-toh **doo**-rah
When is the next tour in English?	Quando è il prossimo tour in inglese? **kwahn**-doh eh eel **proh**-see-moh toor een een-**gleh**-zay

Some sights are tourable only by groups with a guide ***(guida turistica).*** At other sights, booking a guided tour can help you avoid lines. Individuals usually end up on the next Italian tour. To get an English tour, call in advance or check online to see if one's scheduled. You may be able to tag along with a large tour group.

Visiting Sights

opening times	orario d'apertura oh-**rah**-ree-oh dah-pehr-**too**-rah
last entry	ultimo ingresso **ool**-tee-moh een-**greh**-soh
What time does this open / close?	A che ora apre / chiude? ah kay **oh**-rah **ah**-pray / kee-**oo**-day

When is the last entry?	Quando è l'ultimo ingresso? **kwahn**-doh eh **lool**-tee-moh een-**greh**-soh
Do I have to check this / this bag?	Devo lasciare questo / questa borsa? **deh**-voh lah-**shah**-ray **kweh**-stoh / **kweh**-stah **bor**-sah
bag check	deposito per le borse deh-**poh**-zee-toh pehr lay **bor**-say
floor plan	planta pee-**ahn**-tah
floor	piano pee-**ah**-noh
room / large room	sala / salone **sah**-lah / sah-**loh**-nay
collection	collezione koh-leht-see-**oh**-nay
exhibit / exhibition...	esposizione / mostra... eh-spoh-zeet-see-**oh**-nay / **moh**-strah
...temporary / special	...temporanea / speciale tehm-poh-**rah**-neh-ah / speh-**chah**-lay
...permanent	...permanente pehr-mah-**nehn**-tay
café	bar bar
elevator	ascensore ah-shehn-**soh**-ray
toilet	toilette twah-**leh**-tay
Where is ____?	Dov'è ____? doh-**veh** ____
I'd like to see ____.	Mi piacerebbe vedere ____. mee pee-ah-cheh-**reh**-bay veh-**deh**-ray ____
Photo / Video OK?	Foto / Video è OK? **foh**-toh / **vee**-deh-oh eh "OK"
flash / tripod	flash / treppiede "flash" / treh-pee-**eh**-day
Will you take my / our photo?	Mi / Ci fa una foto? mee / chee fah **oo**-nah **foh**-toh
Please let me / us in. (if room or sight is closing)	Per favore, mi / ci faccia entrare. pehr fah-**voh**-ray mee / chee **fah**-chah ehn-**trah**-ray
I promise I'll be fast.	Prometto che sarò veloce. proh-**meh**-toh kay sah-**roh** veh-**loh**-chay

It was my mother's dying wish that I see this.	Ho promesso a mia madre sul letto di morte che avrei visto questo. oh proh-**meh**-soh ah **mee**-ah **mah**-dray sool **leh**-toh dee **mor**-tay kay ah-**vreh**-ee **vee**-stoh **kweh**-stoh

Once at the sight, get your bearings by viewing the ***pianta*** (floor plan). ***Voi siete qui*** means "You are here." Many museums have an official, one-way route that all visitors take—just follow signs for ***percorso della visita*** (direction of visit).

RECREATION AND ENTERTAINMENT

RECREATION

Outdoor Fun

Where is the best place for...?	Dov'è il posto migliore per...? doh-**veh** eel **poh**-stoh meel-**yoh**-ray pehr
...biking	...andare in bicicletta ahn-**dah**-ray een bee-chee-**kleh**-tah
...walking	...passeggiare pah-seh-**jah**-ray
...hiking	...fare trekking / fare escursioni **fah**-ray **treh**-keeng / **fah**-ray eh-skoor-see-**oh**-nee
...running	...correre koh-**reh**-ray
...picnicking	...fare un picnic **fah**-ray oon **peek**-neek
...sunbathing	...prendere il sole **prehn**-deh-ray eel **soh**-lay
Where is...?	Dov'è...? doh-**veh**
...a park	...un parco oon **par**-koh
...playground equipment	...parco giochi **par**-koh **joh**-kee
...a snack shop	...un bar oon bar
...the toilet	...la toilette lah twah-**leh**-tay
Where can I rent...?	Dove posso noleggiare...? **doh**-vay **poh**-soh noh-leh-**jah**-ray
...a bike	...una bici / bicicletta **oo**-nah **bee**-chee / bee-chee-**kleh**-tah
...that	...quello **kweh**-loh

What's a fun activity...?	Qual'è un'attività divertente...? kwah-**leh** oon-ah-tee-vee-**tah** dee-vehr-**tehn**-tay
...for a boy / a girl...	...per un bambino / una bambina... pehr oon bahm-**bee**-noh / **oo**-nah bahm-**bee**-nah
... ____ years old	...di ____ anni dee ____ **ahn**-nee

At most parks, people—usually men—play ***bocce*** (**boh**-chay): Players take turns tossing croquet-size balls into a dirt playing area, with the object of getting them close to the target, a small wooden ball ***(pallino).***

Swimming

Where is a...?	Dov'è un / una...? doh-**veh** oon / **oo**-nah
...swimming pool	...piscina pee-**shee**-nah
...water park	...parco acquatico **par**-koh ah-**kwah**-tee-koh
...(good) beach	...(bella) spiaggia (**beh**-lah) spee-**ah**-jah
...nude beach	...spiaggia nudista spee-**ah**-jah noo-**dee**-stah
Is it safe for swimming?	È sicuro fare un bagno? eh see-**koo**-roh **fah**-ray oon **bahn**-yoh

Bicycling

bicycle / bike	bicicletta / bici bee-chee-**kleh**-tah / **bee**-chee
I'd like to rent a bicycle.	Vorrei noleggiare una bicicletta. voh-**reh**-ee noh-leh-**jah**-ray **oo**-nah bee-chee-**kleh**-tah
two bicycles	due biciclette **doo**-ay bee-chee-**kleh**-tay

Renting

Whether you're renting a bike or a boat, here's what to ask.

Where can I rent a...?	Dove posso noleggiare una...? **doh**-vay **poh**-soh noh-leh-**jah**-ray **oo**-nah
Can I rent a...?	Posso noleggiare una...? **poh**-soh noh-leh-**jah**-ray **oo**-nah
...bike	...bicicletta bee-chee-**kleh**-tah
...boat	...barca **bar**-kah
How much per...?	Quanto costa...? **kwahn**-toh **koh**-stah
...hour	...all'ora ah-**loh**-rah
...half-day	...per mezza giornata pehr **mehd**-zah jor-**nah**-tah
...day	...al giorno ahl **jor**-noh
Is a deposit required?	Ci vuole un deposito? chee **vwoh**-lay oon deh-**poh**-zee-toh

kid's bike	bicicletta da bambino(a) bee-chee-**kleh**-tah dah bahm-**bee**-noh
mountain bike	mountain bike "mountain bike"
helmet	casco **kah**-skoh
map	cartina kar-**tee**-nah
lock	lucchetto loo-**keh**-toh
chain	catena kah-**teh**-nah
pedal	pedale peh-**dah**-lay
wheel	ruota roo-**oh**-tah
tire	gomma **goh**-mah
air / no air	aria / senza aria **ah**-ree-ah / **sehnt**-sah **ah**-ree-ah
pump	pompa **pohm**-pah
brakes	freni **freh**-nee

How does this work?	Come funziona? **koh**-may foont-see-**oh**-nah
How many gears?	Quante marce? **kwahn**-tay **mar**-chay
Is there a bike path?	C'è una pista ciclabile? cheh **oo**-nah **pee**-stah chee-**klah**-bee-lay
I don't like hills or traffic.	Non mi piacciono le salite nè il traffico. nohn mee pee-ah-**choh**-noh lay sah-**lee**-tay neh eel **trah**-fee-koh
I brake for bakeries.	Mi fermo ad ogni pasticceria. mee **fehr**-moh ahd **ohn**-yee pah-stee-cheh-**ree**-ah

Way to Go!

Whether you're biking or hiking, you'll want to know the best way to go.

Can you recommend a route / hike that is...?	Può raccomandare un'itinerario / un'escursione...? pwoh rah-koh-mahn-**dah**-ray oon-ee-tee-neh-**rah**-ree-oh / oon-eh-skoor-see-**oh**-nay
...easy	...facile **fah**-chee-lay
...moderate	...moderato moh-deh-**rah**-toh
...strenuous	...faticoso fah-tee-**koh**-zoh
...safe	...sicuro see-**koo**-roh
...scenic	...panoramico pah-noh-**rah**-mee-koh
...about ____ kilometers	...circa ____ chilometri **cheer**-kah ____ kee-**loh**-meh-tree
How many minutes / hours?	Quante minuti / ore? **kwahn**-tay mee-**noo**-tee / **oh**-ray
uphill / level / downhill	salita / in pianura / discesa sah-**lee**-tah / een pee-ah-**noo**-rah / dee-**sheh**-zah

Hiking

hiking	escursione / trekking eh-skoor-see-**oh**-nay / **treh**-keeng
a hike	un'escursione oon-eh-skoor-see-**oh**-nay
trail	sentiero sehn-tee-**eh**-roh
Where can I buy a...?	Dove posso comprare una...? **doh**-vay **poh**-soh kohm-**prah**-ray **oo**-nah
...hiking map	...cartina dei sentieri kar-**tee**-nah **deh**-ee sehn-tee-**eh**-ree
...compass	...bussola **boo**-soh-lah
Where's the trailhead?	Dov'è il punto di partenza del sentiero? doh-**veh** eel **poon**-toh dee par-**tehnt**-sah dehl sehn-tee-**eh**-roh
How do I get there?	Come ci arrivo? **koh**-may chee ah-**ree**-voh

Most hiking trails are well-marked with signs listing the destination and duration (***ore di cammino,*** literally "hours of walking") or length of the trail ***(lunghezza del percorso).*** Some signs have abbreviations for the degree of difficulty:

T = tourist trail, easy
E = longer, more varied, marked along the way
EE = for experts
EEA = for experts with equipment

ENTERTAINMENT

event guide	guida agli eventi **gwee**-dah **ahl**-yee eh-**vehn**-tee
What's happening tonight?	Che cosa succede stasera? kay **koh**-zah soo-**cheh**-day stah-**seh**-rah
What do you recommend?	Che cosa raccomanda? kay **koh**-zah rah-koh-**mahn**-dah

Where is it?	Dov'è? doh-**veh**
How do I get there?	Come ci arriva? **koh**-may chee ah-**ree**-vah
Is it free?	È gratis? eh **grah**-tees
Are there seats available?	Ci sono ancora dei posti? chee **soh**-noh ahn-**koh**-rah **deh**-ee **poh**-stee
Where can I buy a ticket?	Dove si comprano i biglietti? **doh**-vay see kohm-**prah**-noh ee beel-**yeh**-tee
Do you have tickets for today / tonight?	Avete dei biglietti per oggi / stasera? ah-**veh**-tay **deh**-ee beel-**yeh**-tee pehr **oh**-jee / stah-**seh**-rah
best / cheap seats	posti migliori / economici **poh**-stee meel-**yoh**-ree / eh-koh-**noh**-mee-chee
sold out	tutto esaurito **too**-toh eh-zow-**ree**-toh
When does it start?	A che ora comincia? ah kay **oh**-rah koh-**meen**-chah
When does it end?	A che ora finisce? ah kay **oh**-rah fee-**nee**-shay
Where is the best place to stroll?	Dov'è il posto migliore per una passeggiata? doh-**veh** eel **poh**-stoh meel-**yoh**-ray pehr **oo**-nah pah-seh-**jah**-tah
Where's a good place for...?	Dov'è un buon posto per...? doh-**veh** oon bwohn **poh**-stoh pehr
...dancing	...ballare bah-**lah**-ray
...(live) music	...musica (dal vivo) **moo**-zee-kah (dahl **vee**-voh)
bar with live music	locale con musica dal vivo loh-**kah**-lay kohn **moo**-zee-kah dahl **vee**-voh
nightclub	locale notturno loh-**kah**-lay noh-**toor**-noh
cover charge	coperto koh-**pehr**-toh

free entry	ingresso libero een-**greh**-soh **lee**-beh-roh
concert	concerto kohn-**chehr**-toh
opera	lirica **lee**-ree-kah
symphony	sinfonica seen-**foh**-nee-kah
show	spettacolo speh-**tah**-koh-loh
theater	teatro tee-**ah**-troh

For cheap entertainment, join the locals and ***fare una passeggiata*** (take a stroll) through town. People gather at the town's ***piazza d'incontro*** (meeting place). As you do laps ***(vasche)*** and bump shoulders in the crowd, you'll know why it's also called ***struscio*** (rubbing). On workdays, Italians stroll between work and dinner. On Sundays and holidays, they hit the streets after lunch.

SHOPPING

SHOP TILL YOU DROP

Shop Talk

opening hours	orario d'apertura oh-**rah**-ree-oh dah-pehr-**too**-rah
sale	saldi **sahl**-dee
cheap	economico eh-koh-**noh**-mee-koh
affordable	accessibile ah-cheh-**see**-bee-lay
(too) expensive	(troppo) costoso (**troh**-poh) koh-**stoh**-zoh

Key Phrases: Shopping

How much is it?	Quanto costa? **kwahn**-toh **koh**-stah
I'm just browsing.	Sto solo guardando. stoh **soh**-loh gwar-**dahn**-doh
Can I see more?	Posso vederne di più? **poh**-soh veh-**dehr**-nay dee pew
I'll think about it.	Ci penserò. chee pehn-seh-**roh**
I'll take it.	Lo prendo. loh **prehn**-doh
Do you accept credit cards?	Accettate carte di credito? ah-cheh-**tah**-tay **kar**-tay dee **kreh**-dee-toh
Can I try it on?	Lo posso provare? loh **poh**-soh proh-**vah**-ray
It's too expensive / big / small.	È troppo costoso / grande / piccolo. eh **troh**-poh koh-**stoh**-zoh / **grahn**-day / **pee**-koh-loh

a good value	un buon prezzo oon bwohn **prehd**-zoh
Excuse me.	Scusi. **skoo**-zee
Where can I buy ____?	Dove posso comprare ____? **doh**-vay **poh**-soh kohm-**prah**-ray ____
How much is it?	Quanto costa? **kwahn**-toh **koh**-stah
I'm just browsing.	Sto solo guardando. stoh **soh**-loh gwar-**dahn**-doh
I'd like...	Vorrei... voh-**reh**-ee
Do you have...?	Avete...? ah-**veh**-tay
...more (m / f)	...altri / altre **ahl**-tree / **ahl**-tray
...something cheaper	...qualcosa di meno caro kwahl-**koh**-zah dee **meh**-noh **kah**-roh
...something nicer	...qualcosa di più elegante kwahl-**koh**-zah dee pew eh-leh-**gahn**-tay
Can I see more?	Posso vederne di più? **poh**-soh veh-**dehr**-nay dee pew
This one.	Questo qui. **kweh**-stoh kwee
I'll think about it.	Ci penserò. chee pehn-seh-**roh**
I'll take it.	Lo prendo. loh **prehn**-doh
What time do you close?	A che ora chiudete? ah kay **oh**-rah kee-oo-**deh**-tay
What time do you open tomorrow?	A che ora aprite domani? ah kay **oh**-rah ah-**pree**-tay doh-**mah**-nee

Bargain hunters keep an eye out for ***saldi*** (sales) and ***sconti*** (discounts).

Pay Up

Where do I pay?	Dove si paga? **doh**-vay see **pah**-gah
cashier	cassa **kah**-sah
Do you accept credit cards?	Accettate carte di credito? ah-cheh-**tah**-tay **kar**-tay dee **kreh**-dee-toh

VAT (Value-Added Tax)	IVA (imposta sul valore aggiunto) ee vee ah (eem-**poh**-stah sool vah-**loh**-ray ah-**joon**-toh)
Can I get...?	Posso avere...? **poh**-soh ah-**veh**-ray
I need the paperwork for...	Mi serve il modulo per... mee **sehr**-vay eel **moh**-doo-loh pehr
...a VAT refund	...un rimborso IVA oon reem-**bor**-soh ee vee ah
Can you ship this?	Può spedirmelo? pwoh speh-deer-**meh**-loh

When you're ready to pay, look for a ***cassa*** (cashier). The cashier might ask you something like ***Ha quindici centesimi?*** (Do you have 15 cents?), ***Ce l'ha spicci?*** (Do you have exact change?), or ***Vuole una busta?*** (Do you want a bag?).

If you make a major purchase from a single store, you may be eligible for a VAT refund; for details, see www.ricksteves.com/vat.

WHERE TO SHOP

Types of Shops

Where is a...?	Dov'è un / una...? doh-**veh** oon / **oo**-nah
barber shop	barbiere bar-bee-**eh**-ray
beauty salon	parrucchiere pah-roo-kee-**eh**-ray
bookstore...	libreria... lee-breh-**ree**-ah
used bookstore...	negozio di libri usati... neh-**goht**-see-oh dee **lee**-bree oo-**zah**-tee
...with books in English	...che vende libri in inglese kay **vehn**-day **lee**-bree een een-**gleh**-zay
clothing boutique	boutique di abbigliamento boo-**teek** dee ah-beel-yah-**mehn**-toh
coffee shop	bar bar
department store	grande magazzino **grahn**-day mah-gahd-**zee**-noh

electronics store	negozio di elettronica neh-**goht**-see-oh dee eh-leh-**troh**-nee-kah
flea market	mercato delle pulci mehr-**kah**-toh **deh**-lay **pool**-chee
jewelry store	gioielleria joh-yeh-leh-**ree**-ah
launderette	lavanderia lah-vahn-deh-**ree**-ah
leather shop	pelletteria peh-leh-teh-**ree**-ah
mobile-phone shop	negozio di cellulari neh-**goht**-see-oh dee cheh-loo-**lah**-ree
newsstand	edicola / giornalaio eh-**dee**-koh-lah / jor-nah-**lah**-yoh
open-air market	mercato mehr-**kah**-toh
pharmacy	farmacia far-mah-**chee**-ah
pottery shop	negozio di ceramica neh-**goht**-see-oh dee cheh-**rah**-mee-kah
shoe store	negozio di calzature neh-**goht**-see-oh dee kahlt-sah-**too**-ray
shopping mall	centro commerciale **chehn**-troh koh-mehr-**chah**-lay
souvenir shop	negozio di souvenir neh-**goht**-see-oh dee **soo**-veh-neer
tobacco stand	tabacchi tah-**bah**-kee
toy store	negozio di giocattoli neh-**goht**-see-oh dee joh-**kah**-toh-lee
travel agency	agenzia di viaggi ah-**jehnt**-see-ah dee vee-**ah**-jee
wine shop	negozio di vini neh-**goht**-see-oh dee **vee**-nee

In Italy, shops are often closed for a long lunch (generally daily between 1:00 p.m. and 3:00 or 4:00 p.m.). While most people are familiar with the Spanish term ***siesta*** to describe this relaxed lifestyle, Italians call it ***pausa pranzo*** (lunch break). Many stores in larger cities close for all or part of August—not a good time to plan a shopping spree.

At tobacco shops (known as ***tabacchi,*** often indicated with a big ***T*** sign), you can pay for street parking, buy stamps, and get tickets for buses and subways.

For tips and phrases on shopping for a picnic—at grocery stores or open-air markets—see page 287 in the Eating chapter.

Street Markets

Did you make this?	L'avete fatto voi questo? lah-**veh**-tay **fah**-toh **voh**-ee **kweh**-stoh
Is this made in Italy?	Questo è made in Italy? **kweh**-stoh eh "made in Italy"
How much is it?	Quanto costa? **kwahn**-toh **koh**-stah
Cheaper?	Me lo dà a meno? may loh dah ah **meh**-noh
And if I give you ____? (name price)	E se le do ____? ay say lay doh ____
Cheaper if I buy two or three?	Costa meno se ne compro due o tre? **koh**-stah **meh**-noh say nay **kohm**-proh **doo**-ay oh tray
Good price.	Buon prezzo. bwohn **prehd**-zoh
My last offer.	La mia ultima offerta. lah **mee**-ah **ool**-tee-mah oh-**fehr**-tah
I'll take it.	Lo prendo. loh **prehn**-doh
We'll take it.	Lo prendiamo. loh prehn-dee-**ah**-moh
I'm / We're nearly broke.	Sono / Siamo quasi al verde. **soh**-noh / see-**ah**-moh **kwah**-zee ahl **vehr**-day

It's OK to bargain at street markets, though not every vendor will drop prices. Expect to pay cash and be wary of pickpockets. For help with numbers and prices, see page 190.

WHAT TO BUY

Clothing

clothing	vestiti veh-**stee**-tee
This one.	Questo qui. **kweh**-stoh kwee
Can I try it on?	Lo posso provare? loh **poh**-soh proh-**vah**-ray
Do you have a...?	Avete...? ah-**veh**-tay
...mirror	...uno specchio **oo**-noh **speh**-kee-oh
...fitting room	...un camerino oon kah-meh-**ree**-noh
(It's) too...	(È) troppo... (eh) **troh**-poh
...expensive.	...costoso. koh-**stoh**-zoh
...big / small.	...grande / piccolo. **grahn**-day / **pee**-koh-loh
...short / long.	...corto / lungo. **kor**-toh / **loon**-goh
...tight / loose.	...stretto / largo. **streh**-toh / **lar**-goh
...dark / light.	...scuro / chiaro. **skoo**-roh / kee-**ah**-roh
Do you have a different color / a different pattern?	Avete un colore diverso / una fantasia diversa? ah-**veh**-tay oon koh-**loh**-ray dee-**vehr**-soh / **oo**-nah fahn-tah-**zee**-ah dee-**vehr**-sah
What's it made of?	Di che cosa è fatto? dee kay **koh**-zah eh **fah**-toh
Is it machine washable?	Si può lavare in lavatrice? see pwoh lah-**vah**-ray een lah-vah-**tree**-chay
Will it shrink?	Si ritira? see ree-**tee**-rah
Will it fade in the wash?	Scolora quando si lava? skoh-**loh**-rah **kwahn**-doh see **lah**-vah
Dry clean only?	Solo lavasecco? **soh**-loh lah-vah-**seh**-koh

Types of Clothes and Accessories

For a...	Per un / una... pehr oon / **oo**-nah
...man.	...uomo. **woh**-moh
...woman.	...donna. **doh**-nah
...teenager. (m / f)	...ragazzo / ragazza. rah-**gahd**-zoh / rah-**gahd**-zah
...child. (m / f)	...bambino / bambina. bahm-**bee**-noh / bahm-**bee**-nah
...baby. (m / f)	...neonato / neonata. neh-oh-**nah**-toh / neh-oh-**nah**-tah
I'm looking for a...	Sto cercando un / una... stoh chehr-**kahn**-doh oon / **oo**-nah
I want to buy a...	Vorrei comprare un / una... voh-**reh**-ee kohm-**prah**-ray oon / **oo**-nah
belt	cintura cheen-**too**-rah
bra	reggiseno reh-jee-**zeh**-noh
dress	vestito da donna veh-**stee**-toh dah **doh**-nah
earrings	orecchini oh-reh-**kee**-nee
gloves	guanti **gwahn**-tee
handbag	borsa **bor**-sah
hat	cappello kah-**peh**-loh
jacket	giacca **jah**-kah
jeans	jeans "jeans"
jewelry	gioielli joh-**yeh**-lee
necklace	collana koh-**lah**-nah
nylons	collant **koh**-lahnt
pajamas	pigiama pee-**jah**-mah
pants	pantaloni pahn-tah-**loh**-nee
raincoat	impermeabile eem-pehr-meh-**ah**-bee-lay
ring	anello ah-**neh**-loh
scarf	sciarpa / foulard **shar**-pah / foo-**lard**

shirt	camicia kah-**mee**-chah
shoelaces	lacci da scarpe **lah**-chee dah **skar**-pay
shoes	scarpe **skar**-pay
shorts	pantaloni corti pahn tah **loh** nee **kor** tee
skirt	gonna **goh**-nah
socks	calzini kahlt-**see**-nee
sweater	maglione mahl **yoh** nay
swimsuit	costume da bagno koh-**stoo**-may dah **bahn**-yoh
tie	cravatta krah-**vah**-tah
tights	dei collant **deh**-ee **koh**-lahnt
T-shirt	maglietta mahl-**yeh**-tah
underwear	intimo **een**-tee-moh
wallet	portafoglio por-tah-**fohl**-yoh
watch	orologio oh-roh-**loh**-joh

Clothing Sizes

extra-small	extra-small "extra-small"
small	small "small"
medium	media **meh**-dee-ah
large	large "large"
extra-large	extra-large "extra-large"
I need a bigger / smaller size.	Mi serve una misura più grande / più piccola. mee **sehr**-vay **oo**-nah mee-**zoo**-rah pew **grahn**-day / pew **pee**-koh-lah
What's my size?	Qual'è la mia misura? kwah-**leh** lah **mee**-ah mee-**zoo**-rah

For help converting US sizes to European, see page 552.

Colors

black	nero **neh**-roh
blue	azzurro ahd-**zoo**-roh
brown	marrone mah-**roh**-nay
gray	grigio **gree**-joh
green	verde **vehr**-day
orange	arancio ah-**rahn**-choh
pink	rosa **roh**-zah
purple	viola vee-**oh**-lah
red	rosso **roh**-soh
white	bianco bee-**ahn**-koh
yellow	giallo **jah**-loh
dark(er)	(più) scuro (pew) **skoo**-roh
light(er)	(più) chiaro (pew) kee-**ah**-roh
bright(er)	(più) brillante (pew) bree-**lahn**-tay

SHIPPING AND MAIL

Though you can ship home goods from ***la posta*** (the post office), it may be more reliable to send packages (especially expensive or fragile objects) using DHL, UPS, or FedEx, which can provide tracking numbers. If you just need stamps, you can often get them at the corner ***tabacchi*** (tobacco shop).

post office	posta **poh**-stah
Where is the post office?	Dov'è l'ufficio postale? doh-**veh** loo-**fee**-choh poh-**stah**-lay
stamps	francobolli frahn-koh-**boh**-lee
postcard	cartolina kar-toh-**lee**-nah
letter	lettera **leh**-teh-rah
package	pacco **pah**-koh
window	sportello spor-**teh**-loh
line	fila **fee**-lah

Which window?	Qual'è lo sportello? kwah-**leh** loh spor-**teh**-loh
Is this the line?	È questa la fila? eh **kweh**-stah lah **fee**-lah
I need some stamps.	Mi servono dei francobolli. mee sehr-**voh**-noh **deh**-ee frahn-koh-**boh**-lee
I need to mail a package (to the United States).	Ho bisogno di spedire un pacco (per Stati Uniti). oh bee-**zohn**-yoh dee speh-**dee**-ray oon **pah**-koh (pehr **stah**-tee oo-**nee**-tee)
Pretty stamps, please.	Dei bei francobolli, per favore. **deh**-ee **beh**-ee frahn-koh-**boh**-lee pehr fah-**voh**-ray
Can I buy a box?	Posso comprare una scatola? **poh**-soh kohm-**prah**-ray **oo**-nah **skah**-toh-lah
This big.	Grande così. **grahn**-day koh-**zee**
Do you have tape?	Avete dello scotch? ah-**veh**-tay **deh**-loh "scotch"

TECHNOLOGY

TECH TERMS

Portable Devices and Accessories

I need a...	Mi serve un / una... mee **sehr**-vay oon / **oo**-nah
Do you have a...?	Avete un / una...? ah-**veh**-tay oon / **oo**-nah
Where can I buy a...?	Dove posso comprare un / una...? **doh**-vay **poh**-soh kohm-**prah**-ray oon / **oo**-nah
battery (for my ____)	batteria (per il mio ____) bah-teh-**ree**-ah (pehr eel **mee**-oh ____)
battery charger	carica batterie **kah**-ree-kah bah-teh-**ree**-ay
computer	computer kohm-**poo**-tehr
convertor	convertitore elettrico kohn-vehr-tee-**toh**-ray eh-**leh**-tree-koh
CD / DVD	CD / DVD **chee**-dee / dee-**vee**-dee
ebook reader	libro elettronico **lee**-broh eh-leh-**troh**-nee-koh
electrical adapter	adattatore elettrico ah-dah-tah-**toh**-ray eh-**leh**-tree-koh
flash drive	flash drive "flash drive"
headphones / earbuds	cuffie / auricolari **koo**-fee-ay / ow-ree-koh-**lah**-ree
iPod / MP3 player	iPod / lettore MP3 "iPod" / leh-**toh**-ray **ehm**-ay-pee-tray
laptop	portatile por-**tah**-tee-lay
memory card	memory card "memory card"
mobile phone	cellulare cheh-loo-**lah**-ray

SIM card	carta SIM **kar**-tah seem
speakers (for my ____)	casse (per il mio ____) **kah**-say (pehr eel **mee**-oh ____)
tablet	tablet "tablet"
USB cable / mini-cable	cavo / cavetto USB **kah**-voh / kah-**veh**-toh oo **ehs**-ay bee
video game	videogioco vee-deh-oh-**joh**-koh
Wi-Fi	Wi-Fi **wee**-fee

Familiar brands (like iPad, Facebook, YouTube, Instagram, or whatever the latest craze) are just as popular in Europe as they are back home. Invariably, these go by their English names, sometimes with an Italian accent.

Cameras

camera	macchina fotografica **mah**-kee-nah foh-toh-**grah**-fee-kah
digital camera	macchina fotografica digitale **mah**-kee-nah foh-toh-**grah**-fee-kah dee-jee-**tah**-lay
video camera	videocamera vee-deh-oh-**kah**-meh rah
lens cap	tappo obiettivo **tah**-poh oh-bee-**eh**-tee-voh
film	pellicola peh-**lee**-koh-lah
Can I download my photos onto a CD?	Posso scaricare le mie foto su CD? **poh**-soh skah-ree-**kah**-ray lay **mee**-ay **foh**-toh soo **chee**-dee
Will you take my / our photo?	Mi / Ci fa una foto? mee / chee fah **oo**-nah **foh**-toh
Can I take a photo of you?	Posso farle una foto? **poh**-soh **far**-lay **oo**-nah **foh**-toh
Smile! (sing / pl)	Sorrida! / Sorridete! soh-**ree**-dah / soh-ree-**deh**-tay

You'll find words for batteries, chargers, and more in the previous list.

TELEPHONES

Telephone Terms

telephone	telefono teh-**leh**-foh-noh
phone call...	chiamata... kee-ah-**mah**-tah
...local (within the city)	...urbana oor-**bah**-nah
...domestic (elsewhere in Italy)	...nazionale naht-see-oh-**nah**-lay
...international	...internazionale een-tehr-naht-see-oh-**nah**-lay
...toll-free	...numero verde / freephone **noo**-meh-roh **vehr**-day / free-**foh**-neh
...with credit card	...con la carta di credito kohn lah **kar**-tah dee **kreh**-dee-toh
...collect	...a carico del destinatario ah **kah**-ree-koh dehl deh-stee-nah-**tah**-ree-oh

Key Phrases: Telephones

telephone	telefono teh-**leh**-foh-noh
phone call	chiamata kee-ah-**mah**-tah
mobile phone	cellulare cheh-loo-**lah**-ray
Where is the nearest phone?	Dov'è il telefono più vicino? doh-**veh** eel teh-**leh**-foh-noh pew vee-**chee**-noh
May I use your phone?	Posso usare il telefono? **poh**-soh oo-**zah**-ray eel teh-**leh**-foh-noh
Where is a mobile-phone shop?	Dov'è un negozio di cellulari? doh-**veh** oon neh-**goht**-see-oh dee cheh-loo-**lah**-ree

mobile phone	cellulare cheh-loo-**lah**-ray
mobile number	numero di cellulare **noo**-meh-roh dee cheh-loo-**lah**-ray
landline	numero fisso **noo**-meh-roh **fee**-soh
country code	prefisso per il paese preh-**fee**-soh pehr eel pah-**eh**-zay
area code	prefisso preh-**fee**-soh
phone number	numero di telefono **noo**-meh-roh dee teh-**leh**-foh-noh
extension	numero interno **noo**-meh-roh een-**tehr**-noh
fax	fax fahks

Travelers have several phoning options: A mobile phone provides the best combination of practicality and flexibility. Public pay phones are available, but are becoming rare and require buying an insertable phone card ***(carta telefonica).*** You can also make calls online (using Skype or a similar program) or from your hotel-room phone (using an international PIN card—***carta telefonica prepagata internazionale***). As this is a fast-changing scene, check my latest tips at www.ricksteves.com/phoning.

Italy uses a direct-dial phone system (no area codes). For phone tips—including a calling chart for dialing European numbers—see page 546.

Making Calls

Where is the nearest phone?	Dov'è il telefono più vicino? doh-**veh** eel teh-**leh**-foh-noh pew vee-**chee**-noh
May I use your phone?	Posso usare il telefono? **poh**-soh oo-**zah**-ray eel teh-**leh**-foh-noh
Can you talk for me?	Può parlare per me? pwoh par-**lah**-ray pehr may
It's busy.	È occupato. eh oh-koo-**pah**-toh

It doesn't work.	Non funziona. nohn foont-see-**oh**-nah
out of service	guasto **gwah**-stoh
Try again?	Può riprovare? pwoh ree-proh-**vah**-ray

On the Phone

Hello, this is ____.	Pronto, sono ____. **prohn**-toh **soh**-noh ____
My name is ____.	Mi chiamo ____. mee kee-**ah**-moh ____
Do you speak English?	Parla inglese? **par**-lah een-**gleh**-zay
Sorry, I speak only a little Italian.	Mi dispiace, parlo solo un po' d'italiano. mee dee-spee-**ah**-chay **par**-loh **soh**-loh oon poh dee-tah-lee-**ah**-noh
Speak slowly, please.	Parli lentamente, per favore. **par**-lee lehn-tah-**mehn**-tay pehr fah-**voh**-ray
Wait a moment.	Un momento. oon moh-**mehn**-toh

Italians answer a call by saying ***Pronto*** (Hello). They may ask ***Chi parla?*** (Who is speaking?)

You'll find the phrases you need to reserve a hotel room on page 226, or a table at a restaurant on page 245. To spell your name over the phone, refer to the code alphabet on page 550.

Mobile Phones

Your US mobile phone should work in Europe if it's GSM-enabled, tri-band or quad-band, and on a calling plan that includes international service. Alternatively, you can buy a phone in Europe. If your phone is unlocked ***(sbloccato)***, you can save money by buying a cheap European SIM card (which usually comes with some calling credit) at a mobile-phone shop or a newsstand. After inserting a SIM card in your phone, you'll have a European number and pay lower European rates.

mobile phone	cellulare cheh-loo-**lah**-ray
smartphone	smartphone "smartphone"
roaming	roaming **roh**-meen
text message	SMS **ehs**-ay **ehm**-ay **ehs**-ay
Where is a mobile-phone shop?	Dov'è un negozio di cellulari? doh-**veh** oon neh-**goht**-see-oh dee cheh-loo-**lah**-ree
I'd like to buy...	Vorrei comprare... voh-**reh**-ee kohm-**prah**-ray
...a (cheap) mobile phone.	...un cellulare (economico). oon cheh-loo-**lah**-ray (eh-koh-**noh**-mee-koh)
...a SIM card.	...una carta SIM. **oo**-nah **kar**-tah seem
(prepaid) credit	credito (prepagato) **kreh**-dee-toh (preh-pah-**gah**-toh)
calling time	durata della chiamata doo-**rah**-tah **deh**-lah kee-ah-**mah**-tah
contract	contratto kohn-**trah**-toh
locked / unlocked	bloccato / sbloccato bloh-**kah**-toh / zbloh-**kah**-toh
Is this phone unlocked?	Questo telefono è sbloccato? **kweh**-stoh teh-**leh**-foh-noh eh zbloh-**kah**-toh
Can you unlock this phone?	Può sbloccare questo telefono? pwoh zbloh-**kah**-ray **kweh**-stoh teh-**leh**-foh-noh
How do I...?	Come faccio a...? **koh**-may **fah**-choh ah
...make calls	...fare una chiamata **fah**-ray **oo**-nah kee-ah-**mah**-tah
...receive calls	...ricevere una chiamata ree-**cheh**-veh-ray **oo**-nah kee-ah-**mah**-tah
...send a text message	...mandare un SMS mahn-**dah**-ray oon **ehs**-ay-**ehm**-ay-**ehs**-ay

...check voicemail	...controllare i messaggi vocali kohn-troh-**lah**-ray ee meh-**sah**-jee voh-**kah**-lee
...set the language to English	...impostare in lingua inglese eem-poh-**stah**-ray een **leen**-gwah een-**gleh**-zay
...mute the ringer	...silenziare la suoneria see-lehnt-see-**ah**-ray lah swoh-neh-**ree**-ah
...change the ringer	...cambiare la suoneria kahm-bee-**ah**-ray lah swoh-neh-**ree**-ah
...turn it on	...accenderlo ah-chehn-**dehr**-loh
...turn it off	...spegnerlo spehn-**yehr**-loh

GETTING ONLINE

Internet Terms

Internet access	accesso all'Internet ah-**cheh**-soh ahl-**een**-tehr-neht
Wi-Fi	Wi-Fi **wee**-fee
email	email / posta elettronica "email" / **poh**-stah eh-leh-**troh**-nee-kah
computer	computer kohm-**poo**-tehr
Internet café	café Internet kah-**fay** **een**-tehr-neht
surf the Web	navigare su Internet nah-vee-**gah**-ray soo **een**-tehr-neht
username	username oo-zehr-**nah**-may
password	password "password"
network key	chiave di sicurezza kee-**ah**-vay dee see-koo-**rehd**-zah
secure network	rete sicura **reh**-tay see-**koo**-rah
website	sito Internet **see**-toh **een**-tehr-neht
homepage	homepage oh-meh-**pah**-jeh

Key Phrases: Getting Online

Where is a Wi-Fi hotspot?	Dov'è un hot spot Wi-Fi? doh-**veh** oon "hot spot" **wee**-fee
Where can I get online?	Dove posso connettermi all'Internet? **doh**-vay **poh**-soh koh-neh-**tehr**-mee ahl-**een**-tehr-neht
Where is an Internet café?	Dov'è un café Internet ? doh-**veh** oon kah-**fay een**-tehr-neht
Can I check my email?	Posso controllare la mia email? **poh**-soh kohn-troh-**lah**-ray lah **mee**-ah "email"

download	scaricare skah-ree-**kah**-ray
print	stampare stahm-**pah**-ray
My email address is ____.	Il mio indirizzo email è ____. eel **mee**-oh een-dee-**reed**-zoh "email" eh ____
What's your email address?	Qual'è il suo indirizzo email? kwah-**leh** eel **soo**-oh een-dee-**reed**-zoh "email"

The ***www*** found at the beginning of most URLs is pronounced ***voo-voo-voo,*** and the dot is ***punto.***

Tech Support

Help me, please.	Mi aiuti, per favore. mee ah-**yoo**-tee pehr fah-**voh**-ray
How do I...?	Come faccio a...? **koh**-may **fah**-choh ah
...start this	...accendere questo ah-**chehn**-deh-ray **kweh**-stoh

...get online	...connettermi all'Internet koh-neh-**tehr**-mee ahl-**een**-tehr-neht
...get this to work	...farlo funzionare **far**-loh foont-see-oh-**nah**-ray
...stop this	...fermarlo **fehr**-mar-loh
...send this	...inviare questo een-vee-**ah**-ray **kweh**-stoh
...print this	...stampare questo stahm-**pah**-ray **kweh**-stoh
...make this symbol	...fare questo simbolo **fah**-ray **kweh**-stoh **seem**-boh-loh
...copy and paste	...fare copia e incolla **fah**-ray **koh**-pee-ah eh een-**koh**-lah
...type @	...fare la chiocciola **fah**-ray lah kee-**oh**-choh-lah
This isn't working.	Non funziona. nohn foont-see-**oh**-nah

For do-it-yourself tips, see "Italian Keyboards" on page 345.

Using Your Own Portable Device

If you have a smartphone, tablet computer, laptop, or other wireless device, you can get online at many hotels, cafés, and public hotspots. Most Internet access is Wi-Fi (pronounced **wee**-fee), but occasionally you'll connect by plugging an Ethernet cable directly into your laptop. While Internet access is often free, sometimes you'll have to pay.

laptop	portatile por-**tah**-tee-lay
tablet	tablet "tablet"
smartphone	smartphone "smartphone"
Where is a Wi-Fi hotspot?	Dov'è un hot spot Wi-Fi? doh-**veh** oon "hot spot" **wee**-fee
Do you have Wi-Fi?	Avete la rete Wi-Fi? ah-**veh**-tay lah **reh**-tay **wee**-fee

What is the...?	Qual'è...? kwah-**leh**
...network name	...il network name eel "network" **nah**-may
...username	...lo username loh oo-zehr-**nah**-may
...password	...la password lah "password"
Do I need a cable?	Mi serve un cavo? mee **sehr**-vay oon **kah**-voh
Do you have a...?	Avete un...? ah-**veh**-tay oon
Can I borrow a...?	Posso prendere in prestito un...? **poh**-soh **prehn**-deh-ray een **preh**-stee-toh oon
...charging cable	...cavo per la carica **kah**-voh pehr lah **kah**-ree-kah
...Ethernet cable	...cavo ethernet **kah**-voh **eh**-tehr-neht
...USB cable	...cavo USB **kah**-voh oo **ehs**-ay bee
Free?	Gratis? **grah**-tees
How much?	Quanto costa? **kwahn**-toh **koh**-stah
Do I have to buy something to use the Internet?	Devo comprare qualcosa per usare Internet? **deh**-voh kohm-**prah**-ray kwahl-**koh**-zah pehr oo-**zah**-ray **een**-tehr-neht

Using a Public Internet Terminal

Many hotels have terminals in the lobby for guests to get online; otherwise, an Internet café is usually nearby.

Where can I get online?	Dove posso connettermi all'Internet? **doh**-vay **poh**-soh koh-neh-**tehr**-mee ahl-**een**-tehr-neht
Where is an Internet café?	Dov'è un café Internet? doh-**veh** oon kah-**fay** **een**-tehr-neht

May I use this computer to...?	Posso usare questo computer per...? **poh**-soh oo-**zah**-ray **kweh**-stoh kohm-**poo**-tehr pehr
...get online	...connettermi all'Internet koh-neh-**tehr**-mee ahl-**een**-tehr-neht
...check my email	...controllare la mia email kohn-troh-**lah**-ray lah **mee**-ah "email"
...download my photos	...scaricare le mie foto skah-ree-**kah**-ray lay **mee**-ay **foh**-toh
...print (something)	...stampare (qualcosa) stahm-**pah**-ray (kwahl-**koh**-zah)
boarding passes	carte d'imbarco **kar**-tay deem-**bar**-koh
tickets	biglietti beel-**yeh**-tee
reservation confirmation	conferma della prenotazione kohn-**fehr**-mah **deh**-lah preh-noh-taht-see-**oh**-nay
Free?	Gratis? **grah**-tees
How much (for... minutes)?	Quanto costa (per... minuti)? **kwahn**-toh **koh**-stah (pehr... mee-**noo**-tee)
...10	...dieci dee-**eh**-chee
...15	...quindici **kween**-dee-chee
...30	...trenta **trehn**-tah
...60	...sessanta seh-**sahn**-tah
Can you switch the keyboard to English?	Può impostare la tastiera in inglese? pwoh eem-poh-**stah**-ray lah tah-stee-**eh**-rah een een-**gleh**-zay

If you're using a public Internet terminal, the keyboard, menus, and on-screen commands will likely be designed for Italian speakers. Some computers allow you to make the Italian keyboard work as if it were an American one (look for the box in the lower right-hand corner of the screen to switch to English, or ask the clerk if it's possible).

Italian Keyboards

Italian keyboards differ from American ones. Here's a rundown of how major commands are labeled on an Italian keyboard:

YOU'LL SEE...	IT MEANS...	YOU'LL SEE...	IT MEANS...
Invio	Enter	**Fine**	End
↑	Shift	**Pag ↑**	Page Up
Canc.	Delete	**Pag ↓**	Page Down
←	Backspace	**Alt Gr**	Alternate Graphics
Ins	Insert		

The **Alt** key to the right of the space bar is actually a different key, called **Alt Gr** (for "Alternate Graphics"). Press this key to insert the extra symbol that appears on some keys (such as the # in the lower-right corner of the **à** key).

A few often-used keys look the same, but have different names in Italian:

@ symbol ("snail")	chiocciola	kee-**oh**-choh-lah
dot (.)	punto	**poon**-toh
hyphen (-)	trattino	trah-**tee**-noh
underscore (_)	linea bassa	**lee**-neh-ah **bah**-sah
slash (/)	barra	**bah**-rah

Italian speakers call the @ symbol ***chiocciola*** (snail). When saying an email address, you say ***chiocciola*** in the middle. You'll find the @ symbol next to the letter **L,** sharing space with **ç** and **ò.**

To type @, press **Alt Gr** and **ò** at the same time. If that doesn't work, try copy-and-pasting the @ sign from elsewhere on the page.

HELP!

EMERGENCIES

To phone for help in Italy, dial **113** for English-speaking police or **118** for medical emergencies. If you're lost, see the phrases on page 223.

Medical Help

Help!	Aiuto! ah-**yoo**-toh
Help me, please.	Mi aiuti, per favore. mee ah-**yoo**-tee pehr fah-**voh**-ray
emergency	emergenza eh-mehr-**jehnt**-sah
accident	incidente een-chee-**dehn**-tay
clinic / hospital	clinica / ospedale **klee**-nee-kah / oh-speh-**dah**-lay
Call...	Chiamate... kee-ah-**mah**-tay
...a doctor.	...un dottore. oon doh-**toh**-ray
...the police.	...la polizia. lah poh-leet-**see**-ah
...an ambulance.	...un'ambulanza. oon-ahm-boo-**lahnt**-sah
I / We need...	Ho / Abbiamo bisogno di... oh / ah-bee-**ah**-moh bee-**zohn**-yoh dee
...a doctor.	...un dottore. oon doh-**toh**-ray
...to go to the hospital.	...andare in ospedale. ahn-**dah**-ray een oh-speh-**dah**-lay
It's urgent.	È urgente. eh oor-**jehn**-tay
injured	ferito feh-**ree**-toh
bleeding	sanguinare sahn-gwee-**nah**-ray
choking	soffocare soh-foh-**kah**-ray
unconscious	svenuto sfeh-**noo**-toh
not breathing	non respira nohn reh-**spee**-rah

Key Phrases: Help!

Help!	Aiuto! ah-**yoo**-toh
emergency	emergenza eh-mehr-**jehnt**-sah
clinic / hospital	clinica / ospedale **klee**-nee-kah / oh-speh-**dah**-lay
Call a doctor.	Chiamate un dottore. kee-ah-**mah**-tay oon doh-**toh**-ray
police	polizia poh-leet-**see**-ah
ambulance	ambulanza ahm-boo-**lahnt**-sah
thief	ladro **lah**-droh
Stop, thief!	Fermatelo! Ladro! fehr-**mah**-teh-loh **lah**-droh

Thank you for your help.	Grazie dell'aiuto. **graht**-see-ay dehl-ah-**yoo**-toh
You are very kind.	Lei è molto gentile. **leh**-ee eh **mohl**-toh jehn-**tee**-lay

For health-related words, see the Personal Care and Health chapter.

Theft and Loss

thief	ladro **lah**-droh
pickpocket	borseggiatore bor-seh-jah-**toh**-ray
police	polizia poh-leet-**see**-ah
embassy	ambasciata ahm-bah-**shah**-tah
Stop, thief!	Fermatelo! Ladro! fehr-**mah**-teh-loh **lah**-droh
Call the police!	Chiamate la polizia! kee-ah-**mah**-tay lah poh-leet-**see**-ah

I've been robbed.	Sono stato(a) derubato(a). **soh**-noh **stah**-toh deh-roo-**bah**-toh
We've been robbed.	Siamo stati derubati. see-**ah**-moh **stah**-tee deh-roo-**bah**-tee
We've been robbed. (said by females)	Siamo state derubate. see-**ah**-moh **stah**-tay deh-roo-**bah**-tay
A thief took...	Un ladro ha preso... oon **lah**-droh ah **preh**-zoh
Thieves took...	I ladri hanno preso... ee **lah**-dree **ahn**-noh **preh**-zoh
I've lost my...	Ho perso il mio... / la mia... oh **pehr**-soh eel **mee**-oh / lah **mee**-ah
We've lost our...	Abbiamo perso i nostri... **ah**-bee-ah-moh **pehr**-soh ee **noh**-stree
money	soldi **sohl**-dee
credit / debit card	carta di credito / debito **kar**-tah dee **kreh**-dee-toh / **deh**-bee-toh
passport	passaporto pah-sah-**por**-toh
ticket	biglietto beel-**yeh**-toh
railpass	tessera ferroviaria **teh**-seh-rah feh-roh-vee-**ah**-ree-ah
baggage	bagaglio bah-**gahl**-yoh
purse	borsa **bor**-sah
wallet	portafoglio por-tah-**fohl**-yoh
watch	orologio oh-roh-**loh**-joh
jewelry	gioielli joh-**yeh**-lee
camera	macchina fotografica **mah**-kee-nah foh-toh-**grah**-fee-kah
mobile phone	telefono cellulare teh-**leh**-foh-noh cheh-loo-**lah**-ray
iPod / iPad	iPod / iPad "iPod" / "iPad"
tablet	tablet "tablet"
computer	computer kohm-**poo**-tehr

laptop	portatile por-**tah**-tee-lay
faith in humankind	fiducia nel prossimo fee-**doo**-chah nehl **proh**-see-moh
I want to contact my embassy.	Vorrei contattare la mia ambasciata. voh-**reh**-ee kohn-tah-**tah**-ray lah **mee**-ah ahm-bah-**shah**-tah
I need to file a police report (for my insurance).	Devo fare una denuncia (per la mia assicurazione). **deh**-voh **fah**-ray **oo**-nah deh-**noon**-chah (pehr lah **mee**-ah ah-see-koo-raht-see-**oh**-nay)
Where is the police station?	Dov'è la questura? doh-**veh** lah kweh-**stoo**-rah

In addition to civilian cops, you may also see police clad in dark blue. These are members of Italy's military police, the ***Carabinieri.***

To replace a passport, you'll need to go in person to your embassy. Cancel and replace your credit and debit cards by calling your credit-card company (as of this printing, these are the 24-hour US numbers that you can call collect: Visa—tel. 303/967-1096, MasterCard—tel. 636/722-7111, American Express—tel. 336/393-1111). If you'll want to submit an insurance claim for lost or stolen gear, be sure to file a police report, either on the spot or within a day or two. For more info, see www.ricksteves.com/help. Precautionary measures can minimize the effects of loss—back up your digital photos and other files frequently.

Fire!

fire	fuoco **fwoh**-koh
smoke	fumo **foo**-moh
exit	uscita oo-**shee**-tah
emergency exit	uscita d'emergenza oo-**shee**-tah deh-mehr-**jehnt**-sah
fire extinguisher	estintore eh-steen-**toh**-ray

Call the fire department.	Chiamate i vigili del fuoco. kee-ah-**mah**-tay ee **vee**-jee-lee dehl **fwoh**-koh

HELP FOR WOMEN

Whenever macho males threaten to make leering a contact sport, local women stroll arm-in-arm or holding hands. Wearing conservative clothes and avoiding smiley eye contact can help convey an "I'm not interested" message.

Generally the best way to react to unwanted attention is loudly and quickly.

No!	No! noh
Stop it!	La smetta! lah **zmeh**-tah
Enough!	Basta! **bah**-stah
Don't touch me.	Non mi tocchi. nohn mee **toh**-kee
Leave me alone.	Mi lasci in pace. mee **lah**-shee een **pah**-chay
Go away.	Se ne vada. say nay **vah**-dah
Get lost!	Sparisca! spah-**ree**-skah
Drop dead!	Crepi! **kreh**-pee
Police!	Polizia! poh-leet-**see**-ah

Safety in Numbers

If a guy is bugging you, approach a friendly-looking couple, family, or business for a place to stay safe.

A man is bothering me.	Un uomo mi sta importunando. oon **woh**-moh mee stah eem-por-too-**nahn**-doh
May I...?	Posso...? **poh**-soh
...join you	...unirmi a voi oo-**neer**-mee ah voy

...sit here	...sedermi qui seh-**dehr**-mee kwee
...wait here until he's gone	...aspettare qui finchè va via ah-speh-**tah**-ray kwee feen-**kay** vah **vee**-ah

You Want to Be Alone

I want to be alone.	Voglio stare sola. **vohl**-yoh **stah**-ray **soh**-lah
I'm not interested.	Non sono interessata. nohn **soh**-noh een-teh-reh-**sah**-tah
I'm married.	Sono sposata. **soh**-noh spoh-**zah**-tah
I'm waiting for my husband.	Sto aspettando mio marito. stoh ah-speh-**tahn**-doh **mee**-oh mah-**ree**-toh
I'm a lesbian.	Sono lesbica. **soh**-noh **lehz**-bee-kah
I have a contagious disease.	Ho una malattia contagiosa. oh **oo**-nah mah-lah-**tee**-ah kohn-tah-**joh**-zah

PERSONAL CARE AND HEALTH

PERSONAL CARE

aftershave lotion	lozione dopobarba loht-see-**oh**-nay doh-poh-**bar**-bah
antiperspirant	antitraspirante ahn-tee-trah-spee-**rahn**-tay
breath mints	mentine per l'alito mehn-**tee**-nay pehr **lah**-lee-toh
cologne	colonia koh-**loh**-nee-ah
comb	pettine peh-**tee**-nay
conditioner	balsamo bahl-**sah**-moh
dental floss	filo interdentale **fee**-loh een-tehr-dehn-**tah**-lay
deodorant	deodorante deh-oh-doh-**rahn**-tay
face cleanser	latte detergente **lah**-tay deh-tehr-**jehn**-tay
facial tissue	fazzoletto di carta fahd-zoh-**leh**-toh dee **kar**-tah
fluoride rinse	colluttorio al fluoro koh-loo-**toh**-ree-oh ahl floo-**oh**-roh
hair dryer	phon fohn
hairbrush	spazzola per capelli spahd-**zoh**-lah pehr kah-**peh**-lee
hand lotion	crema per le mani **kreh**-mah pehr lay **mah**-nee
hand sanitizer	igienizzante per le mani ee-jeh-need-**zahn**-tay pehr lay **mah**-nee
lip balm	burro di cacao **boo**-roh dee kah-**kah**-oh

lip gloss	lucidalabbra loo-chee-dah-**lah**-brah
lipstick	rossetto roh-**seh**-toh
makeup	trucco **troo**-koh
mirror	specchio **speh** kee-oh
moisturizer (with sunblock)	crema idratante (con protezione solare) **kreh**-mah ee-drah-**tahn**-tay (kohn proh-teht-see-**oh**-nay soh-**lah**-ray)
mouthwash	colluttorio koh-loo-**toh**-ree-oh
nail clippers	tagliaunghie tahl-yah-**oon**-gee-ay (hard "g")
nail file	limetta per unghie lee-**meh**-tah pehr **oon**-gee-ay (hard "g")
nail polish	smalto per le unghie **zmahl**-toh pehr lay **oon**-gee-ay (hard "g")
nail polish remover	solvente per le unghie sohl-**vehn**-tay pehr lay **oon**-gee-ay (hard "g")
perfume	profumo proh-**foo**-moh
Q-tips (cotton swabs)	cotton fioc **koh**-tohn fee-**ohk**
razor	rasoio rah-**zoh**-yoh
sanitary pads	assorbenti igienici ah-sor-**behn**-tee ee-**jehn**-ee-chee
scissors	forbici **for**-bee-chee
shampoo	shampoo **shahm**-poo
shaving cream	crema da barba **kreh**-mah dah **bar**-bah
soap	sapone sah-**poh**-nay
sunscreen	protezione solare proh-teht-see-**oh**-nay soh-**lah**-ray
suntan lotion	crema solare **kreh**-mah soh-**lah**-ray
tampons	assorbenti interni ah-sor-**behn**-tee een-**tehr**-nee
tissues	fazzoletti di carta fahd-zoh-**leh**-tee dee **kar**-tah
toilet paper	carta igienica **kar**-tah ee-**jehn**-ee-kah

toothbrush	spazzolino da denti spahd-zoh-**lee**-noh dah **dehn**-tee
toothpaste	dentifricio dehn-tee-**free**-choh
tweezers	pinzette peent-**seh**-tay

HEALTH

Throughout Europe, people with simple ailments go first to the pharmacist, who can diagnose and prescribe remedies. Pharmacists are usually friendly and speak English. If necessary, the pharmacist will send you to a doctor or a clinic.

Getting Help

Where is a...?	Dov'è...? doh-**veh**
...pharmacy (open 24 hours)	...una farmacia (aperta ventiquattro ore) **oo**-nah far-mah-**chee**-ah (ah-**pehr**-tah vehn-tee-**kwah**-troh **oh**-ray)
...clinic	...una clinica **oo**-nah **klee**-nee-kah
...hospital	...un ospedale oon oh-speh-**dah**-lay
I am sick.	Sto male. stoh **mah**-lay
He / She is sick.	Lui / Lei sta male. **loo**-ee / **leh**-ee stah **mah**-lay
I / We need a doctor...	Ho / Abbiamo bisogno di un dottore... oh / ah-bee-**ah**-moh bee-**zohn**-yoh dee oon doh-**toh**-ray
...who speaks English.	...che parli inglese. kay **par**-lee een-**gleh**-zay
Please call a doctor.	Per favore, chiami un dottore. pehr fah-**voh**-ray kee-**ah**-mee oon doh-**toh**-ray
Could a doctor come here?	Puo venire qua un dottore? pwoh veh-**nee**-ray kwah oon doh-**toh**-ray
It's urgent.	È urgente. eh oor-**jehn**-tay

Key Phrases: Health

I am sick.	Sto male. stoh **mah**-lay
I need a doctor (who speaks English).	Ho bisogno di un dottore (che parli inglese). oh bee-**zohn**-yoh dee oon doh-**toh**-ray (kay **par**-lee een-**gleh**-zay)
pain	dolore doh-**loh**-ray
It hurts here.	Fa male qui. fah **mah**-lay kwee
medicine	farmaco **far**-mah-koh
Where is a pharmacy?	Dov'è una farmacia? doh-**veh oo**-nah far-mah-**chee**-ah

ambulance	ambulanza ahm-boo-**lahnt**-sah
dentist	dentista dehn-**tee**-stah
health insurance	assicurazione medica ah-see-koo-raht-see-**oh**-nay **meh**-dee-kah
Receipt, please.	La ricevuta, per favore. lah ree-cheh-**voo**-tah pehr fah-**voh**-ray

Ailments

I have...	Ho... oh
He / She has...	Lui / Lei ha... **loo**-ee / **leh**-ee ah
I need medicine for...	Mi serve un farmaco per... mee **sehr**-vay oon **far**-mah-koh pehr
allergy	un'allergia oon-ah-lehr-**jee**-ah
bee sting	una puntura d'ape **oo**-nah poon-**too**-rah **dah**-pay
bites from...	puncture di... poonk-**too**-ray dee
...bedbugs	...cimici **chee**-mee-chee

...a dog	...un cane oon **kah**-nay
...mosquitoes	...zanzare zahnt-**sah**-ray
...a spider	...un ragno oon **rahn**-yoh
...a tick	...una zecca **oo**-nah **zeh**-kah
blisters	le vesciche lay veh-**shee**-kay
body odor	puzzo **pood**-zoh
burn	una bruciatura **oo**-nah broo-chah-**too**-rah
chapped lips	le labbra secche lay **lah**-brah **seh**-kay
chest pains	un dolore al petto oon doh-**loh**-ray ahl **peh**-toh
chills	i brividi ee bree-**vee**-dee
cold	un raffreddore oon rah-freh-**doh**-ray
congestion	una congestione **oo**-nah kohn-jeh-stee-**oh**-nay
constipation	la stitichezza lah stee-tee-**kehd**-zah
cough	la tosse lah **toh**-say
cramps...	i crampi... ee **krahm**-pee
...menstrual	...mestruali meh-stroo-**ah**-lee
...muscle	...muscolari moo-skoh-**lah**-ree
...stomach	...allo stomaco **ah**-loh **stoh**-mah-koh
diarrhea	la diarrea lah dee-ah-**reh**-ah
dizziness	i capogiri ee kah-poh-**jee**-ree
earache	il mal d'orecchi eel mahl doh-**reh**-kee
eczema	un eczema oon ehk-**zeh**-mah
fever	la febbre lah **feh**-bray
flu	l'influenza leen-floo-**ehnt**-sah
food poisoning	l'avvelenamento da cibo lah-veh-leh-nah-**mehn**-toh dah **chee**-boh
gas	l'aria nello stomaco **lah**-ree-ah **neh**-loh **stoh**-mah-koh
hay fever	il raffreddore da fieno eel rah-freh-**doh**-ray dah fee-**eh**-noh

headache	il mal di testa eel mahl dee **teh**-stah
heartburn	il bruciore di stomaco eel broo-**choh**-ray dee **stoh**-mah-koh
hemorrhoids	le emorroidi lay eh-moh-roh-**ee**-dee
hot flashes	le vampate di calore lay vahm-**pah**-tay dee kah-**loh**-ray
indigestion	un'indigestione oon-een-dee-jeh-stee-**oh**-nay
infection	un'infezione oon-een-feht-see-**oh**-nay
inflammation	un'infiammazione oon-een-fee-ah-maht-see-**oh**-nay
insomnia	l'insonnia leen-**soh**-nee-ah
lice	i pidocchi ee pee-**doh**-kee
lightheadedness	i capogiri ee kah-poh-**jee**-ree
migraine	l'emicrania leh-mee-**krah**-nee-ah
motion sickness (car)	il mal di macchina eel mahl dee **mah**-kee-nah
motion sickness (sea)	il mal di mare eel mahl dee **mah**-ray
nausea	la nausea lah **now**-zee-ah
numbness	l'intorpidimento leen-tor-pee-dee-**mehn**-toh
pain	il dolore eel doh-**loh**-ray
pimples	i foruncoli ee for-oon-**koh**-lee
pneumonia	la broncopolmonite lah brohn-koh-pohl-moh-**nee**-tay
pus	il pus eel poos
rash	l'irritazione della pelle lee-ree-taht-see-**oh**-nay **deh**-lah **peh**-lay
sinus problems	la sinusite lah see-noo-**zee**-tay
sneezing	gli starnuti lee star-noo-**tee**
sore throat	il mal di gola eel mahl dee **goh**-lah
splinter	una scheggia **oo**-nah **skeh**-jah

stomachache	il mal di stomaco eel mahl dee **stoh**-mah-koh
(bad) sunburn	una (brutta) scottatura solare **oo**-nah (**broo**-tah) skoh-tah-**too**-rah soh-**lah**-ray
swelling	un gonfiore oon gohn-fee-**oh**-ray
tendonitis	la tendinite lah tehn-dee-**nee**-tay
toothache	il mal di denti eel mahl dee **dehn**-tee
urinary tract infection	un'infezione urinaria oon-een-feht-see-**oh**-nay oo-ree-**nah**-ree-ah
urination (frequent / painful)	un'urinazione (frequente / dolorosa) oon-oo-ree-naht-see-**oh**-nay (freh-**kwehn**-tay / doh-loh-**roh**-zah)
vomiting	il vomito eel **voh**-mee-toh
wart	una verruca **oo**-nah veh-**roo**-kah
I'm going bald.	Perdo i capelli. **pehr**-doh ee kah-**peh**-lee

It Hurts

pain	dolore doh-**loh**-ray
painful	doloroso doh-loh-**roh**-zoh
hurts	fa male fah **mah**-lay
It hurts here.	Fa male qui. fah **mah**-lay kwee
My ____ hurts. (body parts listed next)	Mi fa male il / la ____. mee fah **mah**-lay eel / lah ____
aching	dolorante doh-loh-**rahn**-tay
bleeding	sanguinare sahn-gwee-**nah**-ray
blocked	bloccato bloh-**kah**-toh
broken	rotto **roh**-toh
bruised	contuso kohn-**too**-zoh
chafing	irritazione ee-ree-taht-see-**oh**-nay
cracked	incrinato een-kree-**nah**-toh

fractured	fratturato frah-too-**rah**-toh
infected	infetto een-**feh**-toh
inflamed	infiammato een-fee-ah-**mah**-toh
punctured (rusty nail)	punto (chiodo arruginito) **poon**-toh (kee-**oh**-doh ah-roo-jee-**nee**-toh)
scraped	sbucciato zboo-**chah**-toh
sore	dolorante doh-loh-**rahn**-tay
sprained	distorsione dee-stor-see-**oh**-nay
swollen	gonfio **gohn**-fee-oh
weak	debole deh-**boh**-lay
diagnosis	diagnosi dee-**ahn**-yoh-zee
What can I do?	Cosa posso fare? **koh**-zah **poh**-soh **fah**-ray
Is it serious?	È grave? eh **grah**-vay
Is it contagious?	È contagioso? eh kohn-tah-**joh**-zoh

Body Parts

ankle	caviglia kah-**veel**-yah
appendix	appendice ah-pehn-**dee**-chay
arm	braccio **brah**-choh
back	schiena skee-**eh**-nah
bladder	vescica veh-**shee**-kah
blood	sangue **sahn**-gway
body	corpo **kor**-poh
bone	osso **oh**-soh
bowel movement	movimento intestinale moh-vee-**mehn**-toh een-teh-stee-**nah**-lay
brain	cervello chehr-**veh**-loh
breast	seno **seh**-noh
chest	petto **peh**-toh
ear	orecchio oh-**reh**-kee-oh

elbow	gomito **goh**-mee-toh
eye	occhio **oh**-kee-oh
face	faccia / viso **fah**-chah / **vee**-zoh
finger	dito **dee**-toh
fingernail	unghia **oon**-gee-ah (hard "g")
foot	piede pee-**eh**-day
hand	mano **mah**-noh
head	testa **teh**-stah
heart	cuore **kwoh**-ray
hip	anca **ahn**-kah
kidney	rene **reh**-nay
knee	ginocchio jee-**noh**-kee-oh
leg	gamba **gahm**-bah
lips	labbra **lah**-brah
liver	fegato feh-**gah**-toh
lung	polmone pohl-**moh**-nay
mouth	bocca **boh**-kah
muscles	muscoli moo-**skoh**-lee
neck	collo **koh**-loh
nose	naso **nah**-zoh
ovary	ovaia oh-**vah**-yah
penis	pene **peh**-nay
poop	pupu **poo**-poo
shoulder	spalla **spah**-lah
skin	pelle **peh**-lay
stomach	stomaco **stoh**-mah-koh
teeth	denti **dehn**-tee
testicles	testicoli teh-**stee**-koh-lee
throat	gola **goh**-lah
toe	alluce ah-**loo**-chay
toenail	unghia del piede **oon**-gee-ah (hard "g") dehl pee-**eh**-day

tongue	lingua **leen**-gwah
urine	urina oo-**ree**-nah
uterus	utero **oo**-teh-roh
vagina	vagina vah-**jee**-nah
waist	vita **vee**-tah
wrist	polso **pohl**-soh
right / left	destro(a) / sinistro(a) **deh**-stroh / see-**nee**-stroh

First-Aid Kit and Medications

American name-brand medications are rare in Europe, but you'll find equally good local equivalents. Rather than looking for Sudafed, ask for a ***decongestionante*** (decongestant). Instead of Nyquil, request a ***farmaco per il raffreddore*** (cold medicine). For prescription drugs, ask your doctor for the generic name (for example, atorvastatin instead of Lipitor), which is more likely to be understood internationally. If using a European thermometer, see page 553 for help with temperature conversions.

medicine	farmaco **far**-mah-koh
pill	pillola pee-**loh**-lah
prescription	ricetta ree-**cheh**-tah
pharmacy	farmacia far-mah-**chee**-ah
24-hour pharmacy	farmacia aperta ventiquattro ore far-mah-**chee**-ah ah-**pehr**-tah vehn-tee-**kwah**-troh **oh**-ray
adult diapers (like Depends)	pannoloni pah-noh-**loh**-nee
antacid	antiacido ahn-tee-ah-**chee**-doh
anti-anxiety medicine	farmaco ansiolitico **far**-mah-koh ahn-see-oh-**lee**-tee-koh
antibiotic	antibiotici ahn-tee-bee-**oh**-tee-chee

antihistamine (like Benadryl)	antistaminico ahn-tee-stah-**mee**-nee-koh
aspirin	aspirina ah-spee-**ree**-nah
non-aspirin substitute (like Tylenol)	Saridon **sah**-ree-dohn
bandage	benda **behn**-dah
Band-Aids	cerotti cheh-**roh**-tee
cold medicine	farmaco per il raffreddore **far**-mah-koh pehr eel rah-freh-**doh**-ray
cough drops	caramelle per la tosse kah-rah-**meh**-lay pehr lah **toh**-say
decongestant (like Sudafed)	decongestionante deh-kohn-jeh-stee-oh-**nahn**-tay
diarrhea medicine	farmaco per la diarrea **far**-mah-koh pehr lah dee-ah-**reh**-ah
disinfectant	disinfettante dee-zeen-feh-**tahn**-tay
first-aid cream	pomata antistaminica poh-**mah**-tah ahn-tee-stah-**mee**-nee-kah
gauze / tape	garza / nastro **gart**-sah / **nah**-stroh
hemorrhoid medicine	farmaco per le emorroidi **far**-mah-koh pehr lay eh-moh-roh-**ee**-dee
hydrogen peroxide	acqua ossigenata **ah**-kwah oh-see-jeh-**nah**-tah
ibuprofen (like Advil)	ibuprofene ee-boo-proh-**feh**-nay
inhaler	inalatore een-ah-lah-**toh**-ray
insulin	insulina een-soo-**lee**-nah
itch reliever	pomata antiprurito poh-**mah**-tah ahn-tee-**proo**-ree-toh
laxative	lassativo lah-sah-**tee**-voh
moleskin (for blisters)	feltro / moleskin **fehl**-troh / "moleskin"
mosquito repellant	repellente per zanzare reh-peh-**lehn**-tay pehr zahnt-**sah**-ray

painkiller	analgesico ah-nahl-**jeh**-zee-koh
stomachache medicine	farmaco per il mal di stomaco **far**-mah-koh pehr eel mahl dee **stoh**-mah-koh
support bandage	fascia di sostegno **fah**-shah dee soh-**stehn**-yoh
syringe	siringa see-**reen**-gah
tetanus shot	antitetanica ahn-tee-teh-**tah**-nee-kah
thermometer	termometro tehr-moh-**meh**-troh
Vaseline	vaselina vah-zeh-**lee**-nah
vitamins	vitamine vee-tah-**mee**-nay
Does it sting?	Fa punture? fah poon-**too**-ray
Take one pill every ____ hours for ____ days.	Prenda una pillola ogni ____ ore per ____ giorni. **prehn**-dah **oo**-nah pee-**loh**-lah **ohn**-yee ____ **oh**-ray pehr ____ **jor**-nee

SPECIFIC NEEDS

The Eyes Have It

optician	ottico **oh**-tee-koh
eye / eyes	occhio / occhi **oh**-kee-oh / **oh**-kee
eye drops (for inflammation)	collirio koh-**lee**-ree-oh
artificial tears	lacrime artificiali **lah**-kree-may ar-tee-fee chee-**ah**-lee
glasses	occhiali oh-kee-**ah**-lee
sunglasses	occhiali da sole oh-kee-**ah**-lee dah **soh**-lay
reading glasses	occhiali da lettura oh-kee-**ah**-lee dah leh-**too**-rah
glasses case	custodia per occhiali koo-**stoh**-dee-ah pehr oh-kee-**ah**-lee

(broken) lens	lenti (rotte) **lehn**-tee (**roh**-tay)
to repair	riparare ree-pah-**rah**-ray
to replace	sostituire soh-stee-**twee**-ray
prescription	ricetta ree-**cheh**-tah
contact lenses...	lenti a contatto... **lehn**-tee ah kohn-**tah**-toh
...soft	...morbide **mor**-bee-day
...hard	...dure **doo**-ray
all-purpose solution	liquido unico per lenti a contatto **lee**-kwee-doh **oo**-nee-koh pehr **lehn**-tee ah kohn-**tah**-toh
contact lens case	porta lenti a contatto **por**-tah **lehn**-tee ah kohn-**tah**-toh
I don't see well.	Non vedo bene. nohn **veh**-doh **beh**-nay
nearsighted	miope mee-**oh**-pay
farsighted	presbite prehs-**bee**-tay
20 / 20 vision	visione perfetto vee-zee-**oh**-nay pehr-**feh**-toh

On Intimate Terms

personal lubricant (like KY Jelly)	lubrificante intimo loo-bree-fee-**kahn**-tay **een**-tee-moh
contraceptives	contraccettivi kohn-trah-cheh-**tee**-vee
condoms	preservativi preh-zehr-vah-**tee**-vee
birth-control pills	pillole anticoncezionali pee-**loh**-lay ahn-tee-kohn-cheht-see-oh-**nah**-lee
morning-after pill	pillola del giorno dopo pee-**loh**-lah dehl **jor**-noh **doh**-poh
herpes (inactive)	herpes (non attivo) **ehr**-pays (nohn ah-**tee**-voh)
HIV / AIDS	HIV / AIDS **ah**-kah ee vee / **ah**-eeds

STD (sexually transmitted disease)	MST (malattia sessualmente trasmissibile) **ehm**-ay **ehs**-ay tee (mah-lah-**tee**-ah seh-soo-ahl-**mehn**-tay trahs-mee-**see**-bee-lay)

For Women

menstruation / period	le mestruazioni lay meh-stroo-aht-see-**oh**-nee
tampons	assorbenti interni ah-sor-**behn**-tee een-**tehr**-nee
sanitary pads	assorbenti igienici ah-sor-**behn**-tee ee-**jehn**-ee-chee
I need medicine for...	Mi serve un farmaco per... mee **sehr**-vay oon **far**-mah-koh pehr
...menstrual cramps.	...i crampi mestruali. ee **krahm**-pee meh-stroo-**ah**-lee
...a yeast infection.	...un'infezione da candida. oon-een-feht-see-**oh**-nay dah **kahn**-dee-dah
...a urinary tract infection.	...un'infezione urinaria. oon-een-feht-see-**oh**-nay oo-ree-**nah**-ree-ah
I'd like to see...	Vorrei vedere... voh-**reh**-ee veh-**deh**-ray
...a female doctor.	...una dottoressa. **oo**-nah doh-toh-**reh**-sah
...a female gynecologist.	...una ginecologa. **oo**-nah jee-neh-**koh**-loh-gah
I've missed a period.	Ho saltato il ciclo mestruale. oh sahl-**tah**-toh eel **chee**-kloh meh-stroo-**ah**-lay
pregnancy test	test di gravidanza tehst dee grah-vee-**dahnt**-sah
ultrasound	ecografia eh-koh-grah-**fee**-ah

I am / She is... pregnant.	Sono / È incinta... **soh**-noh / eh een-**cheen**-tah
... ____ weeks / months	...di ____ settimane / mesi. dee ____ seh-tee-**mah**-nay / **meh**-zee
miscarriage	aborto spontaneo ah-**bor**-toh spohn-**tah**-neh-oh
abortion	aborto ah-**bor**-toh
menopause	menopausa meh-noh-**pow**-zah

GERMAN

Versatile, entertaining German is spoken throughout Germany, Austria, and most of Switzerland. In addition, German rivals English as the handiest second language in Scandinavia, the Netherlands, Eastern Europe, and Turkey.

German is kind of a "Lego language." Be on the lookout for fun combination words. A glove is a "hand shoe" ***(Handschuh),*** a peninsula is a "half island" ***(Halbinsel),*** and a skunk is a stinky animal ***(Stinktier).*** It follows that a ***Dummkopf*** (dumb head) is... um... uh...

German pronunciation differs from English in some key ways:

CH sounds like the guttural CH in Scottish loch.
G sounds like G in go. (not like G in gentle)
J sounds like Y in yes.
K is never silent.
S can sound like S in sun or Z in zoo.
SCH sounds like SH in shine.
TH sounds like T in top.
V usually sounds like F in fun.
W sounds like V in volt.
Z sounds like TS in hits.
AU sounds like OW in cow.
ÄU and EU sound like OY in joy.
EI and AI sound like I in light.
IE sounds like EE in seed.

German has a few unusual signs and sounds. The letter **ß** is not a letter B at all—it's interchangeable with "ss." Some of the German vowels are double-dotted with an umlaut. The ***ö*** has a sound uncommon in English. To make the ***ö*** sound, round your lips to say "o," but say "ee." To say ***ü,*** pucker your lips to make an "oo" sound, but say "ee." The German ***ch*** has a clearing-your-throat sound. Say ***Achtung!***

You can communicate a lot with only a few key German phrases. For example, the versatile ***es gibt*** and ***geht das*** have only two syllables apiece, but they can be useful in many situations. Here's how:

Es gibt (which means "there is" and is pronounced ehs gibt) can be used with any noun to create a statement of fact. If you don't know how to say "It's raining," just say ***Es gibt Regen*** (There is rain). And if you reverse the words, it becomes an all-purpose question: ***Gibt es Toilette?*** (Is there a toilet?)

Geht das? (pronounced gayt dahs) literally means "Does this go?"—basically "Is this OK?" It's a handy phrase when combined with a gesture. When showing your sightseeing pass to a museum ticket-taker, it means "Is this ticket valid at your museum?" When pointing to your camera at a market stall, it means "May I please take a picture?" The answer (you hope) will be ***Das geht.*** The globally understood "OK?" works in many of the same situations.

Here's a quick guide to the phonetics in this book:

ah	like A in father
ar	like AR in far
ay	like AY in play
ee	like EE in seed
eh	like E in get
ehr	sounds like "air"
ew	pucker your lips and say "ee"
g	like G in go
kh	like the guttural CH in Achtung
i	like I in hit
ī	like I in light
oh	like O in note
oo	like OO in moon
ow	like OW in cow
oy	like OY in toy
s	like S in sun
ur	like UR in purr
ts	like TS in hits; it's a small explosive sound
zh	like S in treasure

In German, the verb is sometimes at the end of the sentence; for instance, "I'd like to reserve a room" in German is ***Ich möchte ein Zimmer reservieren*** (literally "I'd like a room to reserve"). Note that when you're using the German phrases in this book, some fill-in-the-blank choices will come before the verb at the end.

Germans capitalize all nouns. Each noun has a gender, which determines which "the" you'll use: ***der, die, das, den, dem,*** or ***des.*** This is determined by the grammatical gender of the word, and how it's being used in the sentence. But no traveler is expected to remember which is which. It's OK to just grab whichever "the" comes to mind. In the interest of simplicity, we've occasionally left out the articles. And for brevity, we often drop the all-important "please" from the phrases. Please use "please" (***bitte,*** pronounced **bit**-teh) liberally.

Spoken German varies tremendously by region, with dialects that can differ noticeably within even a small area. Lilting Swiss German is particularly distinctive—and nearly unintelligible to many northern Germans. Swiss Germans speak it around the home, but in schools and at work they speak and write in the standard German used in Germany and Austria (called "High German," or ***Hochdeutsch***). Throughout this book, I've noted if a particular term or phrase is used predominantly or exclusively in a particular region: *(Aus.)* for Austria, *(Switz.)* for Switzerland, and *(Bav.)* for Bavaria—which, while part of Germany, has a dialect all its own.

It's fun to keep an eye out for the various diminutives that German speakers tack on to the end of nouns to make things smaller and/or cuter. Germans usually use ***chen*** or ***lein: Häuschen*** means small house, ***Hündchen*** is a little dog, ***Fraülein*** is a young woman. The Swiss use ***li: Brötli*** to the Swiss is a "little bread"—a roll. Austrians tend to add just ***l*** (a German girl is a ***Mädchen,*** but in Austria she's a ***Mädl***).

Greetings, however, vary the most across regions. Most Germans stick with ***Guten Tag*** (good day, **goo**-tehn tahg). The multilingual Swiss say hi with a cheery ***Grüetzi*** (**grewt**-see), thank you by saying ***Merci*** (**mer**-see), and bid goodbye with ***Ciao.*** And Austrians and Bavarians greet one another with ***Grüss Gott*** (grews goht), which means "May God greet you."

GERMAN BASICS

HELLOS AND GOODBYES

Pleasantries

Hello.	Guten Tag. **goo**-tehn tahg
Do you speak English?	Sprechen Sie Englisch? **shprehkh**-ehn zee **ehng**-lish
Yes. / No.	Ja. / Nein. yah / nīn
I don't speak German.	Ich spreche kein Deutsch. ikh **shprehkh**-eh kīn doytch
I'm sorry.	Es tut mir leid. ehs toot meer līt
Please.	Bitte. **bit**-teh
Thank you.	Danke. **dahn**-keh
Thank you very much.	Vielen Dank. **fee**-lehn dahnk
Excuse me.	Entschuldigung. ehnt-**shool**-dig-oong
OK?	OK? "OK"
OK.	In Ordnung. in **ord**-noong
Good.	Gut. goot
Very good.	Sehr gut. zehr goot
Excellent.	Ausgezeichnet. ows-geht-**sīkh**-neht
You are very kind.	Sie sind sehr freundlich. zee zint zehr **froynd**-likh
No problem.	Kein Problem. kīn proh-**blaym**
It doesn't matter.	Macht nichts. mahkht nikhts
You're welcome.	Bitte. **bit**-teh
Bye. (informal)	Tschüss chewss
Goodbye.	Auf Wiedersehen. owf **vee**-dehr-zay-ehn

Please is a magic word in any language. If you want to buy something, you can point at it and say ***Bitte*** (Please). If you know the word for what you want, such as the bill, simply say ***Rechnung, bitte*** (Bill, please). ***Bitte*** is an all-purpose courtesy word that can also mean "You're welcome" or "May I help you?"

Meeting and Greeting

Hi. (informal)	Hallo. hah-**loh**
Good morning.	Guten Morgen. **goo**-tehn **mor**-gehn
Good day. (Ger.)	Guten Tag. **goo**-tehn tahg
Good day. (Aus.)	Grüss Gott. grews goht
Good day. (Switz.)	Grüezi. **grewt**-see
Good evening.	Guten Abend. **goo**-tehn **ah**-behnt
Good night.	Gute Nacht. **goo**-teh nahkht
Welcome!	Willkommen! vil-**koh**-mehn
Mr.	Herr hehr
Ms.	Frau frow (rhymes with "now")
Miss (under 18)	Fräulein **froy**-līn
My name is ____.	Ich heisse ____. ikh **hī**-seh ____
What's your name?	Wie heissen Sie? vee **hī**-sehn zee
Pleased to meet you.	Sehr erfreut. zehr ehr-**froyt**
How are you?	Wie geht es Ihnen? vee gayt ehs **ee**-nehn
Very well, thank you.	Sehr gut, danke. zehr goot **dahn**-keh
Fine, thanks.	Gut, danke. goot **dahn**-keh
And you?	Und Ihnen? oont **ee**-nehn
Where are you from?	Woher kommen Sie? voh-**hehr koh**-mehn zee
I am from ____.	Ich komme aus ____. ikh **koh**-meh ows ____
I am / We are...	Ich bin / Wir sind... ikh bin / veer zint

Are you...?	Sind Sie...? zint zee
...on vacation	...auf Urlaub owf **oor**-lowb
...on business	...auf Geschäftsreise owf geh-**shehfts**-rī-zeh

Guten Tag (Good day) is the German "Hello," which people say all day long. To be more specific about the time of day, people use the greeting ***Guten Morgen*** (Good morning) before noon. Say ***Guten Abend*** (Good evening) after 6 p.m. and ***Gute Nacht*** (Good night) at bedtime.

Although Austrians and Swiss understand ***Guten Tag,*** they use their own variations to greet each other: ***Grüss Gott*** in Austria (also common in Bavaria) and ***Grüezi*** in Switzerland. In Austria, people sometimes use the all-purpose greeting ***Servus*** (**sehr**-voos)—a holdover from the days of the multilingual Austro-Hungarian Empire.

Moving On

I'm going to ____.	Ich fahre nach ____. ikh **far**-eh nahkh ____
How do I go to ____?	Wie komme ich nach ____? vee **koh**-meh ikh nahkh ____
Let's go.	Auf geht's. owf gayts
See you later!	Bis später! bis **shpay**-tehr
See you tomorrow!	Bis morgen! bis **mor**-gehn
So long! (informal)	Tschüss! chewss
Goodbye.	Auf Wiedersehen. owf **vee**-dehr-zay-ehn
Good luck!	Viel Glück! feel glewk
Happy travels!	Gute Reise! **goo**-teh **rī**-zeh

When saying goodbye, instead of ***auf Wiedersehen,*** some German speakers say ***auf Wiederschauen.*** They both mean the same thing ("until we see each other again"). You may also hear less-formal goodbyes, such as ***Tschüss, Bis später, Bis nachher,*** and even ***Ciao.***

STRUGGLING WITH GERMAN

Who Speaks What?

German	Deutsch doytch
English	Englisch **ehng**-lish
Do you speak English?	Sprechen Sie Englisch? **shprehkh**-ehn zee **ehng**-lish
A teeny weeny bit?	Ein ganz klein wenig? īn gahnts klīn **vay**-nig
Please speak English.	Bitte sprechen Sie Englisch. **bit**-teh **shprehkh**-ehn zee **ehng**-lish
Speak slowly, please.	Bitte sprechen Sie langsam. **bit**-teh **shprehkh**-ehn zee **lahng**-zahm
Repeat?	Noch einmal? nohkh **īn**-mahl
I understand.	Ich verstehe. ikh fehr-**shtay**-eh
I don't understand.	Ich verstehe nicht. ikh fehr-**shtay**-eh nikht
Do you understand?	Verstehen Sie? fehr-**shtay**-ehn zee
You speak English well.	Ihr Englisch ist sehr gut. eer **ehng**-lish ist zehr goot
Does somebody here speak English?	Spricht jemand hier Englisch? shprikht **yay**-mahnt heer **ehng**-lish
I don't speak German.	Ich spreche kein Deutsch. ikh **shprehkh**-eh kīn doytch
I speak a little German.	Ich spreche nur wenig Deutsch. ikh **shprehkh**-eh noor **vay**-nig doytch
What does that mean?	Was bedeutet das? vahs beh-**doy**-teht dahs
How do you say that in German?	Wie heisst das auf Deutsch? vee hīst dahs owf doytch
Write it down?	Aufschreiben? **owf**-shrī-behn

Very German Expressions

Ach so. ahkh zoh	I see.
Achtung! ahkh-**toong**	Attention! / Watch out!
Alles klar. **ahl**-ehs klar	Everything is clear. / I get it.
(Alles) in Ordnung. (**ahl**-ehs) in **ord**-noong	Everything's in order. (OK)
Ausgezeichnet. ows-geht-**sīkh**-neht	Excellent.
Bitte. **bit**-teh	Please. / You're welcome. / Can I help you? (casual)
Es geht. ehs gayt	It's fine. (passable, not great)
Es gibt... ehs gibt	There is... / There are...
gemütlich geh-**mewt**-likh	cozy
Gemütlichkeit geh-**mewt**-likh-kīt	coziness
Genau. geh-**now**	Exactly.
Halt. hahlt	Stop.
Hoppla! **hohp**-lah	Oops!
Kann ich Ihnen helfen? kahn ikh **een**-ehn **hehl**-fehn	Can I help you? (formal)
Kein Problem. kīn proh-**blaym**	No problem.
Kein Wunder. kīn **voon**-dehr	No wonder.

Mach schnell! mahkh shnehl	Hurry up! (informal)
Macht nichts. mahkht nikhts	It doesn't matter. / No problem.
Natürlich. nah-**tewr**-likh	Naturally.
Na ja. nah yah	Oh, well.
Schade. **shah**-deh	Too bad. / That's a shame.
Sicher. **zikh**-ehr	Sure.
Sonst noch etwas? zohnst nohkh **eht**-vahs	Anything else?
Stimmt. shtimt	Correct.
Super. **zoo**-pehr	Great.
Warum nicht? vah-**room** nikht	Why not?
Was gibt's? vahs gibts	What's up?
Was ist los? vahs ist lohs	What's the matter?
Wie geht's? vee gayts	How's it going?
Wunderbar! **voon**-dehr-bar	Wonderful!

Gemütlich (the adjective) and ***Gemütlichkeit*** (the noun) refer to an atmospheric coziness. A candlelit dinner, a friendly pub, a strolling violinist under a grape arbor on a balmy evening...this is ***gemütlich.***

REQUESTS

The Essentials

Can you help me?	Können Sie mir helfen? **kurn**-ehn zee meer **hehl**-fehn
Do you have ____?	Haben Sie ____? **hah**-behn zee ____
I'd like...	Ich hätte gern... ikh **heh**-teh gehrn
We'd like...	Wir hätten gern... veer **heh**-tehn gehrn
...this / that.	...dies / das. dees / dahs
How much (does it cost)?	Wie viel (kostet das)? vee feel (**kohs**-teht dahs)
Is it free?	Ist es kostenlos? ist ehs **kohs**-tehn-lohs
Included?	Inklusive? in-kloo-**zee**-veh
Is it possible?	Ist es möglich? ist ehs **murg**-likh
Yes or no?	Ja oder nein? yah **oh**-dehr nīn
Where are the toilets?	Wo sind die Toiletten? voh zint dee toy-**leh**-tehn
men	Herren **hehr**-ehn
women	Damen **dah**-mehn

To prompt a simple answer, ask ***Ja oder nein?*** (Yes or no?). To turn a word or sentence into a question, ask it in a questioning tone. An easy way to ask "Where are the toilets?" is to say ***Toiletten?***

Where?

Where?	Wo? voh
Where is the...?	Wo ist...? voh ist
...tourist information office	...das Touristeninfo dahs too-**ris**-tehn-in-foh
...train station	...der Bahnhof dehr **bahn**-hohf
Where is a cash machine?	Wo ist ein Geldautomat? voh ist īn **gelt**-ow-toh-maht

Where can I buy ____?	Wo kann ich ____ kaufen? voh kahn ikh ____ **kow**-fehn
Where can I find ____?	Wo kann ich ____ finden? voh kahn ikh ____ **fin**-dehn

You'll find some German words are similar to English if you're looking for a ***Hotel, Restaurant,*** or ***Supermarkt.***

How Much?

How much (does it cost)?	Wie viel (kostet das)? vee feel (**kohs**-teht dahs)
Write it down?	Aufschreiben? **owf**-shrī-behn
I'd like...	Ich hätte gern... ikh **heh**-teh gehrn
...a ticket.	...eine Karte. ī-neh **kar**-teh
...the bill.	...die Rechnung. dee **rehkh**-noong
This much. (gesturing)	So viel. zoh feel
More. / Less.	Mehr. / Weniger. mehr / **vay**-nig-ehr
Too much.	Zu viel. tsoo feel

When?

When?	Wann? vahn
What time is it?	Wie spät ist es? vee shpayt ist ehs
At what time?	Um wie viel Uhr? oom vee feel oor
____ o'clock	____ Uhr ____ oor
open / closed	geöffnet / geschlossen geh-**urf**-neht / geh-**shloh**-sehn
When does this open / close?	Wann ist hier geöffnet / geschlossen? vahn ist heer geh-**urf**-neht / geh-**shloh**-sehn
Is this open daily?	Ist es täglich geöffnet? ist ehs **tayg**-likh geh-**urf**-neht

What day is this closed?	An welchem Tag ist es geschlossen? ahn **vehlkh**-ehm tahg ist ehs geh-**shloh**-sehn
On time?	Pünktlich? **pewnkt**-likh
Late?	Spät? shpayt
Just a moment.	Moment. moh-**mehnt**
now / soon / later	jetzt / bald / später yehtst / bahlt / **shpay**-tehr
today / tomorrow	heute / morgen **hoy**-teh / **mor**-gehn

For tips on telling time, see "Time and Dates" on page 388.

How Long?

How long does it take?	Wie lange dauert es? vee **lahng**-eh **dow**-ehrt ehs
How many minutes / hours?	Wie viele Minuten / Stunden? vee **fee**-leh mee-**noo**-tehn / **shtoon**-dehn
How far?	Wie weit? vee vīt

SIMPLY IMPORTANT WORDS

For numbers, days, months, and time, see the next chapter. For guidance on how to pronounce the German alphabet, see page 550.

Big Little Words

I	ich ikh
you (formal)	Sie zee
you (informal)	du doo
we	wir veer
he	er ehr
she	sie zee
it	es ehs

they	sie zee
and	und oont
at	bei bī
because	weil vīl
but	aber **ah**-behr
by (train, car, etc.)	mit mit
for	für fewr
from	von fohn
here	hier heer
if	ob ohp
in	in in
not	nicht nikht
now	jetzt yehtst
of	von fohn
only	nur noor
or	oder **oh**-dehr
out	aus ows
this	dies dees
that	das dahs
to	nach nahkh
too	zu tsoo
very	sehr zehr

Opposites

good / bad	gut / schlecht goot / shlehkht
best / worst	beste / schlechteste **behs**-teh / **shlehkh**-tehs-teh
a little / a lot	wenig / viel **vay**-nig / feel
more / less	mehr / weniger mehr / **vay**-nig-ehr
cheap / expensive	billig / teuer **bil**-lig / **toy**-ehr
big / small	gross / klein grohs / klīn

hot / cold	heiss / kalt hīs / kahlt
warm / cool	warm / kühl varm / kewl
open / closed	geöffnet / geschlossen geh-**urt**-neht / geh **shloh**-sehn
entrance / exit	Eingang / Ausgang **īn**-gahng / **ows**-gahng
push / pull	drücken / ziehen **drewk**-ehn / **tsee**-ehn
arrive / depart	ankommen / abfahren **ahn**-koh-mehn / **ahp**-fah-rehn
early / late	früh / spät frew / shpayt
soon / later	bald / später bahlt / **shpay**-tehr
fast / slow	schnell / langsam shnehl / **lahng**-zahm
here / there	hier / dort heer / dort
near / far	nah / fern nah / fehrn
inside / outside	drinnen / draussen **drin**-nehn / **drow**-sehn
mine / yours	mein / Ihr mīn / eer
this / that	dies / das dees / dahs
easy / difficult	leicht / schwierig līkht / **shvee**-rig
left / right	links / rechts links / rehkhts
up / down	hoch / runter hohkh / **roon**-tehr
above / below	ober / unter **oh**-behr / **oon**-tehr
young / old	jung / alt yoong / ahlt
new / old	neu / alt noy / ahlt
heavy / light	schwer / leicht shvehr / līkht
dark / light	dunkel / hell **doonk**-ehl / hehl
happy / sad	glücklich / traurig **glewk**-likh / **trow**-rig
beautiful / ugly	schön / hässlich shurn / **hehs**-likh
nice / mean	nett / gemein neht / geh-**mīn**
smart / stupid	klug / dumm kloog / doom
vacant / occupied	frei / besetzt frī / beh-**zehtst**
with / without	mit / ohne mit / **oh**-neh

NUMBERS, MONEY & TIME

NUMBERS

0	null nool
1	eins īns
2	zwei tsvī
3	drei drī
4	vier feer
5	fünf fewnf
6	sechs zehkhs
7	sieben **zee**-behn
8	acht ahkht
9	neun noyn
10	zehn tsayn
11	elf ehlf
12	zwölf tsvurlf
13	dreizehn **drī**-tsayn
14	vierzehn **feer**-tsayn
15	fünfzehn **fewnf**-tsayn
16	sechzehn **zehkh**-tsayn
17	siebzehn **zeeb**-tsayn
18	achtzehn **ahkht**-tsayn
19	neunzehn **noyn**-tsayn
20	zwanzig **tsvahn**-tsig
21	einundzwanzig **īn**-oont-tsvahn-tsig
22	zweiundzwanzig **tsvī**-oont-tsvahn-tsig
23	dreiundzwanzig **drī**-oont-tsvahn-tsig

30	dreissig **drī**-sig
31	einunddreissig **īn**-oont-drī-sig
40	vierzig **feer**-tsig
50	fünfzig **fewnf**-tsig
60	sechzig **zehkh**-tsig
70	siebzig **zeeb**-tsig
80	achtzig **ahkht**-tsig
90	neunzig **noyn**-tsig
100	hundert **hoon**-dehrt
101	hunderteins hoon-dehrt-**īns**
102	hundertzwei hoon-dehrt **tsvī**
200	zweihundert **tsvī**-hoon-dehrt
300	dreihundert **drī**-hoon-dehrt
400	vierhundert **feer**-hoon-dehrt
500	fünfhundert **fewnf**-hoon-dehrt
600	sechshundert **zehkhs**-hoon-dehrt
700	siebenhundert **zee**-behn-hoon-dehrt
800	achthundert **ahkt**-hoon-dehrt
900	neunhundert **noyn**-hoon-dehrt
1000	tausend **tow**-zehnd ("tow" rhymes with "cow")
2000	zweitausend **tsvī**-tow-zehnd
2010	zweitausendzehn **tsvī**-tow-zehnd-**tsayn**
2011	zweitausendelf **tsvī**-tow-zehnd-**ehlf**
2012	zweitausendzwölf **tsvī**-tow-zehnd-**tsvurlf**
2013	zweitausenddreizehn **tsvī**-tow-zehnd-**drī**-tsayn
2014	zweitausendvierzehn **tsvī**-tow-zehnd-**feer**-tsayn
2015	zweitausendfünfzehn **tsvī**-tow-zehnd-**fewnf**-tsayn
2016	zweitausendsechzehn **tsvī**-tow-zehnd-**zehkh**-tsayn

2017	zweitausendsiebzehn **tsvī**-tow-zehnd-**zeeb**-tsayn
2018	zweitausendachtzehn **tsvī**-tow-zehnd-**ahkht**-tsayn
2019	zweitausendneunzehn **tsvī**-tow-zehnd-**noyn**-tsayn
2020	zweitausendzwanzig **tsvī**-tow-zehnd-**tsvahn**-tsig
million	eine Million ī-neh mil-**yohn**
billion	eine Milliarde ī-neh mil-**yar**-deh
number one	Nummer eins **noo**-mehr īns
first	erste **ehr**-steh
second	zweite **tsvī**-teh
third	dritte **drit**-teh
once / twice	ein Mal / zwei Mal īn mahl / tsvī mahl
a quarter	ein Viertel īn **feer**-tehl
a third	ein Drittel īn **drit**-tehl
half / a half	halb / ein Halbes hahlb / īn **hahl**-behs
this much	so viel zoh feel
a dozen	ein Dutzend īn **doot**-sehnd
a handful	eine Hand voll ī-neh hahnt fohl
enough	genug geh-**noog**
not enough	nicht genug nikht geh-**noog**
too much	zu viel tsoo feel
more	mehr mehr
less	weniger **vay**-nig-ehr
50%	fünfzig Prozent **fewnf**-tsig proh-**tsehnt**
100%	hundert Prozent **hoon**-dehrt proh-**tsehnt**

In some dialects, the number ***zwei*** (two) is sometimes pronounced "tsvoh" to help distinguish it from the similar sound of ***drei*** (three).

Remember the nursery rhyme about the four-and-twenty blackbirds? That's how Germans say the numbers from 21 to 99 (e.g., 59 = ***neunundfünfzig*** = nine-and-fifty).

Learning how to say your hotel room number is a good way to practice German numbers. You'll likely be asked for the number frequently (at breakfast, or to claim your key when you return to your room).

MONEY

Germany and Austria use the euro currency. One euro (€) is divided into 100 cents. Germans use the term ***Euro*** (**oy**-roh) and ***Cent*** (tsehnt) as both singular and plural, so €2.50 would be ***zwei Euro fünfzig Cent***—or simply ***zwei fünfzig.***

Switzerland has held fast to its francs (which can be abbreviated as Fr, SF, or CHF). Each franc is divided into 100 smaller units, called ***Rappen*** (abbreviated as Rp, **rah**-pehn) in German.

Use your common cents—***Cent*** and ***Rappen*** are like pennies, and the euro and franc currencies each have coins like nickels, dimes, and half-dollars. There are also €1 and €2 coins.

Cash Machines (ATMs)

To get cash, ATMs are the way to go. Every cash machine (called ***Geldautomat*** in Germany, ***Bankomat*** in Austria and Switzerland) has multilingual instructions. However, the keys might be marked in German: ***Bestätigung*** means confirm, ***Korrektur*** means change or correct, and ***Abbruch*** is cancel.

money	Geld gehlt
cash	Bargeld **bar**-gehlt
card	Karte **kar**-teh
PIN code	PIN-Nummer **pin**-noo-mehr
Where is a...?	Wo ist ein...? voh ist īn
...cash machine	...Geldautomat (Ger.) / Bankomat (Aus., Switz.) **gelt**-ow-toh-maht / **bahnk**-oh-maht

...bank	...Bank bahnk
My debit card has been...	Meine Bankkarte wurde... **mī**-neh **bahnk**-kar-teh **voor**-deh
...demagnetized.	...entmagnetisiert. ehnt-mahg-neh-tee-**zeert**
...stolen.	...gestohlen. geh-**shtoh**-lehn
...eaten by the machine.	...von der Maschine geschluckt. fohn dehr mah-**shee**-neh geh-**shlookt**
My card doesn't work.	Meine Karte geht nicht. **mī**-neh **kar**-teh gayt nikht

Credit and Debit Cards

Credit cards are widely accepted at larger businesses, though smaller shops, restaurants, and guest houses prefer cash. Even if they accept credit cards, some hotels might cut you a discount for paying in cash.

credit card	Kreditkarte kreh-**deet**-kar-teh
debit card	Bankkarte **bahnk**-kar-teh
receipt	Rechnung **rehkh**-noong
handwritten receipt	Quittung **kvit**-toong
sign	unterschreiben **oon**-tehr-schrī-behn
pay	zahlen **tsah**-lehn
cashier	Kasse **kah**-seh
cash advance	Vorschuss in Bargeld **for**-shoos in **bar**-gehlt
Do you accept credit cards?	Akzeptieren Sie Kreditkarten? ahkt-sehp-**teer**-ehn zee kreh-**deet**-kar-tehn
Cheaper if I pay cash?	Billiger wenn ich mit Bargeld bezahle? **bil**-lig-ehr vehn ikh mit **bar**-gehlt beht-**sah**-leh
I do not have a PIN.	Ich habe keine PIN-Nummer. ikh **hah**-beh **kīn**-eh **pin**-noo-mehr

Key Phrases: Money

euro (€)	Euro **oy**-roh
cent	Cent tsehnt
cash	Bargeld **bar**-gehlt
Where is a...?	Wo ist ein...? voh ist īn
...cash machine	...Geldautomat (Ger.) / Bankomat (Aus., Switz.) **gelt**-ow-toh-maht / **bahnk**-oh-maht
...bank	...Bank bahnk
credit card	Kreditkarte kreh-**deet**-kar-teh
debit card	Bankkarte **bahnk**-kar-teh
Do you accept credit cards?	Akzeptieren Sie Kreditkarten? ahkt-sehp-**teer**-ehn zee kreh-**deet**-kar-tehn

Can I sign the receipt instead?	Kann ich stattdessen die Rechnung unterschreiben? kahn ikh staht-**deh**-sehn dee **rehkh**-noong **oon**-tehr-schrī-behn
Print a receipt?	Kassenbon ausdrucken? **kah**-sehn-bohn **ows**-droo-kehn
I have another card.	Ich habe eine andere Karte. ikh **hah**-beh **ī**-neh **ahn**-deh-reh **kar**-teh

Much of Europe is adopting a "chip-and-PIN" system for credit and debit cards, which are embedded with an electronic chip. If a shop window or machine indicates that Visa or MasterCard is accepted, your American card should work. But automated machines that take only ***GeldKarten*** and/or ***EC Karten*** can only handle these chip-embedded cards. If a payment machine won't take your card, look for a cashier who can swipe it instead, or find a machine that takes cash.

TIME AND DATES

Telling Time

In Germany, Austria, and Switzerland, the 24-hour clock (which we call "military time") is used for setting formal appointments (for instance, arrival times at a hotel), for the opening and closing hours of museums and shops, and for train, bus, and boat schedules. Informally, Europeans usually use the same 12-hour clock we do. So they might meet a friend at 3:00 ***am Nachmittag*** (in the afternoon) to catch a train 15 minutes later at 15:15.

What time is it?	Wie spät ist es?	vee shpayt ist ehs
____ o'clock	____ Uhr	____ oor
(in the) morning	(am) Morgen	(ahm) **mor**-gehn
(in the) afternoon	(am) Nachmittag	(ahm) **nahkh**-mit-tahg
(in the) evening	(am) Abend	(ahm) **ah**-behnt
(at) night	(in der) Nacht	(in dehr) nahkht
half	Halb	hahlb
quarter	Viertel	**feer**-tehl
minute	Minute	mee-**noo**-teh
hour	Stunde	**shtoon**-deh
It's... / At...	Es ist... / Um...	ehs ist / oom
...8:00 in the morning.	...acht Uhr morgens.	ahkht oor **mor**-gehns
...16:00.	...sechzehn Uhr.	**zehkh**-tsayn oor
...4:00 in the afternoon.	...vier Uhr nachmittags.	feer oor **nahkh**-mit-tahgs
...10:30 in the evening. ("half-eleven")	...halb elf abends.	hahlb ehlf **ah**-behnts
...a quarter past nine.	...viertel nach neun.	**feer**-tehl nahkh noyn
...a quarter to eleven.	...viertel vor elf.	**feer**-tehl for ehlf
at 6:00 sharp	um Punkt sechs Uhr	oom poonkt zehkhs oor

from 8:00 to 10:00	von acht bis zehn fohn ahkht bis tsayn
noon	Mittag **mit**-tahg
midnight	Mitternacht **mit**-tehr-nahkht
It's my bedtime.	Es ist meine Bettzeit. ehs ist **mī**-neh beht-sīt
I will be / We will be...	Ich bin / Wir sind... ikh bin / veer zint
...back at 11:20.	...um elf Uhr zwanzig zurück. oom ehlf oor **tsvahn**-tsig tsoo-**rewk**
...there by 18:00.	...um achtzehn Uhr dort. oom **ahkht**-tsayn oor dort

Key Phrases: Time and Dates

What time is it?	Wie spät ist es? vee shpayt ist ehs
____ o'clock	____ Uhr ____ oor
minute	Minute mee-**noo**-teh
hour	Stunde **shtoon**-deh
It's...	Es ist... ehs ist
...7:00 in the morning.	...sieben Uhr morgens. **zee**-behn oor **mor**-gehns
...2:00 in the afternoon.	...zwei Uhr nachmittags. tsvī oor **nahkh**-mit-tahgs
When does this open / close?	Wann ist hier geöffnet / geschlossen? vahn ist heer geh-**urf**-neht / geh-**shloh**-sehn
day	Tag tahg
today	heute **hoy**-teh
tomorrow	morgen **mor**-gehn
(this) week	(diese) Woche (**dee**-zeh) **vohkh**-eh
August 21	Einundzwanzigsten August **īn**-oont-tsvahn-tsig-stehn ow-**goost**

Timely Questions

When?	Wann? vahn
At what time?	Um wie viel Uhr? oom vee feel oor
Opening times?	Öffnungszeiten? **urf**-noongs-tsī-tehn
When does this open / close?	Wann ist hier geöffnet / geschlossen? vahn ist heer geh-**urf**-neht / geh-**shloh**-sehn
Is the train / bus...?	Ist der Zug / Bus...? ist dehr tsoog / boos
...early / late	...früh / verspätet frew / fehr-**shpay**-teht
...on time	...pünktlich **pewnkt**-likh
When is check-out time?	Um wie viel Uhr ist Check-out? oom vee feel oor ist "check-out"

It's About Time

now	jetzt yehtst
soon	bald bahlt
later	später **shpay**-tehr
in one hour	in einer Stunde in ī-nehr **shtoon**-deh
in half an hour	in einer halben Stunde in ī-nehr **hahl**-behn **shtoon**-deh
in three hours	in drei Stunden in drī **shtoon**-dehn
early	früh frew
late	spät shpayt
on time	pünktlich **pewnkt**-likh
anytime	jederzeit yay-dehr-**tsīt**
immediately	sofort zoh-**fort**
every hour	jede Stunde / stündlich **yay**-deh **shtoon**-deh / **shtewnd**-likh
every day	jeden Tag **yay**-dehn tahg

daily	täglich **tay**-glikh
last	letzte **lehts**-teh
this	diese **dee**-zeh
next	nächste **nehkh**-steh
before	vor for
after	nach nahkh
May 15	fünfzehnten Mai **fewnf**-tsayn-tehn mī

The Day

day	Tag tahg
today	heute **hoy**-teh
sunrise	Sonnenaufgang zoh-nehn-**owf**-gahng
this morning	heute Morgen **hoy**-teh **mor**-gehn
sunset	Sonnenuntergang zoh-nehn-**oon**-tehr-gahng
tonight	heute Abend **hoy**-teh **ah**-behnt
yesterday	gestern **geh**-stehrn
tomorrow	morgen **mor**-gehn
tomorrow morning	morgen früh **mor**-gehn frew
day after tomorrow	übermorgen **ew**-behr-mor-gehn

The Week

Sunday	Sonntag **zohn**-tahg
Monday	Montag **mohn**-tahg
Tuesday	Dienstag **deens**-tahg
Wednesday	Mittwoch **mit**-vohkh
Thursday	Donnerstag **doh**-nehrs-tahg
Friday	Freitag **frī**-tahg
Saturday	Samstag / Sonnabend (Aus.) **zahms**-tahg / **zohn**-ah-behnt

week	Woche **vohkh**-eh
last week	letzte Woche **lehts**-teh **vohkh**-eh
this week	diese Woche **dee**-zeh **vohkh**-eh
next week	nächste Woche **nehkh**-steh **vohkh**-eh
weekend	Wochenende **vohkh**-ehn-ehn-deh
this weekend	dieses Wochenende **dee**-zehs **vohkh**-ehn-ehn-deh

The Months

month	Monat **moh**-naht
January	Januar / Jänner (Aus.) **yah**-noo-ar / **yeh**-nehr
February	Februar **fay**-broo-ar
March	März mehrts
April	April ah-**pril**
May	Mai mī
June	Juni **yoo**-nee
July	Juli **yoo**-lee
August	August ow-**goost**
September	September zehp-**tehm**-behr
October	Oktober ohk-**toh**-behr
November	November noh-**fehm**-behr
December	Dezember day-**tsehm**-behr

For dates, you can usually take any number, add ***ten*** to the end, then say the month. So June 19 is ***neunzehnten Juni.***

The Year

year	Jahr yar
season	Jahreszeit **yar**-ehs-tsīt
spring	Frühling **frew**-ling
summer	Sommer **zohm**-ehr
fall	Herbst hehrpst
winter	Winter **vin**-tehr

For a list of years, see the "Numbers" section, pages 383-384.

TRANSPORTATION

GETTING AROUND

train	Zug tsoog
suburban railway	S-Bahn **ehs**-bahn
bus	Bus boos
subway	U-Bahn **oo**-bahn
taxi	Taxi **tahk**-see
car	Auto **ow**-toh ("ow" rhymes with "cow")
walk	laufen **low**-fehn ("low" rhymes with "cow")
on foot	zu Fuss tsoo foos
journey / trip	Farhrt fart
Where is the...?	Wo ist...? voh ist
...train station	...der Bahnhof dehr **bahn**-hohf
...bus station	...der Busbahnhof dehr **boos**-bahn-hohf
...bus stop	...die Bushaltestelle dee **boos**-hahl-teh-**shteh**-leh
...subway station	...die U-Bahn-Station dee **oo**-bahn-staht-see-ohn
...taxi stand	...der Taxistand dehr **tahk**-see-shtahnt
I'm going / We're going to ____.	Ich fahre / Wir fahren nach ____. ikh **far**-eh / veer **far**-ehn nahkh ____
What is the cheapest / fastest / easiest way...?	Wie komme ich am günstigsten / schnellsten / einfachsten...? vee **koh**-meh ikh ahm **gewn**-stig-stehn / **shnehl**-stehn / **īn**-fahkh-stehn
...to downtown	...zum Zentrum tsoom tsehn-**troom**

...to the train station	...zum Bahnhof tsoom **bahn**-hohf
...to my / our hotel	...zum meinem / unserem Hotel tsoom **mī**-nehm / **oon**-zeh-rehm "hotel"
...to the airport	...zum Flughafen tsoom **floog**-hah-fehn

In German, there are two different ways of saying "to go." If going somewhere by foot, use ***gehen;*** on wheels, use ***fahren.***

TRAINS

For tips and strategies about rail travel and railpasses in Germany, Austria, and Switzerland, see www.ricksteves.com/rail. Note that many of the following train phrases work for long-distance bus travel as well.

Ticket Basics

ticket	Fahrkarte **far**-kar-teh
reservation	Reservierung / Platzkarte reh-zehr-**veer**-oong / **plahts**-kar-teh
ticket counter	Kartenschalter **kar**-tehn-shahl-tehr
ticket machine	Fahrkartenautomat **far**-kar-tehn-**ow**-toh-maht
to validate	entwerten **ehnt**-vehr-tehn
Where can I buy a ticket?	Wo kann ich eine Fahrkarte kaufen? voh kahn ikh ī-neh **far**-kar-teh **kow**-fehn
Is this the line for...?	Ist hier die Schlange für...? ist heer dee **shlahng**-eh fewr
...tickets	...Fahrkarten **far**-kar-tehn
...reservations	...Reservierungen reh-zehr-**veer**-oong-ehn
...information	...Information in-for-maht-see-**ohn**
One ticket (to ____).	Eine Fahrkarte (nach ____). ī-neh **far**-kar-teh (nahkh ____)

Two tickets.	Zwei Fahrkarten. tsvī **far**-kar-tehn
I want to go to ____.	Ich möchte nach ____. ikh **murkh**-teh nahkh ____
How much (is a ticket to ____)?	Wie viel (kostet eine Fahrkarte nach ____)? vee feel (**kohs**-teht ī-neh **far**-kar-teh nahkh ____)
one-way ticket	Hinfahrkarte **hin**-far-kar-teh
round-trip ticket	Rückfahrkarte **rewk**-far-kar-teh
today / tomorrow	heute / morgen **hoy**-teh / **mor**-gehn

A ticket can also be called a ***Fahrausweis,*** a ***Fahrschein,*** or (in Switzerland) a ***Billett.***

Ticket Specifics

For phrases related to discounts (such as for children, families, or seniors), see page 400.

schedule	Fahrplan **far**-plahn
When is the next train (to ____)?	Wann fährt der nächste Zug (nach ____)? vahn fehrt dehr **nehkh**-steh tsoog (nahkh ____)
What time does it leave?	Um wie viel Uhr fährt er ab? oom vee feel oor fehrt ehr ahp
I'd like / We'd like to leave...	Ich möchte / Wir möchten... abfahren. ikh **murkh**-teh / veer **murkh**-tehn... **ahp**-far-ehn
I'd like / We'd like to arrive...	Ich möchte / Wir möchten... ankommen. ikh **murkh**-teh / veer **murkh**-tehn... **ahn**-koh-mehn
...by ____ o'clock.	...bis ____ Uhr bis ____ oor
...at ____ o'clock...	...um ____ Uhr... um ____ oor

Getting Tickets

When it comes to buying tickets for the bus, train, or subway, the following phrases will come in handy.

Where can I buy a ticket?	Wo kann ich eine Fahrkarte kaufen? voh kahn ikh ī-neh **far**-kar-teh **kow**-fehn
How much (is a ticket to ____)?	Wie viel (kostet eine Fahrkarte nach ____)? vee feel (**kohs**-teht ī-neh **far**-kar-teh nahkh ____)
I want to go to ____.	Ich möchte nach ____. ikh **murkh**-teh nahkh ____
One ticket / Two tickets (to ____).	Eine Fahrkarte / Zwei Fahrkarten (nach ____). ī-neh **far**-kar-teh / tsvī **far**-kar-tehn (nahkh ____)
When is the next train / bus (to ____)?	Wann kommt der nächste Zug / Bus (nach ____)? vahn kohmt dehr **nehkh**-steh tsoog / boos (nahkh ____)
What time does it leave?	Um wie viel Uhr fährt er ab? oom vee feel oor fehrt ehr ahp
Direct?	Direkt? dee-rehkt
Is a reservation required?	Brauche ich eine Reservierung? **browkh**-eh ikh ī-neh reh-zehr-**veer**-oong
I'd like / We'd like to reserve a seat.	Ich möchte / Wir möchten einen Sitzplatz reservieren. ikh **murkh**-teh / veer **murkh**-tehn ī-nehn **zits**-plahts reh-zehr-**veer**-ehn
Can I buy a ticket on board?	Kann ich an Bord Fahrkarten kaufen? kahn ikh ahn bord **far**-kar-tehn **kow**-fehn
Do you give change?	Geben Sie Rückgeld? **gay**-behn zee **rewk**-gehlt

...in the morning / afternoon / evening.	...am Morgen / Nachmittag / Abend ahm **mor**-gehn / **nahkh**-mit-tahg / **ah**-behnt
Is there a...?	Gibt es einen...? gibt ehs ī-nehn
...earlier train	...früheren Zug **frew**-ehr-ehn tsoog
...later train	...späteren Zug **shpay**-tehr-ehn tsoog
...overnight train	...Nachtzug **nahkht**-tsoog
...cheaper train	...günstigeren Zug **gewn**-stig-ehr-ehn tsoog
...express train	...Schnellzug **shnehl**-tsoog
...direct train	...Direktzug dee-**rehkt**-tsoog
Direct?	Direkt? dee-**rehkt**
Is a transfer required?	Muss man umsteigen? moos mahn **oom**-shtī-gehn
How many transfers?	Wie oft muss man Umsteigen? vee oft moos mahn **oom**-shtī-gehn
When? Where?	Wann? Wo? vahn / voh
first / second class	erste / zweite Klasse **ehr**-steh / **tsvī**-teh **klah**-seh
How long is this ticket valid?	Wie lange ist diese Fahrkarte gültig? vee **lahng**-eh ist **dee**-zeh **far**-kar-teh **gewl**-tig
Can you validate my railpass?	Können Sie bitte meinen Fahrschein validieren? **kurn**-ehn zee **bit**-teh **mī**-nehn **far**-shīn vah-lee-**deer**-ehn

You can buy tickets at ticket windows, at machines, or, at larger stations, in the ***Reisezentrum*** (travel center). Be sure you go to the correct window: Head to ***Fahrkarten*** or ***Fahrscheine*** for tickets, ***Reservierungen*** for reservations, ***Inland*** for domestic trips, and ***Ausland*** for international routes. On tickets, ***1.*** (or ***1. Klasse***) means first class, and ***2.*** (or ***2. Klasse***) means second class.

When using ticket machines, you might see these instructions: ***Bitte wählen Sie*** (please select), ***Zahlbar mit...*** (payable with—cash, credit card, etc.), and ***Annahme von Banknoten*** (acceptance of banknotes—where to insert your cash).

Train Reservations

Whether you use a railpass or point-to-point tickets, you can pay a little extra for a ***Reservierung*** (seat reservation). Reserving a seat is often optional, but can be a good idea for busy routes at popular times. Some high-speed international trains require railpass holders to buy a reservation—look for the R symbol in the timetable. If you buy a ticket for a slow train, then decide to take a fast one instead, you might have to pay a ***Zuschlag*** (supplement). If you have a railpass, it already covers supplements on trains in Germany, Austria, and Switzerland.

Is a reservation required?	Brauche ich eine Reservierung? **browkh**-eh ikh ī-neh reh-zehr-**veer**-oong
I'd like / We'd like to reserve...	Ich möchte / Wir möchten... reservieren. ikh **murkh**-teh / veer **murkh**-tehn... reh-zehr-**veer**-ehn
...a seat.	...einen Sitzplatz ī-nehn **zits**-plahts
...an aisle seat.	...einen Sitzplatz am Gang ī-nehn **zits**-plahts ahm gahng
...a window seat.	...einen Sitzplatz am Fenster ī-nehn **zits**-plahts ahm **fehn**-stehr
...two seats.	...zwei Sitzplätze tsvī **zits**-pleht-seh
...a couchette. (sleeping berth)	...einen Liegewagenplatz ī-nehn **lee**-geh-vah-gehn-plahts
...an upper / middle / lower berth.	...einen oberen / mittleren / unteren Liegewagenplatz ī-nehn **oh**-beh-rehn / **mit**-leh-rehn / **oon**-teh-rehn **lee**-geh-vah-gehn-plahts
...two couchettes.	...zwei Liegewagenplätze tsvī **lee**-geh-vah-gehn-pleht-seh

...a sleeper.	...einen Schlafwagenplatz ī-nehn **shlahf**-vah-gehn-plahts
...a sleeper with two beds.	...ein Zweibett-Schlafabteil īn **tsvī**-beht-**schlahf**-ahp-tīl
...the entire train.	...den ganzen Zug dayn **gahnt**-sehn tsoog

Discounts

Is there a cheaper option?	Gibt es eine günstigere Variante? gibt ehs ī-neh **gewn**-stig-ehr-eh vah-ree-**ahn**-teh
discount	Ermässigung ehr-**may**-see-goong
reduced fare	verbilligte Karte fehr-**bil**-lig-teh **kar**-teh
refund	Rückzahlung **rewk**-tsah-loong
Is there a discount for...?	Gibt es eine Ermässigung für...? gibt ehs ī-neh ehr-**may**-see-goong fewr
...children	...Kinder **kin**-dehr
...youths	...Jugendliche **yoo**-gehnd-likh-eh
...seniors	...Senioren zehn-**yor**-ehn
...families	...Familien fah-**meel**-yehn
...groups	...Gruppen **groop**-ehn
...advance purchase	...vorverkauf **for**-fehr-kowf
...weekends	...Wochenende **vohkh**-ehn-ehn-deh
Are there any deals for this journey?	Gibt es Sonderangebote für diese Reise? gibt ehs zohn-dehr-**ahn**-geh-boh-teh fewr **dee**-zeh **rī**-zeh

At the Train Station

Bahnhof (Bf.) means train station. Big cities can have several, but the ***Hauptbahnhof (Hbf.)*** is the main one.

Key Phrases: Trains

(main) train station	(Haupt)Bahnhof (**howpt**-)**bahn**-hohf
train	Zug tsoog
platform	Bahnsteig **bahn**-shtīg
track	Gleis glīs
What track does it leave from?	Von welchem Gleis fährt er ab? fohn **vehlkh**-ehm glīs fehrt ehr ahp
Is this the train to ____?	Ist das der Zug nach ____? ist dahs dehr tsoog nahkh ____
Which train to ____?	Welcher Zug fährt nach ____? **vehlkh**-ehr tsoog fehrt nahkh ____
Can you tell me when (to get off)?	Können Sie mir sagen (wenn ich raus muss)? **kurn**-ehn zee meer **zah**-gehn (vehn ikh rows moos)
transfer	Umsteig **oom**-shtīg
Change here for ____?	Hier umsteigen nach ____? heer **oom**-shtī-gehn nahkh ____

Where is the train station / main train station?	Wo ist der Bahnhof / Hauptbahnhof? voh ist dehr **bahn**-hohf / **howpt**-bahn-hohf
train information	Zugauskunft tsoog-**ows**-koonft
travel center	Reisezentrum **rī**-zeh-tsehn-troom
ticket counter	Kartenschalter **kar**-ten-shahl-tehr
tickets	Fahrkarten **far**-kar-tehn
departure / arrival	Abfahrt / Ankunft **ahp**-fart / **ahn**-koonft
On time?	Pünktlich? **pewnkt**-likh
Late?	Verspätet? fehr-**shpay**-teht
How late?	Wie spät? vee shpayt

platform	Bahnsteig **bahn**-shtīg
track	Gleis glīs
What track does it leave from?	Von welchem Gleis fährt er ab? fohn **vehlkh**-ehm glīs fehrt ehr ahp
waiting room	Wartesaal **var**-teh-zahl
lockers	Schliessfächer **shlees**-fehkh-ehr
baggage check	Gepäckaufgabe geh-**pehk**-owf-gah-beh
tourist information	Touristen information too-**ris**-tehn in-for-maht-see-**ohn**
lost and found office	Fundbüro **foond**-bew-roh
toilets	Toiletten toy-**leh**-tehn

Every sizeable German rail station has a ***Reisezentrum*** (travel center) where you can buy tickets and reservations, get schedule information, and ask questions. You'll either wait in line or take a number ***(Nummer ziehen)***. The number readout screen says ***Anruf*** (number currently being served) and ***Schalter*** (numbered window to report to).

At bigger stations, you might find a ***Bahnhofs-Übersichtsplan*** (train-station floor plan), ***Städteverbindungen*** (information about connections to nearby places), or ***Stadtplan*** (city map).

Each country has its own railway company: German trains are operated by ***Deutsche Bahn*** (***DB,*** day bay); in Austria, it's ***Österreichische Bundesbahn*** (***ÖBB,*** ur bay bay); and Switzerland has the ***Schweizer Bundesbahn*** (***SBB,*** ehs bay bay).

Train and Bus Schedules

European timetables use the 24-hour clock. It's like American time until noon. After that, subtract twelve and add p.m. So 13:00 is 1 p.m., and 19:00 is 7 p.m. Here are common scheduling terms:

ab	from
Abfahrt	departure
an	to
Ankunft	arrival

auch	also
ausser	except
bis	until
etwa ____ Min. später	about ____ minutes late
fährt	goes
Feiertag	holiday
Fernverkehr	long-distance transportation
Gleis (Gl.)	track number / platform
hält nicht überall	does not make every stop
jede	every
Minuten (Min.)	minutes
nach	to
nicht	not
nur	only
Richtung	direction and / or final destination
Samstag	Saturday
Sonntag	Sunday
später	later (than scheduled)
Stunden (Std.)	hours
täglich (tgl.)	daily
tagsüber	during the day
über	via
verspätet	late
Verspätung (Versp.)	delay
von	from
voraussichtlich (Vor.)	estimated (as in an arrival time)
Werktags	Monday-Saturday (workdays)
Wochentags	weekdays
Zeit	time
Ziel	destination
Zug	train (type and number)
1-5 / 6 / 7	Monday-Friday / Saturday / Sunday

Sometimes, instead of using numbers, days of the week are abbreviated as ***Mo*** (Monday), ***Di*** (Tuesday), ***Mi*** (Wednesday), ***Do*** (Thursday), ***Fr*** (Friday), ***Sa*** (Saturday), and ***So*** (Sunday).

All Aboard

In the station, signs direct you ***zu den Zügen*** (to the trains). The electronic train information board posted above the track lists ***Ankunft*** (the time the train arrives), ***Abfahrt*** (when it will depart), and a list of major stops. For express trains, it might say ***hält nicht überall*** (does not make every stop). The ***Wagenstandanzeiger*** (train-car configuration diagram) shows you where to wait for your car along the platform.

Some trains split partway along a journey ***(Zugteilung)***, sending the front ***(vorderer Zugteil)*** and back ***(hinterer Zugteil)*** halves of the train cars to different destinations. If you read schedules carefully—then check signs posted in the window of each train car—you can anticipate this and be sure you wind up on the correct half.

platform	Bahnsteig **bahn**-shtīg
track	Gleis glīs
number	Nummer **noo**-mehr
train car	Wagen **vah**-gehn
conductor	Schaffner **shahf**-nehr
Is this the train to ____?	Ist das der Zug nach ____? ist dahs dehr tsoog nahkh ____
Which train to ____?	Welcher ist der Zug nach ____? **vehlkh**-ehr ist dehr tsoog nahkh ____
Which train car to ____?	Welcher Wagen fährt nach ____? **vehlkh**-ehr **vah**-gehn fehrt nahkh ____
Where is...?	Wo ist...? voh ist
Is this...?	Ist dieser...? ist **dee**-zehr
...my seat	...mein Platz mīn plahts
...first / second class	...erste (1.) / zweite (2.) Klasse **ehr**-steh / **tsvī**-teh **klah**-seh
...the dining car	...der Speisewagen dehr **shpī**-zeh-vah-gehn
...the sleeper car	...der Liegewagen dehr **lee**-geh-vah-gehn
...the toilet	...die Toilette dee toy-**leh**-teh

reserved / occupied / free	reserviert / besetzt / frei **reh**-zehr-veert / **beh**-zehtst / frī
Is this (seat) free?	Ist hier frei? ist heer (plahts) frī
May I / May we...?	Darf ich / Dürfen wir...? darf ikh / **dewr**-fehn veer
...sit here	...hier sitzen heer **zit**-sehn
...open the window	...das Fenster öffnen dahs **fehn**-stehr **urf**-nehn
...eat here	...hier essen heer **eh**-sehn
(I believe) that's my seat.	(Ich glaube) das ist mein Platz. (ikh **glow**-beh) dahs ist mīn plahts ("glow" rhymes with "cow")
These are our seats.	Das sind unsere Plätze. dahs zint **oon**-zeh-reh **pleht**-seh
Save my place?	Halten Sie meinen Platz frei? **hahl**-tehn zee **mī**-nehn plahts frī
Save our places?	Halten Sie unsere Plätze frei? **hahl**-tehn zee **oon**-zeh-reh **pleht**-seh frī
Where are you going?	Wohin fahren Sie? voh-**hin far**-ehn zee
I'm going / We're going to ____.	Ich fahre / Wir fahren nach ____. ikh **far**-eh / veer **far**-ehn nahkh ____
Does this train stop in ____?	Hält dieser Zug in ____? hehlt **dee**-zehr tsoog in ____
When will it arrive?	Wann kommt er an? vahn kohmt ehr ahn
When will it arrive in ____?	Wann kommt er in ____ an? vahn kohmt ehr in ____ ahn
Where is a (handsome) conductor?	Wo ist ein (hübscher) Schaffner? voh ist īn (**hewb**-shehr) **shahf**-nehr
Can you tell me when to get off?	Können Sie mir sagen wenn ich raus muss? **kurn**-ehn zee meer **zah**-gehn vehn ikh rows moos

I need to get off.	Ich muss hier aussteigen. ikh moos heer **ows**-shtī-gehn
How do I open the door?	Wie öffne ich die Tür? vee **urf**-neh ikh dee tewr

Steigen (**shtī**-gehn) is a handy all-purpose word that you can use for various modes of transportation such as trains and buses. Useful terms include ***einsteigen*** (to get on), ***aussteigen*** (to get off), and ***umsteigen*** (to transfer).

As you approach a station on the train, you'll hear an announcement such as ***In wenigen Minuten erreichen wir München*** (In a few minutes, we will arrive in Munich).

LONG-DISTANCE BUSES

A few journeys in Germany, Austria, or Switzerland are better by bus. Many routes are operated by the post office ***(Postbus);*** others, such as Germany's famous ***Romantische Strasse*** (Romantic Road), use tourist buses. While there may be a designated bus station, usually buses simply leave from in front of the train station.

long-distance bus	Fernbus **fehrn**-boos
regional bus	Regionalbus reh-gee-ohn-**ahl**-boos (hard "g")
bus station	Busbahnhof **boos**-bahn-hohf
mega-bus station and public-transit hub	Zentraler Omnibusbahnhof (ZOB) tsehn-**trah**-lehr ohm-nee-boos-**bahn**-hohf (tseht oh bay)
stall / platform	Haltestelle **hahl**-teh-shteh-leh
How many minutes here?	Wie viele Minuten hier? vee **fee**-leh mee-**noo**-tehn heer

For more tips on interpreting schedules, see page 402.

CITY BUSES AND SUBWAYS

Ticket Talk

Most big cities offer deals on transportation, such as one-day tickets, cheaper fares for youths and seniors, or a discount for buying a batch of tickets (which you can share with friends—called ***Mehrfahrkarten Ermässigung***). If you're taking a short trip (usually three stops or fewer), buy a discounted ***Kurzstrecke*** (short stretch ticket). For more discount-related terms, see page 400.

Where can I buy a ticket?	Wo kann ich eine Fahrkarte kaufen? voh kahn ikh ī-neh **far**-kar-teh **kow**-fehn
I want to go to ____.	Ich möchte nach ____. ikh **murkh**-teh nahkh ____
How much (is a ticket to ____)?	Wie viel (kostet eine Fahrkarte nach ____)? vee feel (**kohs**-teht ī-neh **far**-kar-teh nahkh ____)
single trip	Einzelfahrt **īnt**-sehl-fart
short-ride ticket	Kurzstrecke **koorts**-shtreh-keh
day ticket	Tageskarte **tahg**-ehs-kar-teh

Key Phrases: City Buses and Subways

bus	Bus boos
subway	U-Bahn **oo**-bahn
How do I get to ____?	Wie komme ich zu ____? vee **koh**-meh ikh tsoo ____
Which stop for ____?	Welche Haltestelle für ____? **vehlkh**-eh **hahl**-teh-shteh-leh fewr ____
Can you tell me when to get off?	Können Sie mir sagen wenn ich raus muss? **kurn**-ehn zee meer **zah**-gehn vehn ikh rows moos

discounted batch of tickets	Mehrfahrkarten Ermässigung **mehr**-far-kar-tehn ehr-**may**-see-goong
Is this ticket valid for ____ (place name)?	Ist diese Fahrkarte gültig nach ____? ist **dee**-zeh **far**-kar-teh **gewl**-tig nahkh ____
Is there a...?	Gibt es eine...? gibt ehs ī-neh
...day ticket	...Tageskarte **tahg**-ehs-kar-teh
...discount if I buy more tickets	...Preisnachlass, wenn ich mehrere Fahrkarten kaufe prīs-**nahkh**-lahs vehn ikh **meh**-reh-reh **far**-kar-tehn **kow**-feh
Can I buy a ticket on board?	Kann ich an Bord Fahrkarten kaufen? kahn ikh ahn bord **far**-kar-tehn **kow**-fehn
Do you give change?	Geben Sie Rückgeld? **gay**-behn zee **rewk**-gehlt
validate (here)	(hier) entwerten (heer) ehnt-**vehr**-tehn

In many cities, you are required to ***entwerten*** (validate) your ticket by sticking it into a validation machine as you enter the subway station, bus, or tram. If you have an all-day or multi-day ticket, validate it only the first time you use it.

Transit Terms

Big cities can have various types of public transit, including ***U-Bahn*** (***Untergrund-Bahn,*** subway); ***S-Bahn*** (***Schnellbahn,*** suburban train); ***Bus*** (bus); and ***Strassenbahn*** or ***Trambahn,*** or simply ***Tram*** (streetcar / tram).

city bus	Linienbus **leen**-yehn-boos
bus stop	Bushaltestelle **boos**-hahl-teh-**shteh**-leh
bus map	Buslinienplan **boos**-leen-yehn-**plahn**
subway / suburban train	U-Bahn / S-Bahn **oo**-bahn / **ehs**-bahn
subway station	U-Bahn-Station **oo**-bahn-staht-see-ohn

subway map	Netzplan **nehts**-plahn
network map	Linniennetz **leen**-yehn-nehts
subway entrance	U-Bahn-Eingang **oo**-bahn-**īn**-gahng
subway stop	U-Bahn-Haltestelle **oo**-bahn-**hahl**-teh-shteh-leh
subway exit	U-Bahn-Ausgang **oo**-bahn-**ows**-gahng
line (bus or subway number)	Linie (nummer) **leen**-yeh (**noo**-mehr)
direction	Richtung **rikh**-toong
direct	Direkt dee-**rehkt**
connection	Verbindung fehr-**bin**-doong
stop requested	Wagen hält **vah**-gehn hehlt
customer service center	Kundencenter **koon**-dehn-"center"
pickpocket	Taschendieb **tahsh**-ehn-deep

The ***Liniennetz*** (line network) is a map of the city's public transit, often accompanied by the ***Fahrplan*** (timetable) and ***Tarif*** (ticket prices). In large cities, how much you pay may depend on which zone ***(Preisstufe)*** you're in.

At the subway platform or bus stop, you might see a digital information board with these columns: ***Linie*** (line number), ***Ziel*** or ***Richtung*** (end station or direction), and ***Abfahrt in Min.*** (minutes until next departure). At night, most public transit shuts down, but a few ***Nachtlinien*** (night lines) keep running.

Public Transit

How do I get to ____?	Wie komme ich zu ____? vee **koh**-meh ikh tsoo ____
How do we get to ____?	Wie kommen wir zu ____? vee **koh**-mehn veer tsoo ____
Which bus to ____? (short trip within town)	Welcher Bus zu ____? **vehlkh**-ehr boos tsoo ____

TRANSPORTATION | City Buses and Subways

Which bus to ____? **(to different town)**	Welcher Bus nach ____? **vehlkh**-ehr boos nahkh ____
Does it stop at ____?	Hält er in ____? hehlt ehr in ____
Which bus stop for ____?	Welche Haltestelle für ____? **vehlkh**-eh **hahl**-teh-shteh-leh fewr ____
Which subway stop for ____?	Welcher Halt für ____? **vehlkh**-ehr hahlt fewr ____
Which direction for ____?	Welche Richtung nach ____? **vehlkh**-eh **rikh**-toong nahkh ____
Is a transfer necessary?	Muss man umsteigen? moos mahn **oom**-shtī-gehn
When is the...?	Wann fährt der... ab? vahn fehrt dehr... ahp
...first / next / last...	...erste / nächste / letzte... **ehr**-steh / **nehkh**-steh / **lehts**-teh
...bus / subway	...Bus / U-Bahn boos / **oo**-bahn
How often does it run (per hour / day)?	Wie oft fährt er (pro Stunde / Tag)? vee ohft fehrt ehr (proh **shtoon**-deh / tahg)
When does the next one leave?	Wann fährt der nächste? vahn fehrt dehr **nehkh**-steh
Where does it leave from?	Von wo fährt er ab? fohn voh fehrt ehr ahp
Can you tell me when to get off?	Können Sie mir sagen wenn ich raus muss? **kurn**-ehn zee meer **zah**-gehn vehn ikh rows moos
I need to get off here.	Ich muss hier aussteigen. ikh moos heer **ows**-shtī-gehn
How do I open the door?	Wie öffne ich die Tür? vee **urf**-neh ikh dee tewr

If you press the button to request a stop on a bus or tram, a sign lights up that says ***Wagen hält*** (Car is stopping). Upon arrival, you might have to press a button or pull a lever to open the door ***(Tür öffnen)***—watch locals and imitate.

TAXIS

Taxis usually take up to four people and allow you to ride in style—usually in a BMW or Mercedes. If you have trouble flagging down a taxi, ask for directions to a ***Taxistand*** or seek out a big hotel where they're waiting for guests. The simplest way to tell a cabbie where you want to go is by stating your destination followed by "please" ***(Hofbräuhaus, bitte).*** Tipping isn't expected, but it's polite to round up—if the fare is €19, give €20.

Taxi!	Taxi! **tahk**-see
Can you call a taxi?	Können Sie mir ein Taxi rufen? **kurn**-ehn zee meer īn **tahk**-see **roo**-fehn
Where can I get a taxi?	Wo finde ich ein Taxi? voh **fin**-deh ikh īn **tahk**-see
Where is a taxi stand?	Wo ist ein Taxistand? voh ist īn **tahk**-see-shtahnt
Are you free?	Sind Sie frei? zint zee frī
Occupied.	Besetzt. beh-**zehtst**
To ____, please.	Zum ____, bitte. tsoom ____ **bit**-teh
To this address.	Zu dieser Adresse. tsoo **dee**-zehr ah-**dreh**-seh
How much is it to...?	Wie viel kostet es...? vee feel **kohs**-teht ehs
...the airport	...zum Flughafen tsoom **floog**-hah-fehn
...the train station	...zum Bahnhof tsoom **bahn**-hohf
...this address	...zu dieser Adresse tsoo **dee**-zehr ah-**dreh**-seh
Can you take ____ people?	Können Sie ____ Personen mitnehmen? **kurn**-ehn zee ____ pehr-**zoh**-nehn **mit**-nay-mehn
Any extra fee?	Extra Gebühren? "extra" geh-**bew**-rehn
The meter, please.	Das Taxameter, bitte. dahs **tahk**-sah-meh-tehr **bit**-teh

Stop here.	Halten Sie hier. **hahl**-tehn zee heer
Here is fine.	Hier ist gut. heer ist goot
At this corner.	An dieser Ecke. ahn **dee**-zehr **ehk**-eh
The next corner.	An der nächsten Ecke. ahn dehr **nehkh**-stehn **ehk**-eh
Too much.	Zu viel. tsoo feel
My change, please.	Mein Wechselgeld, bitte. mīn **vehkh**-sehl-gehlt **bit**-teh
Keep the change.	Stimmt so. shtimt zoh

FINDING YOUR WAY

Whether you're driving, walking, or biking, these phrases will help you get around.

Route-Finding Phrases

I'm going / We're going to ____. (on foot)	Ich gehe / Wir gehen nach ____. ikh **gay**-eh / veer **gay**-ehn nahkh ____
I'm going / We're going to ____. (on wheels)	Ich fahre / Wir fahren nach ____. ikh **far**-eh / veer **far**-ehn nahkh ____
Do you have...?	Haben Sie...? **hah**-behn zee
...a city map	...einen Stadtplan ī-nehn **shtaht**-plahn
...a road map	...eine Strassenkarte ī-neh **shtrah**-sehn-kar-teh
How many minutes / hours...?	Wie viele Minuten / Stunden...? vee **fee**-leh mee-**noo**-tehn / **shtoon**-dehn
...on foot	...zu Fuss tsoo foos
...by bicycle	...mit dem Rad mit daym raht
...by car	...mit dem Auto mit daym **ow**-toh
How many kilometers to ____?	Wie viele Kilometer sind es nach ____? vee **fee**-leh kee-loh-**may**-tehr zint ehs nahkh ____

What's the... route to Berlin?	Was ist der... Weg nach Berlin? vahs ist dehr... vayg nahkh behr-**leen**
...most scenic	...schönste **shurn**-steh
...fastest	...schnellste **shnehl**-steh
...easiest	...einfachste **ī̄n**-fahkh-steh
...most interesting	...interessanteste in-teh-reh-**sahn**-tehs-teh
Point it out?	Zeigen Sie es mir? **tsī**-gehn zee ehs meer
Where is this address?	Wo ist diese Adresse? voh ist **dee**-zeh ah-**dreh**-seh

You may notice that jaywalking is rare in German-speaking lands—even when there's no traffic. In fact, German has no simple word for jaywalking. Instead, they'd describe it as ***bei Rot über die Ampel gehen*** (crossing on a red light).

Directions

Bigger cities are more likely to have signs pointing you to the ***Zentrum*** (center). In smaller towns, following signs to ***Stadtmitte*** will land you in the heart of things.

downtown	Zentrum / Stadtzentrum / Stadtmitte **tsehn**-troom / **shtaht**-tsehn-troom / **shtaht**-mit-teh
straight ahead	geradeaus geh-rah-deh-**ows**
left / right	links / rechts links / rehkhts
first	erste **ehr**-steh
next	nächste **nehkh**-steh
intersection	Kreuzung **kroy**-tsoong
corner	Ecke **ehk**-eh
block	Häuserblock **hoy**-zehr-blohk
roundabout	Kreisel **krī**-zehl

(main) square	(Markt)platz (**markt**-)plahts
street	Strasse **shtrah**-seh
bridge	Brücke **brew**-keh
road	Strasse **shtrah**-seh
highway	Landstrasse **lahnd**-shtrah-seh
expressway	Autobahn **ow**-toh-bahn
north	Nord nord
south	Süd zewd
east	Ost ohst
west	West vehst

While all roads seem to lead to the little town of ***Ausfahrt,*** that is the German word for exit. Missing a turnoff can cost you lots of time and miles—be alert for ***Autobahn Kreuz*** (interchange) signs.

Lost Your Way

I'm lost. (on foot)	Ich habe mich verlaufen. ikh **hah**-beh mikh fehr-**lowf**-ehn
I'm lost. (by car)	Ich habe mich verfahren. ikh **hah**-beh mikh **fehr**-far-ehn
Excuse me, can you help?	Entschuldigung, können Sie mir helfen? ehnt-**shool**-dig-oong **kurn**-ehn zee meer **hehl**-fen
Where am I?	Wo bin ich? voh bin ikh
Where is ____?	Wo ist ____? voh ist ____
How do I get to ____?	Wie komme ich nach ____? vee **koh**-meh ikh nahkh ____
Can you show me the way?	Können Sie mir den Weg weisen? **kurn**-ehn zee meer dayn vayg **vī**-zehn

SLEEPING

RESERVATIONS

Making a Reservation

reservation	Reservierung reh-zehr-**veer**-oong
Do you have...?	Haben Sie...? **hah**-behn zee
I'd like to reserve...	Ich möchte... reservieren. ikh **murkh**-teh... reh-zehr-**veer**-ehn
...a room for...	...ein Zimmer für... īn **tsim**-ehr fewr
...one person / two people	...eine Person / zwei Personen ī-neh pehr-**zohn** / tsvī pehr-**zoh**-nehn
...today / tomorrow	...heute / morgen **hoy**-teh / **mor**-gehn
...one night	...eine Nacht ī-neh nahkht
...two / three nights	...zwei / drei Nächte tsvī / drī **nehkh**-teh
June 21	einundzwanzigstenJuni īn-oont-**tsvahn**-tsig-stehn **yoo**-nee
How much?	Wie viel? vee feel
Anything cheaper?	Etwas günstigeres? **eht**-vahs **gewn**-stig-ehr-ehs
I'll take it.	Ich nehme es. ikh **nay**-meh ehs
My name is ____.	Ich heisse ____. ikh **hī**-seh ____
Do you need a deposit?	Brauchen Sie eine Anzahlung? **browkh**-ehn zee ī-neh **ahnt**-sah-loong
Do you accept credit cards?	Akzeptieren Sie Kreditkarten? ahkt-sehp-**teer**-ehn zee kreh-**deet**-kar-tehn
Can I reserve with a credit card and pay in cash?	Kann ich mit einer Kreditkarte reservieren, und mit Bargeld bezahlen? kahn ikh mit ī-nehr kreh-**deet**-kar-teh reh-zehr-**veer**-ehn oont mit **bar**-gehlt beht-**sah**-lehn

Accommodations can go by many German names, all of them carrying different connotations. A ***Hotel*** is likely to offer the most amenities, but many a country inn—***Gasthof, Gasthaus,*** or ***Landhaus***—can be plush (or basic, just like hotels). The word ***garni*** in a hotel name means "without restaurant."

In Germany and Austria, look for homeowners renting out their spare rooms—a.k.a. ***Privatzimmer*** or ***Gästezimmer***—usually advertised by a sign simply reading ***Zimmer*** (rooms) or ***Zimmer frei*** (rooms available). Staying in a private home offers double the cultural experience for half the price of a hotel. If a place has no rooms available, you may see a ***belegt*** or ***komplett*** sign, meaning they're ***ausgebucht*** (fully booked). ***Pension*** is a catch-all word for budget accommodations that provide at least breakfast—whether a private home with rooms for rent, a quaint B&B, or a small hotel.

In Germany, Austria, and Switzerland, you're never far from a ***Jugendherberge*** (hostel). In the Alps, rustic accommodations for hikers

Key Phrases: Sleeping

Do you have a room?	Haben Sie ein Zimmer? **hah**-behn zee īn **tsim**-ehr
for one person / two people	für eine Person / zwei Personen fewr ī-neh pehr-**zohn** / tsvī pehr-**zoh**-nehn
today / tomorrow	heute / morgen **hoy**-teh / **mor**-gehn
one night / two nights	eine Nacht / zwei Nächte ī-neh nahkht / tsvī **nehkh**-teh
How much is it?	Wie viel ist es? vee feel ist ehs
hotel	Hotel "hotel"
small hotel	Pension pehn-see-**ohn**
vacancy	Zimmer frei **tsim**-ehr frī
no vacancy	belegt / komplett beh-**lehgt** / kohm-**pleht**

are usually in a ***Hütte*** (hut), with basic beds and hearty food, or in a ***Matratzenlager*** (mattress camp)—a rural dorm.

Getting Specific

I'd like a...	Ich möchte ein...	ikh **murkh**-teh īn
...single room.	...Einzelzimmer.	**īn**-tsehl-tsim-ehr
...double room.	...Doppelzimmer.	**doh**-pehl-tsim-ehr
...triple room.	...Dreibettzimmer.	**drī**-beht-tsim-ehr
...room for ____ people.	...Zimmer für ____ Personen.	**tsim**-ehr fewr ____ pehr-**zoh**-nehn
with / without / and	mit / ohne / und	mit / **oh**-neh / oont
two-person bed with a big mattress	französisches Bett	frahnt-**sur**-seesh-ehs beht
bed with two twin mattresses inside one frame	Doppelbett	**doh**-pehl-beht
separate twin beds	getrennte Betten	geh-**trehn**-teh **beh**-tehn
single bed	Einzelbett	**īnt**-sehl-beht
bed without a footboard	Bett ohne Trittbrett	beht **oh**-neh **trit**-breht
private bathroom	eigenes Bad	**ī**-geh-nehs baht
toilet	Toilette	toy-**leh**-teh
shower	Dusche	**doo**-sheh
bathtub	Badewanne	**bah**-deh-vah-neh
with only a sink	nur mit Waschbecken	noor mit **vahsh**-behk-ehn
shower outside the room	Dusche im Gang	**doo**-sheh im gahng
balcony	Balkon	bahl-**kohn**
view	Ausblick / Aussicht	**ows**-blik / **ows**-sikht
cheap	günstig / preiswert	**gewn**-stig / **prīs**-vehrt
quiet	ruhig	**roo**-eeg

romantic	romantisch roh-**mahn**-tish
on the ground floor	im Erdgeschoss im **ehrd**-geh-shohs
Do you have...?	Haben Sie...? **hah**-behn zee
...an elevator	...einen Aufzug ī-nehn **owf**-tsoog
...air-conditioning	...Klimaanlage **klee**-mah-ahn-lah-geh
...Internet access	...Internetanschluss "Internet"-**ahn**-shloos
...Wi-Fi (in the room)	...WLAN (im Zimmer) **vay**-lahn (im **tsim**-ehr)
...parking	...einen Gastparkplatz ī-nehn **gahst**-park-plahtz
...a garage	...eine Garage ī-neh gah-**rah**-zheh
What is the...?	Was ist die...? vahs ist dee
...email address	...E-mail Adresse "email" ah-**dreh**-seh
...cancellation policy	...Stornierungsbedingung **shtor**-neer-oongs-beh-**ding**-oong

In German-speaking countries, a true double or queen-size bed is relatively rare. Instead, they use this terminology: a ***französisches Bett*** or ***französische Liege*** is a two-person bed with one large mattress; ***Doppelbett*** means two mattresses in the same frame, often sheeted together as one big bed; and ***getrennte Betten*** are beds in separate frames. Taller guests may want to request a ***Bett ohne Trittbrett*** (bed without a footboard).

Nailing Down the Price

price	Preis prīs
May I see the price list?	Darf ich die Preisliste sehen? darf ikh dee **prīs**-lis-teh **zay**-hehn
How much is...?	Wie viel kostet...? vee feel **kohs**-teht
...a room for____ people	...ein Zimmer für____ Personen īn **tsim**-ehr fewr ____ pehr-**zoh**-nehn
...your cheapest room	...Ihr günstigstes Zimmer eer **gewn**-stig-stehs **tsim**-ehr

Is breakfast included?	Frühstück inklusive? **frew**-stewk in-kloo-**zee**-veh
Complete price?	Gesamtpreis? geh-**zahmt**-prīs
Is it cheaper if...?	Ist es günstiger, wenn...? ist ehs **gewn**-stig-ehr vehn
...I stay three nights	...ich drei Nächte bleibe ikh drī **nehkh**-teh **blī**-beh
...I pay in cash	...ich bar bezahle ikh bar beht-**sah**-leh

Arrival and Departure

arrival (date)	Ankunft(datum) **ahn**-koonft(-**dah**-toom)
departure (date)	Abreise(datum) **ahp**-rī-zeh(-**dah**-toom)
I'll come / We'll come...	Ich komme / Wir kommen... ikh **koh**-meh / veer **koh**-mehn
I'll depart / We'll depart...	Ich reise / Wir reisen... ab. ikh **rī**-zeh / veer **rī**-zehn... ahp
...June 16.	...am 16 Juni ahm **zekh**-tsayn-tehn **yoo**-nee
...in the morning / afternoon / evening.	...Morgen früh / am Nachmittag / am Abend **mor**-gehn frew / ahm **nahkh**-mit-tahg / ahm **ah**-behnt
...Friday before 6 p.m.	...Freitag vor sechs Uhr abends **frī**-tahg for zehkhs oor **ah**-behnts
I'll stay...	Ich bleibe... ikh **blī**-beh
We'll stay...	Wir bleiben... veer **blī**-behn
...two nights.	...zwei Nächte. tsvī **nehkh**-teh
We arrive Monday, depart Wednesday.	Wir kommen am Montag, und reisen am Mittwoch ab. veer **koh**-mehn ahm **mohn**-tahg oont **rī**-zehn ahm **mit**-vohkh ahp

For help with saying dates in German, see "Time and Dates," starting on page 388. For a sample of a reservation request email, see page 551.

Confirm, Change, or Cancel

It's smart to call a day or two in advance to confirm your reservation.

I have a reservation.	Ich habe eine Reservierung. ikh **hah**-beh **ī**-neh reh-zehr-**veer**-oong
My name is ____.	Ich heisse ____. ikh **hī**-seh ____
I'd like to... my reservation.	Ich möchte meine Reservierung... ikh **murkh**-teh **mī**-neh reh-zehr-**veer**-oong
...confirm	...bestätigen beh-**shtay**-tig-ehn
...change	...ändern **ehn**-dehrn
...cancel	...stornieren shtor-**neer**-ehn
The reservation is for...	Die Reservierung ist für... dee reh-zehr-**veer**-oong ist fewr
...today / tomorrow.	...heute / morgen. **hoy**-teh / **mor**-gehn
...August 13.	...den dreizehnten August. dayn **drī**-tsayn-tehn ow-**goost**
Did you find the reservation?	Haben Sie die Reservierung gefunden? **hah**-behn zee dee reh-zehr-**veer**-oong geh-**foon**-dehn
Is everything OK?	Ist alles in Ordnung? ist **ah**-lehs in **ord**-noong
See you then.	Bis dann. bis dahn
I'm sorry, but I need to cancel.	Ich bedauere, aber ich muss stornieren. ikh beh-**dow**-eh-reh **ah**-behr ikh moos shtor-**neer**-ehn
Is there a penalty? (for canceling the reservation)	Kostet das eine Gebühr? (für die Stornierung) **koh**-steht dahs **ī**-neh geh-**bewr** (fewr dee shtor-**neer**-oong)
cancellation penalty	Stornogebühr **shtor**-noh-geh-bewr

Depending on how far ahead you cancel a reservation—and on the hotel's cancellation policy—you might pay a penalty.

AT THE HOTEL

Checking In

My name is ____.	Ich heisse ____. ikh **hī**-seh ____
I have a reservation.	Ich habe eine Reservierung. ikh **hah**-beh **ī**-neh reh-zehr-**veer**-oong
one night	eine Nacht **ī**-neh nahkht
two / three nights	zwei / drei Nächte tsvī / drī **nehkh**-teh
Where is...?	Wo ist...? voh ist
...my room	...mein Zimmer mīn **tsim**-ehr
...the elevator	...der Aufzug dehr **owf**-tsoog
...the breakfast room	...das Frühstückszimmer dahs **frew**-shtewks-tsim-ehr
Is breakfast included?	Frühstück inklusive? **frew**-shtewk in-kloo-**zee**-veh
When does breakfast start and end?	Wann beginnt und endet das Frühstück? vahn beh-**gint** oont **ehn**-deht dahs **frew**-shtewk
key	Schlüssel **shlew**-sehl
Two keys, please.	Zwei Schlüssel, bitte tsvī **shlew**-sehl **bit**-teh

Choosing a Room

May I see...?	Darf ich... sehen? darf ikh... **zay**-ehn
...a room	...ein Zimmer īn **tsim**-ehr
...a different room	...ein anderes Zimmer īn **ahn**-deh-rehs **tsim**-ehr
Do you have something...?	Haben Sie etwas...? **hah**-behn zee **eht**-vahs
...larger / smaller	...grösseres / kleineres **grur**-sehr-ehs / **klī**-nehr-ehs

...better / cheaper	...besseres / günstigeres **behs**-ehr-ehs / **gewn**-stig-ehr-ehs
...brighter	...helleres **hehl**-ehr-ehs
...quieter	...ruhigeres **roo**-ee-gehr-ehs
...in the back	...nach hinten hinaus nahkh **hin**-tehn hin-**ows**
...with a view	...mit Aussicht mit **ows**-sikht
...on a lower / higher floor	...auf einer niedrigeren / höheren Etage. owf **ī**-nehr **nee**-drig-ehr-ehn / **hur**-ehr-ehn ay-**tah**-zheh
No, thank you.	Nein, danke. nīn **dahn**-keh
What a charming room!	Was für charmantes Zimmer! vahs fewr shar-**mahn**-tehs **tsim**-ehr
I'll take it.	Ich nehme es. ikh **nay**-meh ehs

Be aware that a room ***mit Aussicht*** (with a view) can also come with more noise. If you want a room on the building's quiet side, specify ***ruhige Seite*** (**roo**-ee-geh **zī**-teh).

At simpler places, you can save money by opting for a room with a ***Badezimmer auf der Etage*** (bathroom down the hall); these places may advertise ***fliessend Wasser*** (running water), meaning there's a sink inside the room...but implying that the toilet and shower aren't.

In Your Room

air-conditioner	Klimaanlage **klee**-mah-ahn-**lah**-geh
alarm clock	Wecker **veh**-kehr
balcony	Balkon bahl-**kohn**
bathroom	Badezimmer **bah**-deh-tsim-ehr
bathtub	Badewanne **bah**-deh-vah-neh
bed	Bett beht
blanket	Decke **dehk**-eh
chair	Stuhl shtool
closet	Kleiderschrank **klī**-dehr-shrahnk

comforter (duvet)	Steppdecke **shtehp**-dehk-eh
crib	Kinderbett **kin**-dehr-beht
door	Tür tewr
electrical adapter	Adapter "adapter"
electrical outlet	Steckdose **shtehk**-doh-zeh
faucet	Wasserhahn **vahs**-ehr-hahn
hair dryer	Haartrockner **har**-trohk-nehr
hanger	Kleiderbügel **klī**-dehr-bew-gehl
lamp	Lampe **lahm**-peh
lightbulb	Glühbirne **glew**-beer-neh
lock	Schloss shlohs
mattress	Matratze **mah**-traht-seh
pillow	Kissen **kis**-ehn
radio	Radio **rah**-dee-oh
remote control...	Fernbediener... **fehrn**-beh-dee-nehr
...for TV	...für den Fernseher fewr dayn **fehrn**-zay-ehr
...for air-conditioner	...für die Klimaanlage fewr dee **klee**-mah-ahn-**lah**-geh
safe	Safe zayf
shampoo	Shampoo "shampoo"
sheets	Bettwäsche **beht**-veh-sheh
shower	Dusche **doo**-sheh
sink	Waschbecken **vahsh**-behk-ehn
sink stopper	Abflussstöpsel **ahp**-floos-shturp-zehl
soap	Seife **zī**-feh
telephone	Telefon tehl-eh-**fohn**
television	Fernseher **fehrn**-zay-ehr
toilet	Toilette toy-**leh**-teh
toilet paper	Toilettenpapier toy-**leh**-tehn-pah-peer
towel (hand)	Handtuch **hahnd**-tookh
towel (bath)	Badetuch **bah**-deh-tookh

wake-up call	Weckruf **vehk**-roof
washcloth	Waschlappen **vahsh**-lah-pehn
water (hot / cold)	Wasser (heisses / kaltes) **vahs**-ehr (**hīs**-ehs / **kahl**-tehs)
window	Fenster **fehn**-stehr

If you don't see remote controls in the room (for the TV or air-conditioner), ask for them at the front desk. A comfortable setting for the air-conditioner is about 20 degrees Celsius (68 °F).

Hotel Hassles

Combine these phrases with the words in the previous table to make simple and clear statements, such as: ***Toilette kaputt*** (Toilet broken).

There is a problem in my room.	Es gibt ein Problem mit meinem Zimmer. ehs gibt īn **proh**-blaym mit **mī**-nehm **tsim**-ehr
Come with me, please.	Kommen Sie mit mir, bitte. **koh**-mehn zee mit meer **bit**-teh
The room is...	Das Zimmer ist... dahs **tsim**-ehr ist
It's...	Es ist... ehs ist
...dirty.	...schmutzig. **shmoot**-sig
...moldy.	...verschimmelt. fehr-**shim**-ehlt
...musty.	...muffig. **moo**-fig
...noisy.	...laut. lowt
...smoky.	...verraucht. fehr-**rowkht**
...stinky.	...stinkig. **shtink**-ig
...too hot / cold.	...zu heiss / zu kalt. tsoo hīs / tsoo kahlt
How can I make the room cooler / warmer?	Wie kann ich das Zimmer kühler / wärmer machen? vee kahn ikh dahs **tsim**-ehr **kewl**-ehr / **vehrm**-ehr **mahkh**-ehn

There's no (hot) water.	Es gibt kein (warmes) Wasser. ehs gibt kīn (**var**-mehs) **vahs**-ehr
I can't open / shut / lock...	Ich kann... nicht öffnen / schliessen / zuschliessen. ikh kahn... nikht **urf**-nehn / **shlee**-sehn / **tsoo**-shlee-sehn
...the door / the window.	...die Tür / das Fenster dee tewr / dahs **fehn**-stehr
How does this work?	Wie funktioniert das? vee foonkt-see-ohn-**eert** dahs
This doesn't work.	Das funktioniert nicht. dahs foonkt-see-ohn-**eert** nikht
broken	kaputt kah-**poot**
When will it be fixed?	Wann wird das repariert? vahn virt dahs reh-pah-**reert**
bedbugs	Wanzen **vahnt**-sehn
mosquitoes	Mücken **mew**-kehn
I'm covered with bug bites.	Ich bin mit Wanzenbissen übersäht. ikh bin mit **vahnt**-sehn-bis-ehn ew-behr-**zayt**
My money...	Mein Geld... mīn gelt
My computer...	Mein Computer... mīn "computer"
My camera...	Meine Kamera... **mī**-neh **kah**-meh-rah
...was stolen.	...wurde gestohlen. **voor**-deh geh-**shtoh**-lehn
I need to speak to the manager.	Ich muss mit dem Chef sprechen. ikh moos mit daym shehf **shprekh**-ehn
I want to make a complaint.	Ich möchte mich beschweren. ikh **murkh**-teh mikh beh-**shvehr**-ehn

Keep your valuables with you, out of sight in your room, or in a room safe (if available). For help on dealing with theft or loss, including a list of items, see page 527.

Hotel Help

Use the "In Your Room" words (on page 422) to fill in the blanks.

I'd like...	Ich hätte gern... ikh **heh**-teh gehrn
Do you have...?	Haben Sie...? **hah**-behn zee
a / another	ein / noch ein īn / nohkh īn
extra	extra "extra"
different	anderes **ahn**-deh-rehs
Please change...	Bitte wechseln Sie... **bit**-teh **vehkh**-zehln zee
Please don't change...	Bitte wechseln Sie nicht... **bit**-teh **vehkh**-zehln zee nikht
...the bath towels / sheets.	...die Badetücher / Bettwäsche. dee **bah**-deh-tewkh-ehr / **beht**-veh-sheh
What is the charge to...?	Was ist der Tarif um das...? vahs ist dehr tah-**reef** oom dahs
...use the telephone	...Telefon zu benutzen tehl-eh-**fohn** tsoo beh-**noot**-sehn
...use the Internet	...Internet zu benutzen "Internet" tsoo beh-**noot**-sehn
Do you have Wi-Fi...?	Haben Sie WLAN...? **hah**-behn zee **vay**-lahn
...in the room / in the lobby	...im Zimmer / in der Lobby im **tsim**-ehr / in dehr "lobby"
Do I need a password?	Brauche ich ein Passwort? **browkh**-eh ikh īn **pahs**-vort
What is the password?	Was ist das Passwort? vahs ist dahs **pahs**-vort
What is the network name?	Wie heisst das Netz? vee hīst dahs nehts
Is there a... nearby?	Gibt es... in der Nähe? gibt ehs... in dehr **nay**-eh

...full-service laundry	...einen Waschsalon mit Dienstleistung ī-nehn **vahsh**-zah-lohn mit **deenst**-līs-toong
...self-service laundry	...einen Waschsalon mit Selbstbedienung ī-nehn **vahsh**-zah-lohn mit zehlpst-beh-**dee**-noong
...pharmacy	...eine Apotheke ī-neh ah-poh-**teh**-keh
...Internet café	...ein Internet-café īn "Internet café"
...grocery store	...einen Supermarkt ī-nehn **zoo**-pehr-markt
...restaurant	...ein Restaurant īn reh-stoh-**rahn**
Which place would you recommend for...?	Welches Lokal empfehlen Sie zum...? **vehlkh**-ehs loh-**kahl** ehmp-**fay**-lehn zee tsoom
...lunch	...Mittagessen **mit**-tahg-eh-sehn
...dinner	...Abendessen **ah**-behnd-eh-sehn
...coffee	...Kaffeetrinken kah-**fay**-trink-ehn
Will you call a taxi for me?	Rufen Sie mir bitte ein Taxi? **roo**-fehn zee meer **bit**-teh īn **tahk**-see
Where can I park?	Wo soll ich parken? voh zohl ikh **par**-kehn
What time do you lock up?	Um wie viel Uhr schliessen Sie ab? oom vee feel oor **shlee**-sehn zee ahp
Please wake me at 7:00.	Wecken Sie mich um sieben Uhr, bitte. **veh**-kehn zee mikh oom **zee**-behn oor **bit**-teh
I'd like to stay another night.	Ich möchte noch eine Nacht bleiben. ikh **murkh**-teh nohkh ī-neh nahkht **blī**-behn
Will you call my next hotel...?	Können Sie bitte mein nächstes Hotel anrufen...? **kurn**-ehn zee **bit**-teh mīn **nekh**-stehs "hotel" **ahn**-roo-fehn

...for tonight	...für heute Abend fewr **hoy**-teh **ah**-behnt
...to reserve	...zum reservieren tsoom reh-zehr-**veer**-ehn
...to confirm	...zum bestätigen tsoom beh-**shtay**-tig-ehn
Will you please call another hotel? (if hotel is booked)	Rufen Sie bitte ein anderes Hotel? **roo**-fehn zee **bit**-teh īn **ahn**-deh-rehs "hotel"
I will pay for the call.	Ich bezahle für den Anruf. ikh beht-**sah**-leh fewr dayn **ahn**-roof

Checking Out

When is check-out time?	Wann muss ich das Zimmer verlassen? vahn moos ikh dahs **tsim**-ehr fehr-**lah**-sehn
Can I check out later?	Kann ich später auschecken? kahn ikh **shpay**-tehr **ows**-"check"-ehn
I'll leave...	Ich fahre... ab. ikh **far**-eh... ahp
We'll leave...	Wir fahren... ab. veer **far**-ehn... ahp
...today / tomorrow.	...heute / morgen **hoy**-teh / **mor**-gehn
...very early.	...sehr früh zehr frew
Can I pay now?	Kann ich jetzt bezahlen? kahn ikh yehtst beht-**sah**-lehn
The bill, please.	Die Rechnung, bitte. dee **rehkh**-noong **bit**-teh
I think this is too high.	Ich glaube das ist zu hoch. ikih **glow**-beh dahs ist tsoo hohkh
Can you explain the bill?	Können Sie die Rechnung erklären? **kurn**-ehn zee dee **rehkh**-noong ehr-**klehr**-ehn

Can you itemize the bill?	Können Sie die Rechnung einzeln aufführen? **kurn**-ehn zee dee **rehkh**-noong **īnt**-sehln **owf**-fewr-ehn
Do you accept credit cards?	Akzeptieren Sie Kreditkarten? ahkt-sehp-**teer**-ehn zee kreh-**deet**-kar-tehn
Is it less if I pay in cash?	Ist es weniger wenn ich bar bezahle? ist ehs **vay**-nig-ehr vehn ikh bar beht-**sah**-leh
Everything was great.	Alles war prima. **ahl**-ehs var **pree**-mah
Can I / Can we...?	Kann ich / Können wir...? kahn ikh / **kurn**-ehn veer
...leave baggage here until ____ o'clock	...das Gepäck bis ____ Uhr hier lassen dahs geh-**pehk** bis ____ oor heer **lah**-sehn

FAMILIES

Do you have a...?	Haben Sie...? **hah**-behn zee
...family room	...ein Familienzimmer īn fah-**meel**-yehn-**tsim**-ehr
...family discount	...eine Familienermässigung ī-neh fah-**meel**-yehn-ehr-**may**-see-goong
...discount for children	...eine Kinderermässigung ī-neh **kin**-dehr-ehr-**may**-see-goong
I have / We have...	Ich habe / Wir haben... ikh **hah**-beh / veer **hah**-behn
...one child.	...ein Kind. īn kint
...two children.	...zwei Kinder. tsvī **kin**-dehr
____ months old	____ Monate alt ____ **moh**-nah-teh ahlt
____ years old	____ Jahre alt ____ **yah**-reh ahlt

Do you accept children?	Sind Kinder willkommen? zint **kin**-dehr vil-**koh**-mehn
Is there a minimum age?	Gibt es ein Mindestalter? gibt ehs īn **min**-deh-shtahl-tehr
I'd like / We'd like a...	Ich hätte gern / Wir hätten gern ein... ikh **heh**-teh gehrn / veer **heh**-tehn gehrn īn
...crib.	...Kinderbett. **kin**-dehr-beht
...extra bed.	...Extrabett. "extra"-beht

AT THE HOSTEL

Europe's cheapest beds are in hostels, open to travelers of any age. Official hostels (affiliated with Hostelling International) are usually big and institutional. Independent hostels are more casual, with fewer rules.

hostel	Jugendherberge **yoo**-gehnd-hehr-behr-geh
dorm bed	Bett im Mehrbettzimmer beht im **mehr**-beht-tsim-ehr
How many beds per room?	Wie viel Betten pro Zimmer? vee feel **beh**-tehn proh **tsim**-ehr
dorm for women only	Mehrbettzimmer nur für Frauen **mehr**-beht-tsim-ehr noor fewr **frow**-ehn
co-ed dorm	gemischte Mehrbettzimmer geh-**mish**-teh **mehr**-beht-tsim-ehr
double room	Doppelzimmer **doh**-pehl-tsim-ehr
family room	Familienzimmer fah-**meel**-yehn-**tsim**-ehr
Is breakfast included?	Frühstück inklusive? **frew**-stewk in-kloo-**zee**-veh
curfew	Sperrstunde **shpehr**-shtoon-deh
membership card	Mitgliedskarte **mit**-gleeds-kar-teh

EATING

RESTAURANTS

Germans eat meals at about the same times as Americans: lunch from about 12:00 to 14:00, and dinner between 18:00 and 21:00.

Dishes—and even the names for basic ingredients—can vary dramatically between Austria, Switzerland, and even specific parts of Germany. In this chapter, I've listed the most widely used terms; in cases where a different term predominates regionally, I've listed a second term, followed by (Aus.) for Austria, (Switz.) for Switzerland, or (Bav.) for Bavaria.

Finding a Restaurant

Where's a good... restaurant nearby?	Wo ist hier ein gutes... Restaurant? voh ist heer īn **goo**-tehs... reh-stoh-**rahn**
...affordable	...günstiges **gewn**-stig-ehs
...local-style	...einheimisches īn-**hī**-mish-ehs
...untouristy	...untouristisches oon-too-**rees**-tish-ehs
...romantic	...romantisches roh-**mahn**-tish-ehs
...vegetarian	...vegetarisches vay-gay-**tar**-ish-ehs
...fast	...schnelles **shnehl**-ehs
...fast food	..."fast food" "fast food"
...self-service	...Selbstbedienungs zehlbst-beh-**dee**-noongs
...Turkish	...türkisches **tewr**-kish-ehs
...Asian	...asiatisches ah-zee-**ah**-tish-ehs
beer garden	Biergarten **beer**-gar-tehn
beer hall	Brauhaus **brow**-hows
with terrace	mit Terrasse mit tehr-**ah**-seh

with a salad bar	mit Salatbar mit **zah**-laht-bar
with candles	bei Kerzenlicht bī **kehrt**-sehn-likht
popular with locals	bei den Einheimischen beliebtes bī dayn īn-**hī**-mish-ehn beh-**leeb**-tehs
moderately priced	nicht zu teuer nikht tsoo **toy**-ehr
splurge	zum Verwöhnen tsoom fehr-**vur**-nehn
Is it better than McDonald's?	Ist es besser als McDonald's? ist ehs **behs**-ehr ahls "McDonald's"

Most German restaurants take a ***Ruhetag*** (day off; **roo**-eh-tahg) each week. Before tracking down a recommended restaurant, call to make sure it's open.

Getting a Table

I'd like...	Ich hätte gern... ikh **heh**-teh gehrn
We'd like...	Wir hätten gern... veer **heh**-tehn gehrn
...a table...	...einen Tisch... ī-nehn tish
...for one / two.	...für eine Person / zwei Personen. fewr ī-neh pehr-**zohn** / tsvī pehr-**zoh**-nehn
...inside / outside.	...drinnen / draussen. **drin**-ehn / **drow**-sehn
...by the window.	...beim Fenster. bīm **fehn**-stehr
...with a view.	...mit Aussicht. mit **ows**-sikht
...a quiet table.	...einen ruhigen Tisch. ī-nehn **roo**-hig-ehn tish
Is this table free?	Ist dieser Tisch frei? ist **dee**-zehr tish frī
May I sit here?	Darf ich hier sitzen? darf ikh heer **zit**-sehn
May we sit here?	Dürfen wir hier sitzen? **dewr**-fehn veer heer **zit**-sehn
How long is the wait?	Wie lang ist die Wartezeit? vee lahng ist dee **var**-teht-sīt

Key Phrases: Restaurants

Where's a good restaurant nearby?	Wo ist hier ein gutes Restaurant? voh ist heer īn **goo**-tehs reh-stoh-**rahn**
I'd like a table for one.	Ich hätte gern einen Tisch für eine Person. ikh **heh**-teh gehrn **ī**-nehn tish fewr **ī**-neh pehr-**zohn**
We'd like a table for two.	Wir hätten gern einen Tisch für zwei. veer **heh**-tehn gehrn **ī**-nehn tish fewr tsvī
Is this table free?	Ist dieser Tisch frei? ist **dee**-zehr tish frī
How long is the wait?	Wie lang ist die Wartezeit? vee lahng ist dee **var**-teht-sīt
The menu (in English), please.	Die Speisekarte (auf Englisch), bitte. dee **shpī**-zeh-kar-teh (owf **ehng**-lish) **bit**-teh
The bill, please.	Die Rechnung, bitte. dee **rehkh**-noong **bit**-teh
Do you accept credit cards?	Akzeptieren Sie Kreditkarten? ahkt-sehp-**teer**-ehn zee kreh-**deet**-kar-tehn

How many minutes?	Wie viele Minuten? vee **fee**-leh mee-**noo**-tehn
Where are the toilets?	Wo sind die Toiletten? voh sint dee toy-**leh**-tehn

When entering a restaurant, you can feel free to seat yourself at any table that isn't marked ***reserviert*** (reserved) or ***Stammtisch*** (special table reserved for regulars).

Reservations

reservation	Reservierung reh-zehr-**veer**-oong
Are reservations recommended?	Muss man reservieren? moos mahn reh-zehr-**veer**-ehn
I'd like to make a reservation...	Ich möchte eine Reservierung... machen. ikh **murkh**-teh ī-neh reh-zehr-**veer**-oong... **mahkh**-ehn
...for myself.	...für mich fewr mikh
...for two people.	...für zwei Personen fewr tsvī pehr-**zoh**-nehn
...for today / tomorrow.	...für heute / morgen fewr **hoy**-teh / **mor**-gehn
...for lunch / dinner.	...fürs Mittagessen / Abendessen fewrs **mit**-tahg-eh-sehn / **ah**-behnd-eh-sehn
...at ____ o'clock.	...um ____ Uhr oom ____ oor
My name is ____.	Ich heisse ____. ikh **hī**-seh
I have a reservation for ____ people.	Ich habe eine Reservierung für ____ Personen. ikh **hah**-beh ī-neh reh-zehr-**veer**-oong fewr ____ pehr-**zoh**-nehn

The Menu

Here are a few food categories and other restaurant lingo you may see on the menu.

menu	Karte / Speisekarte **kar**-teh / **shpī**-zeh-**kar**-teh
The menu (in English), please.	Die Speisekarte (auf Englisch), bitte. dee **shpī**-zeh-kar-teh (owf **ehng**-lish) **bit**-teh
daily special	Tagesgericht / Tagesteller **tah**-gehs-geh-rikht / **tah**-geh-shtehl-ehr

specialty of the house	Spezialität des Hauses **shpayt**-see-ahl-ee-**tayt** dehs **how**-zehs
menu of the day	Tageskarte **tah**-gehs-kar-teh
fixed-price meal	menü meh-**new**
fixed-price meal of the day	Tagesmenü **tah**-gehs-meh-new
multi-course dinner	Mehrgang-Menü **mehr**-gahng-meh-new
half-portion	halbe Portion **hahl**-beh **port**-see-ohn
list of small-portion dishes	kleine Hunger **klī**-neh **hoon**-gehr
children's plate	Kinderteller **kin**-dehr-tehl-ehr
breakfast	Frühstück **frew**-shtewk
lunch	Mittagessen **mit**-tahg-eh-sehn
dinner	Abendessen **ah**-behnd-eh-sehn
dishes (prepared dishes)	Gerichte geh-**rikh**-teh
warm / cold dishes	warme / kalte Gerichte **var**-meh / **kahl**-teh geh-**rikh**-teh
appetizers	Vorspeisen **for**-shpī-zehn
sandwiches	Sandwiches **zehnd**-vich-ehs
bread	Brot broht
salad	Salat zah-**laht**
soup	Suppe **zoo**-peh
first course	erster Gang **ehr**-stehr gahng
main course(s)	Hauptgericht(e) / Hauptgang **howpt**-geh-rikht(-eh) / **howpt**-gahng
meat	Fleisch flīsh
poultry	Geflügel geh-**flew**-gehl
fish	Fisch fish
seafood	Meeresfrüchte **meh**-rehs-frewkh-teh
side dishes	Beilagen **bī**-lah-gehn
vegetables	Gemüse geh-**mew**-zeh

cheese	Käse **kay**-zeh
dessert	Nachspeise / Nachtisch **nahkh**-shpī-zeh / **nahkh**-tish
light lunch	Brotzeit **broht**-sīt
bar snacks	zum Knabbern tsoom keh-**nah**-behrn
drinks menu	Getränkekarte geh-**trehn**-keh-**kar**-teh
beverages	Getränke geh-**trehn**-keh
beer	Bier beer
wine	Wein vīn
cover charge	Eintritt **īn**-trit
service (not) included	Bedienung (nicht) inklusive beh-**dee**-noong (nikht) in-kloo-**zee**-veh
hot / cold	warm / kalt varm / kahlt
comes with	dazu daht-**soo**
choice of	Wahl vahl

You can save money by ordering a ***halbe Portion*** (half-portion), a dish off the ***kleine Hunger*** (small hunger) list, or the ***Tagesmenü*** (fixed-price meal of the day).

Ordering

waiter	Kellner **kehl**-nehr
waitress	Kellnerin **kehl**-neh-rin
I'm ready / We're ready to order.	Ich möchte / Wir möchten bestellen. ikh **murkh**-teh / veer **murkh**-tehn beh-**shtehl**-ehn
I need / We need more time.	Ich brauche / Wir brauchen mehr Zeit. ikh **browkh**-eh / veer **browkh**-ehn mehr tsīt
I'd like / We'd like...	Ich möchte / Wir möchten... ikh **murkh**-teh / veer **murkh**-tehn
...just a drink.	...nur etwas zu trinken. noor **eht**-vahs tsoo **trink**-ehn

...to see the menu.	...die Karte sehen. dee **kar**-teh **zay**-ehn
...to eat.	...essen. **eh**-sehn
Do you have...?	Haben Sie...? **hah**-behn zee
...an English menu	...eine Speisekarte auf Englisch ī-neh **shpī**-zeh-kar-teh owf **ehng**-lish
...a fixed-price meal of the day	...ein Tagesmenü īn tah-gehs-meh-**new**
...half portions	...halbe Portionen **hahl**-beh port-see-**oh**-nehn
...a lunch special	...ein Mittagsmenü īn **mit** tahgs-meh-**new**
What do you recommend?	Was schlagen Sie vor? vahs **shlah**-gehn zee for
What's your favorite dish?	Was ist Ihr Lieblingsessen? vahs ist eer **leeb**-lings-eh-sehn
What is better? (point to menu items)	Was ist besser? vahs ist **behs**-her
What is...?	Was ist...? vahs ist
Is it...?	Ist es...? ist ehs
...good	...gut goot
...affordable	...günstig **gewn**-stig
...expensive	...teuer **toy**-ehr
...local	...typisch **tew**-pish
...fresh	...frisch frish
...fast	...schnell shnehl
...spicy (hot)	...scharf sharf
Is it filling?	Macht das satt? mahkt dahs zaht
What is that? (pointing)	Was ist das? vahs ist dahs
How much?	Wie viel? vee feel
Nothing with eyeballs.	Nichts mit Augen. nihkts mit **ow**-gehn

Can I substitute (something else) for the ____?	Kann ich (etwas anderes) statt ____ haben? kahn ikh (**eht**-vahs **ahn**-deh-rehs) shtaht ____ **hah**-behn
Can I / Can we get it to go?	Kann ich / Können wir das mitnehmen? kahn ikh / **kurn**-ehn veer dahs **mit**-nay-mehn

This is the sequence of a typical restaurant experience: The waiter gives you a menu (***Karte*** or ***Speisekarte***) and then asks if you'd like something to drink ***(Etwas zu trinken?).*** When ready to take your order, the waiter simply says ***Bitte?.*** After the meal, he asks if the meal tasted good ***(Hat's gut geschmeckt?),*** if you'd like dessert ***(Möchten Sie eine Nachspeise?),*** and if you'd like anything else (***Sonst noch etwas?*** or ***Möchten Sie etwas dazu?*** or ***Haben Sie noch einen Wunsch?***). He may also ask ***Sind Sie zufrieden?*** (Are you content?). If you'd like to speak with the server, you'll need to signal for him or her politely.

Tableware and Condiments

I need / We need a...	Ich brauche / Wir brauchen... ikh **browkh**-eh / veer **browkh**-ehn
...napkin.	...eine Serviette. ī-neh zehr-vee-**eht**-eh
...knife.	...ein Messer. īn **mehs**-ehr
...fork.	...eine Gabel. ī-neh **gah**-behl
...spoon.	...einen Löffel. ī-nehn **lurf**-fehl
...cup.	...eine Tasse. ī-neh **tah**-seh
...glass.	...ein Glas. īn glahs
Please, another...	Bitte, noch... **bit**-teh nohkh
...table setting.	...ein Gedeck. īn geh-**dehk**
...plate.	...einen Teller. ī-nehn **tehl**-ehr
silverware	Besteck beh-**shtehk**
carafe	Karaffe kah-**rah**-feh

water	Wasser **vahs**-ehr
bread	Brot broht
large pretzel	Brezel / Brez'n (Bav.) **brayt**-sehl / **brayts**-ehn
butter	Butter **boo**-tehr
margarine	Margarine mar-gah-**ree**-neh
salt / pepper	Salz / Pfeffer zahlts / **pfehf**-ehr
sugar	Zucker **tsoo**-kehr
artificial sweetener	Süssstoff **sews**-shtohf
honey	Honig **hoh**-nig
mustard	Senf zehnf
...mild mustard	...milder Senf **meeld**-ehr zehnf
...semi-hot mustard	...mittelscharfer Senf **mit**-tehl-sharf-ehr zehnf
...hot mustard	...scharfer Senf **sharf**-ehr zehnf
...sweet mustard	...süsser Senf **zews**-ehr zehnf
...sweet-sour mustard	...süss-sauerer Senf **zews**-zow-ehr-ehr zehnf ("zow" rhymes with "cow")
ketchup	Ketchup "ketchup"
mayonnaise	Mayonnaise mah-yoh-**nay**-zeh
toothpick	Zahnstocher **tsahn**-shtohkh-ehr

The Food Arrives

After serving the meal, your server might wish you a cheery ***Guten Appetit!*** Strangers may also say this to you as they pass your table.

That looks delicious!	Das sieht köstlich aus! dahs zeet **kurst**-likh ows
Is this included with the meal?	Ist das im Essen inklusive? ist dahs im **eh**-sehn in-kloo-**zee**-veh

I / We did not order this.	Dies habe ich / Dies haben wir nicht bestellt. dees **hah**-beh ikh / dees **hah**-behn veer nikht beh-**shtehlt**
This is...	Dies ist... dees ist
...dirty.	...schmutzig. **shmoot**-sig
...greasy.	...fettig. **feh**-tig
...salty.	...salzig. **zahlt**-sig
...undercooked.	...zu wenig gekocht. tsoo **vay**-nig geh-**kohkht**
...overcooked.	...zu lang gekocht. tsoo lahng geh-**kohkht**
...cold.	...kalt. kahlt
Please heat this up?	Bitte aufwärmen? **bit**-teh **owf**-vehr-mehn
A little.	Ein bisschen. īn **bis**-yehn
More. / Another.	Mehr. / Noch eins. mehr / nohkh īns
One more, please.	Bitte, noch eins. **bit**-teh nohkh īns
The same.	Das gleiche. dahs **glīkh**-eh
Enough.	Genug. geh-**noog**
Yummy!	Mmmh! mmm
Delicious!	Lecker! **lehk**-ehr
Excellent!	Ausgezeichnet! ows-geht-**sīkh**-neht
My compliments to the chef!	Komplimente an den Koch! kohmp-lim-**ehn**-teh ahn dayn kohkh
Finished.	Fertig. **fehr**-tig
I'm full.	Ich bin satt. ikh bin zaht
Thank you.	Danke. **dahn**-keh

Paying

bill	Rechnung / Zahlen **rehkh**-noong / **tsah**-lehn
The bill, please.	Die Rechnung, bitte. dee **rehkh**-noong **bit**-teh

Together.	Zusammen. tsoo-**zah**-mehn
Separate checks.	Getrennt. geh-**trehnt**
Do you accept credit cards?	Akzeptieren Sie Kreditkarten? ahkt-sehp-**teer**-ehn zee kreh-**deet**-kar-tehn
This is not correct.	Das stimmt nicht. dahs shtimt nikht
Can you explain this?	Können Sie das erklären? **kurn**-ehn zee dahs ehr-**klehr**-ehn
Can you itemize the bill?	Können Sie die Rechnung einzeln aufführen? **kurn**-ehn zee dee **rehkh**-noong **īnt**-sehln **owf**-fewr-ehn
What if I wash the dishes?	Und wenn ich die Teller wasche? oont vehn ikh dee **tehl**-ehr **vah**-sheh
Could I have a receipt, please?	Kann ich bitte einen Beleg haben? kahn ikh **bit**-teh ī-nehn beh-**lehg** **hah**-behn

When you're ready to pay, first get the waiter's attention. Then ask for the bill by saying ***Die Rechnung*** (literally "reckoning") or ***Zahlen, bitte.*** The waiter might ask you ***Zusammen oder getrennt?*** (Together, or separate checks?).

Tipping

The service charge (sometimes called ***Bedienung***) is nearly always included. Tipping is not expected beyond that, though it's polite to round up to the next big coin (10 percent is about right)—this bonus is called ***Trinkgeld,*** literally "drinking money." If you're uncertain whether to tip, ask another customer if tipping is expected.

Rather than leaving loose coins on the table, German, Austrian, and Swiss diners "tip with paper": When paying your bill, tell your server the total amount you want to pay including the tip. For example, if your bill is €13.70 and you're handing over a €20 bill, simply say ***Fünfzehn*** (Fifteen). You'll get €5 change, your server keeps the extra €1.30

(without having to fish around for coins that you'll just give back anyway, and you'll feel very local.

tip	Trinkgeld **trink**-gehlt
service (not) included	Bedienung (nicht) inklusive beh-**dee**-noong (nikht) in-kloo-**zee**-veh
Is tipping expected?	Ist Trinkgeld üblich? ist **trink**-gehlt **ewb**-likh
What percent?	Wie viel Prozent? vee feel proh-**tsehnt**
Keep the change.	Stimmt so. shtimt zoh
Change, please.	Wechselgeld, bitte. vehkh-zehl-**gehlt bit**-teh
This is for you.	Das ist für Sie. dahs ist fewr zee

SPECIAL CONCERNS

In a Hurry

Europeans take their time at meals, so don't expect speedy service. However, if you're in a rush, let your server know.

I'm / We're in a hurry.	Ich habe / Wir haben es eilig. ikh **hah**-beh / veer **hah**-behn ehs **ī**-lig
I'm sorry.	Es tut mir leid. ehs toot meer līt
I must / We must leave...	Ich muss / Wir müssen... gehen. ikh moos / veer **mew**-sehn... **gay**-ehn
...in 30 minutes / in one hour.	...in dreissig Minuten / in einer Stunde in **drī**-sig mee-**noo**-tehn / in **ī**-nehr **shtoon**-deh
Will the food be ready soon?	Ist das Essen bald bereit? ist dahs **eh**-sehn bahlt beh-**rīt**
The bill, please.	Die Rechnung, bitte. dee **rehkh**-noong **bit**-teh

To speed things up, ask for your bill when the waiter brings your food. You could explain ***Es tut mir leid—ich habe es eilig*** (I'm sorry—I'm in a hurry.).

Allergies and Other Dietary Restrictions

allergy	Allergie ah-lehr-**gee** (hard "g")
I'm allergic to...	Ich bin allergisch auf... ikh bin ah-**lehr**-gish owf
I cannot eat...	Ich darf kein... essen. ikh darf kīn... **eh**-sehn
He / She cannot eat...	Er / Sie darf kein... essen. ehr / zee darf kīn... **eh**-sehn
He / She has a life-threatening allergy to...	Er / Sie hat eine lebensbedrohliche Allergie auf... ehr / zee haht ī-neh **lay**-behnz-beh-**droh**-likh-eh ah-lehr-**gee** owf
No...	Keine... **kī**-neh
...dairy products.	...Milchprodukte **milkh**-proh-**dook**-teh
...nuts.	...Nüsse **new**-seh
...peanuts.	...Erdnüsse ehrd-**new**-seh
...walnuts.	...Walnüsse vahl-**new**-seh
...wheat / gluten.	...Weizen / Gluten **vīt**-sehn / "gluten"
...seafood.	...Meeresfrüchte **meh**-rehs-**frewkh**-teh
...shellfish.	...Schalentiere **shahl**-ehn-teer-eh
No salt / sugar.	Kein Salz / Zucker. kīn zahlts / **tsoo**-kehr
I'm a diabetic. (m / f)	Ich bin Diabetiker / Diabetikerin. ikh bin dee-ah-**bay**-tik-ehr / dee-ah-**bay**-tik-eh-rin
He / She is lactose intolerant.	Er / Sie hat eine Laktoseintoleranz. ehr / zee haht ī-neh **lahk**-tohz-in-toh-lehr-**ahnts**
No caffeine.	Koffeinfrei. koh-fay-**in**-frī

No alcohol.	Kein Alkohol. kīn "alcohol"
Organic.	Bio. **bee**-oh

Vegetarian Phrases

Very often, Europeans think vegetarian means "no red meat" or "not much meat." If you're a strict vegetarian, tell your server what you don't eat: Write it out on a card and keep it handy. It can also be helpful to clarify what you do eat.

I'm a...	Ich bin... ikh bin
...vegetarian. (m / f)	...Vegetarier / Vegetarierin. vay-gay-**tar**-ee-ehr / vay-gay-**tar**-ee-eh-rin
...strict vegetarian. (m / f)	...strenger Vegetarier / strenge Vegetarierin. **shtrehng**-ehr vay-gay-**tar**-ee-ehr / **shtrehng**-eh vay-gay-**tar**-ee-eh-rin
...vegan. (m / f)	...Veganer / Veganerin. veh-**gahn**-ehr / veh-**gahn**-eh-rin
Is any meat or animal fat used in this?	Hat es Fleisch oder tierische Fette drin? haht ehs flīsh **oh**-dehr **teer**-ish-eh **feht**-eh drin
What is vegetarian here? (pointing to menu)	Was ist hier vegetarisch? vahs ist heer vay-gay-**tah**-rish
I don't eat...	Ich esse kein... ikh **eh**-seh kīn
I'd like this without...	Ich möchte das ohne... ikh **murhk**-teh dahs **oh**-neh
...meat.	...Fleisch. flīsh
...eggs.	...Eier. ī-ehr
...animal products.	...Tierprodukte. teer-proh-**dook**-teh
I eat...	Ich esse... ikh **eh**-seh
Do you have...?	Haben Sie...? **hah**-behn zee

...anything with tofu	...irgend etwas mit Tofu **eer**-gehnd eht-**vahs** mit toh-**foo**
...veggie burgers	...Veggie-Burger "veggie burger"

Children

Do you have a children's menu?	Haben Sie eine Kinderspeisekarte? **hah**-behn zee ī-neh kin-dehr-**shpī**-zeh-**kar**-teh
children's portions	Kinderportionen **kin**-dehr-port-see-**ohn**-ehn
half-portions	halbe Portionen **hahl**-beh port-see-**ohn**-ehn
a high chair	einen Kinderhocker ī-nehn **kin**-dehr-**hoh**-kehr
a booster seat	einen Kindersitz ī-nehn **kin**-dehr-zits
noodles	Nudeln **noo**-dehln
rice	Reis "rice"
with butter	mit Butter mit **boo**-tehr
without sauce	ohne Sosse **oh**-neh **zoh**-seh
sauce / dressing on the side	Sosse / Salatsosse separat **zoh**-seh / zah-**laht**-zoh-seh zeh-pah-**raht**
pizza...	Pizza... "pizza"
...cheese only	...nur Käse noor **kay**-zeh
...pepperoni	...Salami zah-**lah**-mee
cheese sandwich	Käsebrot **kay**-zeh-broht
toasted cheese sandwich	getoastetes Käsebrot geh-**tohst**-eh-tehs **kay**-zeh-broht
grilled cheese sandwich	gegrilltes Käsebrot geh-**gril**-tehs **kay**-zeh-broht
hot dog	Hot Dog "hot dog"
hamburger	Hamburger **hahm**-boor-gehr
cheeseburger	Cheeseburger **"cheese"**-boor-gehr

French fries	Pommes frites / Pommes pohm frits / **poh**-mehs
ketchup	Ketchup "ketchup"
Small milk.	Kleine Portion Milch. **klī**-neh port-see-**ohn** milkh
Straw(s).	Strohhalm(e). **shtroh**-hahlm(-eh)
More napkins, please.	Mehr Servietten, bitte. mehr zehr-vee-**eht**-ehn **bit**-teh

Remember, to get smaller portions, you can order from the ***kleine Hunger*** (small hunger) section of the menu.

WHAT'S COOKING?

Traditional Germanic food—heavy on potatoes, cabbage, and ***Wurst*** (sausage)—is notoriously starchy and filling. But these days, many locals have become health nuts. On menus, the word ***Fitness*** marks healthy items (such as ***Fitnessteller,*** fitness plate). People in these countries are also quite passionate about choosing ***Bio*** (organic) products. Not only do they eat ***Bio*** fruits and vegetables, but also ***Bio*** bread, ice cream, and schnitzel. A ***Bioladen*** is a store that sells organic products.

Breakfast

I'd like...	Ich hätte gern... ikh **heh**-teh gehrn
We'd like...	Wir hätten gern... veer **heh**-tehn gehrn
breakfast	Frühstück **frew**-shtewk
bread	Brot broht
roll	Brötchen **brurtkh**-yehn
sweet roll	Kleingebäck / Zuckergebäck / Teilchen **klīn**-geh-behk / tsoo-**kehr**-geh-behk / **tīlkh**-yehn
toast	Toast "toast"
butter	Butter **boo**-tehr
jelly	Marmelade mar-meh-**lah**-deh
honey	Honig **hoh**-nig

Key Phrases: What's Cooking?

food	Essen **eh**-sehn
breakfast	Frühstück **frew**-shtewk
lunch	Mittagessen **mit**-tahg-eh-sehn
dinner	Abendessen **ah**-behnd-eh-sehn
bread	Brot broht
cheese	Käse **kay**-zeh
soup	Suppe **zoo**-peh
salad	Salat zah-**laht**
fish	Fisch fish
chicken	Hähnchen / Huhn **hehnkh**-yehn / hoon
meat	Fleisch flīsh
vegetables	Gemüse geh-**mew**-zeh
fruit	Frucht / Obst frookht / ohpst
dessert	Nachspeise **nahkh**-shpī-zeh

cold cuts	Aufschnitt **owf**-shnit
pastry	Gebäck geh-**behk**
croissant	Croissant / Gipfel / Hörnchen krwah-**sahn** / **gip**-fehl / **hurnkh**-yehn
omelet	Omelett ohm-**leht**
egg / eggs	Ei / Eier ī / **ī**-ehr
soft-boiled / hard-boiled eggs	weichgekochte / hartgekochte Eier **vīkh**-geh-kohkh-teh / **hart**-geh-kohkh-teh **ī**-ehr
poached eggs	pochierte Eier **pokh**-eer-teh **ī**-ehr
scrambled eggs	Rühreier **rewr**-ī-ehr
fried eggs...	Spiegeleier... **shpee**-gehl-ī-ehr
...sunny side up	...Sunny Side "sunny side"
...over easy	...beidseitig **bīd**-zī-tig

...easy / medium / well-done	...weich / mittel / gut gebraten vīkh / **mit**-tehl / goot geh-**brah**-tehn
ham	Schinken **shink**-ehn
bacon	Speck shpehk
cheese	Käse **kay**-zeh
yogurt...	Joghurt... **yoh**-goort
...with strawberries	...mit Erdbeeren mit **ehrd**-behr-ehn
cereal	Cornflakes "cornflakes"
granola	Müsli **mewz**-lee
fruit cup	Früchtebecher **frewkh**-teh-behkh-ehr
milk	Milch milkh
coffee / tea	Kaffee / Tee kah-**fay** / tay
fruit juice	Fruchtsaft **frookht**-zahft
orange juice	Orangensaft oh-**rahn**-zhehn-zahft
apple juice	Apfelsaft **ahp**-fehl-zahft
hot chocolate	heisse Schokolade **hī**-seh shoh-koh-**lah**-deh

Sandwiches

The traditional term for a sandwich is ***belegtes Brot*** (literally, "laid bread"), and ***Brötchen*** (roll) can also mean a sandwich. But everyone understands the English word ***Sandwich.***

I'd like a sandwich.	Ich hätte gern ein Sandwich. ikh **heh**-teh gehrn īn **zehnd**-vich
white bread	Weissbrot **vīs**-broht
wheat bread	Dunkelbrot / Vollkornbrot **doon**-kehl-broht / **fohl**-korn-broht
baguette	Baguette "baguette"
cheese	Käse **kay**-zeh
tuna	Thunfisch **toon**-fish
fish	Fisch fish

chicken	Hähnchen **hehnkh**-yehn
turkey	Truthahn / Pute **troot**-hahn / **poo**-teh
cold cuts	Aufschnitt **owf**-shnit
ham	Schinken **shink**-ehn
cured ham	Rohschinken **roh**-shink-ehn
cooked ham	Kochschinken **kokh**-shink-ehn
meat (beef)	Fleisch flīsh
smoked meat	Räuchern **roykh**-ehrn
pork	Schweinefleisch **shvīn**-eh-flīsh
salami	Salami zah-**lah**-mee
spread	Aufstrich **owf**-shtrikh
lard spread	Schmalz shmahlts
egg salad	Eiersalat ī-ehr-zah-laht
lettuce	Kopfsalat **kohpf**-zah laht
tomatoes	Tomaten toh-**mah**-tehn
onions	Zwiebeln **tsvee**-behln
mustard...	Senf... zehnf
...mild / hot / sweet	...mild / scharf / süss meelt / sharf / zews
horseradish	Meerrettich / Kren (Bav. and Aus.) **mehr**-eh-tikh / krehn
mayonnaise	Mayonnaise mah-yoh-**nay**-zeh
peanut butter	Erdnussbutter **ehrd**-noos-boo-tehr
jelly	Marmelade mar-meh-**lah**-deh
on a slice of bread / on a roll	auf eine Schnitte Brot / auf einem Brötchen owf ī-neh **shnit**-teh broht / owf ī-nehm **brurtkh**-yehn
toasted / grilled / heated	getoastet / gegrillt / erwärmt geh-**tohst**-eht / geh-**grilt** / ehr-**vehrmt**
Does this come cold or warm?	Wird das kalt oder warm serviert? virt dahs kahlt **oh**-dehr varm zehr-**veert**

Best of the Wurst

Wurst (sausage) is a Germanic staple. While available at restaurants, it's more commonly eaten at fast-food stands (called ***Würstchenbude*** in Germany, or ***Würstelstand*** in Austria).

Your sausage options go far beyond the hometown hot dog. Some are ***gegrillt*** (grilled), while others are ***gekocht*** (boiled or steamed). Most are pork-based. Generally, the darker the weenie, the spicier it is. Here are just a few of the many types of ***Wurst:***

Bratwurst / Rostbratwurst **braht**-voorst / **rohst**-braht-voorst
generic term for any grilled sausage

Brühwurst **brew**-voorst
generic name for any boiled or steamed sausage

Currywurst "**curry**"-voorst
grilled pork sausage (usually pre-cooked) with a ketchup / curry sauce

Frankfurter **frahnk**-foort-ehr
skinny, pink, boiled sausage—the ancestor of our hot dog

Kochwurst **kohkh**-voorst
generic term for sausages made of pre-cooked ingredients; these are only lightly steamed before eating

Lyoner lee-**oh**-nehr
thicker, shorter Frankfurter, often chopped up with onions and vinegar in Wurstsalat

Nürnberger **newrn**-behr-gehr
short and spicy grilled pork sausage (Bav.)

Weisswurst **vīs**-voorst
boiled white sausage—peel off the casing before you eat it—(Bav.)

Wollwurst **vohl**-voorst
like Weisswurst, but peeled and grilled

At the Sausage Stand

sausage	Wurst voorst
with...	mit... mit

...(sweet / hot) mustard	...(süsser / scharfer) Senf (**zews**-ehr / **sharf**-ehr) zehnf
...sauerkraut	...Sauerkraut **zow**-ehr-krowt
...horseradish	...Meerrettich / Kren (Bav. and Aus.) mehr-**reh**-tikh / krehn
bread	Brot broht
roll	Brötchen **brurtkh**-yehn
roasted potatoes	Bratkartoffeln **braht**-kar-**tohf**-ehln
potato salad	Kartoffelsalat kar-**tohf**-ehl-zah-**laht**

Say Cheese

cheese	Käse **kay**-zeh
cheese shop	Käserei kay-zeh-**rī**
Do you have a cheese that is...?	Haben Sie einen Käse der... ist? **hah**-behn zee **ī**-nehn **kay**-zeh dehr... ist
...mild / sharp	...mild / scharf meelt / sharf
...fresh / aged	...frisch / gealtet frish / geh-**ahl**-teht
...soft / hard	...weich / hart vīkh / hart
...(made) from a cow / sheep / goat	...von Kuhmilch / Schafsmilch / Ziegenmilch (gemacht) fohn **koo**-milkh / **shahfs**-milkh / **tsee**-gehn-milkh (geh-**mahkht**)
sliced	in Scheiben geschnitten in **shī**-behn geh-**shnit**-ehn
smoked	geräuchert geh-**roykh**-ehrt
Can I try a taste?	Kann ich es probieren? kahn ikh ehs **proh**-beer-ehn
What is your favorite cheese?	Was ist Ihr Lieblingskäse? vahs ist eer **lee**-blings-**kay**-zeh
I would like three types of cheese for a picnic.	Ich möchte drei Käsesorten für ein Picknick. ikh **murkh**-teh drī **kay**-zeh-**zor**-tehn fewr īn "picnic"

Choose for me, please.	Wählen Sie bitte für mich. **vay**-lehn zee **bit**-teh fewr mikh
This much. (showing size)	So viel. zoh feel
More. / Less.	Mehr. / Weniger. mehr / **vay**-nig-ehr
Can you please slice it?	Bitte schneiden? **bit**-teh **shnī**-dehn

Soups

In Germany, soup is often served as a first course to the large midday meal ***(Mittagessen).***

soup (of the day)	Suppe (des Tages) **zoo**-peh (dehs **tahg**-ehs)
stew	Eintopf **īn**-tohpf
vegetable soup	Gemüsesuppe geh-**mew**-zeh-zoo-peh
fish soup	Fischsuppe **fish**-zoo-peh
chicken broth	Hühnerbrühe **hew**-nehr-brew-eh
beef broth	Rinderbrühe **rin**-dehr-brew-eh
with noodles	mit Nudeln mit **noo**-dehln
with rice	mit Reis mit "rice"
with dumplings	mit Knödel mit keh-**nur**-dehl

Salads

For a starter, a side dish, or a small appetite, consider a ***grüner Salat*** (mostly lettuce) or—for more variety—***gemischter Salat*** (a.k.a. ***buntner Salat***), a mixed salad of lettuce, fresh and (often) pickled veggies, and a tasty dressing.

salad	Salat zah-**laht**
green salad	grüner Salat **grew**-nehr zah-**laht**

mixed salad	gemischter Salat geh-**mish**-tehr zah-**laht**
potato salad	Kartoffelsalat kar-**tohf**-ehl-zah-**laht**
Greek salad	griechischer Salat **greekh**-ish-ehr zah-**laht**
chef's salad...	gemischter Salat des Hauses... geh-**mish**-tehr zah-**laht** dehs **how**-zehs
...with ham and cheese	...mit Schinken und Käse mit **shink**-ehn oont **kay**-zeh
...with egg	...mit Ei mit ī
plate of various salads	Salatteller zah-**laht**-tehl-ehr
vegetable platter	Gemüseplatte / Gemüseteller geh-**mew**-zeh-plah-teh / geh-**mew**-zeh-tehl-ehr
lettuce	Kopfsalat **kohpf**-zah-laht
cabbage / red cabbage	Kohl / Rotkohl kohl / **roht**-kohl
tomato	Tomate toh-**mah**-teh
onion	Zwiebel **tsvee**-behl
cucumber	Gurke **goor**-keh
carrot	Karotte / Möhre kah-**roh**-teh / **mur**-eh
beet	rote Bete / rote Rübe **roh**-teh **bay**-teh / **roh**-teh **rew**-beh
oil / vinegar	Öl / Essig url / **eh**-sig
dressing (on the side)	Salatsosse (separat) zah-**laht**-zoh-seh (zeh-pah-**raht**)
What is in this salad?	Was ist in diesem Salat? vahs ist in **dee**-zehm zah-**laht**

At a self-serve ***Salatbar*** (salad bar), you'll normally be charged by the size of the plate. Choose a ***Teller*** (plate) that is ***klein*** (small), ***mittel*** (medium), or ***gross*** (large). Budget travelers eat a cheap and healthy lunch by grabbing a small plate and stacking it high.

Fish and Seafood

seafood	Meeresfrüchte **meh**-rehs-**frewkh**-teh
assorted seafood	gemischte Meeresfrüchte geh-**mish**-teh **meh**-rehs-**frewkh**-teh
fish	Fisch fish
shellfish	Schalentiere **shah**-lehn-teer-eh
anchovy	Sardelle zar-**dehl**-eh
carp	Karpfen **karp**-fehn
clam	Muschel **moo**-shehl
cod	Dorsch dorsh
crab	Krabbe **krah**-beh
crayfish	Languste **lahn**-goo-steh
eel	Aal ahl
halibut	Heilbutt **hīl**-boot
herring	Hering / Matjes **hehr**-ing / **maht**-yehs
lobster	Hummer **hoo**-mehr
mackerel	Makrele **mahk**-reh-leh
mussel	Miesmuschel **mees**-moo-shehl
oyster	Auster **ow**-stehr
pike	Hecht hehkht
pikeperch	Zander **tsahn**-dehr
prawn	Garnele / Krevette (Switz.) gar-**neh**-leh / kreh-**veh**-teh
salmon	Lachs lahkhs
sardine	Sardine zar-**dee**-neh
scallop	Jakobsmuschel **yah**-kohbs-moo-shehl
squid	Tintenfisch **tin**-tehn-fish
swordfish	Schwertfisch **shvehrt**-fish
trout	Forelle foh-**rehl**-eh
tuna	Thunfisch **toon**-fish

How much for a portion?	Wie viel für eine Portion? vee feel fewr **ī**-neh port-see-**ohn**
What's fresh today?	Was ist heute frisch? vahs ist **hoy**-teh frish
How do you eat this?	Wie isst man das? vee ist mahn dahs
Do you eat this part?	Isst man diesen Teil? ist mahn **dee**-zehn tīl
Just the head, please.	Nur den Kopf, bitte. noor dayn kohpf **bit**-teh

Poultry

poultry	Geflügel geh-**flew**-gehl
chicken	Hähnchen **hehnkh**-yehn
roast chicken	Brathähnchen / Backhühner (Aus.) / Hendl (Aus.) **braht**-hehnkh-yehn / **bahk**-hew-nehr / **hehnd**-ehl
duck	Ente **ehn**-teh
goose	Gans gahns
turkey	Truthahn / Pute **troot**-hahn / **poo**-teh
breast	Brust broost
thigh / drumstick	Schenkel / Schlegel **shehn**-kehl / **shlay**-gehl
white / dark meat	helles / dunkles Fleisch **hehl**-ehs / **doonk**-lehs flīsh
liver (pâté)	Leber (pastete) **lay**-behr (pah-**steh**-teh)
eggs	Eier **ī**-ehr
free-range	Freilandhaltung frī-lahnd-**hahl**-toong
How long has this been dead?	Wie lange ist dieses Tier schon tot? vee **lahng**-eh ist **dee**-zehs teer shohn toht

Meat

meat	Fleisch flīsh
cold cuts	Aufschnitt **owf**-shnit
salt-cured meat	Pökelfleisch **pur**-kehl-flīsh
smoke-cured meat	Räucherfleisch **roy**-khehr-flīsh
bacon	Speck shpehk
beef	Rindfleisch **rint**-flīsh
beef steak	Beefsteak "beefsteak"
cutlet	Kotelett **koh**-teh-leht
deer	Reh ray
ham	Schinken **shink**-ehn
knuckle (fatty joint)	Haxe / Stelze (Aus.) **hahk**-seh / **shtehlt**-seh
lamb	Lamm lahm
mixed grill	Grillteller **gril**-tehl-ehr
mutton	Hammelfleisch **hah**-mehl-flīsh
ox	Ochse / Ochsenfleisch **ohkh**-seh / **ohkh**-sehn-flīsh
pig	Schwein shvīn
suckling pig	Spanferkel **shpahn**-fehr-kehl

Avoiding Mis-Steaks

alive	lebendig lay-**behn**-dig
raw	roh roh
very rare	blutig **bloo**-tig
rare	rot roht
medium	halbgar **hahlb**-gar
well-done	gar / durchgebraten gar / **durkh**-geh-**brah**-tehn
very well-done	ganz gar gahnts gar

pork	Schweinefleisch **shvī**-neh-flīsh
prosciutto	Schinkenspeck **shink**-ehn-shpehk
rabbit	Kaninchen kah-**neenkh**-yehn
rib steak	Ribsteak "ribsteak"
roast beef	Rinderbraten **rin**-dehr-brah-tehn
sausage / blood sausage	Wurst / Blutwurst voorst / **bloot**-voorst
shoulder	Schulter **shoohl**-tehr
veal	Kalbfleisch **kahlb**-flīsh
venison	Wildbret **veeld**-breht
wild boar	Wildschwein **veeld**-shvīn
Is this cooked?	Ist das gekocht? ist dahs geh-**kohkht**

Veggies

vegetables	Gemüse geh-**mew**-zeh
mixed vegetables	gemischtes Gemüse geh-**mish**-tehs geh-**mew**-zeh
artichoke	Artischocke ar-tish-**oh**-keh
arugula (rocket)	Rucola **roo**-koh-lah
asparagus	Spargel **shpar**-gehl
avocado	Avocado ah-voh-**kah**-doh
bean	Bohne **boh**-neh
beet	rote Bete / rote Rübe **roh**-teh **bay**-teh / **roh**-teh **rew**-beh
broccoli	Brokkoli **broh**-koh-lee
cabbage	Kohl kohl
carrot	Karotte / Möhre kah-**roh**-teh / **mur**-eh
cauliflower	Blumenkohl / Karfiol (Aus.) **bloo**-mehn-kohl / **kar**-fee-ohl
corn	Mais / Kukuruz (Aus.) mīs / **koo**-koo-roots
cucumber (or pickle)	Gurke **goor**-keh

eggplant	Aubergine / Melanzani (Aus.) oh-behr-**zhee**-neh / meh-lahnt-**sah**-nee
endive	Endive ehn-**dee**-veh
fennel	Fenchel **fehnkh**-ehl
garlic	Knoblauch keh-**noh**-blowkh
green bean	grüne Bohne / Fisole (Aus.) **grew**-neh **boh**-neh / fee-**zoh**-leh
leek	Lauch lowkh
lentil	Linse **lin**-zeh
mushroom	Pilz pilts
olive	Olive oh-**lee**-veh
onion	Zwiebel **tsvee**-behl
pea	Erbse **ehrb**-zeh
(green / red / yellow) pepper	(grüner / roter / gelber) Paprika (**grew**-nehr / **roh**-tehr / **gehl**-behr) **pah**-pree-kah
pickle	Essiggurke eh-sig-**goor**-keh
radish	Radiesch rah-**dish**
red cabbage (raw / cooked)	Rotkohl / Blaukraut **roht**-kohl / **blow**-krowt ("blow" rhymes with "cow")
sauerkraut	Sauerkraut **zow**-ehr-krowt
spinach	Spinat shpee-**naht**
tomato	Tomate / Paradeiser (Aus.) toh-**mah**-teh / pah-rah-**dī**-zehr
turnip	weisse Rübe **vī**-seh **rew**-beh
zucchini	Zucchini tsoo-**kee**-nee

Dumplings, Potatoes, and Noodles

dumplings	Knödel keh-**nur**-dehl
potatoes	Kartoffeln / Erdäpfel (Aus.) kar-**tohf**-ehln / **ehrd**-ahp-fehl

roasted potatoes	Bratkartoffeln **braht**-kar-**tohf**-ehln
mashed potatoes	Kartoffelpüree kar-**tohf**-ehl-pew-**ray**
potatoes boiled in salty water	Salzkartoffeln **zahlts** kar **tohf**-ehln
baked potato	Ofenkartoffel **oh**-fehn-kar-**tohf**-ehl
potato pancake	Reibekuchen **rī**-beh-kookh-ehn
hash browns	Rösti (Switz.) **rur**-shtee
French fries	Pommes frites / Pommes pom frits / **poh**-mehs
pasta	Pasta / Teigwaren "pasta" / **tīg**-vah-rehn
noodles	Nudeln **noo**-dehln
spaghetti	Spaghetti "spaghetti"
rice	Reis "rice"

The quintessential Germanic noodle is ***Spätzle***—an egg-and-flour batter that's dripped through a wide-holed sieve into boiling water to create simple but very filling little bits of dough.

Fruits

fruit	Frucht / Obst frookht / ohpst
fruit cup	Früchtebecher **frewkh**-teh-behkh-ehr
fruit smoothie	Frucht Smoothie frookht **smoo**-tee
apple	Apfel **ahp**-fehl
apricot	Aprikose / Marille (Aus.) ahp-rik-**oh**-zeh / mah-**ril**-eh
banana	Banane bah-**nah**-neh
berries	Beeren **behr**-ehn
bilberry	Heidelbeere **hī**-dehl-behr-eh
black currant	schwarze Johannisbeere **shvarts**-eh yoh-hah-nis-**behr**-eh
blackberry	Brombeere **brohm**-behr-eh

blueberry	Blaubeere **blow**-behr-eh ("blow" rhymes with "cow")
cantaloupe	Melone meh-**loh**-neh
cherry	Kirsche **keer**-sheh
...sour cherry	...Sauerkirsche / Weichsel (Aus.) **zow**-ehr-keer-sheh / **vīkh**-sehl
cranberry	Preiselbeere **prī**-zehl-behr-eh
date	Dattel **daht**-ehl
fig	Feige **fī**-geh
grapefruit	Pampelmuse / Grapefruit pahm-pehl-**moo**-zeh / "grapefruit"
grape	Traub trowb
honeydew melon	Honigmelone hoh-nig-meh-**loh**-neh
lemon	Zitrone tsee-**troh**-neh
mango	Mango **mahn**-goh
orange	Apfelsine / Orange ahp-fehl-**zee**-neh / oh-**rahn**-zheh
peach	Pfirsich **pfeer**-zikh
pear	Birne **beer**-neh
persimmon	Persimone pehr-zee-**moh**-neh
pineapple	Ananas **ahn**-ahn-ahs
plum	Pflaume / Zwetsche **pflow**-meh / **tsveht**-sheh
pomegranate	Granatapfel grah-naht-**ahp**-fehl
prune	Backpflaume **bahk**-pflow-meh
raisin	Rosine roh-**zee**-neh
raspberry	Himbeere **him**-behr-eh
red currant	rote Johannisbeere **roh**-teh yoh-hah-nis-**behr**-eh
strawberry	Erdbeere **ehrd**-behr-eh
tangerine	Mandarine mahn-dah-**ree**-neh
watermelon	Wassermelone **vahs**-ehr-meh-loh-neh

Desserts

I'd like...	Ich hätte gern... ikh **heh**-teh gehrn
We'd like...	Wir hätten gern... veer **heh**-tehn gehrn
dessert	Nachspeise / Nachtisch **nahkh**-shpī-zeh / **nahkh**-tish
cookies	Kekse **kayk**-zeh
candy	Bonbons **bohn**-bohns
pastries	Gebäck geh-**behk**
strudel	Strudel **shtroo**-dehl
cake	Kuchen **kookh**-ehn
pie	Torte **tor**-teh
ice cream	Eis īs
a scoop of...	ein Kugel... īn **koo**-gehl
vanilla	Vanille vah-**nee**-leh
chocolate	Schokolade shoh-koh-**lah**-deh
strawberry	Erdbeer **ehrd**-behr
lemon	Zitrone tsee-**troh**-neh
...in a cone	...in einer Waffel in ī-nehr **vah**-fehl
...in a cup	...in einem Becher in ī-nehm **behkh**-ehr
ice cream cake	Eistorte īs-**tor**-teh
sorbet	Sorbet zor-**bay**
pralines	Pralinen prah-**lee**-nehn
cupcake	Cupcake "cupcake"
tart	Törtchen **turtkh**-yehn
whipped cream	Schlagsahne / Schlag / Schlagobers (Aus.) **shlahg**-zah-neh / shlahg / **shlahg**-oh-behrs
chocolate mousse	Schokoladenmousse shoh-koh-**lah**-dehn-moos
pudding	Pudding "pudding"
low calorie	kalorienarm kah-loh-**ree**-ehn-arm
homemade	hausgemacht **hows**-geh-mahkht

We'll split one.	Wir teilen uns eine. veer **tī**-lehn oons **ī**-neh
Two forks / spoons, please.	Zwei Gabeln / Löffel, bitte. tsvī **gah**-behln / **lurf**-fehl **bit**-teh
I shouldn't, but...	Ich sollte nicht, aber... ikh **zohl**-teh nikht **ah**-behr
Delicious!	Köstlich! **kurst**-likh
Yum!	Lecker! **lehk**-ehr

DRINKING

On a menu, you'll find drinks listed under ***Getränkekarte*** (drink menu).

Water

mineral water...	Mineralwasser... min-eh-rahl-**vahs**-ehr
...with / without carbonation	...mit / ohne Gas mit / **oh**-neh gahs
tap water	Leitungswasser **lī**-toongs-vahs-ehr
(not) drinking water	(kein) Trinkwasser (kīn) **trink**-vahs-ehr
Is the water safe to drink?	Ist das Trinkwasser? ist dahs **trink**-vahs-sehr

If you ask for ***Wasser*** in a restaurant, you'll be served mineral water. Germans rarely drink tap water at the table; try the inexpensive, classy ***Mineralwasser*** (also called ***Tafelwasser,*** table water). Bubbly mineral water might be listed on menus or in stores as ***mit Kohlensäure*** (with carbon dioxide) or ***mit Sprudel*** (with bubbles). But when you're requesting it, the easy-to-remember ***mit Gas*** will do the trick. To get water without bubbles, look for ***ohne Kohlensäure / Sprudel / Gas.*** If you have your heart set on free tap water, try asking for ***Leitungswasser*** and be persistent.

Key Phrases: Drinking

drink	Getränk geh-**trehnk**
mineral water	Mineralwasser min-eh-rahl-**vahs**-ehr
tap water	Leitungswasser **lī**-toongs-vahs-ehr
milk	Milch milkh
juice	Saft zahft
coffee	Kaffee kah-**fay**
tea	Tee tay
wine	Wein vīn
beer	Bier beer
Cheers!	Prost! prohst

Milk

milk	Milch milkh
whole milk	Vollmilch **fohl**-milkh
skim milk	Magermilch **mah**-gehr-milkh
cream	Sahne / Obers (Aus.) **zah**-neh / **oh**-behrs
fresh milk	frische Milch **frish**-eh milkh
cold / warm	kalt / warm kahlt / varm
straw	Strohhalm **shtroh**-hahlm
acidophilus	Acidophilus / Kefir ah-**see**-doh-fil-oos / **keh**-feer

Juice and Other Drinks

fruit juice	Fruchtsaft **frookht**-zahft
100% juice	reiner Fruchtsaft **rī**-nehr **frookht**-zahft
orange juice	Orangensaft oh-**rahn**-zhehn-zahft

apple juice	Apfelsaft **ahp**-fehl-zahft
fizzy apple drink	Apfelschorle / Apfelsaft gespritzt (Aus.) **ahp**-fehl-shor-leh / **ahp**-fehl-zahft geh-**shpritst**
grape juice	Traubensaft **trow**-behn-zahft
grapefruit juice	Grapefruitsaft "grapefruit"-zahft
pineapple juice	Ananassaft **ah**-nah-nah-sahft
fruit smoothie	Frucht Smoothie frookht **smoo**-tee
lemon soda	Limonade lee-moh-**nah**-deh
lemonade	frishgemachte Limonade **frish**-geh-**mahkh**-teh lee-moh-**nah**-deh
soda	Limonade lee-moh-**nah**-deh
energy drink	Energy-Drink "energy drink"
with / without...	mit / ohne... mit / **oh**-neh
...sugar	...Zucker **tsoo**-kehr
...ice cubes	...Eiswürfeln īs-**vewr**-fehln

To get a diet drink, use the word "light" instead of "diet" (for instance, Diet Coke is called Coke Light). Coke Zero, which is also diet, is widely available in Europe.

Coffee and Other Hot Drinks

In Germany and Switzerland, coffee is more popular than espresso drinks. Austria, on the other hand, has a thriving café culture.

coffee...	Kaffee... kah-**fay**
...with milk	...mit Milch mit milkh
...with cream	...mit Sahne mit **zah**-neh
...with sugar	...mit Zucker mit **tsoo**-kehr
...with ice cubes	...mit Eiswürfeln mit īs-**vewr**-fehln
black coffee	schwarzer Kaffee **shvarts**-ehr kah-**fay**
coffee with lots of hot milk	Milchkaffee **milkh**-kah-fay

instant coffee	Pulverkaffee / Nescafé **pool**-vehr-kah-fay / "Nescafé"
decaffeinated	koffeinfrei / Kaffee Haag koh-fay-**in**-frī / kah-**fay** hahg
espresso (single)	Espresso "espresso"
double espresso	Doppelter Espresso **dohp**-ehl-ter "espresso"
double espresso with lots of milk	Latte Macchiato **lah**-tay mah-kee-**ah**-toh
cappuccino	Cappuccino "cappuccino"
Americano (espresso with water)	Kaffee verlängert kah-**fay** fehr-**lehng**-ehrt
coffee with ice cream	Eiskaffee **īs**-kah-fay
hot water	heisses Wasser **hī**-sehs **vahs**-ehr
tea	Tee tay
lemon	Zitrone tsee-**troh**-neh
tea bag	Teebeutel **tay**-boy-tehl
herbal tea	Kräutertee **kroy**-tehr-tay
chamomile	Kamillentee kah-**meel**-ehn-tay
black tea	Schwarztee **shvarts**-tay
English breakfast tea	English Breakfast "English breakfast"
green tea	Grüner Tee **grew**-nehr tay
lemon tea	Zitronentee tsit-**roh**-nehn-tay
orange tea	Orangentee oh-**rahn**-zhehn-tay
fruit tea	Früchtetee **frewkh**-teh-tay
peppermint tea	Pfefferminztee **pfehf**-ehr-mints-tay
chai tea	Chai-Tee "chai" tay
hot chocolate	heisse Schokolade / Kakao **hī**-seh shoh-koh-**lah**-deh / kah-**kow**

If you know you'll want a second cup, order ***eine Portion Kaffee*** or ***eine Kanne Kaffee*** (your own little pitcher; **kah**-neh) rather than ***ein Kaffee*** (just a cup). If you order ***ein Kaffee*** and then want a refill, you'll have to pay for an additional cup.

Wine Lingo

Three-quarters of German, Austrian, and Swiss wines are white. The best-known German whites are from the Rhine and Mosel regions, and there are some good reds, especially from the south. In Austria, the wine (85 percent white) from the Danube River Valley is particularly good. Swiss wines are best from the south and west.

wine	Wein vīn
table wine	Tafelwein **tah**-fehl-vīn
house wine	Hausmarke **hows**-mar-keh
local	einheimisch **īn**-hī-mish
of the region	regional reh-gee-ohn-**ahl** (hard "g")
red	rot roht
white	weiss vīs
rosé	Rosé roh-**zay**
sparkling white wine	Sekt zehkt
light / heavy	leicht / schwer līkht / shvehr
sweet	süss zews
semi-sweet	lieblich **leeb**-likh
semi-dry	halbtrocken **hahlb**-trohk-ehn
(very) dry	(sehr) trocken (zehr) **trohk**-ehn
full-bodied	vollmundig fohl-**moon**-dig
mature	trinkreif **trink**-rīf
fruity	fruchtig **frookh**-tig
chilled	gekühlt geh-**kewlt**
at room temperature	Raumtemperatur rowm-tehm-pehr-ah-**toor**
cork	Korken **kor**-kehn
corkscrew	Korkenzieher **kor**-kehnt-see-hehr

vineyard	Weinberg / Weingut **vīn**-behrg / **vīn**-goot
vintage	Lese / Weinlese **lay**-zeh / **vīn**-lay-zeh

The ***Heuriger*** (**hoy**-rig-ehr) is a uniquely Viennese institution: wine gardens in the hills selling their homemade "new wine." The ***Heurigen*** in the Vienna hills also serve a variety of foods at a buffet (sold by weight, often in ***10 dag*** units—that's 100 grams, or about a quarter-pound).

Ordering Wine

I'd like...	Ich hätte gern... ikh **heh**-teh gehrn
We'd like...	Wir hätten gern... veer **heh**-tehn gehrn
...the wine list.	...die Weinkarte. dee **vīn**-kar-teh
...a glass.	...ein Viertel / ein Glas. īn **feer**-tehl / īn glahs
...a small glass.	...ein Achtel / ein kleines Glas. īn **ahkh**-tehl / īn **klī**-nehs glahs
...a carafe.	...eine Karaffe. **ī**-neh kah-**rah**-feh
...a half-bottle.	...eine halbe Flasche. **ī**-neh **hahl**-beh **flah**-sheh
...a bottle.	...eine Flasche. **ī**-neh **flah**-sheh
red wine	Rotwein **roht**-vīn
white wine	Weisswein **vīs**-vīn
What do you recommend?	Was empfehlen Sie? vahs ehmp-**fay**-lehn zee
Choose for me, please.	Wählen Sie bitte für mich. **vay**-lehn zee **bit**-teh fewr mikh
Around ____ euros.	Ungefähr ____ Euro. **oon**-geh-fehr ____ **oy**-roh
Another, please.	Noch eins, bitte. nohkh īns **bit**-teh

Typically, you order a glass of wine by saying ***ein Viertel*** (a quarter liter) or ***ein Achtel*** (an eighth liter). In Switzerland, a ***Pfiff*** is two deciliters of red wine, and a ***Bocalino*** is a small, decorated ceramic jug with two deciliters of a light Swiss red wine called ***Dole.***

Beer

I'd like...	Ich hätte gern... ikh **heh**-teh gehrn
We'd like...	Wir hätten gern... veer **heh**-tehn gehrn
beer	Bier beer
from the tap	vom Fass fom fahs
glass	Glas glahs
mug	Krug kroog
bottle	Flasche **flah**-sheh
liter	Mass mahs
half-liter	Halbes / Krügerl (Aus.) **hahl**-behs / **krew**-gehrl
third-liter	Stange / Seidel (Aus.) **shtahng**-eh / **zī**-dehl
fifth-liter	Pfiff (Aus.) / Herrgöttli (Switz.) pfiff / hehr-**gurt**-lee
local / imported	einheimisches / importiertes **īn**-hī-mish-ehs / im-por-**teer**-tehs
small / large	kleines / grosses **klī**-nehs / **groh**-sehs
low-calorie ("lite") beer	leichtes Bier **līkh**-tehs beer

The most popular Germanic beers belong to four major categories.

helles Bier (**hehl**-ehs beer): Generic name for pale lager
dunkles Bier (**doonk**-lehs beer): Generic name for dark beer
Weissbier (**vīs**-beer) **/ Weizenbier** (**vīt**-sehn-beer): "White" or "wheat" beer
Pilsner (**pilz**-nehr) **/ Pilsener** (**pilz**-ehn-ehr) **/ Pils** (pils): Barley-based, flavorful, light-colored beer

Biergarten Tips

A sprawling, rollicking ***Biergarten***—with long, skinny picnic tables stretching beneath shady chestnut trees—is a memorable way to experience Germanic food and drink.

Biergartens may have some tables with tablecloths; these are part of a restaurant with table service. If you bring your own food (or buy it from self-service stands), you can sit at any table that doesn't have a tablecloth.

Buy your beer first, then your food (so the food doesn't get cold). Most beer gardens have a deposit ***(Pfand)*** system for their big glass steins: You pay €1 extra, and when you're finished, you can take the mug and your deposit token ***(Pfandmarke)*** to the returns clerk ***(Pfandrückgabe)*** for your refund, or leave it on the table and lose your money.

The food is usually ***Selbstbedienung*** or ***Selbstdienst*** (self-service)—a sign may say ***Bitte bedienen Sie sich selbst*** (Please serve yourself). If two prices are listed, ***Schank*** is for self-service, while ***Bedienung*** is for table service. If you have trouble finding cutlery, ask around for ***Besteck.***

In most places, if you order simply ***ein Bier,*** you'll get a half-liter of ***helles*** in a standard glass or mug. In Bavarian beer halls and gardens, the default is ***eine Mass*** (a liter mug—about a quart!).

Some drink menus list exactly how many deciliters you'll get in your glass. A ***5 dl*** beer is a half-liter, or about a pint (16 ounces). Beer can also be listed by the third-liter (about 10 ounces served in a rod-shaped glass) or fifth-liter (about 7 ounces).

Bar Talk

For drinks at reasonable prices, do what the locals do. Visit an atmospheric ***Weinstube*** (wine bar) or ***Biergarten*** (beer garden) to have a drink and chat with friends.

Let's go out for a drink.	Komm, wir gehen etwas trinken. kohm veer **gay**-ehn **eht**-vahs **trink**-ehn
May I buy you a drink?	Darf ich dir einen Drink spendieren? darf ikh deer ī-nehn drink shpehn-**deer**-ehn
My treat.	Ich lade ein. ikh **lah**-deh īn
The next one's on me.	Die nächste Runde geht auf mich. dee **nehkh**-steh **roon**-deh gayt owf mikh
What would you like?	Was hättest du gern? vahs **heh**-tehst doo gehrn
I'll have a ____.	Ich nehme ein ____. ikh **nay**-meh īn ____
I don't drink alcohol.	Ich trinke keinen Alkohol. ikh **trink**-eh **kīn**-ehn "alcohol"
What's the local specialty?	Was ist hier die Spezialität? vahs ist heer dee **shpayt**-see-ahl-ee-**tayt**
Straight.	Pur. poor
with / without ice	mit / ohne Eis mit / **oh**-neh īs
with / without alcohol	mit / ohne Alkohol mit / **oh**-neh "alcohol"
One more.	Noch eins. nohkh īns
Cheers!	Prost! prohst

The bartender will often throw a coaster ***(Bierdeckel)*** down at your place and keep track of your bill by keeping a stroke tally on the coaster. To get your bill, hand your coaster to the bartender.

PICNICKING

While you can opt for a one-stop ***Lebensmittelgeschäft*** (grocery store) or ***Supermarkt*** (supermarket), it's more fun to assemble your picnic ***(Picknick)*** at smaller specialty shops or at a ***Markt*** (open-air market). For a fast snack, stop at an ***Obst*** (fruit stand) or ***Imbiss*** (fast-food stand).

Self-service?	Selbstbedienung? **zehlpst**-beh-dee-noong
Fifty grams.	Fünfzig Gramm. **fewnf**-tsig grahm
One hundred grams.	Hundert Gramm. **hoon**-dehrt grahm
More. / Less.	Mehr. / Weniger. mehr / **vay**-nig-ehr
A piece.	Ein Stück. īn shtewk
A slice.	Eine Scheibe. ī-neh **shī**-beh
Four slices.	Vier Scheiben. feer **shī**-behn
Sliced (fine).	In (feinen) Scheiben. in (**fī**-nehn) **shī**-behn
Half.	Halb. hahlb
bunch (handful)	Bund boont
A bag, please.	Eine Tüte, bitte. ī-neh **tew**-teh **bit**-teh
Ripe for today?	Jetzt reif? yehtst rīf
Can I taste it?	Kann ich es probieren? kahn ikh ehs proh-**beer**-ehn
Does this need to be cooked?	Muss man das kochen? moos mahn dahs **kohkh**-ehn
container	Behälter beh-**hehl**-tehr
plastic...	Plastik... **plah**-steek
...spoon / fork	...Löffel / Gabel **lurf**-fehl / **gah**-behl
paper...	Papier... pah-**peer**
...plate / cup	...Teller / Becher **tehl**-ehr / **behkh**-ehr
Do you have a...?	Haben Sie ein...? **hah**-behn zee īn
Where can I buy / find a...?	Wo kann ich einen... kaufen / finden? voh kahn ikh ī-nehn... **kow**-fehn / **fin**-dehn
...corkscrew	...Korkenzieher **kor**-kehnt-see-hehr
...can opener	...Dosenöffner **doh**-zehn-urf-nehr
...bottle opener	...Flaschenöffner **flahsh**-ehn-urf-nehr

Meat and cheese are sold by the gram. One hundred grams is enough for two sandwiches. If you want a sturdy plastic bag ***(Tüte)***, you'll be charged a small amount. You're expected to bag your own groceries.

At markets, it's considered rude for customers to touch produce; instead, tell the clerk what you want.

MENU DECODER

This handy German-English decoder won't list every word on the menu, but it'll get you ***Bratwurst*** (pork sausage) instead of ***Blutwurst*** (blood sausage).

Menu Categories

When you pick up a menu, you'll likely see these categories of offerings.

Frühstück	Breakfast
Mittagessen	Lunch
Abendessen	Dinner
Vorspeise	Appetizers
Warm	Hot
Kalt	Cold
Sandwiche	Sandwiches
Salate	Salads
Suppen	Soups
Menü / Tagesmenü	Fixed-Price Meal / Fixed-Price Meal of the Day
Spezialitäten	Specialties
Gerichte	Dishes
Hauptgerichte	Main Dishes
Fleisch	Meat
Schweinefleisch	Pork
Geflügel	Poultry
Wild	Game
Fisch	Fish
Meeresfrüchte	Seafood
Beilagen	Side Dishes
Gemüse	Vegetables
Brot	Bread
Getränkekarte	Drink Menu
Weinkarte	Wine List
Nachspeise, Nachtisch	Dessert

Kinderspeisekarte	Children's Menu
Unser	"Our"
Auswahl an	Selection of

And for the fine print:

Eintritt	Cover charge
Trinkgeld (nicht) inklusive	Service (not) included
Steuern inklusive	Tax included

Small Words

aus dem	from the
dazu	served with
in	in
mit	with
nach ____-er Art	in the style of
ohne	without
von	from / of

GERMAN / ENGLISH

There are many dialects within Germany (and Austria and Switzerland), and each region is proud of its own words, so you may find menus employing local terms for some of these items. While charming to Germans, it can render this menu decoder less helpful.

Be prepared for "Lego" words. You might have to split the menu item into its respective parts to figure out its meaning. For example:

Rahmgurkensalat = ***Rahm*** (cream) + ***gurken*** (cucumbers) + ***salat*** (salad) = Cucumber salad with cream dressing

Kalbsleberscheiben = ***Kalbs*** (veal) + ***leber*** (liver) + ***scheiben*** (slices) = Slices of veal liver

If a particular term is used only in one geographical region—or if a specialty is likely to be found only in one place—I've noted that place in parentheses. For example, most Germans and Swiss call potatoes ***Kartoffeln,*** but Austrians call them ***Erdäpfel.***

Aal eel
Abendessen dinner
abgebräunt browned
abgehangen aged (meat)
abgelöscht deglazed
Achtel eighth-liter (wine)
Ahle Wurst salami-like sausage
Ahorn maple
Allgäuer Bergkäse hard, mild cheese with holes
Almdudler Austrian ginger ale
Alsterwasser shandy (lager with lemon soda)
Altbier smooth, balanced amber beer
Altenburger soft, mild goat cheese
Amerikaner flat, round, glazed doughnut
Ananas pineapple
Anis anise
Apfel apple
Apfelmus applesauce
Apfelsaft apple juice
Apfelsine orange (Aus.)
Apfelsosse applesauce
Apfelstrudel apples and raisins in puff pastry
Apfelwein hard cider (Frankfurt)
Appenzeller sharp, hard Swiss cheese
Appenzeller Alpenbitter digestif made from flower and roots (Switz.)
Aprikose apricot
Artischocke artichoke
Aubergine eggplant
Aufschnitt cold cuts

Aufstrich spread
ausgereift ripe; mature
Auslese sweet white wine made from perfectly ripe grapes
Austernpilz oyster mushroom
Bachsaibling brook char
Backe cheek
Backhühner roasted chicken
Backpflaume prune
Banane banana
Bandnudel tagliatelle
Bärenfang / Bärenjäger honey-flavored liqueur
Bärlauch "bear's" (wild) garlic
Barsch bass
Basilikum basil
Basmati-Reis basmati rice
Bauch belly
Bauern farmer-style (from the garden)
Bauernsalat Greek salad (sometimes with sausage)
Bauernsuppe cabbage and sausage soup
Becher small glass
Beere berry
Beerenauslese sweet dessert wine made from overripe grapes
beidseitig "on both sides" (i.e., over-easy eggs)
Beilagen side dishes
Bein shin
Beinwurst sausage made of smoked pork, herbs, and wine
Bergkäse mountain cheese
Berliner / Berliner Ballen jelly doughnut
Berliner Weisse (mit Schuss) Berlin's fizzy, slightly sour wheat beer (with a shot of syrup)
(auf einem) Bett aus (served) on a bed of
Beutelwurst sausage of congealed blood
Bier beer
bio / biologisch organic
Birne pear
Biskuit sponge cake
bitter bitter
blanchiert blanched
Blatt leaf
blättrig leafy
Blaubeere blueberry
Blauburger velvety red wine (Aus.)
Blauburgunder pinot noir
Blauer Portugieser mild, light, tart red wine (Aus.)
Blaufränkisch medium to full-bodied tannic red wine (Aus.)
Blumenkohl cauliflower
Blunzen sausage of congealed blood
blutig very rare meat ("bloody")
Blutwurst sausage of congealed blood
Bock / Bockbier hoppy, bittersweet amber beer (Bav.)
Bockwurst thick pork-and-veal sausage
Bohne bean
Bohne, grüne green bean
Bohnensalat bean salad
Bohnensuppe bean soup

Bosna spicy sausage with onions and sometimes curry (Aus.)
Brat / Braten grilled or roasted
Bratenfett gelatinous fat drippings
Brathähnchen roast chicken
Brathering fried, marinated herring
Bratkartoffeln roasted or grilled potatoes
Bratfett gelatinous fat drippings
Bratwurst grilled sausage (generic term)
Brauner espresso with a little milk (Vienna)
brauner Reis brown rice
Braunschweiger smoky liver sausage
Bregenwurst brain sausage (now rarely made with brain)
Brezel / Brez'n big pretzel (Bav.)
Brille palmier pastry ("eyeglasses")
Brokkoli broccoli
Brombeere blackberry
Brösel crumbs
Brot bread
Brötchen roll
Brotkorb bread basket
Brotzeit light snack served cold; usually a platter of cold cuts and cheeses
Brühe broth
Brühwurst boiled or steamed sausage (generic term)
Brunnenkress watercress
Brust breast
Bruststück brisket
Buchtel yeasty sweet roll filled with jam (Aus.)
Buchweizen buckwheat
Buletten meatballs (Berlin)
Bündner Gerstensuppe creamy barley and vegetable soup (Switz.)
Bündnerfleisch air-cured beef
bunter (Salat) mixed or "multicolored" (salad)
Burenwurst kielbasa-like pork sausage
Butterhörnchen croissant
Butternuss-Kürbis butternut squash
Camembert pungent cow cheese, often deep-fried
Cayennepfeffer cayenne pepper
Cervelat butterflied and grilled sausage (Switz.)
Cervelat Salat Cervelat sausage with onions, cheese, and dressing
Champignon mushroom
Chasselas full, fruity, dry white wine (Switz.)
Chicoree curly endive
chinesisch Chinese
Churer Fleischtorte meat pie (Switz.)
Colaweizen wheat beer and cola
Cremeschnitte Napoleon pastry
Currywurst grilled sausage with curry sauce
Dampfnudel steamed roll
Darm sausage casing

Datschi fruit-topped cake
Dattel date
dazu served with
Debreziner spicy sausage (Aus.)
Diesel lager and cola
Dill dill
Dole light-bodied red wine blend (Switz.)
Döner Dürüm Turkish-style rotisserie meat in a flatbread wrap
Döner Kebab Turkish-style rotisserie meat in pita bread
Döner Teller Turkish-style rotisserie meat on a plate
Dornfelder velvety, often oaky red wine
Dorsch cod
Drei im Weggla / Drei im Weckle three Nürnberger sausages in a bun
Dreierlei three kinds of
Dreikornbrot three-grain bread
Dresdner Eierschecke eggy cheesecake (Dresden)
Duftreis jasmine rice
Dukaten medallions (meat)
dunkel dark
Dünnele Germanic "white" pizza
durch / durchgebraten cooked through (well-done)
Dürüm Kebab Turkish-style rotisserie meat in a flatbread wrap
Dutzend dozen
Ebbelwoi hard cider (Frankfurt)
Edelpilzkäse mild blue cheese
Ei / Eier egg / eggs
Eierkuchen crêpe-like pancake
Eierlikör eggnog-like liqueur
Eiernockerl see Spätzle (Aus.)
Eierschecke eggy cheesecake (Dresden)
Eierschwammerl chanterelle mushroom (Bav. and Aus.)
Eigelb egg yolk
eingelegt pickled; potted (as in potted meat)
einheimisch local
einseitig "on one side" (i.e., eggs sunny side up)
Einspänner coffee with lots of whipped cream (Vienna)
Eintopf stew
Eis ice; ice cream
Eisbecher ice-cream sundae
Eisbier / Eisbock high-alcohol "ice" lager
Eischwerkuchen pound cake
Eiskaffee / Wiener Eiskaffee coffee with vanilla ice cream (Vienna)
Eiskremwaffel ice-cream cone
Eistee iced tea
Eiswein ultra-sweet white dessert wine
Eiswürfeln ice cubes
Eiweiss egg white
Emmentaler hard, mild Swiss cheese
Endive endive
entbeint deboned; boneless
Ente duck
entrahmt skimmed

Erbse pea
Erbsensuppe split pea soup
Erdapfel potato (Aus.)
Erdäpfelpüree mashed potatoes (Aus.)
Erdbeere strawberry
Erdnuss peanut
erster Gang first course
Eskariol escarole
Essen food; meal
Essig vinegar
Essiggurke pickle
Estragon tarragon
Export strong pale lager (beer)
Falafel deep-fried chickpea croquettes
Faschierte ground meat (Aus.)
Faschierte Laibchen large meatballs (Aus.)
(vom) Fass on tap (beer)
Fassbutter churned butter
Feierabend happy hour
Feige fig
fein smooth (texture)
Feingebäck / Feine Backwaren pastry
Feinkostgeschäft delicatessen
Feldsalat lamb's lettuce (mâche)
Fenchel fennel
Fendant tart white wine (Switz.)
Festbier seasonal, dark "Christmas" beer
Fett fat
Fiaker black coffee with kirsch liqueur or rum (Vienna)
Filet Mignon tenderloin
Fisch fish
Fisole green bean (Aus.)
Fladenbrot dense flatbread
Flädle(suppe) soup with strips of savory crêpes
Flammkuchen Germanic "white" pizza
Flanke flank
Flasche bottle
Fleckerl flat egg noodles (Aus.)
Fleisch meat; flesh
Fleischlaberl minced meat patties (Aus.)
Fleischpfanzerl meatballs (Bav.)
Fleischsalat salad of cold cuts, onions, oil, and vinegar
Fleischtorte meat pie
Florentiner crispy round cookie
Forelle trout
Frankfurter hot dog
Franziskaner espresso with a little whipped cream (Vienna)
französisch French
Freilandei(er) free-range egg(s)
Freilandhaltung free-range
Freilandhuhn free-range chicken
Frikadelle large meatball (like a hamburger)
Frikassee fricassee
frisch fresh
frischgepresst freshly squeezed
Frischkäse soft curd cheese with herbs
Frittaten strips of pancake
frittiert deep-fried
Frucht fruit
Früchtebecher fruit cup
fruchtig fruity (wine)

Fruchtsaft fruit juice
Frühstück breakfast
Gämse goat-like antelope
Gang course
Gans goose
ganz gar / ganz durch very well-done (meat)
gar well done (meat)
Garnele prawn
Garnierung garnish
garnitur garnished
Gas carbonation
gealtert aged (cheese)
Gebäck pastry
gebackene baked
gebeizte marinated ("stained")
gebraten browned
Gedärme intestines
gedünstet steamed; stewed
Geflügel poultry
gefüllt stuffed
gegrillt grilled
gehackt minced; chopped
gekocht cooked
Gelbwurst pork and veal sausage, eaten cold ("yellow sausage")
gemästet fattened
gemischt mixed
gemischter Salat mixed salad
Gemüse vegetables
Gemüseplatte / Gemüseteller vegetable platter
Gemüsesuppe vegetable soup
gepökelt salt cured
Gequellde boiled and peeled potatoes
geräuchert smoked; cured
gereift aged (cheese)
Gericht dish (entrée)
geriebene grated / ground
Germknödel sourdough dumpling
geröstet roasted
geröstete Knödel roasted dumpling
geschält peeled
geschmolzen melted
geschmort braised
Geschnetzeltes meat slivers in a rich sauce with noodles or Rösti
gesottene boiled
Gespritzter spritzer (Aus.)
Getränke beverages
Getränkekarte drinks menu
Gewürztraminer aromatic, intense, "spicy" white wine
Gipfel croissant ("summit")
Glas glass
glasiert glazed; coated
Glühwein hot spiced wine
Gluten wheat gluten
glutenfrei gluten-free
Gose acidic light wheat beer (Leipzig)
Granatapfel pomegranate
Gratin au gratin (topped with browned cheese)
Graubrot mixed wheat and rye bread
Grauburgunder pinot gris
Griess semolina (grain)
Griessklösschen / Griessnockerl (Aus.) semolina dumpling

Grillkohle charcoal
Grillteller mixed grill
grob chunky
gross big
Gröstl hash (Aus.)
grün green
grüne Bohne green bean
Grüne Grütze gooseberry fruit pudding
Grüne Sosse green sauce of seven herbs (Frankfurt)
grüner Salat green salad
Grüner Silvaner acidic, fruity white wine
grüner Spargel green asparagus
Grüner Veltliner dry, fruity, light white wine (Aus.)
Grünkohl kale
Grützwurst smoked sausage made of meat, offal, blood, and whole grains (eaten raw or pan-fried)
Gruyère strong-flavored Swiss cheese
Gulasch(suppe) spicy meat stew (goulash) or soup
Gurke cucumber
Gurkensalat cucumbers in vinegar
Gutedel full, fruity, dry white wine (Switz.)
Gutsabfüllung estate bottled (wine)
Hackfleisch minced meat
Hähnchen chicken
halb half
halbgar medium (meat)
halbsüss semi-sweet, medium (wine)
halbtrocken semi-dry (wine)
Hals neck
Hammelfleisch mutton
Handkäse (mit Musik) aged, ricotta-like cheese (served with onions and vinegar)
hartgekocht hard-boiled
Hase rabbit
Haselnuss hazelnut
Hasenpfeffer spicy rabbit stew
Hauptspeise main course
Haus house
Hausfrauen Art "housewife"-style, often with apples, onions, and sour cream
hausgemacht homemade
Haut skin
Haxe / Hax'n knuckle
Hecht pike
Hefe yeast
Hefeweizen cloudy, yeasty wheat beer
Heidelbeere bilberry
heimisch domestic; local
Heilbutt halibut
heiss hot
heisse Schockolade hot chocolate
helles light (beer)
Hend'l roasted chicken
Hering herring
Herrgöttli fifth-liter (Switz.)
herzhaft savory
Herzmuschel cockle
heurig new; this year's (wine)

Heuriger young, often tart "new" wine; also a wine bar with food (Aus.)
Himbeere raspberry
Himbeersoda raspberry soda
Hirn brain
Hirnwurst pork and veal sausage, eaten cold
Hirsch deer
Hochzeitssuppe "wedding soup" of thin broth, meatballs, and noodles
Hoden testicle
Hofente crispy duck
Holunder gespritzt elderberry soda
Honig honey
Hörnchen croissant ("little horn")
Hufe hoof
Hüft hip
Hühnerbrühe chicken broth
Hummer lobster
importiert imported
Ingwer ginger
inklusive included
Innereien organs (innards)
italienisch Italian
Jagdwurst smoky, baloney-like "hunter's sausage"
Jäger hunter-style (with mushrooms and gravy)
Jägermeister anise and herb digestif
Jägertee tea with brandy and rum
Jakobsmuschel scallop
Jasmin-Reis jasmine rice
Joghurt yogurt
Johannisbeere currant
Johannisbeere, rote red currant
Johannisbeere, schwarze black currant
Jungtaube squab (young pigeon)
Kaffee coffee
Kaffee Verkehrt espresso with lots of milk (Vienna)
Kaiserschmarren shredded pancakes with raisins, powdered sugar, and cinnamon
Kakao cocoa
Kalbfleisch veal
Kalbsbries calf sweetbreads (innards)
kalt cold
Kaltschale chilled soup
Kaninchen rabbit
Kännchen small pot of tea
Kaper caper
Kapuziner strong coffee with a dollop of sweetened cream (Vienna)
Karaffe carafe
Kardamom cardamom
Karfiol cauliflower (Aus.)
Karotte carrot
Karpfen carp
Karte menu
Kartoffel potato
Kartoffelbrei mashed potatoes
Kartoffelkäse spread of mashed potatoes, onion, and sour cream
Kartoffelknödel potato dumpling
Kartoffelpuffer potato pancake

Kartoffelpüree mashed potatoes
Kartoffelsalat potato salad
Kartoffelstock mashed potatoes (S. Germ. and Switz.)
Käse cheese
Käse Fondue melted Swiss cheeses eaten with cubes of bread
Käsebrot cheese with bread
Käsekrainer sausage with melted cheese inside (Aus.)
Käseplatte cheese platter
Käseteller cheese platter
Käsespätzle / Kasnocken (Aus.) Spätzle (short egg noodles) with cheese
Kasserole casserole
Kassler salted, slightly smoked pork
Kastanie chestnut
Keks cookie
Kellerbier unfiltered lager
Kern seed; nut
kernlos seedless
Kernöl vegetable oil
Keule drumstick
Kinderteller children's portion
Kirsche cherry
Kirschtomate cherry tomato
klein small
Kleingebäck pastry; sweet roll
Kleinigkeit snack
Klopse meatballs (large)
Klösse big, puffy potato dumpling
Knackwurst / Knockwurst stubby, garlicky sausage
Knipp sausage with offal and grains (see Grützwurst)
Knoblauch garlic
Knoblauchzehe garlic clove
Knödel dumpling
Knöpfle see Spätzle
Knusprig crispy
Knusprig chip
koch- cooked
Kochschinken cooked ham
Kochwurst sausage made of precooked ingredients (steamed before eating)
koffeinfrei decaffeinated
Kohl cabbage
Kohlensäure carbonation
(ohne) Kohlensäure (without) carbonation
Kohlroulade stuffed cabbage leaves
Kohlsprosse Brussels sprout (Aus.)
Kohlwurst lung sausage
Kokosnuss coconut
Kölsch pale, mild, highly fermented beer (Köln)
Konfitüre jam
Königsberger Klopse meatball with capers and potatoes in a white sauce (E. Germ.)
Konserve preserve (n)
Kopenhagner danish
Kopf head
Kopfsalat lettuce
Koriander cilantro (coriander)
Korkenzieher corkscrew
Kornspitz whole-meal bread roll

koscher kosher
Kotelett cutlet; chop
Krabbe crab
kräftig strong
Krakauer Polish sausage, usually eaten cold
Krapfen jelly doughnut (Bav.)
Kraut sauerkraut
Kräuter herbs
Kräutertee herbal tea
Krautsalat cold sauerkraut
Krefelder lager and cola
Kren horseradish (Aus.)
Kreuzkümmel cumin
Kristallweizen clear, filtered, yeast-free wheat beer
Krügerl half-liter (Aus.)
Krümel crumb
Kruste crust
Küche food ("cooking")
Kugel scoop (ice cream)
Kukuruz corn (Aus.)
Kümmel caraway
Kümmelbraten crispy roast pork with caraway
Kürbis squash
Kutteln tripe
Labskaus mushy mix of salted meat, potatoes, often beets, and sometimes herring
Lachs salmon
Lahmacun Turkish-style flatbread topped with vegetables, minced meat, and sauce
Laktose lactose
Lamm lamb
Lammbries lamb sweetbreads (innards)
Lammrücken back of lamb
Landjäger skinny, spicy salami
Languste crayfish
Lauch leek
Lauchzwiebel green onion
Laugen pretzel
lauwarm lukewarm
Lavendel lavender
Leber liver
Leberkäse meatloaf made of pork, beef, and sometimes liver
Leberknödel liver dumpling
Leberknödelsuppe liver dumpling soup
Leberwurst soft, spreadable liver sausage
Lebkuchen gingerbread
leicht light
Leipziger Gose acidic light wheat beer (Leipzig)
Leiterchen spareribs
Lemburger medium to full-bodied tannic red wine (Aus.)
Lende loin
Lendenfilet sirloin
Lendenstück tenderloin of T-bone
Lese vintage (wine)
Liebfraumilch semi-sweet white wine
lieblich sweet (wine)
Limabohne lima bean
Limburger strong-smelling, soft cheese with herbs

Limonade clear soda or lemonade
Linse lentil
Linsen mit Spätzle Spätzle (short egg noodles) with lentils
Linzertorte almond cake with raspberry
Liptauer spicy cheese spread (Aus.)
Lorbeer bay (seasoning)
Lorbeer-Blatt bay leaf
Lunge lung
Lungenbraten tenderloin (Aus.)
Lungwurst lung sausage
Lyoner thick, short hot dog
Magen stomach
Mais corn
Majoran marjoram
Makrele mackerel
Malaga rum-raisin flavor
Malzbier non-alcoholic dark beer
Mandarine tangerine
Mandel almond
Mandelgipfel / Mandelhorn almond croissant
Mangold Swiss chard
Maracuja passion fruit
Maria Theresia coffee with orange liqueur (Vienna)
Marille apricot (Aus.)
mariniert marinated
Mark marrow
Markklösschen / Markknödel (Aus.) marrow dumpling
Marktpreis market price
Marmelade jelly; jam
Märzen(bier) light, malty Oktoberfest beer (Bav.)
Mass liter of beer
Matjesfilet raw herring in yogurt
Maul mouth (of an animal)
Maultaschen ravioli
Meeresfrüchte seafood
Meerrettich horseradish
Mehlprodukte wheat; gluten products
Mehrkorn(brot) multigrain (bread)
Melange espresso with foamed milk (Vienna)
Melanzani eggplant (Aus.)
Melasse molasses
Melone cantaloupe
Merlot del Ticino full-bodied red wine (Switz.)
Mettbrot raw ground pork spread on bread, often with raw onions
Mettwurst spreadable, cured and smoked sausage made from uncooked pork
Metzger(ei) butcher
Miesmuschel mussel
Mikrowelle microwave
Milch milk
Milchkaffee espresso or drip coffee with lots of hot milk
mild mild
Milzwurst / Milzstücken spleen sausage
Mineralwasser mineral water
Minze mint

Mittagessen lunch
Mohn poppy seed
Mohnkuchen poppy-seed cake
Mohr im Hemd chocolate pudding with chocolate sauce
Möhre carrot (Aus.)
Mokka straight, black espresso (Vienna)
Mönchsfisch monkfish
Müllerin (Art) breaded and fried, usually fish
Müller-Thurgau light and flowery white wine
-mus purée
Muschel clam
Muskatnuss nutmeg
Müsli granola cereal
nach ____-er Art in the style of ____
Nachspeise / Nachtisch dessert
Nacken neck
Nährbier barely alcoholic "near beer"
Naturschnitzel veal cutlet served with rice and sauce
Nelke clove
Niere / Nierchen kidney
Nizzasalat Niçoise salad (with tuna)
Nockerl, Salzburger fluffy, baked pudding / flan
Nudel noodle
Nudelsalat pasta salad
Nürnberger short, spicy grilled sausage (Bav.)
Nüsse nuts
Nussgipfel nut croissant
Nusstorte rich walnut cake (Switz.)
Obatzda paprika cheese spread
Obenkartoffel baked potato
Obers cream (Aus.)
Obst fruit
Obstler fruit brandy
Obstsalat fruit salad
Ochse / Ochsenfleisch oxen meat
Ochsenfetzen shredded oxen meat
Ochsenmaulsalat "ox mouth salad" with vinegar, onion, and herbs
Ochsenschwanz oxtail
Ochsenschwanzsuppe oxtail soup
Ofen oven
ofenfrisch oven-fresh
ofengebacken oven-baked
Öl oil
Oliv olive
Oliviersalat Russian salad (potatoes, eggs, vegetables, mayo)
Omelett omelet
Orangensaft orange juice
Oregano oregano
Palatschinke crêpe (Aus.)
Pampelmuse grapefruit
Panaché shandy (lager with lemon soda)
paniert breaded
Papaya papaya
Paprika bell pepper; paprika
Paradeiser tomato (Aus.)

Pellkartoffeln boiled and peeled potatoes
Pergament parchment
Perlhühner guinea fowl
Persimone persimmon
Petersilie parsley
Pfälzer see Lyoner
pfannengebraten sautéed
Pfannkuchen pancake; jelly doughnut (Berlin)
Pfeffer pepper
Pfefferkuchen gingerbread
Pfefferminz peppermint
Pfiff fifth-liter (Aus.)
Pfirsich peach
Pflaume plum
Pflümli plum Schnapps
Pichelsteiner meat and vegetable stew
pikant spicy (hot)
Pilsener / Pils light, hoppy beer
Pilz mushroom
Pinienkern pine nut
Pinkel sausage with offal and grains (see Grützwurst)
pinot blanc semi-dry white wine with a fruity nose (Aus.)
Pistazie pistachio
Pizokel cheesy flour dumpling (Switz.)
Platte platter
pochiert poached
Pökelfleisch salt-cured meat
Pommes (frites) French fries
Portugieser mild, light, tart red wine (Aus.)
Preiselbeere cranberry
Presswurst (also Presssack / Presskopf) headcheese–bits of organ meat in congealed fat or blood
Prinzregententorte chocolate layer sponge cake (Bav.)
Pulverkaffee instant coffee
Pute turkey
Quark sweet curd cheese
Quarkkäulchen small pancakes made of sweet curd cheese and mashed potatoes
Quitte quince
Raclette Swiss cheese melted over vegetables (Switz.)
Radiesch radish
Radler shandy (lager with lemon soda)
Ragout stew
Rahm cream
Rahmsauce / Rahmsosse cream sauce
Ratsherrentopf roasted meat and potato stew
Rauchbier dark, "smoky" beer (Bamberg)
Rauchfleisch / Räucherfleisch smoke-cured meat
Rauchzepferl smoky sausage (Munich)
Rebhuhn partridge
Regensburger see Lyoner
Reh deer
Rehpfeffer deer stew (Aus. and Switz.)
Reibekuchen / Reiberdatschi (Bav.) potato pancake

rein pure
Riesen giant
Riesling fruity, fragrant, elegant white wine
Rind beef
Rinderbraten roast beef
Rinderbrühe beef broth
Rinderlende beef loin
Rinderroulade braised beef rolled up with bacon, onion, and pickles
Rinderschmorbraten pot roast
Rindfleisch beef
Rippe rib
Rivella Swiss soft drink that tastes like chewable vitamins
Roastbeef roast beef
Rogen roe (fish eggs)
Roggen rye
Roggenbier dark-colored rye wheat beer
Roggenmischbrot rye bread
roh raw
Rohkost crudités
Rohrnudel raisin-filled sweet dumpling (Bav. and Aus.)
Rohschinken cured ham
Rotkohl red cabbage
Rollmops pickled herring wrapped around a pickle
Romadur fragrant, soft cow cheese
Römersalat Romaine lettuce
Rosenkohl Brussels sprouts
Rosine raisin
Rosmarin rosemary
Rostbrätel marinated and grilled pork neck
Rostbratwurst grilled sausage (generic term)
Rösti hash browns (Switz.)
rot rare (meat)
Rotbarbe red mullet
rote Bete beet
rote Grütze raspberry and currant pudding
rote Johannisbeere red currant
rote Rübe beet
Rotwein red wine
Rotweiss with ketchup and mayonnaise *(Wurst)*
Rotwurst sausage of congealed blood
Roulade braised beef rolled up with bacon, onion, and pickles
Royal danish
Rücken back
Rucola arugula (rocket)
Rühreier scrambled eggs
Russ (also Russe; Russ'n) wheat beer and lemon soda
Sacher-Torte decadent chocolate layer cake (Vienna)
Safran saffron
saftig juicy
Sahne cream
Sahnemeerrettich horseradish cream
Saibling char (fish)
Salat salad
Salatsosse salad dressing
Salatteller plate of various salads

Salbei sage
Salz salt
Salzburger Nockerl fluffy, baked pudding / flan
Salzkartoffeln potatoes boiled in salty water
sättigend filling
Saubohne fava bean
Sauce sauce
Sauerampfer sorrel
Sauerbraten marinated roast beef
Sauerkirsche sour cherry
Sauerrahm sour cream
Sauerteig sourdough
Saumagen "sow's stomach" stuffed with meat, vegetables, and spices
Saure Zipfel Bratwurst cooked in vinegar and onions
Schaf sheep
Schale shell
Schale Gold espresso with a little cream (Vienna)
Schälen peelings from a plant
Schalentiere shellfish
Schalotte shallot
scharf spicy (hot)
Schäufele oven-roasted pork shoulder with gravy
Schaum foam
Scheibe slice
(in) Scheiben geschnitten sliced
Schenkel thigh
Schinken ham
Schinkenfleckerl ham, egg noodle, and cheese casserole
Schinkenspeck prosciutto
Schlachtplatte / Schlachtschüssel blood sausage, Leberwurst, and other meat over hot sauerkraut ("butcher's plate")
Schlagsahne whipped cream
Schlagobers heavy cream; whipped cream (Aus.)
Schlegel drumstick
Schlögel leg (Aus.)
Schlesisches Himmelreich pork roast, ham, dumplings, and stewed fruit in a white sauce ("Silesian Heaven"–Silesia)
Schlutzkrapfen ravioli
Schmalz lard
Schmalzbrot bread smeared with lard
Schmand sour cream
Schmankerl specialty
Schmaus feast of simple grub
schmelz- melted
Schmutziges lager and cola ("dirty")
Schnauze snout
Schnecken "snail"-shaped pastry roll
Schneeball pie crusts crumpled into a ball (Rothenburg)
schnitt cut; julienne
Schnittlauch chive
Schnittlauchbrot bread with cream cheese and diced chives
Schnitzel thinly sliced pork or veal
Schokolade chocolate

Scholle whitefish
Schoppe hard cider (Frankfurt)
Schorle spritzer; wine cooler
Schulter shoulder
Schupfnudeln thick, finger-sized potato noodles
Schwammerl large mushroom (Bav. and Aus.)
Schwarzbier very dark ("black"), chocolaty lager
Schwarzbrot dark rye bread
schwarze Johannisbeere black currant
Schwarzer straight, black espresso (Vienna)
Schwarzwälder Kirschtorte Black Forest cake—chocolate, cherries, and cream
Schwarzwurst sausage of congealed blood
Schweinebraten roasted pork with gravy
Schweinefleisch pork
Schweinenacken pork neck
Schweinerollbraten roasted pork belly
Schweinerüssel pork snout
Schweinshaxe / Schweinshax'n pork knuckle
Schweinswurst pork sausage (generic term)
Schweizer Käse Swiss cheese
Schweizer Wurstsalat chopped-up sausage with onions and Swiss cheese in oil and vinegar
Schwenker grilled on an open fire
Seeanemone anemone
Seebarsch sea bass
Seehecht hake
Seeteufel monkfish
Seezunge sole (fish)
Seidel third-liter (Aus., beer)
Sekt sparkling wine
Semmel roll (Bav. and Aus.)
Semmelknödel bread dumpling
Senf mustard
Serbische Bohnensuppe bean soup (Aus.)
Silvaner acidic, fruity white wine
Sonnenblume sunflower
Sonnenblumenkerne sunflower seeds
Sorbet sherbet
Sosse sauce
Sossklopse meatballs with capers and potatoes in a white sauce (E. Germ.)
Späne shavings
Spanferkel roast suckling pig
Spargel (grüner / weisser) asparagus (green / white); "Spargel" alone is usually white
Spätburgunder pinot noir
Spätlese "late harvest" wine (sweet)
Spätzle short egg noodles
Speck fatty bacon
Specklinsen lentils with bacon
Speckpfannkuchen large, savory crêpe with bacon

Speckwirsing heavy greens in bacon and cream sauce
Speisekarte menu
Spezial strong pale lager (beer)
Spezialität specialty
Spiegeleier fried eggs
Spiess; Spie skewer
Spinat spinach
Spitze tip; point
Sprudel carbonation (bubbly water)
(ohne) Sprudel without carbonation (still water)
sprudelnd sparkling
St. Saphorin lovely, fruity white wine (Switz.)
Stange third-liter (beer)
Stangenspargel stem of asparagus
Starkbier "strong beer" (usually Bockbier)
Steckerlfisch entire fish grilled on a stick
Steinbutt turbot
Stelze knuckle (Aus.)
Stint smelt
Stippgrütze sausage with offal and grains (see Grützwurst)
Stollen sweet Christmas bread
Stolzer Heinrich grilled sausage in beer sauce (Berlin)
Strauch bush; vine
Strauchtomaten vine-ripened tomatoes
Streichwurst meat spread
Streifen strips
Streuselkuchen coffee cake squares
Stück piece
Sülze aspic (jellied meat stock)
Suppe soup
Surhaxe roasted marinated pork knuckle
süss sweet
Süsswaren sweets (usually pastry)
Tablett tray
Tafelspitz broth-boiled beef with apples and horseradish
Tafelwasser mineral water ("table water")
Tafelwein table wine
Tagesgericht special of the day
Tageskarte menu of the day
Tagesmenü fixed-price meal of the day
Tasse cup
Tee tea
Teewurst air-dried sausage
Teilchen sweet roll
Teller plate
Teufelsalat "devil's salad" with beef, mayo, Tabasco, and tomato
Thunfisch tuna
Thüringer long, skinny, peppery grilled sausage
Thüringer Rotwurst blood-sausage variation of Thüringer
Thymian thyme
Tilapia tilapia
Tilsiter mild, tangy, firm cheese

Tiroler Bauernschmaus various meats with sauerkraut, potatoes, and dumplings
Tirolerwurst sliced smoked sausage (Aus.)
Tomate tomato
Topfen sweet cheese curds (Aus.)
Topfenstrudel puff pastry filled with sweet cheese and raisins (Aus.)
Törtchen tart
Torte cake
Traube grape
Traubenblatt grape leaf
Traubensaft grape juice
trocken dry (wine)
Trockenbeerenauslese exceptionally sweet wine made from grapes that have frozen and shriveled on the vine
Truthahn turkey
türkische Pizza flatbread topped with vegetables, minced meat, and sauce ("Turkish pizza")
typisch local ("typical")
überbacken scalloped (baked in layers); au gratin
Vanille vanilla
Vanillepudding custard
Veganer vegan
Vegetarier vegetarian
verbrannt burned
Verlängerter espresso with hot water (Vienna)
Vermicell chestnut mousse in noodle shape (Switz.)
Viertel quarter-liter (wine)
Vinaigrette vinaigrette
Vogerlsalat lamb's lettuce (mâche) (Aus.)
Vollkornbrot dark bread, whole wheat
vollmundig full-bodied (wine)
Vorderviertel chuck
Vorspeise appetizers
Wachtel quail
Wachtelei(er) quail egg(s)
Waffel cone; waffle
wahlweise choice of
Waldbauernflade rustic flatbread
Waldviertler smoked sausage (Aus.)
Walnuss walnut
Wasser water
Wasserkresse watercress
Wassermelone watermelon
Weckle roll (S. Germ.)
weich soft (cheese)
weichgekocht soft-boiled
Weichsel sour cherry (Aus.)
Weihnachtsbier seasonal, dark "Christmas" beer
Wein wine
Weinberg vineyard
Weinkarte wine list
Weinlese vintage (wine)
Weinprobe wine tasting
(vom) Weinstock from the vine
Weintraube grape (wine)
weiss white
Weissbier wheat beer
Weissbrot light bread
weisse Rübe turnip

weisser Spargel white asparagus
Weisswein white wine
Weisswurst boiled veal sausage
Weizen wheat
Weizenbier wheat beer
Wiener breaded and fried ("Viennese style")
Wienerwurst / Wienerli see Frankfurter
Wiener Eiskaffee coffee with vanilla ice cream (Vienna)
Wiener Schnitzel breaded, pan-fried veal
wild wild
Wild / Wildfleisch game
Wildbret venison
Wildhuhn game hen
Wildschwein wild boar
Windbeutel cream puff
Wirsing Savoy cabbage
Wittling whiting (fish)
Wollwurst skinless, grilled Weisswurst
Würfel cube
Wurst sausage
Wurstsalat chopped-up sausage with onions in oil and vinegar
Wurzel root
Wurzelgemüse root vegetables
würzig spicy (flavorful)
Yufka Turkish-style rotisserie meat in a flatbread wrap
Zahnstocher toothpick
Zander pikeperch
zart tender; lightly
zerlassen melted
Ziege goat
Ziegenkäse goat cheese
Zimt cinnamon
Zipfel end; tip
Zitrone lemon
Zitrus citrus
Zucchini zucchini
Zucker sugar
Zuckergebäck pastry; sweet roll
zum Mitnehmen to go
Zunge tongue
Zweigelt light, spicy, floral red wine (Aus.)
Zwetschge plum
Zwetschgenknödel fried plum dumpling
Zwickelbier unfiltered lager
Zwiebel onion
Zwiebelbraten pot roast with onions
Zwiebelringen onion rings
Zwiebelwurst liver and onion sausage

SIGHTSEEING

WHERE?

Where is / are the...?	Wo ist / sind...? voh ist / zint
tourist information office	das Touristeninfo dahs too-**ris**-tehn-in-foh
toilets	die Toiletten dee toy-**leh**-tehn
main square	der Hauptplatz dehr **howpt**-plahts
city center	das Zentrum dahs tsehn-**troom**
old town center	die Altstadt dee **ahlt**-shtaht
entrance	der Eingang dehr **īn**-gahng
exit	der Ausgang dehr **ows**-gahng
town hall	das Rathaus dahs **raht**-hows
museum	das Museum dahs moo-**zay**-um
art gallery	die Pinakothek dee pee-nah-koh-**tehk**

Key Phrases: Sightseeing

ticket	Eintrittskarte **īn**-trits-kar-teh
How much is it?	Wie viel kostet das? vee feel **kohs**-teht dahs
Is there a tour (in English)?	Gibt es eine Führung (auf Englisch)? gibt ehs **ī**-neh **few**-roong (owf **ehng**-lish)
At what time?	Um wie viel Uhr? oom vee feel oor
When?	Wann? vahn
What time does this open / close?	Um wie viel Uhr ist hier geöffnet / geschlossen? oom vee feel oor ist heer geh-**urf**-neht / geh-**shloh**-sehn

painting gallery	die Gemäldegalerie dee geh-**mehl**-deh-gah-leh-**ree**
cathedral	der Dom / die Kathedrale / das Münster dehr dohm / dee kah-teh-**drah**-leh / dahs **mewn**-stehr
church	die Kirche dee **keerkh**-eh
castle	die Burg dee boorg
palace	das Schloss dahs shlohs
royal residence	die Residenz dee reh-zee-**dehnts**
best view	der beste Ausblick dehr **behs**-teh **ows**-blik
viewpoint	der Aussichtspunkt dehr **ows**-sikhts-poonkt

German has a number of ways to say "tourist information office"—you're likely to see ***Touristen-Informationszentrum, Besucherinfozentrum, Tourismusbüro, Fremdenverkehrsamt,*** and more. Most German speakers, however, will understand what you mean if you just ask for the ***Touristeninfo.***

AT SIGHTS

Tickets and Discounts

ticket desk	Kasse **kah**-seh
ticket	Eintrittskarte **īn**-trits-kar-teh
combo-ticket	Kombi-ticket **kohm**-bee-"ticket"
price	Preis prīs
discount	Ermässigung ehr-**may**-see-goong
Is there a discount for...?	Gibt es eine Ermässigung für...? gibt ehs **ī**-neh ehr-**may**-see-goong fewr
...children	...Kinder **kin**-dehr
...youths	...Jugendliche **yoo**-gehnd-likh-eh
...students	...Studenten shtoo-**dehn**-tehn

...families	...Familien fah-**meel**-yehn
...seniors	...Senioren zehn-**yor**-ehn
...groups	...Gruppen **groop**-ehn
I am...	Ich bin... ikh bin
He / She is...	Er / Sie ist... ehr / zee ist
... ____ years old.	... ____ Jahre alt. ____ **yah**-reh ahlt
...extremely old.	...extrem alt. eks-**trehm** ahlt
Is the ticket good all day?	Gilt die Eintrittskarte den ganzen Tag? gilt dee **īn**-trits-kar-teh dayn **gahnt**-sehn tahg
Can I get back in?	Kann ich wieder hinein? kahn ikh **vee**-dehr hin-**īn**

You may be eligible for a discount at tourist sights, in hotels, or on buses and trains—ask.

In some cities, several worthwhile sights are covered by a single combo-ticket. Figure out which sights you plan to visit, then do the arithmetic to see if the combo-ticket will save you money.

Information and Tours

information	Information / Auskunft in-for-maht-see-**ohn** / **ows**-koonft
tour	Führung **few**-roong
in English	auf Englisch owf **ehng**-lish
Is there a...?	Gibt es...? gibt ehs
...city walking tour	...eine geführte Stadtführung ī-neh geh-**fewr**-teh shtaht-**fewr**-oong
...audioguide	...ein Audioguide īn **ow**-dee-oh-"guide"
...local guide (I can hire)	...einen Stadtführer (den ich buchen kann) ī-nehn **shtaht**-fewr-ehr (dayn ikh **bookh**-ehn kahn)

...city guidebook	...einen Reiseführer für die Stadt ī-nehn **rī**-zeh-fewr-ehr fewr dee shtaht
...museum guidebook	...einen Museumsführer ī-nehn moo-**zay**-ums-fewr-ehr
Is it free?	Ist es kostenlos? ist ehs **kohs**-tehn-lohs
How much is it?	Wie viel kostet das? vee feel **kohs**-teht dahs
How long does it last?	Wie lange dauert es? vee **lahng**-eh **dow**-ehrt ehs
When is the next tour in English?	Wann ist die nächste Führung auf Englisch? vahn ist dee **nehkh**-steh **few**-roong owf **ehng**-lish

Stadtführer means "city guide." As in English, it can refer either to a guidebook or a live tour guide.

Some sights are tourable only by groups with a guide. Individuals usually end up with the next German tour. To get an English tour, call in advance to see if one's scheduled. Individuals can often tag along with a large English tour group.

Visiting Sights

opening times	Öffnungszeiten **urf**-noongs-tsī-tehn
last entry	letzter Einlass / letzter Eintritt **lehts**-tehr **īn**-lahs / **lehts**-tehr **īn**-trit
What time does this open / close?	Um wie viel Uhr ist hier geöffnet / geschlossen? oom vee feel oor ist heer geh-**urf**-neht / geh-**shloh**-sehn
When is the last entry?	Wann ist letzter Einlass? vahn ist **lehts**-tehr **īn**-lahs
Do I have to check this?	Muss ich das an der Garderobe abgeben? moos ikh dahs ahn dehr **gar**-deh-roh-beh **ahp**-gay-behn

bag check	Garderobe **gar**-deh-roh-beh
floor plan	Orientierungsplan oh-ree-ehn-**teer**-oongs-plahn
floor	Etage / Stock ay-**tazh**-eh / shtock
collection	Sammlung **zahm**-loong
exhibition	Ausstellung **ows**-shtehl-oong
temporary exhibit / permanent exhibit	Sonderausstellung / Dauerausstellung **zohn**-dehr-ows-shtehl-oong / **dow**-ehr-ows-shtehl-oong
café	Café "café"
elevator	Aufzug **owf**-tsoog
toilets	Toiletten toy-**leh**-tehn
Where is ____?	Wo ist ____? voh ist ____
I'd like to see ____.	Ich möchte gerne ____ sehen. ikh **murkh**-teh **gehr**-neh ____ **zay**-hehn
Photo / Video OK?	Ist Fotografieren / Videofilmen OK? ist **foh**-toh-grah-**feer**-ehn / **vee**-deh-oh-fil-mehn "OK"
(No) flash.	(Kein) Blitz. (kīn) blits
(No) tripod.	Stativ (verboten). shtah-**teef** (fehr-**boh**-tehn)
Will you take my / our photo?	Machen Sie ein Foto von mir / uns? **mahkh**-ehn zee īn **foh**-toh fohn meer / oons
Please let me / us in! (if room or sight is closing)	Bitte, lassen Sie mich / uns hinein! **bit**-teh **lah**-sehn zee mikh / oons hin-**īn**
I promise I'll / we'll be fast.	Ich verspreche, mich / uns zu beeilen. ikh fehr-**shprehkh**-eh mikh / oons tsoo beh-**ī**-lehn

I promised my mother on her deathbed that I'd see this.	Ich habe meiner Mutter am Sterbebett versprochen, das zu sehen. ikh **hah**-beh **mī**-nehr **moo**-tehr ahm **shtehr**-beh-beht fehr-**shprohkh**-ehn dahs tsoo **zay**-hehn

Once at the sight, get your bearings by viewing the ***Orientierungsplan*** (floor plan). ***Standort*** means "You are here." Many museums have an official, one-way route that all visitors take—just follow signs for ***Rundgang.***

RECREATION AND ENTERTAINMENT

RECREATION

Outdoor Fun

Where is the best place for...?	Wo kann man am besten...? voh kahn mahn ahm **behs**-tehn
...biking	...Fahrrad fahren **far**-ahd **far**-ehn
...walking	...spazieren shpaht-**seer**-ehn
...hiking	...wandern **vahn**-dehrn
...running	...joggen **"jog"**-ehn
...picnicking	...picknicken "picnic"-ehn
...sunbathing	...sonnen **zohn**-ehn
Where is...?	Wo ist...? voh ist
...a park	...ein Park īn park
...a playground	...ein Spielplatz īn **shpeel**-plahts
...a snack shop	...ein Imbiss Laden īn **im**-bis **lah**-dehn
Are there toilets nearby?	Gibt es Toiletten in der Nähe? gibt ehs toy-**leh**-tehn in dehr **nay**-heh
Where can I rent...?	Wo kann ich... mieten? voh kahn ikh... **mee**-tehn
...a bike	...ein Fahrrad īn **far**-ahd
...that	...das dahs
What's a fun activity...?	Was ist eine lustige Aktivität...? vahs ist ī-neh **loos**-tig-eh ahk-tiv-ee-**tayt**
...for a (____-year-old) boy	...für einen (____-jährigen) Jungen fewr ī-nehn (____-**yeh**-rig-ehn) **yoong**-ehn
...for a (____-year-old) girl	...für ein (____-jähriges) Mädchen fewr īn (____-**yeh**-rig-ehs) **mayds**-yehn

At bigger parks, you can sometimes rent a paddleboat ***(Tretboot)*** or rowboat ***(Ruderboot),*** or see a puppet show (***Puppenspiel*** or ***Mario-nettentheater***)—fun to watch in any language. Many of the bigger parks also sport a family-friendly ***Biergarten.***

Swimming

swimming (n)	Baden / Schwimmen **bah**-dehn / **shvim**-mehn
Where is a...?	Wo ist ein...? voh ist īn
...swimming pool	...Schwimmbad **shvim**-baht
...water park	...Wasserpark **vahs**-ehr-park
...(good) beach	...(guter) Strand (**goo**-tehr) shtrahnt
...nude beach	...FKK-Strand ehf-kah-**kah**-shtrahnt
Is it safe for swimming?	Ist es sicher zu schwimmen? ist es **zikh**-hehr tsoo **shvim**-mehn?

German has two words for swimming, depending on how seriously it's done: If you're just out for a dip, it's ***Baden*** (think bathing), whereas ***Schwimmen*** is the better word for doing laps in a pool. At nearly any beach—and even in many city parks—German women enjoy going topless. Truly nude beaches are marked ***FKK,*** which stands for ***Frei-körper Kultur*** (Free Body Culture).

Bicycling

bicycle	Fahrrad / Velo (Switz.) **far**-ahd / **feh**-loh
I'd like to rent a bicycle.	Ich möchte ein Fahrrad mieten. ikh **murkh**-teh īn **far**-ahd **mee**-tehn
two bicycles	zwei Fahrräder tsvī **far**-ray-dehr
kid's bike	Kinderrad **kin**-dehr-ahd
mountain bike	Mountainbike "mountain bike"
helmet	Helm hehlm

Renting

If you're renting a bike or a boat, here's what to ask.

Where can I rent a...?	Wo kann ich ein... mieten? voh kahn ikh īn... **mee**-tehn
Can I rent a...?	Kann ich ein... hier mieten? kahn ikh īn... heer **mee**-tehn
...bike	...Fahrrad **far**-ahd
...boat	...Boot boht
How much per...?	Wie viel pro...? vee feel proh
...hour	...Stunde **shtoon**-deh
...half-day	...halben Tag **hahl**-behn tahg
...day	...Tag tahg
Do you need a deposit?	Brauchen Sie eine Kaution? **browkh**-ehn zee **ī**-neh kowt-see-**ohn**

map	Karte **kar**-teh
lock	Schloss shlohs
chain	Kette **keh**-teh
pedal	Pedale peh-**dah**-leh
wheel	Rad rahd
tire	Reifen **rī**-fehn
air / no air	Luft / keine Luft looft / **kī**-neh looft
pump	Pumpe **poom**-peh
brakes	Bremsen **brehm**-zehn
How does this work?	Wie funktioniert das? vee foonk-see-ohn-**eert** dahs
How many gears?	Wie viele Gänge? vee **fee**-leh **gehng**-eh
Is there a bike path?	Gibt es einen Radweg? gibt ehs **ī**-nehn **rahd**-vayg

I don't like hills or traffic.	Ich mag keine Hügel oder Autoverkehr. ikh mahg **kī**-neh **hew**-gehl **oh**-dehr **ow**-toh-fehr-kehr
I brake for bakeries.	Ich bremse für Bäckereien. ikh **brehm**-zeh fewr behk-eh-**rī**-ehn

Hiking

hiking	Wandern **vahn**-dehrn
a hike	eine Wanderung **ī**-neh **vahn**-dehr-oong
trail	Wanderweg **vahn**-dehr-vayg

Way to Go!

Whether you're biking or hiking, you'll want to know the best way to go.

Can you recommend a route / a hike that is...?	Können Sie eine Route / einen Weg empfehlen der... ist? **kurn**-ehn zee **ī**-neh **row**-teh / **ī**-nehn vayg ehmp-**fay**-lehn dehr... ist
...easy	...leicht līkht
...moderate	...mässig anstrengend **may**-sig **ahn**-shtrehng-ehnd
...strenuous	...anstrengend **ahn**-shtrehng-ehnd
...safe	...sicher **zikh**-hehr
...scenic	...schön shurn
...about ____ kilometers	...ungefähr ____ Kilometer **oon**-geh-fehr ____ kee-loh-**may**-tehr
How many minutes / hours?	Wie viele Minuten / Stunden? vee **fee**-leh mee-**noo**-tehn / **shtoon**-dehn
uphill / level / downhill	bergauf / flach / bergab behrg-**owf** / flahkh / behrg-**ahp**

Where can I buy...?	Wo kann ich... kaufen? voh kahn ikh... **kow**-fehn
...a hiking map	...eine Wanderkarte ī-neh **vahn**-dehr-kar-teh
...a compass	...einen Kompass ī-nehn **kohm**-pahs
Where's the trailhead?	Wo ist der Startpunkt? voh ist dehr **shtart**-poonkt
How do I get there?	Wie komme ich dorthin? vee **koh**-meh ikh dort-**hin**

Most hiking trails are well-marked with signs listing the destination and the duration in hours ***(Std.)*** and minutes ***(Min.)***. When choosing trails, you'll reach more scenery (and expend more effort) if you take the ***Panoramaweg*** (panoramic trail) or the ***Höhenweg*** (high trail). Join the locals on their ***Volksmärsche*** (people's marches)—group hikes through the wilderness.

ENTERTAINMENT

event guide	Kulturprogramm kool-**toor**-proh-grahm
What's happening tonight?	Was ist heute abend los? vahs ist **hoy**-teh **ah**-behnt lohs
What do you recommend?	Was empfehlen Sie? vahs ehmp-**fay**-lehn zee
Where is it?	Wo ist es? voh ist ehs
How do I get there?	Wie komme ich dorthin? vee **koh**-meh ikh dort-**hin**
How do we get there?	Wie kommen wir dorthin? vee **koh**-mehn veer dort-**hin**
Is it free?	Ist es gratis? ist ehs **grah**-tis?
Are there seats available?	Gibt es noch Platz? gibt ehs nohkh plahts
Where can I buy a ticket?	Wo kann ich eine Karte kaufen? voh kahn ikh ī-neh **kar**-teh **kowf**-ehn

Do you have tickets for today / tonight?	Haben Sie Karten für heute / heute Abend? **hah**-behn zee **kar**-tehn fewr **hoy**-teh / **hoy**-teh **ah**-behnt
best / cheap seats	beste / günstige Plätze **behs**-teh / **gewn**-stig-eh **pleht**-seh
sold out	ausverkauft **ows**-fehr-kowft
When does it start?	Wann fängt es an? vahn fehngt ehs ahn
When does it end?	Wann endet es? vahn **ehn**-deht ehs
Where is a good place to take a stroll?	Wo kann man hier gut spazierengehen? voh kahn mahn heer goot shpaht-**seer**-ehn-gay-ehn
Where's a good place for (live) music?	Wo gibt es hier guten (Live-)Musik? voh gibt ehs heer **goo**-tehn ("live"-)moo-**zeek**
Where can you go dancing around here?	Wo kann man hier Tanzen gehen? voh kahn mahn heer **tahn**-tsehn **gay**-ehn
bar with live music	Bar mit Live-Musik bar mit "live"-moo-**zeek**
nightclub	Nachtklub **nahkht**-kloob
(no) cover charge	(kein) Eintritt (kīn) **īn**-trit
concert	Konzert kohn-**tsehrt**
opera	Oper **oh**-pehr
symphony	Symphonie zim-foh-**nee**
show	Vorführung **for**-few-roong
theater	Theater tay-**ah**-tehr
cabaret	Kabarett kah-bah-**reht**
stage	Bühne **bew**-neh

SHOPPING

SHOP TILL YOU DROP

Shop Talk

opening hours	Öffnungszeiten urf-noongs-**tsī**-tehn
sale	Schlussverkauf **shloos**-fehr-kowf
special offer	Angebot **ahn**-geh-boht
cheap	billig **bil**-lig
affordable	günstig **gewn**-stig
(too) expensive	(zu) teuer (tsoo) **toy**-ehr
good-value	preiswert **prīs**-vehrt
Pardon me.	Entschuldigung. ehnt-**shool**-dig-oong
Where can I buy ____?	Wo kann ich ____ kaufen? voh kahn ikh ____ **kow**-fehn
How much is it?	Wie viel kostet das? vee feel **kohs**-teht dahs
I'm just browsing.	Ich sehe mich nur um. ikh **zay**-eh mikh noor oom
We're just browsing.	Wir sehen uns nur um. veer **zay**-ehn oons noor oom
I'd like...	Ich hätte gern... ikh **heh**-teh gehrn
Do you have...?	Haben Sie...? **hah**-behn zee
...more	...mehr mehr
...something cheaper	...etwas günstiger **eht**-vahs **gewn**-stig-ehr
...something nicer	...etwas schöner **eht**-vahs **shurn**-ehr
May I see more?	Darf ich mehr sehen? darf ikh mehr **zay**-ehn
This one.	Dieses. **dee**-zehs

Key Phrases: Shopping

How much is it?	Wie viel kostet das? vee feel **kohs**-teht dahs
I'm just browsing.	Ich sehe mich nur um. ikh **zay**-eh mikh noor oom
May I see more?	Darf ich mehr sehen? darf ikh mehr **zay**-ehn
I'll think about it.	Ich überlege es mir. ikh ew-behr-**lay**-geh ehs meer
I'll take it.	Ich nehme es. ikh **nay**-meh ehs
Do you accept credit cards?	Akzeptieren Sie Kreditkarten? ahkt-sehp-**teer**-ehn zee kreh-**deet**-kar-tehn
May I try it on?	Darf ich es anprobieren? darf ikh ehs **ahn**-proh-beer-ehn
It's too expensive / big / small.	Es ist zu teuer / gross / klein. ehs ist tsoo **toy**-ehr / grohs / klīn

I'll think about it.	Ich überlege es mir. ikh ew-behr-**lay**-geh ehs meer
I'll take it.	Ich nehme es. ikh **nay**-meh ehs
What time do you close?	Um wie viel Uhr schliessen Sie? oom vee feel oor **shlee**-sehn zee
What time do you open tomorrow?	Wann öffnen Sie morgen? vahn **urf**-nehn zee **mor**-gehn

Bargain hunters keep an eye out for sales: ***Angebot*** (special offer; you'll see this word everywhere), ***Sonder-Preis*** (special price), or ***Sonder-angebot*** (extra-special offer).

German speakers have three ways to say "inexpensive." ***Billig*** (cheap) can have a negative connotation. ***Preiswert*** means "worth the price." And ***günstig*** (affordable) implies a good deal. You may see ads promoting a product as ***gut und günstig*** (good and affordable).

Pay Up

Where do I pay?	Wo kann ich zahlen? voh kahn ikh **tsah**-lehn
cashier	Kasse **kah**-seh
Do you accept credit cards?	Akzeptieren Sie Kreditkarten? ahkt-sehp-**teer**-ehn zee kreh-**deet**-kar-tehn
Value-Added Tax (VAT)	Mehrwertsteuer (Mwst) **mehr**-vehrt-shtoy-ehr
Is a VAT refund possible here?	Ist das "Tax Free" Schema hier möglich? ist dahs "tax free" **shay**-mah heer **murg**-likh
Do you have the paperwork for a VAT refund?	Haben Sie ein "Tax Free" Formular? **hah**-behn zee īn "tax free" for-moo-**lar**
Can you ship this?	Können Sie das versenden? **kurn**-ehn zee dahs fehr-**zehn**-dehn

When you're ready to pay, look for a ***Kasse*** (cashier). The cashier might ask you something like ***Haben Sie fünfzehn Cent?*** (Do you have 15 cents?) or ***Möchten Sie eine Tüte?*** (Would you like a bag?). At larger stores such as supermarkets, a flimsy little bag (***Beutel,*** **boy**-tehl) is usually free, but if you want a sturdier ***Tüte*** (**tew**-teh) or ***Plastiktüte,*** you'll be charged a token amount.

If you make a major purchase from a single store, you may be eligible for a VAT refund; for details, see www.ricksteves.com/vat. While the German word for the Value-Added Tax is a mouthful, all shopkeepers recognize the English words "tax free" to mean the system that allows tourists to get a refund.

WHERE TO SHOP

Types of Shops

Where is a...?	Wo ist...? voh ist
barber shop	ein Herrenfriseur īn **hehr**-ehn-friz-**ur**
beauty salon / hair salon	ein Schönheitssalon / Friseursalon īn **shurn**-hīts-sah-**lohn** / friz-**ur**-zah-**lohn**
bookstore...	eine Buchhandlung... ī-neh **bookh**-hahnd-loong
used bookstore...	eine Secondhand-Buchhandlung... ī-neh "second hand"-**bookh**-hahnd-loong
...with books in English	...mit englischen Büchern mit **ehng**-lish-ehn **bewkh**-ehrn
camera shop	ein Photoladen īn **foh**-toh-lah-dehn
clothing boutique	ein Kleiderladen īn **klī**-dehr-lah-dehn
coffee shop	ein Kaffeeladen īn kah-**fay**-lah-dehn
department store	ein Kaufhaus īn **kowf**-hows
electronics store	ein Elektronikgeschäft īn eh-lehk-**troh**-nik-geh-**sheft**
flea market	ein Flohmarkt īn **floh**-markt
jewelry store	ein Schmuckgeschäft īn **shmook**-geh-shehft
launderette	ein Waschsalon īn **vahsh**-zah-lohn
mobile-phone shop	ein Handyladen īn **hehn**-dee-lah-dehn
newsstand	ein Kiosk / Zeitungsstand īn **kee**-ohsk / **tsī**-toongs-shtahnt
open-air market	ein Markt īn markt
pharmacy	eine Apotheke ī-neh ah-poh-**tay**-keh
shoe store	ein Schuhladen īn **shoo**-lah-dehn
shopping mall	ein Einkaufszentrum īn **īn**-kowfs-tsehn-troom
souvenir shop	ein Souvenirladen īn zoo-veh-**neer**-lah-dehn

toy store	ein Spielzeugladen īn **shpeel**-tsoyg-lah-dehn
travel agency	eine Reiseagentur ī-neh **rī**-zeh-ah-gehn-**toor**
wine shop	eine Weinhandlung ī-neh **vīn**-hahnt-loong

In Germany, most shops are open from about 9:00 until 18:00-20:00 on weekdays, but close early on Saturday (about 12:00 in towns and as late as 17:00 in bigger cities). In small towns, a few shops may take a mid-afternoon break on weekdays (roughly between 12:00 and 14:00). Throughout Germany, most shops close entirely on Sundays. For tips and phrases on shopping for a picnic—at grocery stores or open-air markets—see page 470.

WHAT TO BUY

Clothing

clothing	Kleider **klī**-dehr
This one.	Dieses. **dee**-zehs
May I try it on?	Darf ich es anprobieren? darf ikh ehs **ahn**-proh-beer-ehn
Do you have a...?	Haben Sie einen...? **hah**-behn zee ī-nehn
...mirror	...Spiegel **shpee**-gehl
...fitting room	...Anprobe **ahn**-proh-beh
It's too...	Es ist zu... ehs ist tsoo
...expensive.	...teuer. **toy**-ehr
...big / small.	...gross / klein. grohs / klīn
...short / long.	...kurz / lang. koorts / lahng
...tight / loose.	...eng / weit. ehng / vīt
...dark / light.	...dunkel / hell. **doon**-kehl / hehl

Do you have a different color / a different pattern?	Haben Sie eine andere Farbe / ein anderes Muster? **hah**-behn zee ī-neh **ahn**-deh-reh **far**-beh / īn **ahn**-deh-rehs **moos**-tehr
What's this made of?	Was ist das für ein Material? vahs ist dahs fewr īn mah-teh-ree-**ahl**
Is it machine washable?	Ist es waschmaschin-enfest? ist ehs **vahsh**-mah-sheen-ehn-**fehst**
Will it shrink?	Läuft es ein? loyft ehs īn
Will it fade in the wash?	Ist die Farbe waschmaschinenfest? ist dee **far**-beh **vahsh**-mah-sheen-ehn-**fehst**
Dry clean only?	Nur trocken reinigen? noor **troh**-kehn **rī**-nig-ehn

For a list of colors, see page 512.

Types of Clothes and Accessories

For a...	Für... fewr
...man.	...einen Herren. ī-nehn **hehr**-ehn
...woman.	...eine Dame. ī-neh **dah**-meh
...teenager. (m / f)	...einen Jungen / ein Mädchen. ī-nehn **yoong**-ehn / īn **mayds**-yehn
...child. (m / f)	...einen Buben / ein Mädchen. ī-nehn **boo**-behn / īn **mayds**-yehn
...baby.	...ein Baby. īn "baby"
I'm looking for a...	Ich suche... ikh **zookh**-eh
I would like a...	Ich möchte... ikh **murkh**-teh
belt	einen Gürtel ī-nehn **gewr**-tehl
bra	einen BH (Büstenhalter) ī-nehn bay hah (**bewst**-ehn-hahl-tehr)
dress	ein Kleid īn klīt
earrings	Ohrringe **or**-ring-eh

gloves	Handschuhe	**hahnt**-shoo-eh
handbag	eine Handtasche	ī-neh **hahnt**-tah-sheh
hat	einen Hut	ī-nehn hoot
jacket	eine Jacke	ī-neh **yah**-keh
jeans	Jeans	"jeans"
jewelry	Schmuck	shmook
necklace	Halsband	**hahls**-bahnt
nylons	Strümpfe	**shtrewmp**-feh
pajamas	einen Pyjama	ī-nehn pew-**jah**-mah
pants	eine Hose	ī-neh **hoh**-zeh
raincoat	einen Regenmantel	ī-nehn **ray**-gehn-mahn-tehl
ring	Ring	ring
scarf	einen Schal	ī-nehn shahl
shirt	ein Hemd	īn hehmt
shoelaces	Schnürsenkel	**shnewr**-zehn-kehl
shoes	Schuhe	**shoo**-eh
shorts	eine kurze Hose	ī-neh **koort**-seh **hoh**-zeh
skirt	einen Rock	ī-nehn rohk
socks	Socken	**zoh**-kehn
sweater	einen Pullover / Pulli	ī-nehn "pullover" / **poo**-lee
swimsuit	einen Badeanzug	ī-nehn **bah**-deh-ahn-tsoog
tie	eine Krawatte	ī-neh krah-**vah**-teh
tights	Strümpfe	**shtrewmp**-feh
T-shirt	ein T-shirt	īn **tay**-shirt
underwear	eine Unterwäsche	ī-neh **oon**-tehr-veh-sheh
wallet	ein Geldbeutel	īn **gehlt**-boy-tehl
watch	Uhr	oor

Clothing Sizes

extra-small	extra klein "extra" klīn
small	klein klīn
medium	mittelgross **mit**-tehl-grohs
large	gross grohs
extra-large	extra gross "extra" grohs
I need a bigger / smaller size.	Ich brauche eine grössere / kleinere Grösse. ikh **browkh**-eh ī-neh **grur**-seh-reh / **klī**-neh-reh **grur**-seh
What's my size?	Was ist meine Grösse? vahs ist **mī**-neh **grur**-seh

For help converting US sizes to European, see page 552.

Colors

black	schwarz shvahrts
blue	blau blow (rhymes with "cow")
brown	braun brown
gray	grau grow (rhymes with "cow")
green	grün grewn
orange	orange oh-**rahn**-zheh
pink	rosa **roh**-zah
purple	lila **lee**-lah
red	rot roht
white	weiss vīs
yellow	gelb gehlb
dark / darker	dunkel / dunkler **doon**-kehl / **doon**-klehr
light / lighter	hell / heller hehl / **hehl**-ehr
bright / brighter	mit satten Farben / mit satteren Farben mit **zah**-tehn **far**-behn / mit **zah**-teh-rehn **far**-behn

SHIPPING AND MAIL

If you need to ship packages home, head for ***die Post*** (the post office). Otherwise, you can often get stamps at a ***Kiosk*** (newsstand), stamp machine (yellow, labeled ***Briefmarken***), or ***Tabak*** (tobacco shop). The German Postal Service is called the ***Deutsche Post;*** in Austria, it's the ***Österreichische Post;*** and Switzerland has the ***Swiss Post.***

post office	die Post dee pohst
Where is the post office?	Wo ist die Post? voh ist dee pohst
stamps	Briefmarken **breef**-mar-kehn
postcard	Postkarte **pohst**-kar-teh
letter	Brief breef
package	Paket pah-**kayt**
counter / window	Schalter **shahl**-tehr
line	Schlange **shlahng**-eh
At which counter is ____?	An welchem Schalter ist ____? ahn **vehlkh**-ehm **shahl**-tehr ist ____
Is this the line for ____?	Ist hier die Schlange für ____? ist heer dee **shlahng**-eh fewr ____
I need stamps.	Ich brauche Briefmarken. ikh **browkh**-eh **breef**-mar-kehn
I want to mail a package.	Ich will ein Packet versenden. ikh veel īn pah-**kayt** fehr-**zehn**-dehn
to America / USA	nach Amerika / USA nahkh ah-**mehr**-ee-kah / oo ehs ah
Pretty stamps, please.	Hübsche Briefmarken, bitte. **hewb**-sheh **breef**-mar-kehn **bit**-teh
Can I buy a box?	Kann ich einen Karton kaufen? kahn ikh ī-nehn kar-**tohn** **kow**-fehn
This big.	So gross. zoh grohss
Do you have tape?	Haben Sie Klebeband? **hah**-behn zee **klay**-beh-bahnd

TECHNOLOGY

TECH TERMS

Portable Devices and Accessories

I need a...	Ich brauche... ikh **browkh**-eh
Do you have a...?	Haben Sie...? **hah**-behn zee
Where can I buy a...?	Wo kann ich... kaufen? voh kahn ikh... **kow**-fehn
battery (for ____)	eine Batterie (für ____) ī-neh bah-teh-**ree** (fewr ____)
battery charger	ein Batterieladegerät īn bah-teh-**ree**-lah-deh-geh-**rayt**
charger	ein Ladegerät īn **lah**-deh-geh-**rayt**
computer	einen Computer ī-nehn "computer"
convertor	einen Konverter ī-nehn kohn-**vehr**-tehr
CD / DVD	eine CD / DVD ī-neh tsay-**day** / day-fow-**day**
ereader	einen e-Reader ī-nehn "ereader"
electrical adapter	einen Adapter ī-nehn "adapter"
flash drive	einen Flashdrive ī-nehn "flashdrive"
headphones / earbuds	Kopfhörer **kohpf**-hur-ehr
iPod / MP3 player	einen iPod / Mp3-Spieler ī-nehn "iPod" / ehm-pay-**drī**-shpeel-ehr
laptop	einen Laptop ī-nehn "laptop"
memory card	eine Memory-Karte ī-neh "memory"-**kar**-teh
mobile phone	ein Handy īn **hehn**-dee
SIM card	eine SIM-Karte ī-neh **sim**-kar-teh

speakers (for ___)	Lautsprecher (für ___) **lowt**-sprehkh-ehr (fewr ___)
tablet	ein Tablet īn "tablet"
(mini) USB cable	ein (mini-) USB-Kabel īn (**mee**-nee) oo-ehs-**bay**-**kah**-behl
video game	ein Videospiel īn **vee**-day-oh-shpeel
Wi-Fi	WLAN **vay**-lahn

Many tech items have both a German name and an English-derived name that is at least understood, if not even more commonly used than the German. An electrical adapter, for example, may be labeled as a ***Stromwandler*** in a store, or a memory card may be labeled as a ***Speicherkarte***...but if you use their English names, German speakers will understand you.

Familiar brands (like iPad, Facebook, YouTube, Instagram, or whatever the latest craze) are just as popular in Europe as they are back home. Invariably, these go by their English names, sometimes with a German accent.

Cameras

camera	Kamera **kah**-meh-rah
digital camera	Digitalkamera deeg-ee-**tahl**-**kah**-meh-rah
video camera	Videokamera **vee**-day-oh-**kah**-meh-rah
lens cap	Objektivdeckel ohb-yehk-**teef**-dehk-ehl
film	Film film
Can I download my photos onto a CD?	Kann ich meine Fotos auf eine CD herunterladen? kann ikh **mī**-neh **foh**-tohs owf **ī**-neh tsay-**day** hehr-**oon**-tehr-lah-dehn
Will you take a photo of me / us?	Machen Sie ein Foto von mir / uns? **mahkh**-ehn zee īn **foh**-toh fohn meer / oons

Can I take a photo of you?	Kann ich ein Foto von Ihnen machen? kahn ikh īn **foh**-toh fohn **ee**-nehn **mahkh**-ehn
Smile!	Lächeln! **laykh**-ehln

You'll find words for batteries, chargers, and more in the previous list.

TELEPHONES

Telephone Terms

telephone	Telefon tehl-eh-**fohn**
phone call	Telefonanruf tehl-eh-**fohn**-ahn-roof
local call	Ortsgespräch **orts**-geh-shprehkh
domestic call	Inlandsgespräch **in**-lahnds-geh-**shprehkh**
international call	Auslandsgespräch **ows**-lahnds-geh-**shprehkh**
toll-free	gebührenfrei geh-**bewr**-ehn-frī
with credit card	mit Kreditkarte mit kreh-**deet**-kar-teh
collect call	R-Gespräch **ehr**-geh-shprehkh
mobile phone	Handy **hehn**-dee
mobile number	Handynummer **hehn**-dee-noo-mehr
landline	Festnetz **fehst**-nehts
toll charged	gebührenpflichtig geh-**bewr**-ehn-**pflikh**-tig
country code	Landesvorwahl **lahn**-dehs-for-vahl
area code	Vorwahl **for**-vahl
local number	Lokalnummer loh-**kahl**-noo-mehr
fax	Fax fahx

Travelers have several phoning options; of these, a mobile phone provides the best combination of practicality and flexibility. Public pay phones are available, but are becoming rare, and some work only with an insertable phone card (***chipKarte,*** chip-kar-teh). Look for public phones at cheap calling shops in train station neighborhoods. You can also make calls online (using Skype or a similar program) or from

Key Phrases: Telephones

telephone	Telefon tehl-eh-**fohn**
phone call	Telefonanruf tehl-eh-**fohn**-ahn-roof
mobile phone	Handy hehn-dee
Where is the nearest phone?	Wo ist das nächste Telefon? voh ist dahs **nehkh**-steh tehl-eh-**fohn**
May I use your phone?	Darf ich Ihr Telefon benutzen? darf ikh eer tehl-eh-**fohn** beh-**noot**-sehn
Where is a mobile-phone shop?	Wo ist ein Handyladen? voh ist īn hehn-dee-**lah**-dehn

your hotel-room phone using a cheap international phone card (***billige Telefonkarte,*** **bil**-lig-eh tehl-eh-**fohn**-kar-teh). As this is a fast-changing scene, check my latest tips at www.ricksteves.com/phoning.

Germany and Austria use area codes while Switzerland has a direct-dial phone system (no area codes). For phone tips—including a calling chart for dialing European numbers—see page 548.

Making Calls

Where is the nearest phone?	Wo ist das nächste Telefon? voh ist dahs **nehkh**-steh tehl-eh-**fohn**
May I use your phone?	Darf ich Ihr Telefon benutzen? darf ikh eer tehl-eh-**fohn** beh-**noot**-sehn
Can you talk for me?	Können Sie für mich sprechen? **kurn**-ehn zee fewr mikh **shprehkh**-ehn
It's busy.	Besetzt. beh-**zehtst**
It doesn't work.	Es funktioniert nicht. ehs foonkt-see-ohn-**eert** nikht
out of service	ausser Betrieb ow-sehr beh-**treeb**
Try again?	Noch einmal versuchen? nohkh **īn**-mahl fehr-**zookh**-ehn

If the number you're calling is out of service, you'll hear a recording: ***Kein Anschluss unter dieser Nummer.***

On the Phone

Hello, this is ____.	Hallo, ich bin ____. **hah**-loh ikh bin ____
My name is ____.	Ich heisse ____. ikh **hī**-seh ____
Do you speak English?	Sprechen Sie Englisch? **shprehkh**-ehn zee **ehng**-lish
Sorry, I speak only a little German.	Tut mir leid, ich spreche nur wenig Deutsch. toot meer līt ikh **shprehkh**-eh noor **vay**-nig dotych
Speak slowly, please.	Sprechen Sie bitte langsam. **shprehkh**-ehn zee **bit**-teh **lahng**-zahm
Wait a moment.	Moment mal. moh-**mehnt** mahl

In German-speaking countries, it's polite to identify yourself by name at the beginning of every phone conversation—whether you're making or receiving the call. If you call your friend Günther Schmitt, he may answer ***Schmitt, Hallo*** or ***Schmitt hier.***

You'll find the phrases you need to reserve a hotel room on page 415, or a table at a restaurant on page 434. To spell your name over the phone, refer to the code alphabet on page 550.

Mobile Phones

Your US mobile phone should work in Europe if it's GSM-enabled, tri-band or quad-band, and on a calling plan that includes international service. Alternatively, you can buy a phone in Europe. While pay-as-you-go phones are fairly uncommon in the US, most European mobile phones come with no commitment—which means it's easy to get a cheap phone for a short trip. In any mobile phone store, ask for ***ein Handy mit Prepaid-Guthaben.***

If your phone is unlocked (***entsperrt*** or ***frei***), you can save money by buying a cheap European SIM card (which usually comes with some calling credit) at a mobile-phone shop or a newsstand. After inserting a SIM card in your phone, you'll have a European number and pay lower European rates.

mobile phone	Handy **hehn**-dee
smartphone	Smartphone "smartphone"
roaming	Roaming "roaming"
text message	SMS "SMS"
Where is a mobile-phone shop?	Wo is ein Handyladen? voh ist īn **hehn**-dee-**lah**-dehn
I'd like to buy...	Ich möchte... kaufen. ikh **murkh**-teh... **kow**-fehn
...a (cheap) mobile phone.	...ein (billiges) Handy īn (**bil**-lig-ehs) **hehn**-dee
...a mobile phone with prepaid credit.	...ein Handy mit Prepaid-Guthaben īn **hehn**-dee mit "prepaid"-**goot**-hah-behn
...a SIM card.	...eine SIM-Karte ī-neh **sim**-kar-teh
prepaid card	Prepaidkarte "prepaid"-**kar**-teh
prepaid credit	Guthaben **goot**-hah-behn
calling time	Sprechzeit **shprehkh**-tsīt
(without) contract	(ohne) Vertrag (**oh**-neh) fehr-**trahg**
locked / unlocked	gesperrt / entsperrt geh-**shpehrt** / **ehnt**-shpehrt
Is this phone unlocked?	Ist dieses Handy entsperrt? ist **dee**-zehs **hehn**-dee **ehnt**-shpehrt
Can you unlock this phone?	Können Sie dieses Handy entsperren? **kurn**-ehn zee **dee**-zehs **hehn**-dee **ehnt**-shpehr-ehn
How can I...?	Wie kann ich...? vee kahn ikh
...make calls	...telefonieren teh-leh-fohn-**eer**-ehn
...receive calls	...Gespräche annehmen geh-**shprehk**-eh **ahn**-nay-mehn

...send a text message	...texten "**text**"-ehn
...check voicemail	...Voicemail anhören "voicemail" **ahn**-hur-ehn
...set the language to English	...die Sprache auf Englisch wechseln dee **sprahkh**-eh owf **ehng**-lish **vehkh**-sehln
...change the ringer	...den Klingelton wechseln dayn **kleeng**-ehl-tohn **vehkh**-sehln
...turn it on	...es anschalten ehs **ahn**-shahl-tehn
...turn it off	...es abschalten ehs **ahp**-shahl-tehn

GETTING ONLINE

Internet Terms

Internet access	Internetanschluss "Internet"-**ahn**-shloos
Wi-Fi	WLAN **vay**-lahn
email	E-Mail "email"
computer	Computer "computer"
Internet café	Internetcafé "Internet café"
surf the Web	im Internet surfen im "Internet" **zoor**-fehn
username	Benutzername beh-**noot**-sehr-**nah**-meh
password	Passwort **pahs**-vort
network key	Netzwerkschlüssel **nehts**-vehrk-shlew-sehl
secure network	passwort-geschütztes WLAN **pahs**-vort-geh-**shewts**-tehs **vay**-lahn
website	Website "website"
homepage	Homepage "homepage"
download	herunterladen hehr-**oon**-tehr-**lah**-dehn
print	drucken **droo**-kehn

Key Phrases: Getting Online

Where is a Wi-Fi hotspot?	Wo ist ein WLAN? voh ist īn **vay**-lahn
Where can I get online?	Wo komm ich ins Internet? voh kohm ikh ins "Internet"
Where is an Internet café?	Wo ist ein Internetcafé? voh ist īn "Internet café"
May I check my email?	Darf ich meine E-Mail lesen? darf ikh **mī**-neh "email" **lay**-zehn

My email address is ____.	Meine E-Mail-Adresse ist ____. **mī**-neh "email"-ah-**dreh**-seh ist ____
What's your email address?	Was ist Ihre E-Mail-Adresse? vahs ist **ee**-reh "email"-ah-**dreh**-seh

The www found at the beginning of most URLs is pronounced **vay vay vay** (three W's).

Tech Support

Help me, please.	Helfen Sie mir, bitte. **hel**-fehn zee meer **bit**-teh
How can I...?	Wie...? vee
...start this	...starte ich das **shtar**-teh ikh dahs
...get online	...komme ich ins Internet **koh**-meh ikh ins "Internet"
...get this to work	...kriege ich das ans Laufen **kree**-geh ikh dahs ahns **low**-fehn
...stop this	...beende ich das beh-**ehn**-deh ikh dahs
...send this	...schicke ich das **shik**-eh ikh dahs

...print this	...drucke ich das **droo**-keh ikh dahs
...make this symbol	...mache ich dieses Symbol **mahkh**-eh ikh **dee**-zehs zim-**bohl**
...copy and paste	...kopiere und füge ich ein koh-pee-**ehr**-eh oont **fewg**-eh ikh īn
...type @	...geht At / Klammeraffe gayt "at" / **klah**-mehr-ah-feh
This doesn't work.	Das funktioniert nicht. dahs foonkt-see-ohn-**eert** nikht

For do-it-yourself tips, see "German Keyboards" on page 524.

Using Your Own Portable Device

If you have a smartphone, tablet computer, laptop, or other wireless device, you can get online at many hotels, cafés, and public hotspots. Most Internet access is Wi-Fi (which German speakers usually call ***WLAN,*** pronounced **vay**-lahn), but occasionally you'll connect by plugging an Ethernet cable directly into your laptop. While Internet access is often free, sometimes you'll have to pay.

laptop	Laptop "laptop"
tablet	Tablet "tablet"
smartphone	Smartphone "smartphone"
Where is a Wi-Fi hotspot?	Wo ist ein WLAN? voh ist īn **vay**-lahn
Do you have Wi-Fi?	Haben Sie WLAN? **hah**-behn zee **vay**-lahn
What is the...?	Was ist...? vahs ist
...network name	...der Netzname dehr **nehts**-nah-meh
...username	...der Benutzername dehr beh-**noot**-sehr-**nah**-meh
...password	...das Passwort dahs **pahs**-vort
Do I need a cable?	Brauche ich ein Kabel? **browkh**-eh ikh īn **kah**-behl

Do you have a...?	Haben Sie ein...? **hah**-behn zee īn
May I borrow a...?	Darf ich ein... ausleihen? darf ikh īn... **ows**-lī-ehn
...charging cable	...Stromkabel **strohm**-kah-behl
...Ethernet cable	...Ethernetkabel **ay**-tehr-neht-**kah**-behl
...USB cable	...USB-Kabel oo-ehs-**bay**-**kah**-behl
Is it free?	Ist es kostenlos? ist ehs **kohs**-tehn-lohs
How much?	Wie viel? vee feel
Do I have to buy something to use the Internet?	Muss ich etwas kaufen um das Internet zu benutzen? moos ikh **eht**-vahs **kow**-fehn oom dahs "Internet" tsoo beh-**noot**-sehn

Using a Public Internet Terminal

Many hotels have terminals in the lobby for guests to get online; otherwise, an Internet café is usually nearby.

Where can I get online?	Wo kann man hier ins Internet? voh kahn mahn heer ins "Internet"
Where is an Internet café?	Wo ist ein Internetcafé? voh ist īn "Internet café"
May I use this computer to...?	Darf ich diesen Computer benutzen...? darf ikh **dee**-zehn "computer" beh-**noot**-sehn
...get online	...um ins Internet zu kommen oom ins "Internet" tsoo **koh**-mehn
...check my email	...um meine E-Mails zu lesen oom **mī**-neh "emails" **tsoo** lay-zehn
...upload my photos	...um meine Fotos hochzuladen oom **mī**-neh **foh**-tohs **hohkh**-tsoo-**lah**-dehn
...download my photos	...um meine Fotos herunterzuladen oom **mī**-neh **foh**-tohs hehr-**oon**-tehr-tsoo-**lah**-dehn

...print something	...um etwas zu drucken oom **eht**-vahs tsoo **drook**-ehn
boarding passes	Bordkarten **bord**-kar-tehn
train tickets	Fahrscheine **far**-shīn-eh
a reservation confirmation	eine Bestätigung ī-neh beh-**shtay**-tig-oong
Is it free?	Ist es kostenlos? ist ehs **kohs**-tehn-lohs
How much (for... minutes)?	Wie viel (für... Minuten)? vee feel (fewr... mee-**noo**-tehn)
...10	...zehn tsayn
...15	...fünfzehn **fewnf**-tsayn
...30	...dreissig **drī**-sig
...60	...sechzig **zehkh**-tsig
Can you switch the keyboard to English?	Könnten Sie die Tastatur auf englisch umstellen? **kurn**-tehn zee dee tah-stah-**toor** owf **ehng**-lish **oom**-shtehl-ehn

If you're using a public Internet terminal, the keyboard, menus, and on-screen commands will likely be designed for German speakers. Some computers allow you to make the German keyboard work as if it were an American one (look for the box in the lower right-hand corner of the screen to switch to English, or ask the clerk if it's possible).

German Keyboards

German keyboards differ from American ones (for example, you'll find the German letter *ß* in place of the hyphen (-) key, and the **Z** and **Y** keys are reversed). The multilingual Swiss use a different keyboard from the standard German and Austrian one. Here's a rundown of how major commands are labeled on a German keyboard:

YOU'LL SEE...	IT MEANS...	YOU'LL SEE...	IT MEANS...
◄┘	Enter	←	Backspace
↑	Shift	**Einfg**	Insert
Strg	Ctrl	**Pos 1**	Home
↓	Caps Lock	**Ende**	End
Num↓	Num Lock	**Bild ↑**	Page Up
→|	Tab	**Bild ↓**	Page Down
Entf	Delete		

A few often-used keys look the same, but have different names in German:

@ sign	At / At-zeichen / Klammeraffe eht / eht-**tsīkh**-ehn / **klah**-mehr-ah-feh
dot (.)	Punkt poonkt
hyphen (-)	Bindestrich **bin**-deh-shtrikh
underscore (_)	Unterstrich **oon**-tehr-shtrikh
slash (/)	Schrägstrich **shrehg**-shtrikh

The **Alt** key to the right of the space bar is actually different from our key; it's called **Alt Gr** (for Alternate Graphics). Press this key to insert the extra symbol that appears on some keys (such as the **€** in the corner of the **E** key). To type **@,** press **Alt Gr** and **Q** at the same time. If that doesn't work, try copying and pasting the @ sign from elsewhere on the page.

German speakers have several names for @. Most common is the anglicized ***At-zeichen*** (at-sign; when reading off an email address, they'll simply say "at" the way we do). It's sometimes more creatively called ***Klammeraffe*** (monkey hug) or ***A-Affenschwanz*** (A with a monkey tail).

HELP!

EMERGENCIES

To phone for help in Germany or Austria, dial **112** for police or medical emergencies. In Switzerland, dial **112** for medical emergencies or **117** for police. If you're lost, see the phrases on page 412.

Medical Help

Help!	Hilfe! **hil**-feh
Help me, please.	Helfen Sie mir, bitte. **hehl**-fehn zee meer **bit**-teh
emergency	Notfall **noht**-fahl
accident	Unfall **oon**-fahl
clinic / hospital	Klinik / Krankenhaus **klee**-nik / **krahn**-kehn-hows
Call...	Rufen Sie... **roo**-fehn zee
...a doctor.	...einen Arzt. ī-nehn artst
...the police.	...die Polizei. dee poh-leet-**sī**
...an ambulance.	...einen Krankenwagen. ī-nehn **krahnk**-ehn-vah-gehn
I need / We need...	Ich muss / Wir müssen... ikh moos / veer **mew**-sehn
...to get to the doctor.	...zum Arzt. tsoom artst
...to go to the hospital.	...ins Krankenhaus. ins **krahn**-kehn-hows
It's urgent.	Es ist dringend. ehs ist **dring**-ehnt
injured	verletzt fehr-**lehtst**
blood	Blut bloot
choking	erstickt ehr-**shtikt**
unconscious	bewusstlos beh-**voost**-lohs

Key Phrases: Help!

Help!	Hilfe! **hil**-feh
emergency	Notfall **noht**-fahl
clinic / hospital	Klinik / Krankenhaus **klee**-nik / **krahn**-kehn-hows
Call a doctor.	Rufen Sie einen Arzt. **roo**-fehn zee ī-nehn artst
police	Polizei poh-leet-**sī**
ambulance	Krankenwagen **krahnk**-ehn-vah-gehn
thief	Dieb deep
Stop, thief!	Halt, Dieb! hahlt deep

isn't breathing	atmet nicht **aht**-meht nikht
Thank you for your help.	Danke für Ihre Hilfe. **dahn**-keh fewr **ee**-reh **hil**-feh
You are very kind.	Sie sind sehr freundlich. zee zint zehr **froynd**-likh

For other health-related words, see the Personal Care and Health chapter.

Theft and Loss

thief	Dieb deep
pickpocket	Taschendieb **tahsh**-ehn-deep
police	Polizei poh-leet-**sī**
embassy	Botschaft **boht**-shahft
Stop, thief!	Halt, Dieb! hahlt deep
Call the police!	Rufen Sie die Polizei! **roo**-fehn see dee poh-leet-**sī**

I've been robbed.	Ich bin beraubt worden. ikh bin beh-**rowbt vor**-dehn
We've been robbed.	Wir sind beraubt worden. veer zint beh-**rowbt vor**-dehn
A thief took...	Ein Dieb hat... genommen. īn deep haht... geh-**noh**-mehn
Thieves took...	Die Diebe haben... genommen. dee **dee**-beh **hah**-behn... geh-**noh**-mehn
I've lost my...	Ich habe meine... verloren. ikh **hah**-beh **mī**-neh... fehr-**lor**-ehn
We've lost our...	Wir haben unsere... verloren. veer **hah**-behn **oon**-zeh-reh... fehr-**lor**-ehn
money	Geld gehlt
credit card(s)	Kreditkarte(n) kreh-**deet**-kar-teh(n)
passport / passports	Pass / Pässe pahs / **peh**-seh
train ticket(s)	Fahrkarte(n) **far**-kar-teh(n)
plane ticket(s)	Flugkarte(n) **floog**-kar-teh(n)
railpass(es)	Railpass(es) "railpass(es)"
baggage	Gepäck geh-**pehk**
purse	Handtasche **hahnt**-tahsh-eh
wallet	Brieftasche **breef**-tahsh-eh
watch	Uhr oor
jewelry	Schmuck shmook
camera	Kamera **kah**-meh-rah
mobile phone	Handy **hehn**-dee
iPod / iPad	iPod / iPad "iPod" / "iPad"
tablet	Tablet "tablet"
computer	Computer "computer"
laptop	Laptop "laptop"
faith in humankind	Glauben an die Menschheit **glow**-behn ahn dee **mehnsh**-hīt

I'd like to contact my embassy.	Ich möchte meine Botschaft kontaktieren. ikh **murkh**-teh **mī**-neh **boht**-shahft kohn-tahk-**tee**-rehn
I need to file a police report (for my insurance).	Ich muss einen Polizeireport (für meine Versicherung) erstellen. ikh moos **ī**-nehn poh-leet-**sī**-reh-port (fewr **mī**-neh fehr-**zikh**-ehr-oong) ehr-**shtehl**-ehn
Where is the police station?	Wo ist die Polizeiwache? voh ist dee poh-leet-**sī**-vahkh-eh

To replace a passport, you'll need to go in person to your embassy. Cancel and replace your credit and debit cards by calling your credit-card company (as of this printing, these are the 24-hour US numbers that you can call collect: Visa—tel. 303/967-1096, MasterCard—tel. 636/722-7111, American Express—tel. 336/393-1111). If you'll want to submit an insurance claim for lost or stolen gear, be sure to file a police report, either on the spot or within a day or two. For more info, see www.ricksteves.com/help. Precautionary measures can minimize the effects of loss—back up your digital photos and other files frequently.

Fire!

fire	Feuer **foy**-ehr
smoke	Rauch rowkh
exit	Ausgang **ows**-gahng
emergency exit	Notausgang **noht**-ows-gahng
fire extinguisher	Feuerlöscher **foy**-ehr-lur-shehr
Call the fire department.	Rufen Sie die Feuerwehr. **roo**-fehn zee dee **foy**-ehr-vehr

The word ***Not,*** which you'll see everywhere, does not mean "not." It means emergency (literally "need"). You might see ***Notruf*** (emergency call), ***im Notfall*** (in case of emergency), ***Notausgang*** (emergency exit), and so on. That last one can be especially confusing. If you know the word for exit is ***Ausgang,*** you may think ***Notausgang*** means "not exit"—when, in fact, in an emergency you'd do exactly the opposite.

HELP FOR WOMEN

Generally the best way to react to unwanted attention is loudly and quickly.

No!	Nein! nīn
Stop it!	Hören Sie auf! **hur**-ehn zee owf
Stop it! (less polite)	Hör auf! hur owf
Knock it off!	Lassen Sie das! **lah**-sehn zee dahs
Enough!	Das reicht! dahs rīkht
Don't touch me.	Fassen Sie mich nicht an. **fah**-sehn zee mikh nikht ahn
Leave me alone.	Lassen Sie mich in Ruhe. **lah**-sehn zee mikh in **roo**-heh
Go away.	Gehen Sie weg. **gay**-ehn zee vayg
Get lost!	Hau ab! how ahp
Back off!	Verschwinde! fehr-**shvin**-deh
Police!	Polizei! poh-leet-**sī**

Safety in Numbers

If a guy is bugging you, approach a friendly-looking couple, family, or business for a place to stay safe.

A man is bothering me.	Ein Mann belästigt mich. īn mahn beh-**lehs**-tigt mikh
May I...?	Darf ich...? darf ikh
...join you	...mich zu Ihnen setzen mikh tsoo **ee**-nehn **zeht**-sehn
...sit here	...mich setzen mikh **zeht**-sehn
...wait here until he's gone	...hier warten bis er fort ist heer **var**-tehn bis ehr fort ist

You Want to Be Alone

I want to be alone.	Ich will alleine sein. ikh vil ah-**lī**-neh zīn
I'm not interested.	Ich habe kein Interesse. ikh **hah**-beh kīn in-teh-**rehs**-eh
I'm married.	Ich bin verheiratet. ikh bin fehr-**hī**-rah-teht
I'm waiting for my husband.	Ich warte auf meinen Mann. ikh **var**-teh owf **mī**-nehn mahn
I'm a lesbian.	Ich bin lesbisch. ikh bin **lehz**-bish
I have a contagious disease.	Ich habe eine ansteckende Krankheit. ikh **hah**-beh ī-neh **ahn**-shtehk-ehn-deh **krahnk**-hīt

PERSONAL CARE AND HEALTH

PERSONAL CARE

aftershave lotion	Aftershave "aftershave"
antiperspirant	Antitranspirant ahn-tee-trahn-speer-**ahnt**
breath mints	Minz-Bonbons (für frischen Atem) **mints**-bohn-bohns (fewr **frish**-ehn **ah**-tehm)
cologne	Herrenduft **hehr**-ehn-dooft
comb	Kamm kahm
conditioner	Haarspülung **har**-shpew-loong
dental floss	Zahnseide **tsahn**-zī-deh
deodorant	Deodorant / Deo day-oh-doh-**rahnt** / **day**-oh
face cleanser	Gesichtsseife geh-**zikht**-sī-feh
facial tissue	Papiertaschentuch pah-**peer**-tahsh-ehn-tookh
fluoride rinse	Fluor-Mundspülung **floo**-or-**moond**-shpew-loong
hair dryer	Haartrockner **har**-trohk-nehr
hairbrush	Haarbürste **har**-bewr-steh
hand lotion	Handlotion **hahnt**-loh-see-**ohn**
hand sanitizer	Hand-Desinfizierer **hahnt**-deh-zin-fit-**seer**-ehr
lip balm	Lippenbalsam **lip**-ehn-bahl-zahm
lip gloss	Lipgloss "lip gloss"
lipstick	Lippenstift **lip**-ehn-shtift

makeup	Makeup / Schminken "makeup" / **shmink**-ehn
mirror	Spiegel **shpee**-gehl
moisturizer (with sunblock)	Feuchtigkeitscreme (mit Sonnenschutz) **foykh**-tig-kīts-**kreh**-meh (mit **zoh**-nehn-shoots)
mouthwash	Mundwasser **moont** vahs ehr
nail clipper	Nagelschere **nah**-gehl-sheh-reh
nail file	Nagelfeile **nah**-gehl-fī-leh
nail polish	Nagellack **nah**-gehl-lahk
nail polish remover	Nagellackentferner **nah**-gehl-lahk-ehnt-**fehr**-nehr
perfume	Parfum / Damenduft par-**foom** / **dah**-mehn-dooft
Q-tips (cotton swabs)	Wattestäbchen **vah**-teh-shtayb-shehn
razor	Rasierapparat rah-**zeer**-ahp-ah-raht
sanitary pads	Damenbinden **dah**-mehn-bin-dehn
scissors	Schere **sheh**-reh
shampoo	Shampoo **shahm**-poo
shaving cream	Rasierschaum rah-**zeer**-showm
soap	Seife **zī**-feh
sunscreen	Sonnenschutz **zoh**-nehn-shoots
suntan lotion	Sonnenöl **zoh**-nehn-url
tampons	Tampons **tahm**-pohns
tissues	Taschentücher / Tempos **tah**-shehn-tewkh-ehr / **tehm**-pohs
toilet paper	Toilettenpapier toy-**leh**-tehn-pah-peer
toothbrush	Zahnbürste **tsahn**-bewr-steh
toothpaste	Zahnpasta **tsahn**-pah-stah
tweezers	Pinzette pin-**tseh**-teh

Many toiletries include the word ***Pflege*** (care)—such as ***Mundpflege*** (mouth care), ***Haarpflege*** (hair care), and ***Gesichtspflege*** (facial care).

A hair dryer may also be called a ***Föhn*** (furn) for the warm wind that blows over the Alps.

HEALTH

Throughout Europe, people with simple ailments go first to the pharmacist, who can diagnose and prescribe remedies. Pharmacists are usually friendly and speak English. If necessary, the pharmacist will send you to a doctor or a clinic.

Getting Help

Where is a...?	Wo ist...? voh ist
...(all-night) pharmacy	...eine Apotheke (mit Nachtdienst) ī-neh ah-poh-**tay**-keh (mit **nahkht**-deenst)
...medical clinic	...eine Klinik ī-neh **klee**-nik
...hospital	...ein Krankenhaus īn **krahn**-kehn-hows
I am sick.	Ich bin krank. ikh bin krahnk
He / She is sick.	Er / Sie ist krank. ehr / zee ist krahnk
I need a doctor...	Ich brauche einen Arzt... ikh **browkh**-eh ī-nehn artst
We need a doctor...	Wir brauchen einen Arzt... veer **browkh**-ehn ī-nehn artst
...who speaks English.	...der Englisch spricht. dehr **ehng**-lish shprikht
Please call a doctor.	Bitte rufen Sie einen Arzt. **bit**-teh **roo**-fehn zee ī-nehn artst
Could a doctor come here?	Kann der Arzt hierherkommen? kahn dehr artst heer-**hehr**-koh-mehn
It's urgent.	Es ist dringend. ehs ist **dring**-ehnd
It's an emergency!	Es ist ein Notfall! ehs ist īn **noht**-fahl
ambulance	Krankenwagen **krahnk**-ehn-vah-gehn
dentist	Zahnarzt **tsahn**-artst

Key Phrases: Health

I am sick.	Ich bin krank. ikh bin krahnk
I need a doctor (who speaks English).	Ich brauche einen Arzt (der Englisch spricht). ikh **browkh**-eh ī-nehn artst (dehr **ehng**-lish shprikht)
pain	Schmerz shmehrts
It hurts here.	Hier tut es weh. heer toot ehs vay
medicine	Medikament meh-dee-kah-**mehnt**
Where is a pharmacy?	Wo ist eine Apotheke? voh ist ī-neh ah-poh-**tay**-keh

health insurance	Krankenversicherung **krahn**-kehn-fehr-**zikh**-ehr-oong
Receipt, please.	Quittung, bitte. **kvit**-toong **bit**-teh

Even in small towns, pharmacies take turns staying open all night, and most have a sign on the window directing you to one that's open—look for ***Notdienst*** (emergency service) or ***Nachtdienst*** (night service). In a pinch, a ***Notzart*** (emergency doctor) may drive to the scene.

Ailments

I have...	Ich habe... ikh **hah**-beh
He / She has...	Er / Sie hat... ehr / zee haht
I need medication for a...	Ich brauche ein Medikament für... ikh **browkh**-eh īn meh-dee-kah-**mehnt** fewr
allergy	eine Allergie ī-neh ah-lehr-**gee** (hard "g")
bee sting	einen Bienenstich ī-nehn **bee**-nehn-stikh
bite	einen Biss ī-nehn bis
...bedbug bite	...einen Wanzenbiss ī-nehn **vahnt**-sehn-bis

...dog bite	...einen Hundebiss ī-nehn **hoon**-deh-bis
...mosquito bite	...einen Mückenstich ī-nehn **mew**-kehn-stikh
...spider bite	...einen Spinnenbiss ī-nehn **shpin**-ehn-bis
...tick bite	...einen Zeckenbiss ī-nehn **tseh**-kehn-bis
blisters	Blasen **blah**-zehn
body odor	Körpergeruch **kur**-pehr-geh-rookh
burn	eine Verbrennung ī-neh fehr-**breh**-noong
chapped lips	aufgesprungene Lippen **owf**-geh-shproong-eh-neh **lip**-ehn
chest pains	Schmerzen in der Brust **shmehrt**-sehn in dehr broost
chills	Kälteschauer **kehl**-teh-show-ehr ("show" rhymes with "cow")
cold	eine Erkältung ī-neh ehr-**kehl**-toong
congestion	Schnupfen **shnoop**-fehn
constipation	Verstopfung fehr-**shtohp**-foong
cough	Husten **hoo**-stehn
cramps	Krämpfe **krehmp**-feh
...muscle cramps	...Muskelkrämpfe **moos**-kehl-krehmp-feh
...stomach cramps	...Bauchkrämpfe **bowkh**-krehmp-feh
...menstrual cramps	...Monatskrämpfe **moh**-nahts-krehmp-feh
diarrhea	Durchfall **doorkh**-fahl
dizziness	Schwindel **shvin**-dehl
earache	Ohrenschmerzen **or**-ehn-shmehrt-sehn
eczema	Ekzem **ehk**-tsehm
fever	Fieber **fee**-behr
flu	die Grippe dee **grip**-eh
food poisoning	Lebensmittelvergiftung **lay**-behns-mit-tehl-fehr-**gift**-oong
gas	Darmgas **darm**-gahs

hay fever	Heuschnupfen **hoy**-shnoop-fehn
headache	Kopfschmerzen **kohpf**-shmehrt-sehn
heartburn	Sodbrennen **sohd**-breh-nehn
hemorrhoids	Hämorrhoiden heh-moh-roh-**ee**-dehn
hot flashes	Hitzeschübe **hit**-seh-shew-beh
indigestion	Verdauungsstörung fehr-**dow**-oongs-shtur-oong
infection	eine Infektion ī-neh in-fehk-see-**ohn** .
inflammation	eine Entzündung ī-neh ehnt-**sewn**-doong
insomnia	Insomnie in-sohm-**nee**
lice	Läuse **loy**-zeh
lightheaded	schwindlig **shvind**-lig
migraine	Migräne mee-**gray**-neh
motion sickness	Bewegungskrankheit beh-**vay**-goongs-krahnk-hīt
nausea	Übelkeit **ew**-behl-kīt
numbness	Taubheit **towb**-hīt
pain	Schmerz shmehrts
pimples	Pickel "pickle"
pneumonia	Lungenentzündung **loong**-ehn-ehnt-**sewn**-doong
pus	Eiter ī-tehr
rash	einen Ausschlag ī-nehn **ows**-shlahg
sinus problems	Sinusitis zee-**noo**-zee-tis
sneezing	Niesen **nee**-zehn
sore throat	Halsschmerzen **hahls**-shmehrt-sehn
splinter	Splitter **shplit**-ehr
stomachache	Magenschmerzen **mah**-gehn-shmehrt-sehn
(bad) sunburn	(üblen) Sonnenbrand (**ew**-blehn) **zoh**-nehn-brahnt

swelling	eine Schwellung ī-neh **shvehl**-oong
tendinitis	Tendinitis tehn-din-**ee**-tis
toothache	Zahnschmerzen **tsahn**-shmehrt-sehn
urinary tract infection	Harnwegsinfekt **harn**-vayg-zin-**fehkt**
urination (frequent / painful)	Urinieren (häufiges / schmerzvolles) oo-ree-**neer**-ehn (**hoy**-fig-ehs / **shmehrts**-foh-lehs)
vomiting	Übergeben ew-behr-**gay**-behn
warts	Warzen **vart**-sehn
I'm going bald.	Mir fallen die Haare aus. meer **fahl**-ehn dee **hah**-reh ows

It Hurts

pain	Schmerz shmehrts
painful	schmerzhaft **shmehrts**-hahft
hurts	tut weh toot vay
It hurts here.	Hier tut es weh. heer toot ehs vay
My ____ hurts. (body parts listed next)	Das ____ tut weh. dahs ____ toot vay
aching	schmerzend **shmehrt**-sehnt
bleeding	blutend **bloo**-tehnd
blocked	blockiert bloh-**keert**
broken	gebrochen geh-**broh**-khen
bruised	geprellt geh-**prehlt**
chafing	aufreibend **owf**-rī-behnt
cracked	angebrochen **ahn**-geh-broh-kehn
fractured	frakturiert frahk-toor-**eert**
infected	infiziert in-fit-**seert**
inflamed	entzündet ehnt-**sewn**-deht

punctured (rusty nail)	punktiert (verrosteter Nagel) poonk-**teert** (fehr-**rohs**-teh-tehr **nah**-gehl)
scraped	gekratzt geh-**krahtst**
sore	wund voont
sprained	verstaucht fehr-**shtowkht**
swollen	geschwollen geh-**shvohl**-ehn
weak	schwach shvahkh
diagnosis	Diagnose dee-ahg-**noh**-zeh
What can I do?	Was kann ich tun? vahs kahn ikh toon
Is it serious?	Ist es schlimm? ist ehs shlim
Is it contagious?	Ist es ansteckend? ist ehs **ahn**-shtehk-ehnt

The warm wind called the ***Föhn*** periodically blows across the Alps from the Mediterranean, sparking pressure changes. Many locals complain that this interferes with their ***Kreislauf*** (circulation), causing some to feel run-down and get headaches. They call this ***Föhnkrankheit*** (***Föhn*** sickness).

Body Parts

ankle	Fussgelenk **foos**-geh-lehnk
appendix	Blinddarm **blin**-darm
arm	Arm arm
back	Rücken **rew**-kehn
bladder	Blase **blah**-zeh
blood	Blut bloot
bone	Knochen keh-**nohkh**-ehn
bowel movement	Stuhlgang **shtool**-gahng
brain	Gehirn geh-**hirn**
breast	Brust broost
chest	Brust broost
ear	Ohr or

elbow	Ellbogen **ehl**-boh-gehn
eye	Auge **ow**-geh
face	Gesicht geh-**zikht**
finger	Finger **fing**-ehr
fingernail	Fingernagel **fing**-ehr-nah-gel
foot	Fuss foos
hand	Hand hahnt
head	Kopf kohpf
heart	Herz hehrts
hip	Hüfte **hewf**-teh
kidney	Niere **neer**-reh
knee	Knie keh-**nee**
leg	Bein bīn
lips	Lippen **lip**-ehn
liver	Leber **lay**-behr
lung	Lunge **loong**-eh
mouth	Mund moont
muscle	Muskel **moos**-kehl
neck	Nacken **nahk**-ehn
nose	Nase **nah**-zeh
ovary	Eierstock **ī**-ehr-stock
penis	Penis **peh**-nees
poop	Stuhl shtool
shoulder	Schulter **shool**-tehr
skin	Haut howt
stomach	Magen **mah**-gehn
teeth	Zähne **tsay**-neh
testicles	Hoden **hoh**-dehn
throat	Hals hahls
toe	Zehe **tsay**-eh
toenail	Zehnagel **tsay**-nah-gel
tongue	Zunge **tsoong**-eh

urine	Urin oo-**reen**
uterus	Gebärmutter geh-**bayr**-moo-tehr
vagina	Vagina **vahg**-ee-nah
waist	Taille **tīl**-yeh
wrist	Handgelenk **hahnt**-geh-lehnk
right / left	rechte / linke **rehkh**-teh / **link**-eh

First-Aid Kit and Medications

American name-brand medications are rare in Europe, but you'll find equally good local equivalents. Rather than looking for Sudafed, ask for a ***Dekongestivum*** (decongestant). Instead of Nyquil, request a ***Grippemittel*** (cold medicine). For prescription drugs, ask your doctor for the generic name (for example, atorvastatin instead of Lipitor), which is more likely to be understood internationally. If using a European thermometer, see page 553 for help with temperature conversions.

medicine	Medikament meh-dee-kah-**mehnt**
pill	Pille **pil**-eh
prescription	Rezept ray-**tsehpt**
refill	Erneuerung ehr-**noy**-ehr-oong
pharmacy	Apotheke ah-poh-**tay**-keh
all-night pharmacy	Apotheke mit Nachtdienst ah-poh-**tay**-keh mit **nahkht**-deenst
antacid	Mittel gegen Sodbrennen **mit**-ehl **gay**-gehn **sohd**-breh-nehn
anti-anxiety medicine	Beruhigungsmittel beh-**roo**-ee-goongs-mit-tehl
antibiotic	Antibiotika ahn-tee-bee-**oh**-tee-kah
antihistamine (like Benadryl)	Antihistaminikum ahn-tee-hees-tah-**meen**-ee-koom
aspirin	Aspirin ah-spir-**een**

non-aspirin substitute (like Tylenol)	Paracetamol (brand name: Ben-u-ron) pah-rah-**seh**-tah-mohl (**behn**-oo-rohn)
adult diapers (like Depends)	Schutzhose **shoots**-hoh-zeh
bandage	Verband fehr-**bahnt**
Band-Aids	Pflaster **flahs**-tehr
cold medicine	Grippemittel **grip**-eh-mit-ehl
cough drops	Hustenbonbons **hoo**-stehn-bohn-bohns
decongestant (like Sudafed)	Dekongestivum day-kohn-**gehs**-tee-foom
diarrhea medicine	Durchfallmedikament **doorkh**-fahl-meh-dee-kah-**mehnt**
disinfectant	Desinfektionsmittel dehs-in-fehkt-see-**ohns**-mit-tehl
first-aid cream	Erste-Hilfe-Salbe **ehr**-steh-**hil**-feh-**zahl**-beh
gauze / tape	Verband fehr-**bahnt**
hemorrhoid medicine	Hämorrhoiden Salbe heh-moh-roh-**ee**-dehn **zahl**-beh
hydrogen peroxide	Wasserstoffperoxid vahs-ehr-shtohf-peh-rohk-**seed**
ibuprofen	Ibuprofen ee-boo-**proh**-fehn
inhaler	Inhalator / Asthmaspray in-hah-**lah**-tor / **ahst**-mah-shpray
insulin	Insulin een-soo-**leen**
itch reliever	Anti-Juckreizmittel **ahn**-tee-**yook**-rīts-mit-tehl
laxative	Laxativ lahks-ah-**teef**
moleskin (for blisters)	Pflaster gegen Blasen **flahs**-tehr **gay**-gehn **blah**-zehn
mosquito repellant	Mückenschutzmittel **mew**-kehn-shoots-mit-tehl
painkiller	Schmerzmittel **shmehrts**-mit-tehl

stomachache medicine	Magenschmerzmittel **mah**-gehn-shmehrts-mit-ehl
support bandage	Stützverband **shtewts**-fehr-bahnt
syringe	Spritze **shprit**-seh
tetanus shot	Tetanusimpfung **tayt**-ah-noo-zim-foong
thermometer	Thermometer tehr-moh-**may**-tehr
Vaseline	Vaseline / Mineralsalbe fah-zeh-**lee**-neh / min-eh-**rahl**-zahl-beh
vitamins	Vitamine fee-tah-**mee**-neh
Does it sting?	Brennt es? brehnt ehs
Take one pill every ____ hours for ____ days.	Täglich eine Pille einnehmen, alle ____ Stunden, bis zu ____ Tagen. **tayg**-likh ī-neh **pil**-eh **īn**-nay-mehn **ahl**-eh ____ **shtoon**-dehn, bis tsoo ____ **tah**-gehn

SPECIFIC NEEDS

The Eyes Have it

optician	Optiker **ohp**-tee-kehr
eye(s)	Auge(n) **ow**-geh(n)
eye drops (for inflammation)	Augentropfen **ow**-gehn-trohp-fehn
artificial tears	Tränenersatzmittel **tray**-neh-nehr-**zahts**-mit-tehl
glasses	Brille **bril**-eh
sunglasses	Sonnenbrille **zoh**-nehn-bril-eh
reading glasses	Lesebrille **lay**-zeh-bril-eh
glasses case	Brillen-Etui **bril**-ehn-eht-**vee**
(broken) lens	(zerbrochenes) Brillenglas (tsehr-**brohkh**-eh-nehs) **bril**-ehn-glahs
to repair	reparieren reh-pah-**reer**-ehn
replacement	Ersatz "ersatz"

prescription	Brillenrezept **bril**-ehn-ray-tsehpt
contact lens(es)	Kontaktlinse(n) kon-**tahkt**-lin-zeh(n)
soft lenses	weiche Linsen **vīkh**-eh **lin**-zehn
hard lenses	harte Linsen **har**-teh **lin**-zehn
all-purpose solution	Salzlösung **zahlts**-lur-zoong
contact lens case	Kontaktlinsenbehälter kon-**tahkt**-lin-zehn-beh-**hehl**-tehr
I don't see well.	Ich kann schlecht sehen. ikh kahn shlehkht **zay**-ehn
nearsighted	kurzsichtig **koort**-sikh-tig
farsighted	weitsichtig **vīt**-sikh-tig
20 / 20 vision	perfekte Dioptrie pehr-**fehk**-teh dee-ohb-**tree**

On Intimate Terms

personal lubricant (like KY Jelly)	Gleitmittel **glīt**-mit-tehl
contraceptives	Verhütungsmittel fehr-**hewt**-oongs-mit-tehl
condoms	Kondome kohn-**doh**-meh
birth control pills	Verhütungspille fehr-**hewt**-oongs-pil-eh
prescription refill	Wiederholungsrezept vee-dehr-**hoh**-loongs-ray-**tsept**
morning-after pill	Morning-After-Pille "morning after" **pil**-eh
herpes (inactive)	Herpes (latent) **hehr**-pays (lah-**tehnt**)
HIV / AIDS	HIV / AIDS hah ee fow / "AIDS"
STD (sexually transmitted disease)	Geschlechtskrankheit geh-**shlehkhts**-krahnk-hīt

For Women

menstruation	Menstruation	mehn-stroo-ah-see-**ohn**
period	Periode	pehr-ee-**oh**-deh
tampons	Tampons	**tahm**-pohns
sanitary pads	Damenbinden	**dah**-mehn-bin-dehn
I need medicine for...	Ich brauche ein Medikament für...	ikh **browkh**-eh īn meh-dee-kah-**mehnt** fewr
...menstrual cramps.	...Monatskrämpfe.	**moh**-nahts-krehmp-feh
...a yeast infection.	...eine Pilzeninfektion.	ī-neh **pilt**-sehn-in-fehkt-see-**ohn**
...a urinary tract infection.	...einen Harnwegsinfekt	ī-nehn **harn**-vayg-zin-**fehkt**
cranberry juice	Preiselbeersaft	**prī**-zehl-behr-zahft
I'd like to see a female...	Ich möchte gern zu einer...	ikh **murkh**-teh gehrn tsoo **ī**-nehr
...doctor.	...Ärztin.	**ayrts**-tin
...gynecologist.	...Gynäkologin.	gew-neh-koh-**loh**-gin (hard "g")
I've missed a period.	Ich habe meine Tage nicht bekommen.	ikh **hah**-beh **mī**-neh **tah**-geh nikht beh-**koh**-mehn
pregnancy test	Schwangerschaftstest	**shvahng**-ehr-shahfts-tehst
ultrasound	Ultraschall	**ool**-trah-shahl
I am / She is... pregnant.	Ich bin / Sie ist... schwanger.	ikh bin / zee ist... **shvahng**-ehr
... ____ weeks / ____ months / ____ trimester	...im ____ Wochen / ____ Monate / ____ Trimester	im ____ **vohkh**-ehn / ____ **moh**-nah-teh / ____ tree-**meh**-stehr
miscarriage	Fehlgeburt	**fayl**-geh-boort
abortion	Abtreibung	**ahp**-trī-boong
menopause	Menopause	may-noh-**pow**-zeh

APPENDIX

LET'S TALK TELEPHONES

Dialing Within Europe

France, Italy, and **Switzerland** use direct-dial phone systems (without area codes). That means phone numbers can be dialed direct throughout these countries. For example, the number of one of my recommended hotels in Nice is 04 97 03 10 70. That's exactly what you dial, whether you're calling it from across the street or across the country.

Understand the various prefixes of phone numbers. In France, any number beginning with 06 or 07 is a mobile phone and costs more to dial. France's toll-free numbers start with 0800, but any 08 number that does not have a 00 directly following is a toll call.

Italy's landlines start with 0, and mobile lines start with 3. The country's toll-free lines begin with 80. These 80 numbers—called ***freephone*** or ***numero verde*** (green number)—can be dialed free from any phone without using a phone card. Any Italian phone number that starts with 8 but isn't followed by a 0 is a toll call.

Germany and **Austria,** like much of the US, use an area-code dialing system. To make domestic calls within the same area code, just dial the local number; but if you're calling outside your area code, you have to dial both the area code (which starts with a 0) and the local number. For example, Munich's area code is 089 and the number of one of my recommended Munich hotels is 545-9940. To call the hotel within Munich, you'd dial 545-9940. To call it from Frankfurt, you'd dial 089/545-9940. If you're calling a German or Austrian mobile phone, you must always dial the complete number.

The French phrase for area code is ***code de zone,*** and the phrase for country code is ***code du pays.*** The Italian word for area code is ***prefisso,*** and the phrase for country code is ***prefisso per il paese.*** The German word for area code is ***Vorwahl*** and the word for country code is ***Landesvorwahl.***

Dialing Internationally

To make an international call, follow these steps:

- Dial the international access code (00 if you're calling from Europe, 011 from the US or Canada). If you're dialing from a mobile phone, you can replace the international access code with +, which works regardless of where you're calling from. (On many mobile phones, you can insert a + by pressing and holding the 0 key.)
- Dial the country code of the country you're calling (33 for France, 39 for Italy, 49 for Germany, 43 for Austria, 41 for Switzerland, or 1 for the US or Canada).
- Dial the local number (but for countries that use area codes, such as Germany and Austria, first dial the area code). Keep in mind that calling many countries requires dropping the initial zero of the phone number (this applies to France). For Italy and Switzerland, you include the initial zero of the local number. The European calling chart in this chapter lists specifics per country.

Calling from the US to France: Dial 011 (the US international access code), 33 (France's country code), then the French number without its initial zero.

Calling from the US to Italy: Dial 011 (the US international access code), 39 (Italy's country code), then the Italian phone number.

Calling from the US to Germany: Dial 011 (the US international access code), 49 (Germany's country code), then the area code (without its initial 0) and the local number.

Calling from the US to Austria: Dial 011 (the US international access code), 43 (Austria's country code), then the area code (without its initial 0) and the local number.

Calling from the US to Switzerland: Dial 011 (the US international access code), 41 (Switzerland's country code), then the local number (without its initial 0).

Calling from any European country to the US: To call my office in Edmonds, Washington, from anywhere in Europe, I dial 00 (Europe's international access code), 1 (the US country code), 425 (Edmonds' area code), and 771-8303.

European Calling Chart

Just smile and dial, using this key:
AC = Area Code, LN = Local Number.

European Country	Calling long distance within...	Calling from the US or Canada to...	Calling from a European country to...
Austria	AC + LN	011 + 43 + AC (without the initial zero) + LN	00 + 43 + AC (without the initial zero) + LN
Belgium	LN	011 + 32 + LN (without initial zero)	00 + 32 + LN (without initial zero)
Britain	AC + LN	011 + 44 + AC (without initial zero) + LN	00 + 44 + AC (without initial zero) + LN
France	LN	011 + 33 + LN (without initial zero)	00 + 33 + LN (without initial zero)
Germany	AC + LN	011 + 49 + AC (without initial zero) + LN	00 + 49 + AC (without initial zero) + LN
Gibraltar	LN	011 + 350 + LN	00 + 350 + LN
Ireland	AC + LN	011 + 353 + AC (without initial zero) + LN	00 + 353 + AC (without initial zero) + LN
Italy	LN	011 + 39 + LN	00 + 39 + LN

European Country	Calling long distance within...	Calling from the US or Canada to...	Calling from a European country to...
Morocco	LN	011 + 212 + LN (without initial zero)	00 + 212 + LN (without initial zero)
Netherlands	AC + LN	011 + 31 + AC (without initial zero) + LN	00 + 31 + AC (without initial zero) + LN
Portugal	LN	011 + 351 + LN	00 + 351 + LN
Spain	LN	011 + 34 + LN	00 + 34 + LN
Switzerland	LN	011 + 41 + LN (without initial zero)	00 + 41 + LN (without initial zero)

- The instructions above apply whether you're calling to or from a European landline or mobile phone.
- If calling from any mobile phone, you can replace the international access code with "+" (press and hold 0 to insert it).
- The international access code is 011 if you're calling from the US or Canada.
- To call the US or Canada from Europe, dial 00, then 1 (country code for US and Canada), then the area code and number. In short, 00 + 1 + AC + LN = Hi, Mom!

THE ALPHABET

If you need to spell your name over the phone (to reserve a room or book a restaurant reservation), this chart will come in handy.

	French	Italian	German
A	ah	ah	ah
B	bay	bee	bay
C	say	chee	tsay
D	day	dee	day
E	uh	ay	ay / eh
F	"f"	**ehf**-ay	"f"
G	zhay	jee	gay
H	ahsh	**ah**-kah	hah
I	ee	ee	ee
J	zhee	ee **loon**-gah	yoht
K	kah	**kah**-pah	kah
L	"l"	**ehl**-ay	"l"
M	"m"	**ehm**-ay	"m"
N	"n"	**ehn**-ay	"n"
O	"o"	oh	"o"
P	pay	pee	pay
Q	kew	koo	koo
R	ehr	**ehr**-ay	ehr
S	"s"	**ehs**-ay	"s"
T	tay	tee	tay
U	ew	oo	oo
V	vay	vee	fow
W	doo-bluh-vay	**dohp**-yoh-voo	vay
X	"x"	eeks	eeks
Y	ee-grehk	**eep**-see-lohn	**ewp**-sil-ohn
Z	zehd	**zeht**-ah	tseht

German also uses these vowels with umlauts: ***Ä*** (eh / ay), ***Ö*** (ur), and ***Ü*** (ew).

What Your Hotelier Wants to Know

If you'd like to reserve by email, your hotel needs to know the following information: number and type of rooms (i.e., single or double); number of nights; date of arrival (written day/month/year); date of departure; and any special needs (such as bathroom in the room, cheapest room, twin beds vs. one big bed, crib, air-conditioning, quiet, view, ground floor, no stairs, and so on). Here's a sample email I'd send to make a reservation.

From: rick@ricksteves.com
Sent: Today
To: info@hotelcentral.com
Subject: Reservation request for 19-22 July

Dear Hotel Central,

I would like to reserve a double room for 2 people for 3 nights, arriving 19 July and departing 22 July. If possible, I would like a quiet room with a bathroom inside the room.

Please let me know if you have a room available and the price.

Thank you!
Rick Steves

The hotel will reply with its room availability and rates for your dates. This is not a confirmation—you must email back to say that you want the room at the given rate, and you'll likely be asked for your credit-card number for a deposit.

NUMBERS AND STUMBLERS

Here are a few things to keep in mind:

- Europeans write a few of their numbers differently than we do. 1= 1, 4= 4, 7= 7.
- In Europe, dates appear as day/month/year.
- Commas are decimal points, and decimal points are commas. A dollar and a half is $1,50, one thousand is 1.000, and there are 5.280 feet in a mile.
- When counting with fingers, start with your thumb. If you hold up your first finger to request one item, you'll probably get two.
- What Americans call the second floor of a building is the first floor in Europe.
- On escalators and moving sidewalks, Europeans keep the left "lane" open for passing. Keep to the right.

Clothing Sizes

When shopping for clothing, use these US-to-European comparisons as general guidelines (but note that no conversion is perfect).

Women's dresses and blouses: Add 30 (US size 10 = EU size 40)
Men's suits and jackets: Add 10 (US size 40 regular = EU size 50)
Men's shirts: Multiply by 2 and add about 8 (US size 15 collar = EU size 38)
Women's shoes: Add about 30 (US size 8 = EU size 38½)
Men's shoes: Add 32-34 (US size 9 = EU size 41; US size 11 = EU size 45)
Children's clothing: Small children, subtract 1 (US size 10 = EU size 9); juniors, subtract 4 (US size 14 = EU size 10)
Girls' shoes: Add 16-17 (US size 10 = EU size 26); over size 13 use women's sizes
Boys' shoes: Add 17.5-18 (US size 11 = EU size 29); over size 13 use men's sizes

Metric Conversions

A kilogram is 2.2 pounds, and 1 liter is about a quart, or almost four to a gallon. A kilometer is six-tenths of a mile. I figure kilometers to miles by cutting the kilometers in half and adding back 10 percent of the original (120 km: 60 + 12 = 72 miles, 300 km: 150 + 30 = 180 miles).

Temperature Conversion

For a rough conversion from Celsius to Fahrenheit, double the number and add 30. For weather, remember that 28°C is 82°F—perfect. For health, 37°C is just right.

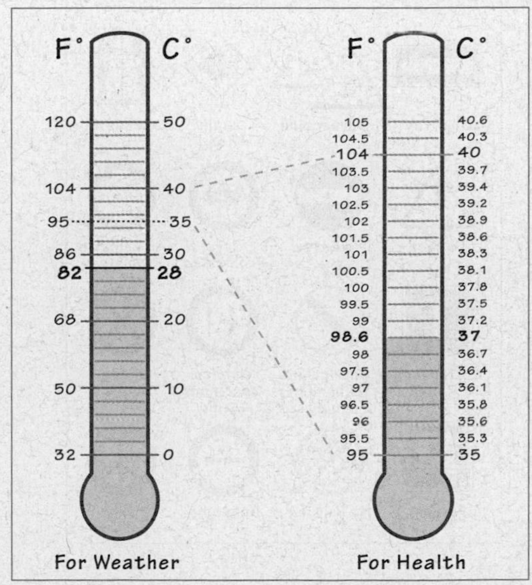

STANDARD ROAD SIGNS

AND LEARN THESE ROAD SIGNS

Speed Limit (km/hr)

Yield

No Passing

End of No Passing Zone

One Way

Intersection

Main Road

Expressway

Danger

No Entry

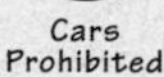
Cars Prohibited

All Vehicles Prohibited

No Through Road

Restrictions No Longer Apply

Yield to Oncoming Traffic

No Stopping

Parking

No Parking

Customs

Peace

TEAR-OUT CHEAT SHEETS

French Basics

Tear out this sheet of French survival phrases and keep it in your pocket to use in case you're caught without your phrase book.

Good day.	Bonjour. bohn-zhoor
Mr.	Monsieur muhs-yuh
Mrs.	Madame mah-dahm
Miss	Mademoiselle mahd-mwah-zehl
Do you speak English?	Parlez-vous anglais? par-lay-voo ahn glay
Yes. / No.	Oui. / Non. wee / nohn
I don't speak French.	Je ne parle pas français. zhuh nuh parl pah frahn-say
I'm sorry.	Désolé. day-zoh-lay
Please.	S'il vous plaît. see voo play
Thank you.	Merci. mehr-see
You're welcome.	De rien. duh ree-an
Excuse me. (to get attention)	Excusez-moi. ehk-skew-zay-mwah
Excuse me. (to pass)	Pardon. par-dohn
OK?	Ça va? sah vah
No problem.	Pas de problème. pah duh proh-blehm
Very good.	Très bien. treh bee-an
Goodbye.	Au revoir. oh ruh-vwahr
How much is it?	Combien? kohn-bee-an
Write it?	Ecrivez? ay-kree-vay
euro (€)	euro uh-roh
zero	zéro zay-roh
one / two	un / deux uhn / duh
three / four	trois / quatre trwah / kah-truh
five / six	cinq / six sank / sees

seven / eight	sept / huit seht / weet
nine / ten	neuf / dix nuhf / dees
Can you help me?	Vous pouvez m'aider? voo poo-vay meh-day
I'd like...	Je voudrais... zhuh voo-dray
We'd like...	Nous voudrions... noo voo-dree-ohn
...this.	...ceci. suh-see
...a ticket.	...un billet. uhn bee-yay
...the bill.	...l'addition. lah-dee-see-ohn
Where is a cash machine?	Où est un distributeur? oo ay uhn dee-stree-bew-tur
Where are the toilets?	Où sont les toilettes? oo sohn lay twah-leht
men / women	hommes / dames ohm / dahm
Is it free?	C'est gratuit? say grah-twee
Included?	Inclus? an-klew
Is it possible?	C'est possible? say poh-see-bluh
entrance / exit	entrée / sortie ahn-tray / sor-tee
At what time does this open / close?	À quelle heure c'est ouvert / fermé? ah kehl ur say oo-vehr / fehr-may
Just a moment.	Un moment. uhn moh-mahn
now	maintenant man-tuh-nahn
soon / later	bientôt / plus tard bee-an-toh / plew tar
today	aujourd'hui oh-zhoor-dwee
tomorrow	demain duh-man
Sunday	dimanche dee-mahnsh
Monday	lundi luhn-dee
Tuesday	mardi mar-dee
Wednesday	mercredi mehr-kruh-dee
Thursday	jeudi zhuh-dee
Friday	vendredi vahn-druh-dee
Saturday	samedi sahm-dee

French Restaurants

I'd like / We'd like...	Je voudrais / Nous voudrions... zhuh voo-dray / noo voo-dree-ohn
...to reserve...	...réserver... ray-zehr-vay
...a table for one / two.	...une table pour un / deux. ewn tah-bluh poor uhn / duh
Is this table free?	Cette table est libre? seht tah-bluh ay lee-bruh
How long is the wait?	Combien de temps faut-il attendre? kohn-bee-an duh tahn foh-teel ah-tahn-druh
The menu (in English), please.	La carte (en anglais), s'il vous plaît. lah kart (ahn ahn-glay) see voo play
breakfast	petit déjeuner puh-tee day-zhuh-nay
lunch	déjeuner day-zhuh-nay
dinner	dîner dee-nay
service (not) included	service (non) compris sehr-vees (nohn) kohn-pree
to go	à emporter ah ahn-por-tay
with / without	avec / sans ah-vehk / sahn
and / or	et / ou ay / oo
fixed-price meal	menu / prix fixe muh-new / pree feeks
special of the day	plat du jour plah dew zhoor
specialty of the house	spécialité de la maison spay-see-ah-lee-tay duh lah may-zohn
appetizers	hors d'oeuvres or duh-vruh
What do you recommend?	Qu'est-ce que vous recommandez? kehs kuh voo ruh-koh-mahn-day
first course (soup, salad)	entrée ahn-tray
main course (meat, fish)	plat principal plah pran-see-pahl
bread	pain pan

cheese	fromage	froh-mahzh
sandwich	sandwich	sahnd-weech
soup	soupe	soop
salad	salade	sah-lahd
meat	viande	vee-ahnd
chicken	poulet	poo-lay
fish	poisson	pwah-sohn
seafood	fruits de mer	frwee duh mehr
fruit	fruit	frwee
vegetables	légumes	lay-gewm
dessert	dessert	day-sehr
mineral water	eau minérale	oh mee-nay-rahl
carafe of tap water	une carafe d'eau	ewn kah-rahf doh
milk	lait	lay
(orange) juice	jus (d'orange)	zhew (doh-rahnzh)
coffee	café	kah-fay
tea	thé	tay
wine	vin	van
red / white	rouge / blanc	roozh / blahn
glass / bottle	verre / bouteille	vehr / boo-tay
beer	bière	bee-ehr
Cheers!	Santé!	sahn-tay
More. / Another.	Plus. / Un autre.	plew / uhn oh-truh
The same.	La même chose.	lah mehm shohz
Finished.	Terminé.	tehr-mee-nay
The bill, please.	L'addition, s'il vous plaît.	lah-dee-see-ohn see voo play
Do you accept credit cards?	Vous prenez les cartes?	voo pruh-nay lay kart
tip	pourboire	poor-bwahr
Delicious!	Délicieux!	day-lee-see-uh

Italian Basics

Tear out this sheet of Italian survival phrases and keep it in your pocket to use in case you're caught without your phrase book.

Good day.	Buon giorno. bwohn **jor**-noh
Mr.	Signore seen-**yoh**-ray
Mrs.	Signora seen-**yoh**-rah
Miss	Signorina seen-yoh-**ree**-nah
Do you speak English?	Parla inglese? **par**-lah een-**gleh**-zay
Yes. / No.	Si. / No. see / noh
I don't speak Italian.	Non parlo l'italiano. nohn **par**-loh lee-tah-lee-**ah**-noh
I'm sorry.	Mi dispiace. mee dee-spee-**ah**-chay
Please.	Per favore. pehr fah-**voh**-ray
Thank you.	Grazie. **graht**-see-ay
You're welcome.	Prego. **preh**-goh
Excuse me. (to get attention)	Mi scusi. mee **skoo**-zee
Excuse me. (to pass)	Permesso. pehr-**meh**-soh
It's not a problem.	Non c'è problema. nohn cheh proh-**bleh**-mah
Good.	Bene. **beh**-nay
Goodbye.	Arrivederci. ah-ree-veh-**dehr**-chee
How much (does it cost)?	Quanto (costa)? **kwahn**-toh (**koh**-stah)
Write it for me?	Me lo scrive? may loh **skree**-vay
euro (€)	euro eh-**oo**-roh
zero	zero **zeh**-roh
one / two	uno / due **oo**-noh / **doo**-ay
three / four	tre / quattro tray / **kwah**-troh
five / six	cinque / sei **cheen**-kway / **seh**-ee
seven / eight	sette / otto **seh**-tay / **oh**-toh

nine / ten	nove / dieci **noh**-vay / dee-**eh**-chee
Can you help me?	Può aiutarmi? pwoh ah-yoo-**tar**-mee
I'd like / We'd like...	Vorrei / Vorremmo... voh-**reh**-ee / voh-**reh**-moh
...that.	...quello. **kweh**-loh
...a ticket.	...un biglietto. oon beel-**yeh**-toh
...the bill.	...il conto. eel **kohn**-toh
Where is a cash machine?	Dov'è un bancomat? doh-**veh** oon **bahn**-koh-maht
Where is the toilet?	Dov'è la toilette? doh-**veh** lah twah-**leh**-tay
men	uomini / signori **woh**-mee-nee / seen-**yoh**-ree
women	donne / signore **doh**-nay / seen-**yoh**-ray
Is it free?	È gratis? eh **grah**-tees
Is it included?	È incluso? eh een-**kloo**-zoh
Is it possible?	È possibile? eh poh-**see**-bee-lay
entrance / exit	entrata / uscita ehn-**trah**-tah / oo-**shee**-tah
What time does this open / close?	A che ora apre / chiude? ah kay **oh**-rah **ah**-pray / kee-**oo**-day
now / soon / later	adesso / presto / più tardi ah-**deh**-soh / **preh**-stoh / pew **tar**-dee
today / tomorrow	oggi / domani **oh**-jee / doh-**mah**-nee
Sunday	domenica doh-**meh**-nee-kah
Monday	lunedì loo-neh-**dee**
Tuesday	martedì mar-teh-**dee**
Wednesday	mercoledì mehr-koh-leh-**dee**
Thursday	giovedì joh-veh-**dee**
Friday	venerdì veh-nehr-**dee**
Saturday	sabato **sah**-bah-toh

Italian Restaurants

I'd like / We'd like...	Vorrei / Vorremmo... voh-**reh**-ee / voh-**reh**-moh
...to reserve...	...prenotare... preh-noh-**tah**-ray
...a table for one / two.	...un tavolo per uno / due. oon **tah**-voh-loh pehr **oo**-noh / **doo**-ay
Is this table free?	È libero questo tavolo? eh **lee**-beh-roh **kweh**-stoh **tah**-voh-loh
How long is the wait?	Quanto c'è da aspettare? **kwahn**-toh cheh dah ah-speh-**tah**-ray
The menu (in English), please.	Il menù (in inglese), per favore. eel meh-**noo** (een een-**gleh**-zay) pehr fah-**voh**-ray
breakfast	colazione koh-laht-see-**oh**-nay
lunch	pranzo **prahnt**-soh
dinner	cena **cheh**-nah
service (not) included	servizio (non) incluso sehr-**veet**-see-oh (nohn) een-**kloo**-zoh
cover charge	coperto koh-**pehr**-toh
to go	da portar via dah por-**tar vee**-ah
with / without	con / senza kohn / **sehnt**-sah
and / or	e / o ay / oh
fixed-price menu	menù fisso meh-**noo fee**-soh
daily specials	piatti del giorno pee-**ah**-tee dehl **jor**-noh
specialty of the house	specialità della casa speh-chah-lee-**tah deh**-lah **kah**-zah
What do you recommend?	Che cosa raccomanda? kay **koh**-zah rah-koh-**mahn**-dah
appetizers	antipasti ahn-tee-**pah**-stee
first course(s) (pasta, soup)	primo piatto / primi **pree**-moh pee-**ah**-toh / **pree**-mee
main course(s) (meat, fish)	secondo piatto / secondi seh-**kohn**-doh pee-**ah**-toh / seh-**kohn**-dee

bread	pane **pah**-nay
cheese	formaggio for-**mah**-joh
sandwich	panino pah-**nee**-noh
soup	zuppa **tsoo**-pah
salad	insalata een-sah-**lah**-tah
meat	carni **kar**-nee
chicken	pollo **poh**-loh
fish	pesce **peh**-shay
seafood	frutti di mare **froo**-tee dee **mah**-ray
vegetables	verdure vehr-**doo**-ray
fruit	frutta **froo**-tah
dessert	dolce **dohl**-chay
mineral water	acqua minerale **ah**-kwah mee-neh-**rah**-lay
tap water	acqua del rubinetto **ah**-kwah dehl roo-bee-**neh**-toh
milk	latte **lah**-tay
coffee / tea	caffè / tè kah-**feh** / teh
wine	vino **vee**-noh
red / white	rosso / bianco **roh**-soh / bee-**ahn**-koh
glass / bottle	bicchiere / bottiglia bee-kee-**eh**-ray / boh-**teel**-yah
beer	birra **bee**-rah
Cheers!	Cin cin! cheen cheen
More. / Another.	Di più. / Un altro. dee pew / oon **ahl**-troh
The same.	Lo stesso. loh **steh**-soh
Finished.	Finito. fee-**nee**-toh
The bill, please.	Il conto, per favore. eel **kohn**-toh pehr fah-**voh**-ray
Do you accept credit cards?	Accettate carte di credito? ah-cheh-**tah**-tay **kar**-tay dee **kreh**-dee-toh
tip	mancia **mahn**-chah
Delicious!	Delizioso! deh-leet-see-**oh**-zoh

German Basics

Keep this sheet of German survival phrases in your pocket, handy to memorize or use if you're caught without your phrase book.

Good day.	Guten Tag. **goo**-tehn tahg
Mr.	Herr hehr
Ms.	Frau frow (rhymes with "now")
Miss (under 18)	Fräulein **froy**-līn
Do you speak English?	Sprechen Sie Englisch? **shprehkh**-ehn zee **ehng**-lish
Yes. / No.	Ja. / Nein. yah / nīn
I don't speak German.	Ich spreche kein Deutsch. ikh **shprehkh**-eh kīn doytch
I'm sorry.	Es tut mir leid. ehs toot meer līt
Please.	Bitte. **bit**-teh
Thank you.	Danke. **dahn**-keh
You're welcome.	Bitte. **bit**-teh
Excuse me.	Entschuldigung. ehnt-**shool**-dig-oong
No problem.	Kein Problem. kīn proh-**blaym**
Very good.	Sehr gut. zehr goot
Goodbye.	Auf Wiedersehen. owf **vee**-dehr-zay-ehn
How much is it?	Wie viel kostet das? vee feel **kohs**-teht dahs
Write it down?	Aufschreiben? **owf**-shrī-behn
euro (€)	Euro **oy**-roh
zero	null nool
one / two	eins / zwei īns / tsvī
three / four	drei / vier drī / feer
five / six	fünf / sechs fewnf / zehkhs
seven / eight	sieben / acht **zee**-behn / ahkht
nine / ten	neun / zehn noyn / tsayn
Can you help me?	Können Sie mir helfen? **kurn**-ehn zee meer **hehl**-fehn

I'd like...	Ich hätte gern... ikh **heh**-teh gehrn
We'd like...	Wir hätten gern... veer **heh**-tehn gehrn
...this.	...dies. dees
...a ticket.	...eine Karte. ī-neh **kar**-teh
...the bill.	...die Rechnung. dee **rehkh**-noong
Where is a cash machine?	Wo ist ein Geldautomat? voh ist īn **gehlt**-ow-toh-maht
Where are the toilets?	Wo sind die Toiletten? voh zint dee toy-**leh**-tehn
men / women	Herren / Damen **hehr**-ehn / **dah**-mehn
Is it free?	Ist es kostenlos? ist ehs **kohs**-tehn-lohs
Included?	Inklusive? in-kloo-**zee**-veh
Is it possible?	Ist es möglich? ist ehs **murg**-likh
entrance / exit	Eingang / Ausgang **īn**-gahng / **ows**-gahng
When does this open / close?	Wann ist hier geöffnet / geschlossen? vahn ist heer geh-**urf**-neht / geh-**shloh**-sehn
Just a moment.	Moment. moh-**mehnt**
now	jetzt yehtst
soon / later	bald / später bahlt / **shpay**-tehr
today	heute **hoy**-teh
tomorrow	morgen **mor**-gehn
Sunday	Sonntag **zohn**-tahg
Monday	Montag **mohn**-tahg
Tuesday	Dienstag **deens**-tahg
Wednesday	Mittwoch **mit**-vohkh
Thursday	Donnerstag **doh**-nehrs-tahg
Friday	Freitag **frī**-tahg
Saturday	Samstag **zahms**-tahg

German Restaurants

I'd like a table for one.	Ich hätte gern einen Tisch für eine Person. ikh **heh**-teh gehrn ī-nehn tish fewr ī-neh pehr-**zohn**
We'd like a table for two.	Wir hätten gern einen Tisch für zwei. veer **heh**-tehn gehrn ī-nehn tish fewr tsvī
I'd like to make a reservation...	Ich möchte eine Reservierung... machen. ikh **murkh**-teh ī-neh reh-zehr-**veer**-oong... **mahkh**-ehn
...for myself / for two people.	...für mich / für zwei Personen fewr mikh / fewr tsvī pehr-**zoh**-nehn
Is this table free?	Ist dieser Tisch frei? ist **dee**-zehr tish frī
How long is the wait?	Wie lang ist die Wartezeit? vee lahng ist dee **var**-teht-sīt
The menu (in English), please.	Die Speisekarte (auf Englisch), bitte. dee **shpī**-zeh-kar-teh (owf **ehng**-lish) **bit**-teh
breakfast	Frühstück **frew**-shtewk
lunch	Mittagessen **mit**-tahg-eh-sehn
dinner	Abendessen **ah**-behnd-eh-sehn
service (not) included	Bedienung (nicht) inklusive beh-**dee**-noong (nikht) in-kloo-**zee**-veh
cover charge	Eintritt **īn**-trit
to go	zum Mitnehmen tsoom **mit**-nay-mehn
with / without	mit / ohne mit / **oh**-neh
and / or	und / oder oont / **oh**-dehr
fixed-price meal	Menü meh-**new**
daily special	Tagesgericht **tah**-gehs-geh-rikht
specialty of the house	Spezialität des Hauses **shpayt**-see-ahl-ee-**tayt** dehs **how**-zehs
What do you recommend?	Was schlagen Sie vor? vahs **shlah**-gehn zee for
appetizer	Vorspeise **for**-shpī-zeh
first course	erster Gang **ehr**-stehr gahng

main course	Hauptgang **howpt**-gahng
bread	Brot broht
cheese	Käse **kay**-zeh
sandwich	Sandwich **zehnd**-vich
soup	Suppe **zoo**-peh
salad	Salat zah-**laht**
meat	Fleisch flīsh
poultry	Geflügel geh-**flew**-gehl
fish	Fisch fish
seafood	Meeresfrüchte **meh**-rehs-**frewkh**-teh
fruit	Obst ohpst
vegetables	Gemüse geh-**mew**-zeh
dessert	Nachspeise **nahkh**-shpī-zeh
mineral water	Mineralwasser min-eh-rahl-**vahs**-ehr
tap water	Leitungswasser **lī**-toongs-vahs-ehr
milk	Milch milkh
(orange) juice	(Orangen)Saft (oh-**rahn**-zhehn-)zahft
coffee	Kaffee kah-**fay**
tea	Tee tay
wine	Wein vīn
red / white	rot / weiss roht / vīs
glass / bottle	Glas / Flasche glahs / **flah**-sheh
beer	Bier beer
Cheers!	Prost! prohst
More. / Another.	Mehr. / Noch eins. mehr / nohkh īns
The same.	Das gleiche. dahs **glīkh**-eh
Finished.	Fertig. **fehr**-tig
The bill, please.	Die Rechnung, bitte. dee **rehkh**-noong **bit**-teh
Do you accept credit cards?	Akzeptieren Sie Kreditkarten? ahkt-sehp-**teer**-ehn zee kreh-**deet**-kar-tehn
tip	Trinkgeld **trink**-gehlt
Delicious!	Lecker! **lehk**-ehr

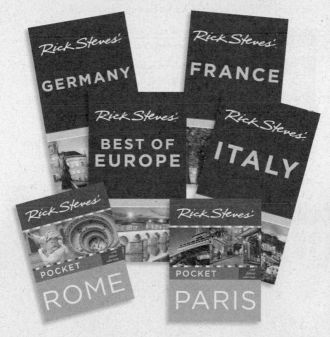

NOW AVAILABLE: eBOOKS, DVD & BLU-RAY

TRAVEL CULTURE

Europe 101
European Christmas
Postcards from Europe
Travel as a Political Act

eBOOKS

Nearly all Rick Steves guides are available as eBooks. Check with your favorite bookseller.

RICK STEVES' EUROPE DVDs

11 New Shows 2013-2014
Austria & the Alps
Eastern Europe
England & Wales
European Christmas
European Travel Skills & Specials
France
Germany, BeNeLux & More
Greece, Turkey & Portugal
Iran
Ireland & Scotland
Italy's Cities
Italy's Countryside
Scandinavia
Spain
Travel Extras

BLU-RAY

Celtic Charms
Eastern Europe Favorites
European Christmas
Italy Through the Back Door
Mediterranean Mosaic
Surprising Cities of Europe

PHRASE BOOKS & DICTIONARIES

French
French, Italian & German
German
Italian
Portuguese
Spanish

JOURNALS

Rick Steves' Pocket Travel Journal
Rick Steves' Travel Journal

PLANNING MAPS

Britain, Ireland & London
Europe
France & Paris
Germany, Austria & Switzerland
Ireland
Italy
Spain & Portugal

Rick Steves guidebooks are published by Avalon Travel, a member of the Perseus Books Group. Rick Steves books and DVDs are available at bookstores and through online booksellers.

Avalon Travel
a member of the Perseus Books Group
1700 Fourth Street, Berkeley, CA 94710, USA

Printed in China by RR Donnelley.

Sixth edition. First printing February 2014.

ISBN-13: 978-1-61238-204-3

For the latest on Rick's lectures, guidebooks, tours, and public television series, contact Europe Through the Back Door, P.O. Box 2009, Edmonds, WA 98020, tel. 425/771-8303, fax 425/771-0833, www.ricksteves.com, rick@ricksteves.com.

Europe Through the Back Door
Managing Editor: Risa Laib
Editorial & Production Manager: Jennifer Madison Davis
Series Manager: Cathy Lu
Editors: Glenn Eriksen, Tom Griffin, Cameron Hewitt, Suzanne Kotz, Carrie Shepherd, Gretchen Strauch
Editorial Assistant: Jessica Shaw
Editorial Interns: Andrés Garza, Caitlin Fjelsted, Valerie Gilmore, Samantha Oberholzer, Rebekka Shattuck, Candace Winegrad
Translation: Scott Bernhard, Mary Campbell Bouron, Francesca Caruso, Paul Desloover, Margaret Hemmen, Julia Klimek, Marijan Krišković, Niels Kuchenbuch, Sabine Leteinturier, Michelle Martin, Martin Minich,

Fabian Rüger, Arnaud Servignat, Heidi Van Sewell, Steve Smith, Vanessa Valles, Karoline Vass
Lead Researcher: Cameron Hewitt
Research Assistance: Hamida Awa, Gregoire Bouron, Malawi Bouron, Mary Campbell Bouron, Tommaso Fuzier Cayla, Julie Coen, Joanna Gates, Thierry Gauduchon, David C. Hoerlein, Gaby Holder, Heather Locke, Luca Martilli, Pascal Mievre, Paola Migliorini, Kelly Raye, Georg Reichlmayr
Graphic Content Director: Laura VanDeventer
Maps & Graphics: David C. Hoerlein, Twozdai Hulse, Lauren Mills, Dawn Tessman Visser

Avalon Travel
Senior Editor and Series Manager: Madhu Prasher
Editor: Jamie Andrade
Associate Editors: Nikki Ioakimedes, Annette Kohl
Assistant Editor: Maggie Ryan
Proofreader: Kelly Lydick
Production & Typesetting: McGuire Barber Design
Cover Design: Kimberly Glyder Design
Maps & Graphics: Kat Bennett, Mike Morgenfeld

Photography: Dominic Bonuccelli, Cameron Hewitt, Steve Smith, Rick Steves, Laura VanDeventer
Front Cover Photo: © Casa del Vino, Florence, Italy
© Giorgio Cosulich/Getty Images
Title Page Photo: Montmartre © nobleIMAGES/Alamy
Pages 1, 175, 367 Photos: © Purestock/Royalty-free